T0367839

HOLY DRACULA... THE CHRISTIAN KNIGHT

JESUS MUNOZ

If I cannot prove with these facts, which are written in the annals of human history, that Jesus Christ is considered God in the West thanks to Dracula's fight against Christ's enemies, you are right to call me insane, a fake, a liar. My reputation and credibility are at stake.

authorHOUSE®

AuthorHouse™ LLC
1663 Liberty Drive
Bloomington, IN 47403
www.authorhouse.com
Phone: 1-800-839-8640

Credit for painting: Guillermo Villanueva

Published by AuthorHouse   08/06/2013

ISBN: 978-1-4918-0467-4 (sc)
ISBN: 978-1-4918-0468-1 (hc)
ISBN: 978-1-4918-0469-8 (e)

Library of Congress Control Number: 2013913540

DEDICATION

I dedicate this novel to my publisher AuthorHouse: to Ella Centino for their valuable huge and timely advice; to Rudy Thomas for their invaluable words of encouragement, to my coordinator Richard VanDeventer, to Sarah Smith for their insightful comments; and to all members of this excellent team of professionals, who with their valuable work made it possible for my novel came into the hands of my readers appreciable.

1

Zapolva a beautiful Wallachian widow, said to her youngest daughter, "Neagoe, go get some wood from the shed."

When Logofat, her new husband, heard her order, he bid her farewell, saying, "I am going to work—I have a lot to do." He took his wife by the shoulders, kissed her quickly on the mouth, and left hurriedly.

Neagoe pretended she had not heard. Her mother began scolding her: "What do I have to do to get your attention? Didn't you hear me? Go get the firewood!"

Neagoe did not like to leave her mother's side; it was the only place she felt secure. Fearfully, she headed to the shed. As she quickly arranged the firewood in her slender arms, she felt a strong hand on her shoulder and heard, as if it were coming from beyond the grave, the dry voice of her stepfather: "Glad to see you Neagoe"

Neagoe's little knees began to buckle; she wanted to drop the firewood and run, but she couldn't. Now she knew how a mouse felt when it faced a snake. "My mom sent me to get firewood," she answered in a faltering voice. "If I don't go back soon, she is going to come looking for me."

Ignoring her words, the beast jerked her toward him, sending the wood clattering to the floor. He unbuckled his pants with one hand, and with the other he grabbed her violently by the hair. "Damn it—you're Satan's temptation," he growled. "I really want you!"

Neagoe resisted, but that only encouraged him more. She knew that she was about to revisit the painful and terrifying hell she feared so dreadfully. Desperately, in a low voice, she pleaded, "My God, help me!" Unfortunately, there was nothing in this world or the next that could protect her from that evil demon.

When Zapolva began to suspect that her daughter had disobeyed her and gone to play, she decided to go get the firewood herself. But when she entered the shed and heard desperate panting, she recognized the noises her husband made when they became intimate. She knew she was about to confirm her longtime suspicion: Logofat was cheating on her with another woman. She advanced stealthily toward the noise to surprise him, and suddenly a nightmare materialized before her, the most dreadful scene she ever could have imagined. For a moment she was speechless and petrified, and then a river of adrenaline ran through her body, giving her strength she had never felt before. She threw herself at the vile rapist with the force of a hurricane, shrieking, "Devil's letch!" Then she was upon him, scratching him with her nails and biting him in the neck.

The demon threw Neagoe to the floor as if she were a rag doll; her head barely missed a rock. Then he took her mother by the hair, threw her aside, and began beating her savagely in the face. "Damned old witch!" he screamed. "Who do you think you are?"

Zapolva felt her loose teeth with her tongue. Everything was spinning—this wasn't the time to faint!—but she felt herself losing control. She clung desperately to consciousness, trying to fight, trying to defend her child, but she couldn't raise her arms. Her efforts were futile; everything was a blur. Finally, pulling strength from her weakness, she screamed until it seemed her throat would tear, and then she fainted.

Jobst, a strong blacksmith who was her neighbor, heard the scream and ran to the shed. When he saw the nightmarish scene he began beating the letch, yelling, "Why don't you hit me, you son of a demon?" His shouts were so loud that more neighbors ran to the place, and everyone's reaction was the same: all the rage that the monstrous crime had generated turned into a savage beating joined by spitting and insults. The situation began to get out of control, and the suddenly dangerous crowd decided to take the law into their own hands. Now the torturer became a victim as some neighbors placed a rope around Logofat's neck to hang him.

The letch, horrified, saw his sad and certain destiny, the day and the way he was going to die.

Some soldiers who were passing by on patrol approached, and the commander of the group shouted, "Stand back, in the name of Dracula! You cannot take the law into your own hands—justice is a function of the authorities!" The soldiers' drawn swords were a powerful argument to obey them.

A townsman named Hugues began complaining bitterly. "This damned letch raped a girl and savagely beat her mother! We want real justice! But if we take him to the vovoid, the town council will simply impose a strong fine, and he will be free. It's always the same!"

"I could not care less what you think," the commander said imperiously. "Justice will be done according to the law!"

"Let us go see Dracula!" Hugues shouted, looking around at his neighbors. "We want to hear his sentence!"

So the crowd set forth, and the news of their mission spread through the town like wildfire. As the townspeople made their way to see Dracula, other neighbors joined the procession out of curiosity. They wanted to know if the vovoid would indeed keep his promise to impose justice.

Dracula received the mass of subjects and asked, "Why was this man beaten?"

Zapolva stepped forward holding her daughter, and with a mouth full of blood answered with difficulty, "This monster has raped my little child."

When Dracula saw the savagely beaten woman holding the little girl with blood running down her legs, he didn't need to see more evidence. Furious, he turned to the beast and said in a loud, clear voice, "You know my law: the ones who steal, rape, kill, or betray me will be impaled! You raped a child. On Sunday after Mass, you will die." Then, turning back to his subjects, he promised them, "If my law is not carried out, I will stop being Dracula—and you can call me 'Dog'-." He called to the commander of the guard. "Chain this beast!" he said. "He must not receive spiritual assistance. And do not allow him to kill himself!"

Hugues gave a loud yell: "Long life to our vovoid!"

"Long life!" his neighbors answered in unison, and the crowd dispersed.

As they walked back to their homes, Hugues said excitedly to Jobst, "Finally we have a governor who will defend us from the unfairness of the town council."

Jobst nodded, saying, "Do not even mention those damn Saxons. They fix everything with money."

Nude and chained to the wall, the rapist felt that even his soul was aching. The pain was beyond his nightmares; he never imagined that one man could suffer so much. He was in hell.

When he heard that Logofat was to be impaled, the priest showed up in the dungeon and told the guard, "I came to confess the prisoner."

"It´s the governor's order that this delinquent die as he deserves—with no spiritual assistance," the guard answered. "Please, Father, go with God."

Unable to perform his sacred mission, the priest sent his blessing from afar, absolving the sins of his pious parishioner in the name of him who, more than anyone, knew the man's vulnerable heart. The victim received that blessing from his uncomfortable position, after silently watching the sainted man walk away.

Every Saturday Logofat dutifully confessed his sins, and even though they were always the same, he always swore he had truly repented, and the infinite mercy of Christ, through his glorious sacrifice and the shedding of his precious blood, always reached Logofat, giving him divine forgiveness.

Suddenly, like a lightning bolt, a brilliant idea hit him: he was going to get out of that hell, and no one was going to stop him.

At home with Neagoe, Zapolva bandaged the wound on her daughter's head, saying. "My little girl, don't be afraid anymore. That mean man is going to die impaled."

"I don't believe it, mom," the little one answered. "No one punishes rapists. Logofat promised to kill us all if you found out what he was doing to me."

"Trust in Dracula's law," her mother replied. "This governor is so strong that I am sure no one will defy him."

Neagoe's older sister was scared. She also had been a victim of her stepfather's lust, and the secret was killing her. Her fear had turned her into an insecure young girl who was frightened of all men, even the ones who approached her with honest intentions. Every Sunday she saw her executioner take Holy Communion with devotion and in silence, and she always pleaded to the Christ of the temple, "Tell me, my God, who is protecting this beast? Why is there no justice for me?" And a desperate prayer came from the deepest part of her soul: "Help me, my God! I trust you completely."

Dracula was determined to carry out his law. The Saxons had to understand that from now on, justice was his; he had the power now

The next day, the Saxon members of the town council met with Dracula. One of them, Moses, addressed him: "We have set the amount of twenty silver coins to release the prisoner."

Unsurprised by the mercenary attitude of the exploiters, Dracula looked at them coldly. "Why don't we charge thirty?" he proposed sarcastically. "Like the amount for which Judas sold our Christ!"

That irony upset them; Moses took a deep breath and then, so as not to offend the new vovoid, answered, "Fine. Let it be thirty."

Dracula was enraged. "There were human beings hurt here!" he shouted furiously. "They are suffering and crying out for justice! Is this the way to impose it? All this is going to change. Nothing and no one will save this bastard rapist from his punishment. He will die impaled on Sunday!"

The Saxons didn't accept the verdict and continued to argue heatedly for several hours. When the vovoid noticed their intransigence, he announced, "From this day forward, this clique called the town council is hereby dissolved!" He turned around and stormed out, leaving the once-powerful men shaking with rage.

When Dracula had gone, Moses turned to the other Saxons. "Who does that moron think he is? Without our support he can never be ruler!" At that moment they started plotting to overthrow him; they had the money to support his enemies and to buy weapons and hire mercenaries. Dracula had renewed his longstanding enmity with the wicked Saxons, who would be his sworn enemies even after God had taken him to his kingdom.

The decisive moment had arrived. Sunday Mass had ended, and the sharp noise of the drum started to resound in the main square, inviting the townsfolk to witness the new justice Dracula had established in Wallachia.

In the place of the impalement, a seat had been reserved up front so the victims and other people affected by the crime could observe Logofat's execution. The soldiers were prepared, as were the stake, the grease, and the horses. And the vultures, although scattered now, would not take long to arrive at the banquet. The entire population of the town had gathered,.

The accused arrived chained in a wooden cage, from which he was pulled without ceremony. The letch seemed calm, even fearless, a broad smile on his evil face. His attitude showed confidence that he was not going to die that day. One by one he looked directly at his victims threateningly and defiantly, smiling the whole time.

When Neagoe saw that cynical smile, she wanted to run away from that place and seek shelter—but where? She was more frightened now than ever. Her feelings puzzled her; something inside her heart told her that the bastard was going to escape impalement, despite the new rule. She sought refuge in her mother's arms, saying, "mom, I still have the same feeling—Dracula is going to release Logofat!"

Zapolva secretly felt the same way, but trying to comfort Neagoe, she hugged her tight without saying a word.

The drum and the crowd fell silent when Dracula appeared; everyone was anxiously waiting for him to reconfirm his fair sentence. With a look of contempt in his deep-green eyes, Dracula gazed at the rapist and, in a determined voice, repeated, "You know my law—it is clear. The ones who steal, kill, rape, or betray me will die impaled! You raped—therefore you will die impaled, immediately!" He turned to his soldiers, "Impale him!" he shouted.

The condemned man received the sentence without fear, the cynical, tight smile not leaving his face. Then he raised his head. "I want to say my last words!" he shouted. Then, with a challenging tone, he addressed Dracula: "You are the highest ecclesiastical authority in Wallachia! You are the defender of our God Jesus Christ, of his law and his faith! And it is him you have to obey! Your law is very clear: the ones who steal, kill, rape, and betray you will die impaled. But that is your law. I tell you that there is another law that is above yours: the law of God. And it says any sinner will receive forgiveness if there is repentance, because our Christ died on the cross and shed his blood for that forgiveness. I am very repentant, and there isn't a sin, no matter how monstrous, that is worth more than one drop of the savior's precious blood. By the blood of Christ, you have to forgive me! Real justice comes only from our God, and our sins are judged in the final judgment, in front of our real and only judge, our Christ!"

Dracula was prepared for everything except an argument so solidly supported. The crowd stood in dead silence, stunned by that brilliant defense.

The letch felt victory within his grasp. He waited, not doubting his imminent release.

An insignificant and simple trial had turned into a dilemma of moral values to Dracula. On the one hand there was the rapist, who wanted divine justice and his freedom; on the other there were the people, who wanted real justice and the impalement of a beast. Dracula felt the collective gaze of his subjects; his prestige and the future of justice in Wallachia depended on his decision. What was he going to do? If he applied his law, he would be stepping on the law of God, and the sacrifice of his Christ would be worthless—and Dracula wished with all his might to be its greatest defender. He concluded that it must be his God whom he would serve, even if he had to change his name and the world turned against him.

7

Everything was clear now to the judge. He raised his right hand and prepared to announce his verdict, which the townspeople craved as a thirsty man craves water.

The inscrutable energy of quantum physics, by which future events affect the past in a way that our logical minds can never comprehend, made a strange move on December 25, 1431. On that day, in Sigishoara, there was born a boy who would become the most hardened defender of Christianity. As the Western world celebrated the birth of Jesus Christ, Dracula arrived among us.

2

Since the Emperor Constantine felt the need to be Christian, he did it in the Roman style: in the year 325, by his order at the historic Council of Nicaea, Jesus Christ was declared God, and Christianity was established all over the Western world. Over the following centuries Christ's divinity was challenged by all kinds of renegades, infidels, and heretics, but it was also defended by a great number of brave men, martyrs, heroes, and philosophers who didn't hesitate to sacrifice their blood and even their lives for it—among them Saul of Tarsus, Joseph of Arimathea, Augustine of Hippo, Pope Damascus I, Cyriacus and Paula, Leoncio of Tripoli, Ovidio, Tarcisius, Isidore of Chios, Eusebius of Nicomedia, Pepin the Brief and his son Charlemagne, Pius II, Sigismund of Luxemburg, Janos Hunyadi, Mikhail Szilagyi . . . and Dracula

---

In 1408, the Hungarian king Sigismund of Luxemburg appeared before Pope Gregory XII at the Vatican. "I've always admired and respected the crusader knights—their history, their legendary bravery, and their military fight for the Christian faith," he said. "I ask for your authorization to create and establish an order to defend the faith of our Christ."

"Tell me about your project," the Holy Father said.

"I wish to establish a semimonastic military order," Sigismund said. "We will invite kings, princes, and prominent military men to join us, and we will defend the Christian faith from heresy and infidelity with the strength of our weapons. We'll call it the Order of the Dragon in tribute to Saint George, who killed the dragon with his powerful sword."

"You have my authorization," the pope told him, "From now on, I appoint you master of the Order of the Dragon, and I wish you all the success in the world. Kneel and receive my blessing."

3

Both the Ottoman sultan and the king of Hungary were trying to force into vassalage the ruler of Wallachia, Mircea the Great, grandfather of Dracula. Desperate for a solution to his problem, Mircea asked his two sons for their opinions of his oppressors.

Alexandru Aldea, his firstborn, spoke: "I think we should ally openly with the Ottoman sultan—he is stronger—and we should tell Sigismund to go to hell."

Vlad II, Alexandru's half-brother, said, "I think we should ally with the king of Hungary. He believes in Christ."

"We have had good relations with both rulers," Mircea told them. "We pay tribute to the sultan, and besides paying Sigismund, we also have allowed him to establish the catholic church in Wallachia. As a result, they both respect us. But I am really worried that the moment will come when they will ask us to choose sides—and we will end up going to war with one of them."

"If there is going to be a war, let it be against the Ottomans!" Vlad shouted.

"Better it be against the king!" refuted Alexandru—and, as usual, the argument continued between the half-brothers.

Mircea watched them, thinking, *Are they always going to be like that? Maybe I should let them argue to see if, for once, they reach an agreement.* When he saw that, instead, they were on the verge of a fistfight, he screamed, "Enough! Both of you shut up and do what I say! For the moment, we will continue doing the same thing we've been doing, although I am really worried. Why do you always force me to control you with violence? What will become of you when I am gone?"

When Mircea died, his sons inherited his lineage. Soon afterward, several emissaries of the king of Hungary, escorted by well-nourished soldiers, arrived in Wallachia and delivered into the sons' hands a sealed envelope sent by the powerful ruler. The emissaries would rest that day, and the next they were to leave with the sons' response.

Mircea's sons opened the envelope in private: it was an invitation to join the Order of the Dragon.

Flattered, Vlad remarked, "I've always wanted to belong to an order like this one."

Alexandru looked worried. He was silent for a few moments and then said, "If we become members of that order and the sultan finds out, we will almost certainly have a war against the Ottomans."

"We have to be brave and face Murad!" Vlad said. "He is an enemy of our God. If he wants war, we will give him war! Anyway, we won't be fighting alone. Let us join the order, Alexandru!"

Again Alexandru remained silent awhile before responding. "I am not sure about my Christian faith," he finally said. "For instance, I don't think that Jesus died on the cross, and I don't believe that absurdity about the forgiveness of sins. I feel Islam is more authentic than Christianity, and it is tolerant of all religions. If we join the sultan, our people will be able to believe what they wish; we would never have a papal inquisition. I think the Ottomans are right. And besides, the sultan's army is a lot more powerful than all the Christians put together."

Vlad stared skeptically at his half-brother, and then, taking a deep breath, asked him, "Are you telling me that you doubt the divinity of our Christ?" He sat in silence, waiting for an answer.

Alexandru did not want to answer such questions. Why waste his time arguing? He was the vovoid; he had no obligation to take into consideration his brother's opinion. Right now he was quietly hating Vlad, who had always criticized his decisions. If Alexandru had to choose between Murad and Sigismund, he would not hesitate to improve his relations with the Ottoman sultan. Alexandru's agile mind quickly devised a plan. "You will go with the king," he said, "and you'll tell him that I'll be ordained later. Meanwhile, you'll become a member of the Order of the Dragon."

Being the good military man he was, Vlad II fulfilled the order gladly. At midnight of February 8, 1431, in the main hall of the imperial castle of Nuremberg, king of Hungary Sigismund of Luxemburg, master of the Order of the Dragon, along with the knights of the order, prepared to welcome three new members.

The master was in the middle of the main entrance hall, in the place of honor. On the wall above him was the emblem of the Order of the Dragon, and on top of that, lighted by two big torches, was a great crucifix. Standing around the initiates were the knights in their ceremonial suits, validating with their presence the importance of the event. And standing in front of the master were the candidates: Prince Ladislas of Poland, Prince Lazarevic of Serbia, and Prince Vlad II from Wallachia. A cross hung upon each man's chest, and upon each man's shoulders lay two capes: a red one representing the blood of the martyrs who had fallen defending the Christian faith, and on top of that a black one representing the power of Christ over his enemies.

The elaborate ritual of initiation was moving forward, with each prince swearing faithfulness and loyalty to the Holy Father in the Vatican and to the king of the Romans and his wife and children, born and unborn. Then the great master headed toward Vlad, stopped in front of him, and held a huge sword before him with its blade pointing toward heaven. "On your knees!" he ordered.

The prince obeyed, and then, in a ceremonious voice, the master said, "I, Sigismund of Luxemburg, King of the Romans, in the name of God the Father almighty, his only son Jesus Christ, and the Holy Spirit, appoint you, Vlad, knight of the Order of the Dragon." As he spoke, the king rested the blade on the initiate's right shoulder. "You will continue to defend our God with all your heart and all your resources, and you will not hesitate to give your life, your children, your wife, your land, and your power for him. He gave them to you, and you owe them to him!" Then he switched the blade to the prince's left shoulder, saying, "From now on and until your death, you will be a dracul knight of the Order of the Dragon."

The unspoken acceptance of each initiate was indicated by the absolute silence of the knights witnessing the ceremony. Among the most prominent were Janos Hunyadi, the White Knight known as the most powerful defender of Christianity at that time and a bitter enemy of the Ottomans, and his brother-in-law, the great Mikhail Szilagyi

Immediately after each initiation, the king produced a gold necklace shaped like a dragon biting its tail, symbolizing the victory of Christ over evil; at the bottom was a red cross with the Latin inscription *O Quam Misericoris est Desus y Justus y Pio*. He placed the necklace on the initiate's neck and then raised a small dagger whose gold handle was carved with the symbol of a dragon. Offering a solemn prayer, the king gave the weapon to the initiate, saying, "Keep this dagger as a symbol of your belonging to our order, and honor it by bathing it with the blood of heretics and infidels. You'll account for it with your life!" He performed the same ritual with all three aspirants, each of whom was ceremoniously invested with the same honorable charge.

"From now on," the king said, "you will profess Catholicism and allow the Catholic Church to be established and flourish in your kingdom. You will defend the pope and everything he represents."

A scream resounded inside Vlad's head: *No! I am an Orthodox!* But had it escaped his throat, it would have assured his immediate expulsion from the order—and now he needed his fellow knights in order to face the Ottomans who were threatening him. Besides, he was not the vovoid of Wallachia at the moment. So he kept silent and accepted the order against his will. He was happy to become a Dracul knight, because it served his own interests.

At the end, the king said to Vlad, "Your mission will be to defend Wallachia from our enemies, the Ottomans; therefore, I appoint you military governor of Transylvania."

Alexandru Aldea went on with the second part of his plan, and while Vlad was fulfilling his orders, he traveled to the Ottoman Empire to strengthen his relations with the sultan. Alexandru was received the way any ally would be: with a bounty of succulent and exotic dishes and a suite of young women willing to satisfy his every wish. Then Murad II asked him, "What about your brother, Vlad—where is he?"

Trying to make his hated brother look bad, Alexandru said, "I could not prevent him from going to see King Sigismund. He went there with the intention of becoming a knight of the Order of the Dragon."

Curious, the sultan asked, "What kind of order is that?"

"It's a semimonastic order; its objective is to defend the Christian faith."

"And have you been ordained?"

"I never will!" Alexandru answered emphatically, "My heart belongs to Allah; I don't agree with the Christian religion, its institutions, and its absurd ideas about the forgiveness of sins."

"Then you are willing to swear before a Bible and the Koran that you will be faithful to me, and as proof you will renew your pact with me?" the sultan asked.

"Gladly."

And so the pact was signed: each year Alexandru would deliver to the empire ten thousand gold coins and one thousand children between seven and fourteen years old to be part of the sultan's army. These children would become ferocious Janissaries.

Vlad II returned to Wallachia as a dracul knight, and from that moment on, the people called him by a new name, Dracul. He established his base in Sigishoara because of its central location, flying a banner showing a dragon biting its tail. Alexandru was furious but stayed silent. He wanted to take his half-brother's title away from him and kill him immediately, but if he did, he would surely start a war against the king of the Romans.

Dracul visited the Saxon town of Sibiu, where there lived an especially talented gunsmith named Jared. "We have to make more powerful weapons," Dracul told him. "The enemy's army is getting stronger and bigger."

"In China they have a special powder that ignites to make beautiful cascades of brilliant light in the night sky," Jared said. "They are experimenting with it for military purposes."

Dracul pressed some gold coins into his hand. "Take these and go there," he said. "Do some research, buy that powder, and do whatever it takes to develop that technology. We must have better weapons."

"No need to say that again—I'll leave immediately," Jared said.

At the end of their discussion, the clever Saxon added, "We have made a delicious banquet in your honor. We hope you like it."

After eating sumptuously, Dracul went to congratulate the cooks on the excellent meal; they were pleased by his courtesy. Finally he bid farewell to his friends and returned to Sigishoara.

4

A group of knights of the Order of the Dragon could be seen in the distance, and the heart of one humble peasant began beating fast and hard. When the knights passed in front of her, she only had eyes for their leader, the powerful military governor of Transylvania. She bowed to show her respect, like the other peasants, watching him out of the corner of her eye. He was the man of her dreams. Whenever he left her sight, her heart seemed to leave her chest. That happened every time she saw him.

Behind the soldiers there was a group of children riding sticks and holding other sticks at their waists, pretending they were riding spirited steeds and carrying terrifying swords. They trailed the soldiers for a short stretch, imitating their heroes.

Dracul noticed the beautiful woman in the crowd and realized she was watching him discreetly. He briefly returned her look with a gentlemanly salute. The peasant felt she would die—a salute just for her? It was like a dream! The secret love burned in her chest, and she realized with sadness that he was a thief who had stolen her heart. He was the one who caused the tremendous pain in her chest every time she thought of him . . . and she thought of him all day. She wanted to forget him, but the more she tried, the more she realized that the most wretched traitor was inside her: it was her own damned heart. The innocent peasant was Cupid's victim; her nights went by slowly, her dreams both a torment and an opportunity to be with her charming prince. Those dreams were a pressure valve, relieving her torture, and they were her worst torment. She would go to sleep touching herself. Nature is a powerful thing. The woman's thoughts were powerful, too, making their quantum movement toward Dracul without his even knowing it, creating a love trap.

Dracul frequently passed through that village and searched for that look, those beautiful blue eyes. Why did she look at him that way? He asked around about the woman and found her address. She lived with her big family in a small shack.

Feeling she had reached the limits of her willpower, the woman decided to throw herself into the arms of the thief and abandon herself to nature. But what if she did it and was rejected? What would her parents say? What would her friends say? She cursed her beloved, hating him for causing her so much pain. And yet she could not stop loving him. Another night of hell awaited her.

———◆◆◆———

Dracul arrived at his house after an agitating day, ready to rest. But first he decided to satisfy his vigorous nature. His beautiful wife was lying in bed, and so, looking at her lustfully, he got undressed and approached her.

Trying to distract him from his intentions, she said loudly, "How did it go, my love?"

Vlad leaned down and whispered in her ear: "I fixed all my problems but one." He put his arms around her waist and pulled her toward him. Looking into her eyes, he said hoarsely, "But I am going to fix it right now. You look more beautiful than ever."

The woman felt her husband's power, and when she saw his intentions she answered mildly, "Thank you—you look handsome, too." She kissed him quickly on the mouth and added sharply, "Have a good night, my love." With that she tried to move away immediately.

Vlad was persistent. "Good night?" he said mischievously. "I am going to give you a good night!" He tried to kiss her on the mouth.

Knowing that after that kiss would come another and another, and no one was going to stop him until he was satisfied, his wife extended her arms and used them as a barrier. "Honey," she said in an imploring tone, "I am very tired. I had an especially difficult day today. Can you 'understand'? What if we leave this for tomorrow?"

"You said the same thing yesterday, and the day before yesterday," he complained, "and the truth is I really want you. You're not going to get away from me today!"

The woman turned her back, but her husband hugged her and started kissing her neck. So again she faced him and used her arms as a barrier, insisting, "I am really tired—and you are insatiable! Please. I promise tomorrow I'll do everything you want."

17

"Not another day," he demanded, upset now. "Come close. I love you."

At that his wife fairly screamed at him, "I love you, too, but can you not 'understand' that my head is hurting? Let me sleep. I'll do whatever you want tomorrow, not today. That's my last word." With that she turned around and covered her head with the blanket.

Dracul was confused. He loved his wife dearly, but she did not seem to understand that he was about to burst. He pulled back the blanket and tried to force her to fulfill her marital obligations, but she refused so vigorously that the whole thing erupted in a big argument. "I am not a God that 'understands'!" he yelled. "I am an animal that needs a woman! Please give me what I am asking for—I need it!"

The woman turned and answered furiously, "Do whatever you want. I don't care!"

Dracul jumped out of bed, got dressed, and got on his horse with no destination in mind. The issue with his wife was so exasperating that he could not begin to understand it. After all, he loved her; she was a good woman and the selfless mother of his sons.

As he struggled with uncertainty, destiny decided to play a trick on him.

Riding aimlessly, the powerful military governor of Transylvania was looking to the moonlight for a solution to his problem. His reproductive system did not give in to his intention to rest, and kept its rigid posture. Then the memory of those beautiful and enigmatic blue eyes came to his mind like lightning.

Meanwhile, in her little shack, the overwhelming power of lust tormented the peasant woman. She could not remove from her mind thoughts of the powerful knight she could only have in her dreams. She touched herself, hating and loving him, without knowing that the strength of her thoughts had led the defenseless Dracul to her doorstep.

Standing outside the shack, he knocked on the thin door with determination. The loud noise woke the peasant from her erotic thoughts.

"Who is knocking at this hour?" came the voice of an older man. Everyone else in the shack was afraid, wondering the same thing.

The answer to their question was another knock on the door, this time stronger.

The older man lit a torch and took up a plow to face the intruder, his family hiding behind him. When the peasant opened the door he could not believe it: in front of him was the powerful military governor of Transylvania, the great Dracul, without an escort! Unsure whether what he saw was dream or reality, he lowered his humble weapon and bowed his head. "Forgive me, my lord," he said shyly. "I did not know it was you. How can I serve you?"

With the daring of a prince, Dracul stepped into the shack and, taking the girl by the hand, asked, "Can we talk for a little while?" The peasant girl could not believe it. She could not stop staring at his eyes, and she felt she was in the middle of a dream. She was speechless.

Her father brought her back from her reverie. "He asked you if you could talk! Are you deaf?"

There were no more words, no questions, nothing. Dracul took her to a barn at the back of the shack.

The moonlight illuminated the two lovers as the girl looked Dracul in the eyes. "Thief, you stole my heart," she said softly, and she gave him a long, passionate kiss.

Her kiss unleashed a storm inside Dracul, who sensed the lust of that inexperienced woman. The storm became a hurricane that swirled around the two lovers. Nature shook them. Blood, pain, sweat, and tears further fueled their passion—once, and then another, and another, and another time. Finally, happy and satisfied, Dracul asked, "What is your name?"

"Caltuna," the girl answered quietly, looking at him steadily.

"Your name is as pretty as you are," Dracul said. He was silent for a moment and then asked, "Why didn't you tell me you were a maiden?"

"Because you are the prince of my dreams," she said simply. "I always imagined giving my virtue to the man I love the most." She sighed, stretching. "I feel like I am in a dream—and I don't want to wake up!" Dracul felt himself falter, and then his inner fire blazed again and he threw himself over his lover—and that's the way sunrise surprised them.

When he took Caltuna back to her shack, her entire family was awake, hungry for news of their relative.

Dracula turned to the older man, Caltuna's father. "From tomorrow on," he said, "you will live in a decent home I will provide for you. You will not be in need. Caltuna is from now on my lover, and she belongs only to me. No man except you and her brothers may talk to her. No man will see her. And she will not work. That is the word of the military governor of Transylvania."

When Caltuna heard his words, which marked her as his possession, she cried from excitement. She can not believe so happiness.

Dracul spent all his free time with her, and she wanted nothing more than to be with him.

In November 1453, Caltuna gave her beloved prince the product of their love. Dracul was happy: he had another child, a beautiful blond boy with blue eyes, who looked very much like his beautiful mother. Dracul had him baptized with the name of Wladislaus Calugarul. Through this formal recognition by his father, the child was being validated as a candidate to the throne. The people would call him Vlad Calugarul; later the world would know him as Vlad the Monk.

Caltuna was happy; she knew that sooner or later her son was going to rule Wallachia and she would be immensely influential—rich and powerful like she had never imagined.

5

Dracul visited Jared again. "What improvements have you made in your work?" he asked.

"You're not going to believe it," the gunsmith said. "You have to see it with your own eyes." And he led Dracul outside, where he had one small cannon, and fired it off.

"This is incredible!" Dracul exclaimed. "It's a devil's weapon!"

"And we are just getting started," Jared added proudly. "We experimented with bigger cannons, but the strength of the gunpowder breaks them. To fix the problem we are experimenting with new alloys, and when we find the right one, we are going to fabricate a great cannon— you'll be able to conquer the world with it! In the meantime, though, we need more money to buy more gunpowder and metals."

Dracul was elated, saying, "I am astonished by your improvements. Here are more gold coins, and I congratulate you!" As was customary, before he left he enjoyed a delicious banquet, and at the end he went to the kitchen to compliment the cooks for their wonderful work.

6

A great part of the sultan's powerful army headed toward Wallachia.

Dracul was in the training field when Balac, one of his faithful boyars, arrived wide-eyed and breathless. "My lord," he gasped, "I found out a retinue of Ottoman soldiers is coming—and this time they mean to kill you!"

Realizing that his half-brother had betrayed him, Dracul addressed his boyars said, "Those of you who follow me must do so of your own will. We are going to defend the faith of our Christ against our new enemy—my brother, Alexandru." He quickly found out who really were his faithful boyars, and there were many. With this large retinue, he planned to travel to see the king of Hungary, Sigismund of Luxemburg. But first he went to get his two sons.

After greeting the king, Dracul said, "My lord, my half-brother is going to attack us with the Ottomans."

Enraged, Sigismund began cursing in his mother tongue. "You should leave immediately to fight against him!" he said angrily. "I am going to give you some of my men, and you must dethrone the traitor!" He paused for a long time and then added in a calmer voice, "You know, my life's desire was to have a male son, but God only blessed me with my daughter, Isabel. Give me the pleasure of having your sons brighten my existence with their company."

Dracul knew the real reason for that petition: the ruler wanted the children as collateral, a guarantee that Dracul would not betray him. And since he did not have the least intention of doing so, Dracul thought that was an excellent idea; in fact, he remembered that when he was a child, his father had also left him as collateral with the same Sigismund. The association evoked pleasant memories of his enjoyable stay at the royal court, surrounded by luxury, a good education, and all the fine things in life. "My lord," Dracul said, "you were like a father to me. You honor me with your desire, and to fulfill it will be more than a pleasure. Although my children are very close and are always together, I need one to stay home and learn the military arts and rule his people, and in that way to keep on serving you."

"You're right," the King said. "I grant you the grace to choose which one you will take with you."

Mircea and Vlad III looked at their father plaintively; one of them was going to receive, without deserving it, the most wonderful punishment he could ever imagine.

Dracul, whose preference for his firstborn was well known, took him by the shoulder, saying, "I am taking Mircea!" Vlad's eyes filled with tears.

The next day Dracul said good-bye to Vlad, who asked him with tears in his eyes, "Dad, have I not been a good boy? Haven't I said my prayers? What did I do wrong? I don't want to stay here!"

Dracul, a good father, answered him lovingly. "Son, you are descended from a dynasty of rulers, and you should behave accordingly. When I was ten years old, your grandfather left me with king Sigismund, and I received an excellent education. I learned court manners, philosophy, literature, Greek, Latin, Italian—and Maria, his wife, taught me French. I went to Prague, Nuremberg, Rome, and other places. I also learned combat techniques. This place was the best school of my life. I am leaving you in the hands of a friend. The king was like a father to me, and now he will be the same for you. You will learn many things that will help you, in the right time, to be a wise, intelligent, and fair ruler. Trust me: someday I'll be back, I promise you! Then you will be able to understand that this sacrifice was worth it."

Vlad trusted his father completely. He knew that if he put his heart and soul in his father's hands, his father would never fail him. Despite his young age, he understood that his father was making the decision for his own good and for the good of his people. Vlad hugged Mircea, and both of them cried like the children they were. Finally, when they could cry no more, they accepted their destiny, their sad separation.

Before saying good-bye to Vlad, Dracul told him, "Son, I know you are only five, but try to have strong relations with these friends. They are good people. However, they are Catholic, and you must hold on to your Orthodox faith." Then, giving Vlad his blessing, Dracul left. At that moment Vlad III felt like a prisoner, although he was following in the footsteps of his father.

⬥

Father Nicolas instructed the boy in the new religious orthodoxy and gave him his first lesson: "The first thing I am going to correct is the way you make the sign of the cross. From now on you'll make it crossing the thumb with the forefinger and the rest of the fingers straight."

Vlad leaned everything quickly. He soon knew all the saints and virgins, but the most important thing he learned was that his new God, Jesus Christ, was still the same. The Holy Trinity was three different people, but there was only one real God, who did not change. He clearly understood the problem of the Filioque: to the Orthodox, the Holy Spirit came from the Father through the Son, and to the Catholics it came from the Father or the Son. Despite his young age, Vlad was surprised that this insignificant difference had caused so many fights and conflicts throughout history. Was it really so difficult for Christians and Orthodox to understand that there was only one God, Jesus Christ, and if the power of the Holy Spirit came from one or the other or from both, at the end it was manifested as the strength of God? Why was that such an issue? Still, he had promised his father that he would hold on to his Orthodox faith, and he did. In his mind he could understand and reconcile both doctrines without trouble. He was sure of one thing: he had great faith in Christ, and he prayed for his loved ones every night.

In the king's court Vlad learned four languages, philosophy, history, and other valuable knowledge that would help him throughout his life, and he studied and practiced the refined manners of the court. From a very young age, therefore, he was a complete little gentlemen; he knew how to treat everyone correctly, like the most skillful and respected court member.

Time went by that way for a child of royal lineage: lots of learning but little play. Vlad also mastered the technique of behaving like a chameleon; he could profess the Orthodox and Catholic doctrines readily and without confusing the two. Anyone who saw him profess the Catholic faith never would have never imagined that his faithful heart was Orthodox.

7

"Attack! Let us defend the faith of our God!" That was the scream that came from Dracul's throat in Albis. But the soldiers who were joining him were not enough to defeat the enemy. When he saw they were surpassed in number by the Ottomans, he said to his bugler, "Play retreat!"

Later, exhausted and with his army decimated, Dracul arrived before the king and told him, "We were defeated by Alexandru and his allies."

Sigismund spoke to the military governor of Transylvania and said, "You must join Dracul. Together you have to defeat our enemy." Then, addressing Dracul, the king said, "If your half-brother, the traitor, has allies, know that you are not alone. Here is a bag with gold coins to buy weapons and achieve the victory."

In the town of Amlas, Dracul made an economic transaction with the Saxons, exchanging gold for military armaments. In December Dracul defeated his half-brother and took him prisoner. "Bring me Alexandru!" he said to his boyars. "I want to speak with him." The order was immediately carried out, and there, in his home, he asked his brother, "Why did you make an alliance with our enemies?"

"Because they are stronger," Alexandru said, "and because my real God is Allah."

"But that's not the God of our parents. That is a savage god!"

"Savage is your god, Jesus Christ," Alexandru answered furiously, "who not only leaves without justice the victims of criminals but also rewards the crime with his divine grace if the sinner says he has repented, and who forgives the same sin not just once but a thousand times if another cynical, maybe fake, and without a doubt cowardly apology is uttered. That kind of justice, that godly attitude, is to me a grotesque mockery of the victim. How is it possible that a representative of that God can hear a criminal's confession and then the victim's plea for restitution—if restitution is even possible—and then give, indiscriminately, divine forgiveness for the crime that was not even committed against him? Doesn't the representative become an accomplice of the sinner by recognizing the crime, forgiving him, and not denouncing him to the authorities? Does your god or that representative care about the victim's pain and thirst for justice? What will stop a criminal if he knows perfectly well that he can commit the same sin as often as he wants, or do the greatest atrocity imaginable, and he'll always find forgiveness through the blood sacrifice of your unfair god?"

"Instead of bravely facing the consequences of his vile actions and suffering the punishment that the law of his society imposes, the sinner conveniently seeks impunity, and he knows where to find it. The only thing he has to do is show his cowardly repentance before his partial judge, who will always impose the ridiculous punishment of repeating like a parrot a prayer to that god. That judge indubitably becomes an accomplice to those crimes. When the crime is theft, the two discreetly share the loot, and the part that belongs to the representative of your god is disguised by the word *alms*. That is what you call divine justice?"

"They say your god is the owner of all the gold and silver, all the wealth in the world, and yet his representatives are always begging . . . I don't understand them. In Islam, every man is responsible for his own actions before Allah, who is a strong and fair God."

When Dracul heard those heretical words, he understood that his brother had been poisoned by the sultan's religion. He was silent for a moment and then said, "Our father raised us in the Christian Orthodox faith, and we have to defend our Christ. We are not alone; there are many nations that support us. Rectify your beliefs, and don't allow a savage god to take their place."

In response to his proposal he received a look full of hatred followed by a long pause; that silence by Alexandru spoke a thousand words.

Breaking the silence, Dracul asked him, "Why did you ally with the Ottomans?"

"Because of their power. That is my real god! The Ottomans held me with it, and now you can take it away from me and feel supported by the failures of the Order of the Dragon and their allies. Enjoy your victory for now, because soon my allies will come and place me back on my throne."

Dracul was so enraged that his single word exploded from his chest like a volcano erupting: "Traitor!" The shout echoed through the house.

Realizing his half-brother was unarmed, Alexandru seized the opportunity to snatch a sword being displayed on the wall, and he stared directly at him.

Dracul knew that when he had asked the guard to leave him alone, he had made a big mistake; he had trusted his half-brother, and because he was in his own house, he was unarmed. He turned to grab his own sword, but it was out of reach.

Alexandru's eyes were sparkling with a strange glow. In a low, determined voice, he said, "I am going to kill you . . . like I should have done a long time ago." Then he let out a shriek and threw himself onto Dracul, sword raised high.

In a fraction of a second, Dracul remembered the dagger that had been given to him during his ordination. He took it out and threw it at the traitor, plunging it straight into his heart. The enemy stopped, his sword clattering to the floor. Then he put his hands to his chest and collapsed.

Dracul quickly took the sword from his enemy, but that wasn't necessary. The cowardly aggressor was lying in the fetal position, preparing to face his final judgment. Dracul leaned over and took the dagger out of his brother's chest; it was covered with blood. With an indescribable emotion he knelt down, lifted the dagger with both hands, and with head bowed and eyes closed, prayed, "My God, today I have baptized my dagger with infidel blood. From the depths of my being, I promise you I will not waste an opportunity to honor it in your name."

When he left; he went to the town council, comprised of Saxons, who had gathered to discuss the succession of the new ruler. Knowing that they would be the real power behind the power, they authorized Dracul as the new vovoid of Wallachia.

8

Little Vlad III was hiding behind a screen, reading a book, when arrived. Hunyadi was joined by six soldiers, each of them carrying two bags of gold. The soldiers placed the bags on a table and left. When the two men were alone, the king hugged Hunyadi and kissed him on the cheek, saying, "Thank you very much, my son. What would I do without your help?"

"Dad helping you is my greatest pleasure," Hunyadi answered warmly. "I know that all your efforts are directed to the defense of the faith of our Christ."

Vlad might as well have been struck by lightning. Janos Hunyadi a bastard son of king Sigismund? He ran away from that place without being seen, asking God for the strength to keep that secret.

On December 9, 1437, little Vlad was crying before the corpse of the one he considered his second father; now it was Sigismund's turn to appear before his final judgment. Without his great support, Vlad felt alone. He became quiet, doing nothing but read, pray, and study at the top of a tower, watching the horizon with the hope that someday his father would come back for him.

9

On March 6, 1438, the silence of the tower was interrupted by a joyful shout: "Son!"

His heart nearly leaping from his chest, Vlad III tossed aside the book he was reading and threw himself into the arms of his father, tears running down his face. Shocked by his own crying, he said, "Dad—I can't believe it!" Then he turned to hug Mircea. "Brother," he said, "I have missed you so much!" Vlad stepped back and looked at his father, anguished. "Are you going to take me home with you?"

"Yes," answered his loving father. "And we are not going to be apart, ever again."

That night the three of them prayed together, and then the father blessed his sons. "I am very happy," said little Vlad III. "Can you tell me a story?"

"Gladly, Son," said his father, and with the boys eager to listen with all their attention, the tale began: "When the Christians took Jerusalem in the first crusade, special defenders of Christianity appeared. They were known as Knights Templar, and they dressed in white with a huge red cross on their back and chest. These were warrior monks who defended the faith of our God, and they purified their swords with infidel blood. One day . . ."

Vlad III was amazed, carried away by the story. He wished with all his heart to someday become like one of these legendary characters who defended the faith of Christ with the power of their sword. Vlad's thoughts would follow the quantum path and direct his yearned-for destiny: to become the most ferocious defender of Christ.

Vlad II reached the end of his story, and father and sons exchanged blessings and went to bed happy. When they went back home, was as if they'd never been apart.

In Wallachia the reunited brothers were inseparable. They studied all morning, and in the afternoon they played. One day Mircea had an idea for a new game: "Let's pretend we are spies. What if we start by spying on the vovoid to discover his connection with the Ottoman enemies?"

Vlad III nodded, adding excitedly, "You lead the action, and I'll follow your orders!"

And that's what they did, riding their ponies with the discretion that the delicate mission deserved. They spied on the supposed enemy, following him at a distance as he left their home and rode unescorted to a nice house, where a beautiful woman came out to meet him with a passionate kiss. At that moment a little blond boy came running from behind the house, chasing a chick, and the woman called, "Vlad, your father is here!" The boy interrupted his play and ran to meet his father, giving him a kiss on the cheek. Then the three of them went inside the house.

The scene was like a bombshell to the young spies; they looked at each other in silence, not daring to ask the thousand questions that came all at once into their heads: Who was that woman? Where did that boy come from? Why did their father kiss them? Was that brat their half-brother? Why did their father go to that house instead of being with his real family?

Feelings of jealousy and hatred toward the two strangers who had stolen the love of their father flourished inside the brothers, whose first inclination was to kill them. They brothers kept spying and learned that the woman was their father's lover and the child was his son, to whom he'd given his legal name. The boy was called Vlad Calugarul.

After assimilating such unpleasant news, Mircea stared at his brother and said mockingly, "You are Vlad, just like that Vlad! Vlad! Vlad! Vlad!"

Enraged, Vlad threw himself at Mircea and started beating on him furiously. Mircea roared with laughter, enjoying the rage of his beloved brother, and to the further humiliation of the little one he said, "You punch like a woman!"

"Like a woman?" Vlad shouted, gathering his strength for a renewed assault. "Take that! And that! And that!" But the only thing Vlad achieved was to make his big brother laugh harder.

Finally Vlad stopped, exhausted and breathless. Mircea looked at him, eyebrows raised. "Are you done yet?" he asked. "Now it's my turn!" And he held Vlad tightly, immobilizing the little boy and increasing his sense of rage and helplessness. "You're mine, Wladislaus!" he said. But after this display of arrogance and brute force, Mircea gave his little brother a warm hug. "My dear Vlad," he said, smiling. "What would I do without you? I love you."

Vlad's anger evaporated, replaced by powerful, pure love. The brothers understood that their love was stronger than all other passions.

Mircea took Vlad by the shoulders and said, "We must keep the secret so we don't cause suffering to our mom. Promise me you won't say a word about this!"

"I promise," Vlad said. "What about you?"

"I promise, too," Mircea answered.

For weeks afterward they viewed their father with a certain distrust and anger, but time helped cure their displeasure, and eventually everything went back to normal.

One day the brothers went deep into the forest, pretending to be explorers. (Actually they knew the area very well.) When they were crossing a river, Vlad found a beautiful little stone and remarked, "Look at this beauty!"

"Let me see it," said Mircea.

"It's mine," Vlad said mockingly, showing it to him from far away, "and I won't let you have it!"

"I don't need to ask you for it," Mircea warned, walking toward him. "You're going to give it to me right now." And with that Vlad was dispossessed of his incredible find.

"Take that . . . and that!" Another shower of blows fell upon Mircea, who only laughed, enraging Vlad to the point of tears.

Mircea gave his younger brother a cynical smile. "Do you see now that I'm stronger than you? That is why I am always right! And this stone is the tribute I demand from you to protect you from your enemies." He put the treasure in his pocket.

Vlad's blood boiled, and he answered Mircea with another share of blows. When he was too tired to continue, he said, "Give me my rock . . . or I'll tell dad you're a thief!"

"You can't do that," Mircea complained. "Our dad has forbidden us to steal!"

"And what did you do, Mircea? Steal from me! You'll see—when we get home I'm going to tell on you."

Faced with such a threat, Mircea had no choice but to return the stone, saying, "Take your filthy stone. You're a crybaby, Wladislaus!" Vlad took it, a smile lighting his face.

When the boys arrived home, Vlad told his parents, "Look what a pretty stone I found!"

"It's really beautiful!" their mother said.

Mircea asked Vlad again and again for that stone, and Vlad would tease him by showing it to him from a distance but not letting him touch it. Vlad would have given Mircea his very life if he had asked for it—but the little round stone? Never! It was too gratifying to see Mircea really mad.

10

Dracul remarked to one of his boyars, Ivan, "I am really worried. Now that the emperor has died, who is going to lead us in battle against the sultan?"

"No one better than Hunyadi," Ivan answered. "He was the emperor's right hand, and it was well known that he even donated a lot of his own money to meet the expenses of his government."

"Janos is both wealthy and brave," agreed Dracul. "Let's wait for him to get organized; I am sure that at the right time he will present to us his strategy against our enemy."

The three archbishops and four archdukes who made up the town council in Hungary, representing the interests of the powerful, had gathered to appoint a new king. One of the men said, "The stupidest thing we have done was to rush our last election without properly evaluating the candidates. We chose Sigismund quickly, and you can see how that came out!"

There were murmurs of agreement among the councilmen, who had been very uncomfortable with the fact that they couldn't control Sigismund as they pleased; he had made decisions without consulting them.

Another councilman said, "We must take the time we need to find a man we can manage to suit our interests."

Everyone concurred: they would take the necessary time to look for the right puppet to occupy the position of king of Hungary.

Meanwhile, on March 15, 1438, envoys of the powerful Sultan Murad II, protected by a huge retinue of Ottoman Janissaries, appeared before the vovoid of Wallachia. The chief falconer envoy in charge said, "We come on behalf of our master with the intention of making a pact. You shall deliver to the sultan ten thousand gold coins per year and one thousand children of conscription, and in exchange you will have peace and our support in case another ruler wants to subjugate you."

Dracul, obviously worried, answered, "That is a very high tribute. We cannot pay it."

"We'll take Wallachia if you don't sign right now," the envoy said. "The bulk of our army is just outside the town; your people will be ours, and we will be able to sell them as slaves. You won't be able to avoid it!"

Dracul had no good options. He was being forced to make a pact breaking the oath he had made before the Order of the Dragon, and that was a nightmare for him. Now who would help him? Where would he find support? He felt alone, convinced that his people's safety had to come first. Reluctantly he answered, "You don't leave me another choice . . . I'll sign the pact."

Dracul informed all of Wallachia that next year they would have to pay tribute according to the terms of the pact, and each village was given an assigned amount it had to contribute. Thus the inhabitants of Wallachia again became slaves of the powerful Ottoman sultan.

A year passed, and again an enormous retinue representing the Ottoman interests appeared, this time with the intention of collecting the tribute. Dracul took his two sons with him so they could see firsthand the most difficult part of governing. They went together with their oppressors, traveling to each village and charging the impoverished peasants, who paid in unhappy silence.

When it was the peasant Kardotas's turn to pay tribute, the humble man told them, "My daughter has been sick from a strange disease, so I took her to the doctor. I spent all I had, and so I had to borrow some money," he added with tears in his eyes. "No matter how hard we tried, we couldn't cure her, and she died. I hope you understand."

Moved, Dracul turned to the man in charge of collecting the tribute. "This is a very special case where we must show some understanding," he said. "This innocent man has had enough punishment with the death of his daughter."

The man in charge stared at Dracul in silence. Then he turned to his soldiers and in a loud voice commanded, "Do what you have to do!"

Dracul, anguished, interjected. "But this poor—"

"Beat him! Burn his possessions! Rape his women! And take his sons to the conscription!" yelled the Ottoman. Then, addressing Dracul, he said furiously, "If we start to accept excuses in place of tributes, everyone is going to want to pay with them. And excuses have no value!"

Vlad III watched the cowardly and unfair action in silence; he wanted to give his own money to the peasant, but he could have been punished for doing so.

Kardotas knelt down and, with tears in his eyes, implored, "Forgive me!" A strong blow to the head made him see stars, and then the shower of blows began. Other soldiers threw themselves upon his women and raped them in the presence of the townspeople, while still others burned his house and crops. Because they were so little, his sons were not chained and taken away.

At the end of the exemplary punishment, everyone understood the lesson: there was no reason that would justify not paying the tribute, and the only way to avoid it was to die.

An Ottoman in charge ordered, "The children between seven and fourteen years of age will stand here!" and the order was fulfilled against everyone's will. "Chain this one and that one, and those two! These will be the Janissaries of the sultan's army!"

Then came the screaming, the fainting, the angry shouts and more aggressive manifestations of disapproval. Desperate and powerless, parents watched their beloved children chained and led away, surely never to be seen again. For the poor parents, it was worse than death.

Vlad III witnessed how the poor innocents were punished and robbed, how, in fact, the ones who did not pay had perfectly good reasons. He watched and absorbed every detail, especially the faces of the debtors. He wanted to erase the images from his memory, but he could not.

When collection was complete, Dracul spoke to the inhabitants of each village, telling them, "We'll work all year to have peace that will continue to reign over Wallachia. Every time you save money for the payment of next year's tribute, do it with joy, because thanks to this payment, we're free!"

When the collectors left his village, Cybar said to Bardat, "The son of the devil says we're free . . . how cynical!"

"We are more enslaved than ever," Bardat said.

"The slaves are more fortunate than we are," Cybar said. "They just work hard, and in exchange their masters protect them, feed them, give them shelter, and worry about them."

When they arrived at Tirgoviste, Vlad III challenged Mircea, "I dare you to ask Father why he didn't charge tribute to the Saxons."

"Are you crazy? If I do, he'll beat me. *You* ask him!"

That night Vlad III lay in bed, waiting. He had already said his prayers, his mother had given him her blessing, and now he was waiting for his father's blessing so he could sleep. When his father did not arrive, Vlad got a bad feeling. Stealthily entering his father's room, he heard murmured prayers interrupted by sobbing. He advanced a little farther and saw his father, kneeling in front of a crucifix, his face bathed in tears. The little one felt the weight of the world upon his shoulders. The strongest man he knew was crying! "Daddy," he asked shyly, "why are you crying?"

His father looked up and gets surprise him, too distraught to try to conceal his grief from his young son. "I love my people with all my heart," he said, "and look what these bastards have forced me to do, to give them the little wealth we generate. Even worse is seeing how they hurt our people and take our children, who might then become our enemies someday. That is really sad, my son. Yet I don't have the strength to stop them! Emperor Sigismund died, and those bastards came upon us like vultures. If one day you become vovoid, do not give in! Seek alliances and fight! It is really hard to love my people and know that they think I am a traitor; it hurts me so much to know that they call me 'son of the devil' behind my back, when I am only trying to save them from slavery and death."

Vlad III did not ask anything else, and he did not say anything. He just stayed by his father's side until he fell asleep.

11

The beautiful Princess Cneajna had fulfilled her duties as a mother, and now she decided to fulfill her obligations as a wife. Wearing a simple but attractive robe—with his fiery temperament, her husband did not need a lot of motivation—she waited patiently until late at night, when he finally arrived home. With a sweet and slightly throaty voice she greeted him, "Good evening, honey . . . how was work?"

Approaching his wife, Dracul answered, "Fine my love." and he gave her a respectful kiss on the forehead.

Cneajna flirtatiously moved her gown aside to show off her feminine attributes, but Dracul just said, "Cover yourself, honey. The night is cold and you can get sick."

When he got in bed, she moved herself close to him. "I am cold," she said. So he got up, found more blankets, and put them over her. Then he got into bed again and said, "Have a good night," turning his back to her and settling in to sleep.

Cneajna was puzzled; her passionate husband had rejected her. That wasn't like him. The night was a long torment for her as she wondered what was happening. Jealousy she'd never felt before started to stir in her heart.

The next morning she pulled aside Vailissa, one of her damsels. "When my husband leaves the palace, follow him," she ordered. "My heart tells me there is another woman between us."

Vailissa fulfilled her princess's orders and soon discovered the existence of the beautiful young Caltuna. The damsel returned to Cneajna and informed her of the facts. Cneajna now faced a great dilemma: whether to reject her husband and devote herself to her children, or to fight for his love. She decided to fight. That night when her husband arrived, Cneajna put aside her modesty and emerged from the bedroom naked, giving him a sultry look.

Seeing the aggressiveness of that beautiful woman, Dracul felt his heart pound. *Is this mouthwatering animal really my selfless and demure wife?* Inside him a strange fire had sparked, heating up his passionate temperament.

Still gazing at him, Cneajna caressed herself without shame and, with feline movements, headed to the bed.

Cneajna's plan had worked: using her most primal feminine weapons to keep her husband, she had started a battle. That battle was unrelenting, and Dracul was happy. He loved his self-sacrificing and now aggressive, temperamental, and sexy wife, and he also was trapped in the passionate clutches of his hot lover.

And the love battle bore fruit. Dracul's wife gave him another child, a blond boy with blue eyes and skin as white as sea foam; he would be the last and most beautiful of Dracul's four children. He was baptized with the name Rudolf and was called by the traditional nickname. Radu The world would know him as the Beautiful.

12

Albert of Habsburg, Archduke of Austria, married Isabel, daughter of the late Emperor Sigismund, in 1439. Feeling entitled to occupy the throne, he crowned himself holy Roman emperor and appointed as general governor of Transylvania, Janos Hunyadi.

A great retinue of soldiers, led by Dracul, arrived in Transylvania, where the leader was received by his brother Dragon. "You don't know how happy I am to know that you will be the governor of Transylvania!" Dracul said effusively. Then, giving Janos a warm hug, he added, "Congratulations on your appointment!"

"Thank you!" the warrior answered. "But now we have to make plans to face our enemy."

Dracul told Janos of his desperate situation. "I cannot stand the Ottomans any longer," he said. "They forced me to sign a pact impoverishing us further, and my people are on the verge of misery. But if we refuse to pay, they will attack us and enslave us. How I miss Sigismund . . . with his support I felt secure."

The White Knight answered, "He's not here, but inside of us there's his precious and brave spirit. We will make an alliance, and you should not pay that unfair tribute, which only enriches and strengthens our enemy. The sultan has plans to expand his presence in other places, so while he solves those problems we will strengthen and organize ourselves. If by refusing to pay the tribute you are attacked, you will not be alone!"

Dracul was happy. Finally there was another warrior in power, a brave man who was not afraid of the powerful sultan and would give Dracul his unconditional support. Dracul sent some emissaries to the Ottoman Empire with a letter that said,

Murad II,

Wallachia is extremely impoverished and can no longer pay the tribute to which we had agreed. I promise not to attack you under any circumstances. I am not, and never will be, your enemy.

Signed,
Wladislaus II, Dracul

When the Sultan Murad II received the letter he told his counselors, "As soon as I subdue the ones we have pending, I've decided to subdue this rebel. What do you think?"

The counselors deliberated, and their representative told him, "We believe your decision is wise."

13

In the year 1441, Vlad III and Mircea joined their father and traveled to the town of Sibiu, where Jared, the Saxon gunsmith, told them, "We have found a way for the cannon to send the bullet farther, but we have not yet found a way to keep the gunpowder from cracking the cannon."

"Your job is to find a way," Dracul told him. "Keep researching. We need this cannon tomorrow!"

"I wish I could give it to you today," Jared said. "But we are not talking about just any weapon. What I can assure you is that when we fix the problem, you'll have the weapon that will conquer the world."

After inspecting the gunsmith's work and his improvements on the cannon, and giving him more money and metals to continue with the tests, Dracul and his sons enjoyed the traditional farewell meal. As usual, everything was delicious, and at the end, Dracul went to the kitchen, joined by his sons, and congratulated the cooks.

14

Murad II was known for dressing conservatively and obeying the law of the Koran. A devoted Ottoman, he was considered a sacred warrior for Islam but was tolerant of other religions, as well as savages and pagans. He treated his servants with kindness, as if they were his relatives.

He was also a skillful politician, economist, and strategist. His spy ring worked perfectly and informed him that it was possible to take the Fortress of Smederevo.

That vulnerable fortress, defended by George Brankovic, fell to the Ottomans. Now Brankovic had to pay the price of defeat, and that was, without a doubt, more painful than the battle itself.

Mara, George's beautiful sister, defended her two children like an animal. When Murad II saw her he was deeply impressed; her violet eyes were one of a kind. The sultan had had many women, but not one had had eyes like those. Murad stared at her and then turned to one of his servants. "I want that woman in my harem," he said.

Mara seized her children and said, "Either you take me with my children, or I will kill myself!"

"Let her take her children," the sultan ordered.

After a few months in captivity, Mara's son Gregory devised a plan. "We have to find a way to run away to our people," he told his brother, Stephen. "Then we will come back to rescue our mother."

There was no need to convince Stephen. At their first opportunity, the brothers stole a horse and rode away to their longed-for freedom.

When the sultan came out of the harem, he was informed by a servant, "My lord, Mara's children have escaped!"

Murad was furious. "And you stayed here like an idiot to inform me without doing anything? Kill this good-for-nothing!" he yelled.

"Wait, my lord! They have been detained, and they are ready to receive their punishment."

"Take their eyes out!" the sultan ordered.

Amidst screaming and tears, the order was fulfilled. With this action the sultan was telling his subjects, "Look what I do to my adopted children. If I do that to them, what might I do to you if you disobey me?"

15

In 1442 the Ottoman sultan said to his counselors, "Now we are going to attack Hunyadi. Let us put Dracul's fidelity to a test."

The counselors agreed, saying, "It is a good opportunity to learn if he is a friend or an enemy."

The sultan attacked Hunyadi in Transylvania, and the White Knight suffered many casualties in his army. In response to this aggression, the Christians organized a crusade against the infidel enemy, assembling soldiers of different nationalities. German, Russian, Austrian, Polish, Serbian, and Hungarian troops gathered together, commanded by the recently elected King Ladislas III of Poland and representing the interests of the Vatican, the Cardinal Giuliani Cesarini.

Hunyadi traveled to Tirgoviste, where he extended an invitation to his brother Dragon: "The crusade is ready. Gather your army and join us!"

"How many soldiers are going?" Dracul asked.

"Twenty thousand, plus your men."

Dracul frowned. "Do you know the size of the sultan's army? Facing him with that number would be suicide. Let us get more men!"

Hunyadi answered him with another question, "You are afraid? You're a knight of the Order of the Dragon! Remember your oath. It is time to give your life, and your children's lives, if necessary, with the men you have. Let's go to the crusade!"

"I refuse to fight with such a small army," Dracul responded categorically.

"Damned coward—get out of Wallachia!" Hunyadi screamed. "You don't deserve to be called Christian! Guards—take this coward out of Wallachia!"

Dracul could say nothing else. He took his three legitimate children and was exiled without a destination.

Hunyadi met with the members of the town council of Wallachia and appointed as new vovoid the council's recommendation, Basarab II. He was a member of the Danesti family, who were bitter enemies of the Draculesti family.

The crusade had its first victory when Sofia of Bulgaria was reclaimed and the Ottomans were forced to withdraw. The battle was fought over a rough winter, and both armies froze to the bones. Due to the heavy snowstorms, the Catholic army sought refuge in Brankovic's Belgrade, over the Danube, but along the way they had to tear apart their carts and burn them for warmth, and most of their horses died from exposure. When a desperate Murad II proposed a truce, it was welcomed by the Catholics.

16

The sultan now knew that Dracul was not his enemy and, in fact, had lost his power for having refused to attack the Ottomans. So the sultan decided to look for Dracul, whom he needed as a trustworthy ally. His spies quickly located the exiled governor, who was soon visited by Ottoman emissaries. "You must join us and go to the sultan immediately!" they said.

Afraid for his children, Dracul took advantage of the fact that Mircea was buying supplies at the market in town. "We'll go right away," he said, and with the rest of his family he immediately set out for the Ottoman Empire, knowing that Mircea would have a better chance of surviving alone than in the hands of his enemies.

During the journey, Dracul kept repeating the same warning to Vlad: "Son, don't ever let our enemy deceive you. He'll lie to you, telling you that he is your friend, that he will always protect you. But he will only want your money, your women, and your children, so he can turn them into Janissary warriors and worshipers of his savage god. Don't you ever believe him! Be cautious and learn from the chameleon, who deceives everyone but only cares and fights for its interests and its family. Son, we are the defenders of Christ; the most important thing to us is our Orthodox religion. If you have to accept the Catholics, do it because we need them— the Order of the Dragon compels us to be Catholics—but your heart must remain faithful to the Orthodox faith. Always fight against the infidel Ottomans and heretics, and if you have to turn in one of them, transform yourself. Be like the chameleon! In the end, do what you have to do, and what is primordial: defend the faith of our God, and your Orthodox religion, even if you have to deceive, kill, or torture in order to do so."

Their arrival in the Ottoman Empire was incredible. Dracul was welcomed like a great governor; the sultan Murad II received his ally in person with his traditional religious greeting, Ottoman style. Then he said, "I welcome you and your honorable family!"

"I feel overwhelmed by these unmerited honors," Dracul said.

"Unmerited?" answered the sultan. "Don't you know my spies informed me that you lost your power in Wallachia because you didn't attack me? Don't you worry, by the glory of Allah, or my name is not Murad, I promise you I'll place you back in power again." They continued talking as if they were great friends, and in the palace around them a celebration began without them noticing. Soon the atmosphere was lively, with beautiful women performing exotic dances in lovely clothes and transparent veils. People came and went; it was a sea of food and women, the amount and variety of which were overwhelming. Finally night arrived, and a room and several women were given to each guest to satisfy his every desire.

Vlad III didn't know if he was in a dream or in the heaven promised by his religion. But his father was not pleased at his sons' exposure to such excess. Not even as a vovoid could he have had those luxuries—and Radu, especially, was just a confused boy who was being turned against his will into a man in the middle of his childhood.

Dracul also knew that this reception would come at a high price; surely he would be reinstated in power and therefore forced to pay to his enemy some tribute of money and children. He wasn't wrong.

Three days later, the sultan told him, "Everything has to come to an end, and we have to keep on building for the sake of our subjects. Again, I thank you for not attacking me; that shows that you are faithful. Therefore I am going to reinstate you in Wallachia's power—but don't forget that you have to pay the annual tribute we had agreed upon."

The request came like a bombshell. "That tribute is too high!" Dracul exclaimed. "Can't we cut it in half? It's too much—we don't have that much money. And you are going to leave us without any children!"

"Too much money?" the sultan asked. "What—are *you* going to pay it? No, your people are going to pay it—and with that tribute you are going to assure the peace and prosperity of your people! Remember that I also have expenses. My army works 365 days a year, war or peace, and I have to pay their full wages. A lot of children? Are you forgetting that those will be the Janissaries who will defend your people? They are going to be better off than anyone. And besides, you are going to recover your power!"

Dracul kept silent, searching for an argument against the tribute, but he couldn't find any that was convincing. "Can we negotiate a reduction of the tribute?" he asked.

The sultan stared at him and answered drily, "Do you think I am a stallholder in the marketplace? Why are you haggling? Do you want me to double the amount I am proposing, or do you wish to cause war between our people? Do you want to recover Wallachia? Anyway, either you pay it or I'll make Basarab pay it—whoever is in power." He paused for a moment and then concluded, "Take it or leave it."

Dracul felt trapped. Again his enemy was subduing him with his strength. Dracul answered quietly, "All right. Let it be what you are proposing."

"We'll have to sign a treaty allowing the free trade of merchandise between Ottomans and Wallachians," the sultan said. "We'll assure the peace, and the Ottoman Empire will protect you militarily against foreign invaders. In exchange, the tribute established will be paid." Both men signed two copies of the document, and each kept one.

The sultan was satisfied with the transaction, but Dracul, still fearful, was anxious to escape the tense atmosphere. He stood up. "My lord, like you said, you have business to attend to. It was a pleasure making this deal with you."

The sultan did not move. "Sit down," he said, and his tone was deadly calm. "I haven't said we are done."

Dracul's blood ran cold. Feeling like he was stuck in a nightmare, he fulfilled the sultan's order and sat down, trying to disguise his impatience.

The sultan asked softly, "What guarantee do I have that you are going to fulfill the promise you have signed here?"

"We are two gentlemen," answered Dracul. "There are no lies between us."

The sultan stared at him with a deep, inquisitive look, and then he asked, "And what about the oath you made to the Order of the Dragon, with your god, Jesus Christ, as a witness, to fight heretics and the Ottoman Empire? Doesn't that count? Why are you telling me that there is more value in a treaty you made with an infidel Ottoman than in the promises to your order?" He was silent again and then he asked, "Is Christ more powerful than, Allah?"

Dracul knew how to deceive; he could lie to the devil himself. But this question had only one answer, and besides, he knew that whatever he said, his powerful enemy was going to do as he pleased. He answered bravely, "No, my lord . . . my Christ is more powerful to me."

The sultan, although grounded in the Koran, was tolerant of savage religions. He looked Dracul in the eye and was quiet for a long time. Then, taking a deep breath, he said; "You will leave your children with me; they will be treated as if they were my own. But if you fail me, I will take out their eyes . . . and then I will impale them."

Dracul felt a chill run through his body. His worst fears had come true, perfected and materialized as a living nightmare: his children were at the mercy of his enemy, and all he could do was obey.

———◆———

At the end of the negotiation, Dracul went to see his children. When he saw them he hugged them with special warmth.

Vlad, who was particularly perceptive, intuitive, and smart, asked timidly, "What's wrong, Father?" But their father kept hugging them with a strange intensity, not answering his question.

Vlad knew that something bad, really bad, had happened, and his mind was filled with terrifying thoughts—his father dead, he and his brother abandoned in the middle of the desert, and other things of the sort. But knowing that his father was in the middle of a emotional crisis, Vlad did not want to press him further and cause more pain just to satisfy his idle curiosity. So he remained silent, hugging his father tightly.

After a while, the father placed his children in front of him and said, "From now on you will live with the sultan. He is our executioner, disguised as our father. He wants to make us believe that he is our friend and that his god is the real one. But listen carefully: I have to go back to our people. Obey him, but do not let the seed of Islam be planted in your hearts; we're Christians, and we have to defend our God, and our Orthodox faith."

Vlad III already knew that; it was very clear for him. But knowing the fickle attitude his brother Radu always assumed, he said to his father; "I understand perfectly well, but what about Radu? What are we going to do with him?"

Dracul knew his children, knew that Radu did not care much about the faith. In fact he steadfastly refused to pray, went unwillingly to religious ceremonies, and was apathetic to everything concerning religion. "Son, I don't think your brother cares about our problems," Dracul said. "It is very likely that he will follow the easy way. But you are my strength; I put my faith in you. I am sure that you will defend Christ and our Orthodox Faith."

"Father, I love my God, and if I have to become a chameleon and act like an Ottoman or a demon to defend him, I will. I'll deceive Satan himself."

Dracul was left speechless. What he had explained to his son so many times had now been explained to him, but more clearly. Taking advantage of the fact that Radu was out playing, Dracul took Vlad by the arm and said, "Come with me, Son."

17

On January 10, 1443, Dracul and Vlad III entered a small room. Dracul closed the door and locked it; they were completely alone. From among his clothes the father took out a crucifix and held it up high on a wall. Then he ordered his son, "Kneel down before our God."

Vlad III obeyed and adopted the same attitude as his father, folding his arms and prostrating himself before Christ.

Dracul began to pray: "My God, before you I ordain my son as knight of the Order of the Dragon. There are no witnesses due to the circumstances that you already know; but you who know and see everything, testify this holy ordinance made in your honor and glory." Then they stood up and Dracul said to his son, "Place your right hand on your heart and answer: do you swear to be faithful and promise to defend with your blood and your life our God?"

"I swear!" Vlad answered.

"Do you swear to be faithful to the holy Orthodox Church, agreeing to make pacts with the Catholics as long as the objective is the defense of the faith of our God?"

"I swear!"

"Do you swear to answer the call of the knights of the Order of the Dragon when they request your help, and without doubt shed your blood for the defense of our God?"

"I swear!"

"On your knees!"

Vlad obeyed. Dracul took his sword in both hands, and pointing it to the sky said a silent prayer. Then he placed it on the right shoulder of the initiate and said with a strong voice, "By the power invested in me by the Holy Roman Emperor Sigismund of Luxemburg, and having as witness our God, I appoint you knight of the Order of the Dragon, in the name of God the Father, his only son, Jesus Christ, and the Holy Spirit." Then he moved the sword to the left shoulder and ordained the initiate: "You will defend God with all your soul and all your being until there is not a drop of blood in your body. You will not hesitate to sacrifice your life, your future children, your future wife, your family, your land, and your power for him. He gave them to you, and you owe them to him."

He changed the blade to the right shoulder and said, "From now on and until your death, you will be a knight Dracul, and for being the son of a knight Dracul, from now you will be known as Dracula, defender of the faith of our God."

The initiate was excited: at that very moment he was no longer Vlad III, but Dracula. He felt a current of energy course through his strong young body. Now he was a real crusader knight.

Then the father took the dagger he had received when he was ordained, the dagger with the gold handle with the symbol of the dragon—his most valuable treasure, which he had never allowed anyone else to touch. And with a powerful and ceremonious voice, he said, "Dracula, receive and keep this dagger as a symbol of your membership in the Order of the Dragon. I have bathed and purified it with the blood of an infidel. Keep honoring it! But be careful—from now on you must be cautious. You might even have to offer it to the service of your enemy. Do it when you have to deceive him. But remember that in the deepest part of your heart, your faith in our Lord will always be firm as a rock."

Dracula could not believe it. He was feeling like a new man: more mature, more responsible, more committed, and he was barely an adolescent. Closing his eyes he made a silent prayer: "My Christ, you are my only God. From now on and until the day of my death, I will be the greatest defender of your faith. I promise to give you everything I possess, and I beg you to grant me the honor and glory of your enemies taking my life as I defend your faith, and of dying with your holy name on my lips." The strength of his thoughts was forming a true warrior of Christianity and shaping his destiny.

At the end of the ceremony, father and son talked about the Order of the Dragon, and Dracul explained in great detail everything related to it. He told the boy how he had baptized his holy dagger with the blood of his half-brother, and then more infidels and heretics came to witness its strength with their deaths.

To Dracula, the whole thing still felt like a dream. He had been secretly ordained by the man he admired and loved the most, right in the midst of their infidel enemies, with the only witness the most important being of all, Christ.

Dracul spent all day with his children, knowing that he probably would never see them again. That night he did not want to sleep; he would have time to do that later. For now he'd better enjoy every minute with his boys, so he told them their favorite stories. Radu fell asleep early, but Dracula wanted to make the most of this time with his father; he, too, had the dark feeling that those were their last moments together on earth. His father gave him the same words of advice over and over again, and Dracula listened to him patiently and gladly, thinking, *My father might repeat himself like a parrot, but I would listen to the same thing forever if I could just have him with me my whole life.* There was an incredible, intense love consolidating between them.

At one point Dracula begged his father, "Please tell Mircea I love him very much! Tell him that when I get out of this prison, we won't just pretend to kill Ottomans; we will make a crusade to fight them. He will be the leader, and I will be his right-hand man, and we will kill them by the thousands. Our games are over!" He took from his bag the little round stone that he'd found that day with Mircea, the one they had fought about for so long, and, giving it to his father, he said in a soft voice, "Give this to Mircea, and tell him never to forget me and to pray for me every night, as I will do for him. Also, tell my mother that I love her, and that the next time she sees me I will be a powerful crusader knight."

Dracul was satisfied with his son, who in spite of his young age was mature and trustworthy. Everything about him was admirable. Dracul was astonished by him; he was sure that eventually, he and Mircea would make an excellent team to govern Wallachia.

"I promise you that at our first opportunity I will escape to Wallachia with Radu," the boy said.

Dracul looked stricken. "Don't even think about it!" he said. "The nephews of George Brankovic tried it, and the sultan had their eyes gouged out. He will show no mercy."

Dracula fell silent, pitying those poor prisoners. Then, with Radu sleeping soundly nearby, Dracula hugged his father tightly as stars appeared in the night sky. In that way—among his father's words of advice, recommendations, stories, hugs, and tender kisses—the boy slept. Far too soon the sun appeared on the horizon, and as neither the feelings nor the wishes of mortal beings could stop the relentless passing of time, Dracul prepared to bid farewell to his sons for the last time. He tried repeatedly to wake Radu, but he was fast asleep. So, with a sad look and a hollow voice, Dracul told his son, "I am leaving . . . I'll be back as soon as I can."

Dracula answered him, "Good-bye, Father, and may our Lord be with you and protect you wherever you are. Please give me your blessing." And he knelt down to receive it.

Dracul blessed his son, mounted his horse, and left.

——◆≫◆——

On January 11, 1443, Dracula watched his father slowly depart, joined by a large escort. As the group moved farther away, the boy felt an intense pain in his chest. An instinct that almost never failed him was telling him that they had said their last good-bye. He could not help it: his eyes filled with tears and he cried abundantly as his beloved father disappeared on the horizon. It was the second time Dracula had been left as a prisoner; again he was a guarantee of the faithful fulfillment of a pact with his bitter enemies.

His father, meanwhile, sensed that his sons would very likely die at the hands of those murderers. He knew how Europeans thought; he would not be able to keep the peace alone, and at the people's first uprising, his children would end up blinded and impaled. Without a powerful army to take back the piece of his heart the sultan had stolen from him, he was helpless. That helplessness turned into desperation, and the desperation turned into tears. Dracul's hardened face was getting wet in that dry weather, and he felt worse than those peasants had when their children were taken for the conscription, because he was sure his sons were going to die excruciating deaths. Seeking comfort in his immense pain, he started to pray, becoming so focused on his petitions he got lost in the horizon that was Edirne.

In that place, faith in Allah was instilled in him and he was instructed in the Koran and Islamic tradition. And like a chameleon, Dracul deceived his enemies and made them believe he had turned into a pious Ottoman. They did not miss the opportunity to remind him that his children were collateral in the pact that he had made with them, and during his stay in Edirne he witnessed much impalement. It became a mental reminder of the destiny that awaited his sons if he disobeyed.

18

Murad II addressed the boys in their own language: "From now on, consider yourselves my sons. You are more than my guests! Get comfortable with your new family. I would really like you to call me Father one day." The sultan smiled warmly at Vlad. "It is difficult for me to pronounce your names. What can I call you besides Wladislaus?"

"Call me Dracula," Vlad suggested.

The sultan looked at his brother. "And what about you?"

"Me? Radu," answered the boy

"No! We will call you cel Frumos [the Beautiful]." The sultan laughed then, adding, "You'll learn your new language with us, and you'll meet your new and powerful God. And in time, I am sure that you'll learn to worship him."

Inside Dracula's head there was a protective shield against that proposal. Remembering his father's words, he opened his eyes and recognized the enemy, knowing he had to wear the chameleon's skin and deceive him. With a smile on his face, he asked, "How many languages do you speak, Father?"

"Four of my empire," the sultan replied proudly, "and I am studying your language."

"Father," Dracula said, "I promise to speak your language as you do, and to study the sacred verses of the Koran, and to seek with all my heart, until I find it, the flame of faith in our God, Allah."

The sultan was happy with the good disposition of his prisoner.

The next day the brothers were summoned to the sultan's presence. "I introduce you my son, Mehemed II," he told them. "I want you to treat each other as brothers and to learn what you can from each other."

Mehemed regarded them with his dark eyes, impressed by the masculine beauty of his new brothers. Without saying a word, he greeted them with a salute, in the Ottoman style; the visitors responded in the same manner. Little by little the brothers would learn their new customs.

Said the sultan, "This is your teacher, Ali. He will teach you the knowledge that will help you. I want you to start your classes immediately.

Ali took the guests away to another room, saying, "You will stop dressing in the clothes you are wearing. This will be your new wardrobe."

Dracula was fascinated when he saw the new clothes they were going to wear. He never would have imagined that the Turks could have such refined taste. The clothes seemed to have come out of an elegant fairytale. He quietly decided he was going to dress like that for the rest of his life.

Murad II told his counselors, "When those boys grow up, they'll learn their new religion and customs, and at the right time I'll place them on Wallachia's throne, because they have royal blood. That way they will change their people's faith, and little by little the place will turn to Islam."

"But aren't they traitors?" one counselor asked.

"Their father has never been a traitor," the sultan answered. "When he rebelled against me it was because he was desperate for the lack of money, and he did it in a peaceful way. He has never taken up weapons against us, and when he was forced to, he refused. As a result he lost his power in Wallachia. He was exiled, along with all his family. I think that, with time, we'll find that we've made an excellent investment. And besides, we will then have an entrance to conquer all of Europe."

The professor, Ali, started his lesson. Radu the Beautiful learned quickly, as any intelligent boy would. But Dracula was especially gifted, and in a short period of time he started to understand and speak their language. "Do you speak another language?" the professor asked him, intrigued.

"Five, not counting the one I am learning."

Ali was impressed, and knowing that he could get more from Dracula, he started to put more pressure on his student. Dracula learned everything with great ease. Before long he was speaking their ottoman language fluently and seeking out unusual words and obscure idioms to learn. He improved his accent to the point that he spoke like any other Turk, and then he began learning other languages spoken in that empire.

Dracula started to go to the school for Janissaries. From across the empire, children between the ages of seven and fourteen were brought there to learn their new language as well as philosophy, history, logic, mathematics, and every military art. After six years of education and military training, they were ready to become strong, well-rounded soldiers, the cream of the Ottoman army.

Mehemed II became Dracula's inseparable friend; he often joined Dracula on the training field. With the passage of time their friendship continued to grow, until one night when they stood on one of the palace terraces, as the moonlight played over the visitor's face, Mehemed felt a strange desire, an uncontrollable attraction to the mysterious young man. Mehemed looked him in the eyes and, without saying a word, took Dracula by the shoulders and slowly approached him with his eyes closed and his lips slightly open, with the clear intention of kissing him.

Dracula, disconcerted, pushed him aside. "What is wrong with you?"

Mehemed II answered softly, "I feel a fire inside me that only you can put out."

Dracula was horrified. "We are men! Those relationships are forbidden by the Koran. Behave like a man . . . or I'll tell our father!"

Mehemed II covered his face with his hands. What had he done? It was the first time he had shown his true sexual leaning, and everything had turned out wrong. Taking a deep breath he began begging: "For my father, for the love of Allah . . . don't say anything! Father would kill me!"

When Dracula saw him so scared, he told him, "I promise you I'll keep quiet. I'll pretend this night never happened—but behave like a man!"

After that Dracula began putting some distance between them, watching sadly when Radu began to have get closer to Mehemed. When he found out that they had consummated that relationship, he confronted his brother. "Have you gone crazy, Radu? What you are doing is a sin in all religions! If our father knew, he would be ashamed of you!"

Radu answered him in Turkish. "Do not meddle in my life. I never interfere in yours."

Dracula was trying to decide what to do. He knew his brother had a sexual deviation and couldn't do anything to avoid it. He was just like that, and Dracula loved him and had to support him. Therefore he tolerated the situation; he had no other choice.

As he knelt down facing Mecca, his arms outstretched on the floor, anyone who saw Dracula would have seen a pious Ottoman Turk worshiping Allah. But inside his head, Dracula was praying fervently to his real and only God, Jesus Christ. *Lord, I am among your enemies. Although it seems I am being unfaithful, in my mind and in my heart there is only one real God, and that is you. Allow me to be the most ferocious crusader knight to defend your sacred name. Protect Father, Mircea, and Mother, and show the light to Radu so he might find your path and not get lost in the dark of a false religion. I beg this of you, and of your holy Father and the Holy Spirit.* At the end of the prayer he made a final salutation and then went back to the military camp.

Dracula's trainers saw that he had the makings of a great warrior and a chief falconer (a highest rank in the Ottoman army), and they taught him all the Turkish strategies. He learned perfectly and completely the Turkish way to make war: when to attack, withdraw, and counterattack. He also learned the techniques of impalement. After analyzing the skills he had learned, he sought ways to improve them. But he never shared that self-taught knowledge with his enemies; he kept it for himself for the time when he would have to fight against them.

A passionate Sultan Murad II entered the palace bedchamber joined by six slaves prepared to please him. But when he pushed aside the curtain, he felt his potency drain away. Everything became blurred, and he felt faint. The most shameful and monstrous scene he ever could have imagined was before him, and his knees began to buckle. Regaining his strength, he asked, stunned, "What is happening here?"

The lovers were petrified. They tried to move, but their fear wouldn't let them.

The sultan recovered from the shock, pulling Radu off Mehemed's naked body and throwing him across the room. "Despicable swine!" he screamed.

The slaves covered their faces with their hands, peering through their fingers at that sinful relationship.

The sultan was speechless. The first thing that came to his head was to kill the sodomites, but he did not want to lose his valuable heir. He could sentence his son to suffer an exemplary punishment, but that wasn't the solution, either; to do that would also cast dishonor and shame upon himself. He would lose everyone's respect, and they would point and laugh at him behind his back. No, he thought, his son should die.

Or there was another choice: he could accept his son, even with his deviation, forgiving him and letting the world follow its course . . . but what about the slaves? They had seen everything, and they would expose his shame to all the empire. Regardless of what he decided, they must die. He left the bedchamber and came back with a soldier, telling him, "Behead these slaves in this room!" Addressing the slaves, he said, "If you speak before dying, this soldier will die, too. On your conscience will be the blood of this innocent man!"

The soldier did not understand, but afraid to ask questions, he grabbed a slave and beheaded her with two strokes of his sword. The others were screaming, horrified, without daring to say what they had witnessed. When the executioner finished with the sixth, the sultan said to him, "Have this mess cleaned! And you two"—addressing the sodomites—"come with me!"

The two lovers were trembling and aghast; because of their lust, six innocent women had died. Later they understood why: with this sacrifice, the good name and prestige of the sultan and the empire had been saved.

The sultan took the young men to an empty chamber and turned angrily to his son. "Now explain to me," he demanded, "why you are a sodomite!"

Mehemed could not find the words to explain. He felt ashamed, fearful, and repentant, and he did not know what to say. The guilt and confusion did not allow him to put his ideas into order. Taking a deep breath, he begged, "Forgive me, Father! I have filled you with shame, and I have covered your hands with blood. But believe me when I tell you that I cannot avoid my sexual preference. I cannot modify it. I have tried to, on many occasions, but it is beyond my strength. I never before had relations with a man in the empire, because I didn't want to embarrass you. I do not understand my nature, but that's what it is: I feel an attraction toward men. The day I met Dracula and Radu, my heart beat as it never had before. After a while I approached Dracula romantically, but he scolded me, saying our religion forbids it, and he threatened to denounce me to you. We never spoke of the issue again."

"Then Dracula knows about your deviation?" asked the sultan, alarmed.

"Yes, Father," Mehemed answered softly.

"And he knows about your sexual relationship with his brother?"

"Yes, Father."

"And how come that swine is an accomplice in all this?" asked the sultan.

"He said and did everything he could to change us, but believe me, Father, it is not a matter of advice or knowledge of the facts. In the end he ended up accepting our relationship, though not condoning it."

The sultan thought for a while and then summoned Dracula to his presence. "Tell me what you think about the relationship between your brother and my son!" he said furiously.

Dracula's white face turned red, and he answered, "The Koran does not allow me to lie, but it allows me to keep silence. I would appreciate it, Father, if you would change the question."

Murad was taken aback by this answer. *Fine,* he thought. "What would you do if you were in my place at this moment and you found out the real sexual preference of your son?"

Dracula took a breath and then answered unhurriedly: "It seems you have found out about the relations between my brother and your son. If I were you, first I would place my blood before my passions. Father, Mehemed is a very good son. He always refers to you with deep respect and reverent love. When you grow old you'll find support in him, and even before then, if you have a serious problem you'll be able to lean on him. He is your blood! And if someday you must entrust your life to someone, he is the one to assume custody. I, in your place, would accept and love him as he is. When you die, a river of tears will be shed in your memory, but your son's will be the most honest tears of all. After your death he will honor your memory and ask Allah to take your soul. Besides, Mehemed is an intelligent and daring warrior during training . . . it is difficult for me to say this, but I feel he is a better soldier than me. I am sure he will bring you glory, honor, and respect.

"We all came to this world with some flaw. Even you have a physical flaw, and it is not your fault: you made your son! He is not *guilty* of his difference—be reasonable and understand. Have you ever wondered how I feel because my brother is a sodomite? Just like you, I feel shame and dishonor, but my blood comes before my passions, and I love my brother above all else." Saying this, Dracula hugged Radu. "Brother," he said, "I will always love you and protect you, and I will gladly give my life for yours!"

The sultan considered in silence the arguments that the very mature boy was proposing. "You are right," he said, "but I am making an effort to teach my son to be a brave warrior . . . and he turned out to be a poof!"

Mehemed was now very frightened, and Radu was deathly pale.

Looking the sultan in the eyes, Dracula said, "The greatest warrior that ever existed on the face of the earth, the bravest, most audacious warrior, was Achilles—and he had relations with his cousin, Petroclus. Julius Caesar—the conqueror and military genius, the esteemed ruler of the Roman Empire—loved men as well as women. He declared, '*Vir omnia mulieris et mulier omnia virorum,*' which in Turkish means, 'I am the man of all women and the woman of all men.' The Roman emperors Augustus and the powerful Augustus Caesar were also homosexuals. You admire Alexander the Great, saying that of all the historical characters, he is your favorite? Well, that man has been considered by many to be the best military strategist and the bravest, boldest, and most intelligent military leader ever, with every positive attribute you could grant. At age thirty-three he had never known defeat and ruled the greatest empire ever known. He also had a lover; his name was Hephaestion. All of them were brave and audacious warriors, and they were all sodomites—like my two brothers, Radu and Mehemed."

Murad gazed steadily at Dracula. "How do you know so much?" he asked.

"When I lived with my beloved and revered father, Sigismund of Luxemburg, whom Allah has now in his kingdom, I had access to such knowledge. And just as you are turning me into a true Ottoman warrior, he walked me through the path of a scholar. I have always liked to read whatever I can, and thanks to Allah, I never forget anything."

The sultan was silent, pleasantly surprised to hear Dracula speak of the emperor and refer to him so respectfully. The boy had also acknowledged that Murad was turning him into a real warrior, so it was likely that when he spoke about the sultan with others, he would refer to him with the same kind of respect—"my beloved and revered father, Murad II." He started digesting the information that his stepson had given him, and then, in a solemn voice, said to Mehemed, "You have come back to life today. Give thanks to Dracula, who defended you. If he hadn't, you would be dead by now!" He then turned to the defender and said, "You're absolutely right!"

Dracula looked over at Mehemed and Radu. "Your relationship is not a reason to be proud," he said firmly. "We shall keep it as a secret; your behavior fills us with shame. However, we cannot change nature with words. I want us to swear by the most sacred being there is, our God Allah, that no one here will ever say what happened this day. The secret we share will go with us to the grave."

They all agreed and solemnly swore by Allah, and then Dracula scolded the lovers again: "And you, be discreet with your relationship! Let no one suspect a thing. The prestige of the Ottoman Empire and the good name of the Draculesti dynasty are at stake."

The Ottoman sultan was fascinated by the way Dracula had cobbled together a happy resolution to the problem. "From now on," he said, "you will be my personal counselor. Despite your youth you are intelligent, agile, skillful, prudent, discreet, wise, and talented, and thanks to Allah, you are on our side. And I promise you that, as sure as Mohammad and Jesus are prophets, when you turn eighteen, I will place you on Wallachia's throne so that land will know the real God. I make you this promise in the name of Allah!"

Dracula was very happy, he had saved his brother from a certain death; he had impressed the sultan, who appointed him his personal counselor; he had saved Mehemed's life with a compromise; and, most important, he had convinced all of them that he was a real Ottoman, when in his heart was alive the flame of his faith in Christ.

19

On October 6, 1443, in Edirne, Dracul was joined by ecclesiastical representatives of the Ottoman Empire, who commanded him to make a ceremonious oath. Directing him to place his right hand on the Koran, they asked him, "Do you swear to be faithful to Allah and to the sultan, and never to rise up against the Ottoman Empire?"

"I swear!" Dracul said, and then they brought out a Bible and had him repeat the oath, this time with Jesus Christ as witness.

The imam told him, "Although you'll give freedom to your people to profess whatever religion they wish, your subjects will turn one by one to Islam when they see your fervor."

Then they headed to Wallachia, escorted by a large army.

The cold winter turned into a hell in Wallachia. Basarab II was being overthrown, and the Saxon town council gladly gave their authorization for Dracul to be named new vovoid when they found out that the interests of the people they represented would be completely respected. Dracul immediately delivered a proclamation explaining why he had left his sons with the Ottomans: "I did it to assure peace with the Ottoman Empire, and to keep it we shall continue to pay the yearly tribute."

Murad II had a very efficient spy network. If Dracul had made alliances with the knights of the Order of the Dragon, he would have summoned them to an open war against the sultan, and he wouldn't have demanded payment of the tribute next year. Murad would have known of this immediately and blinded and impaled Dracul's children without thinking twice.

Dracul gave an excited shout. "My beloved son!" he cried, and he ran to hug Mircea.

"Where are my brothers?" Mircea asked breathlessly.

"The sultan forced me to leave them as a guarantee that we won't attack him," Dracul said. "If we do, he will blind and impale them."

Mircea was enraged. "Damn him—let's go rescue them!"

"Wait, Son, it's not that easy. You don't know the sultan's powerful army and sophisticated weapons. Besides, he is immensely rich, thanks to the tribute he charges in every place he subdues. We have to act carefully. The first thing is to prepare the people to pay the tribute next year." Dracul glanced around them. "Where is your mother?"

Mircea eyes filled and he answered in a soft voice, "She died." There was a long silence.

Dracul felt his own eyes fill with tears, but he held them back with a lot of effort. Then, trying to be strong, he took out of his bag the little round stone. "Your brother sent you this little gift. He asked me to beg you to forgive him for not giving it to you sooner. He said that not until you were separated did he realize the great and true love he feels for you."

Mircea held the stone tight in his hand and two tears trailed down his cheeks; he felt powerless to rescue Vlad. He murmured, "My brother . . . someday we're going to be together forever." Trying to overcome his pain, he suggested a plan. "This time we are going to go to the Saxons and ask them to help us to pay the tribute."

Father and son went to the town council, and Dracul addressed their leader with a moving plea that came from depths of his heart: "My children are prisoners of the Ottomans. Please, I need you to help us pay the tribute to our enemies while we rescue them. If we don't, my sons will die blinded and impaled."

A loud silence and impassive expressions answered his petition. The *no* that could have been said with two simple letters was said instead with their cold attitude. Dracul and Mircea left that place saddened, disappointed, and desperate.

20

Dracul, Mircea, and Ivan Stokovich, the most faithful boyar of the Draculesti family, visited the Saxon gunsmith, Jared, who told them desperately, "The small cannons work to perfection; but we cannot find the right alloy for the gunpowder not to break the great cannon."

Dracul held firm. "Keep looking," he said. "You have to find the solution to this problem—here is more money." And he gave him a bag of gold coins. Dracul needed the money to rescue his children, but this project was also of vital importance.

A beautiful pedigree puppy approached Jared, who took it in his hands and, smiling at his best client and friend, said, "This dog's name is Dracul."

In that place and at that time, it was customary to give a dog the name of your greatest friend or your bitterest enemy. On this occasion, with Jared's action, the ties of friendship and trade between him and Dracul were strengthened. They shared a bountiful dinner as the perfect finale to their reunion—and at the end as usual, Dracul congratulated the cooks on the excellent meal.

21

On October 26, 1443, Hunyadi arrived in Tirgoviste escorted by his powerful army. He was furious: his candidate to the throne of Wallachia had been overthrown by the exiled Dracul with the help of Hunyadi's bitter enemies, the Ottoman Turks. He was also outraged because Dracul, a knight of the Order of the Dragon, had made a pact with his enemy. Hunyadi made a big display with his appearance in Tirgoviste, facing the vovoid and demanding, "What have you done, traitor?"

"I had no choice," Dracul replied calmly. "I am glad to see you again."

"Don't be a hypocrite, Dracul! You must have a powerful reason to have taken sides with the enemy and broken the oath of the Dragons."

"My children are prisoners of Murad II, and if I attack him, he is going to blind them and impale them." Dracul felt his voice falter. "He forced me to sign a treaty and make an oath, with Christ as witness, that I'll never attack him. Besides, facing him with our armies would be suicide."

Hunyadi spoke like the brave warrior he was. "I am not afraid of any enemy, or of death—which, when it comes, will surely lead me to the presence of my Lord. If the sultan has weapons and a powerful army, I have a heart that wishes to stop beating in the defense of my faith."

Dracul felt the same, but unlike Hunyadi, he had pawned his children, and if he made a mistake, he would lose them. He answered with deep silence.

The White Knight told him, "We are organizing a great crusade to take the Port of Varna. We will rescue your children from there, but you must join us with your men so we do not fail in our attempt."

"The sultan made me swear on a Bible and before our Christ that I would never attack him," Dracul repeated.

"That oath has no value because it comes from the enemies of the Cross. I will do what it takes for the Holy Father in the Vatican to release you from it."

Dracul was not telling the truth: that he did not attack his enemy for fear of losing his children to tortuous deaths. Trying to discern the strength of Hunyadi's army, he asked, "How many soldiers do you estimate are going to the crusade?"

"Approximately fifty thousand."

Dracul gave an astonished gasp. "That is insane!"

"Why?" Hunyadi asked impatiently.

"In that port there are going to be no fewer than one hundred thousand soldiers with weapons that are newer and more powerful than ours. I tell you, this is going to be suicide! We have to look for more soldiers."

"More soldiers?" Hunyadi shouted. "You'd better look for more courage. You are a coward!"

Quickly, Dracul drew his sword and put its tip to the throat of the White Knight. "Take back what you said or you'll die right here. I will hold you responsible for the slaughter that is about to happen—and for the death of my children!"

Hunyadi, who was braver than he was handsome, screamed, "And you are going to kill the one who can rescue your children!" With that he lifted his head, daring Dracul to plunge it into his throat.

Dracul, realizing that the desperate fear of losing his children had nearly driven him to murder, lowered his sword, ashamed. "Forgive me, Brother—I am desperate. I fear I am going to lose my boys in the cruelest way you could imagine . . . Please put yourself in my shoes!"

"Vlad, we were born to die," the noble knight declared. "That is the law of our God. Remember that death is only a companion who will guide us to his presence. If your children die, they will do it at the hands of our enemies for the glory of God. It is to heaven they will go!"

Dracul understood that, but he couldn't accept it. He wanted his children in this world, not in the celestial one. But he kept his dissatisfaction to himself, and after a few brief exchanges of opinion, they bid one another farewell.

Hunyadi sent some emissaries to Pope Eugene IV, who dissolved the oath Dracul had made to the Ottomans. Then he let his brother Dragon know.

Alliances in Europe were changing. Eugene IV, seeking to extend the Christian faith, organized a holy crusade which would be led by Cardinal Guiliano Cesarini. Joining it were a contingent of poorly armed Hungarians, Polish, Bosnians, Croatians, Romans, and Russians, led by the young king of Poland, Ladislas IV Jagello, and supported by Hunyadi. The organization set, they looked for the right time to put the warriors into action.

Hunyadi sent Dracula a proclamation that said, "We are going to Varna's crusade. It is impossible to run away and inconceivable to give up. We are going to fight bravely and honorably with the weapons we have."

The Dragons were waiting for the arrival of the army of King Ladislas and Cardinal Cesarini. Then all would be accounted for, and the crusade could start.

On November 1, 1444, Hunyadi summoned Dracul to join them in Nicopolis. When Dracul saw that Hunyadi had just, thirty-four thousand men, he thought, *This is going to be a massacre.* Nevertheless, he had given his word to support the crusade, so he agreed to send Mircea with four thousand soldiers.

Before Mircea left, Dracul said, "Son, try not to go up front, and be discreet when you show the banner of the Dragon. I recommend that you look for a place to attack and then stay in the rear guard—if the sultan identifies you, he will kill your brothers. If you are in the great battle and you see that it is lost, give the order to your soldiers to retreat. You are going straight into a mousetrap!"

Mircea, who was braver than his father, answered, "I am going to fight with all my heart to achieve the victory and to continue moving forward to rescue my brothers."

Dracul was thoughtful and worried. After a moment he said, "Son, listen to me—be discreet! Do not show the banner of the Dragon, and stay in the rear guard. You are going to lose this battle! Think of your brothers: they are going to be blinded and impaled!"

But Mircea wanted to show his father that he also was knowledgeable, and kneeling down, he begged him, "Father, let God guide my hand, and give me your blessing!"

And so the father blessed his son, who joined the Crusade of Varna.

The crusaders provoked both admiration and fear wherever they went. In Bulgaria, some townspeople cheered the great King Ladislas as their liberator; but those were the same opportunists who cheered any invading army, and in doing so avoided plunder, robbery, and rape. Most Bulgarians fled, imploring Dracul for his mercy. More and more people arrived with their oxcarts, begging for asylum. Dracul, thinking of his children, accepted those refugees, offering his lands as a home. He did the same for the Turks from Edirne and Gallipoli.

Hunyadi congratulated Cardinal Cesarini, saying, "Your decision to break our ten-year truce with the Turks is the smartest one I've ever heard."

The cardinal smiled. "Can you imagine the power and wealth our enemies would have accumulated during that time?"

"Without a doubt, if we wait for ten years to attack them, they will be so strong we will never be able to defeat them."

On November 3 the crusaders passed by Petretz. Mircea said to Hunyadi, "I ask for your permission to attack this town and test our cannon."

"You have my permission," Hunyadi said, "but if you haven't taken the town by tomorrow, leave it. Our objective is Varna!"

"Thank you," Mircea said. He looked at the town, which was protected by a huge, inaccessible moat. He turned to his soldiers and yelled, "For the glory of our God . . . attack!"

When the cannon roared, the noise was so loud that some of the crusaders crossed themselves out of respect and fear. Then assault ladders appeared, and the inhabitants began defending themselves. While the battle raged, a soldier from another army told Mircea, "I know the way to enter that place!"

"Tell me how!"

"I need something in exchange," the soldier said.

"What do you want?" Mircea asked.

"I was a baker in this place, and there is a very bad man there who killed part of my family. My body still bears scars from the punishments he gave me. I want you to deliver the justice I want."

"You will have what you are asking for," Mircea promised.

"Follow me!" said the soldier, and Mircea obliged, trailing the soldier until he stopped in some heavy woods and pointed to a cave. "When I was a slave and we were under siege," the soldier said, "we got food through this place."

The population of Petretz was taken; the soldier apprehended his punisher; and the army commanded by Mircea, with another victory in their military career, joined the rear guard of the great crusader army.

22

On November 10, 1444, in Varna, thirty-eight thousand Christian soldiers met eighty-four thousand Ottoman Turk soldiers. The die was cast: war was unavoidable.

Ottoman sultan Murad II was leading his army from a prudent distance. Surrounded by his personal guard, he was giving commands, and his soldiers obeyed them blindly. With the superior numbers of his retinue, there was no doubt that the Ottomans would get the victory.

King Ladislas IV summoned Hunyadi. "You will lead the army," he said. "And may the hand of God lead your orders and actions!"

Hunyadi read to his men the proclamation everyone had heard: "We are going to Varna's crusade. It is impossible to run away and inconceivable to give up . . ." Then he ordered a surprise frontal attack, which got him exactly what he had expected: panic among his numerous enemies. Hunyadi's military strategy was exceptional. That battle, despite two-to-one odds favoring the Ottomans, was leading straight to their defeat. Mikhail Szilagyi blindly followed the orders of his commanding officer, and it promised to be a victory for Christianity.

Suddenly a strong wind blew and heavy rain began to fall. The sultan knew the battle was lost: he watched in horror as his army withdrew in fear from the brave crusaders. Finally he ordered the retreat. It was a total defeat for the Turks.

The Wallachians seized the opportunity to plunder the wealth the sultan had in his tent. That act consummated the Christians' victory.

King Ladislas, overcome by the euphoria and exuberance that came with youth, felt like a winner. Convinced that his name would be written in gold letters in the universal history of Christianity, he threw himself bravely at his enemy with his sword drawn. Hunyadi watched, admiring the passion with which his king was defending his faith; but when he evaluated the risk the young man was taking, he shouted, "Stay back, my king! Go back!"

Undeterred, the king tasted the glory of victory and waded into the middle of the battle. But the ground was wet, and the king's horse slipped and fell in the mud. Hunyadi saw Ladislas in trouble and, with the bravery of a lion, went to protect and help him. He jumped from his steed, suffering an enemy blow to his right arm, and with some difficulty picked up the young man and unceremoniously began carrying him away from the worst of the battle. The king was slender, but his armor was reinforced and very heavy. When the young king looked up and saw Hunyadi, he felt secure. He was in the hands of the greatest and most experienced knight in the crusade.

Hunyadi, severely wounded, made a superhuman effort to get the king onto his horse and transport him to a safe place. In the heat of the battle he did not care about the new wounds his enemies were giving him. He just had one thought in mind: to save his king!

An Ottoman knight was about to finish off a Christian soldier when he saw the king in trouble. To the amazement of his nearly dead prey, the Ottoman stopped what he was doing, let go of his shield, and threw himself at the young monarch, who was still in Hunyadi's arms. With difficulty the enemy lifted the young man by the hair with one hand, and with the other he decapitated him, screaming, "I have killed your king!"

Hunyadi was now living a nightmare. In his arms lay the decapitated body of his king. As his blood mixed with the monarch's, he felt a hatred toward his enemies like he had never felt, and he began to attack them even more viciously than before.

The Ottoman who decapitated the king did not fight anymore; he just rode through the battle, holding up the grisly head and screaming like a madman, "I have killed your king!" With this action he wrought the complete demoralization of the crusader army. When the Christians saw the head of their monarch, they started to lose confidence and run away from the battle. Hunyadi urged them to keep fighting until they achieved victory, but the news spread like wildfire, and soon what had been an assured victory turned into a complete defeat for the Christians.

When Mircea saw that the course of the battle was changing, he withdrew his men from the fight and they ran away with a considerable amount of loot.

Hunyadi was severely wounded; his body had been primary target of his enemy's weapons. But that was not his first battle, and the wounds he obtained in battle were also his trophies and his greatest pride. He knew he had two choices: he could be taken prisoner and await a dark and uncertain destiny and surely a dishonorable death, or he could retreat from the battlefield and keep defending Christ. He chose the second.

At the end of the battle came the plundering of the corpses, which almost always had something valuable on them, as the soldiers kept in their pockets what they treasured most. When the Ottomans arrived at the corpse of King Ladislas, they took his valuable armor and threw his body carelessly on top of other dead. That is how the great king was buried, in a common grave at the church of Varna. He was twenty-one when he died, and the remains of the heroic warrior would never be found. Two tombs were made for him: one in Varna, Bulgaria, and the other in the Cathedral of Wawel in Krakow.

Murad II summoned the soldier who had killed the king. "Do you know what you did?" he asked.

"I fulfilled my duty to serve my sultan," answered the brave soldier.

"I will promote you in rank because of your action. I thank Allah that you are with us!"

The sweet taste of victory did not sicken the Ottomans, who happily enchained the defeated, saying, "With so many slaves, we are going to become rich!"

"You are not going to sell me, you damned devil's Turks!" yelled a soldier as he put up resistance against his captors. He had landed several of his punches when suddenly he felt a strong blow to the head. By the time he awoke, he had already been mutilated; without arms and legs he would suffer an excruciating death. Other soldiers, seeing their destiny in that unfortunate man, decided to cooperate with their punishers.

Cardinal Guiliano Cesarini also was taken prisoner, but he was not like the others; his elaborate armor showed his elevated military rank. With a strong voice he challenged his captors in their language. "Infidels! Do you know what you are doing?"

The Ottomans looked at him curiously and then approached him in silence.

Pointing at them and without lowering his voice, he declared, "Damned infidel Turks! May your souls burn forever in hell if you touch just one of my hairs!"

One of the braver Ottomans stepped toward him. "Take off that armor!"

"Don't you dare to touch me! Your soul is in danger of going to hell—and if you go there, thousands of demons will torture you for all eternity!"

The Turk laughed, and in a mocking tone responded, "Are you the owner of hell? And your employee is Satan? And his demons obey you?"

"Quiet, blasphemous Turk. You are going to hell!"

"Who are you calling blasphemous? Son of the devil! Go ahead and ask your demons for help, because you are going to undress."

"I am the representative of God!" the cardinal shouted, enraged.

"But your employees are demons. Undress!" And the cardinal received a beating while he was forced to take off his valuable armor. "Look how skinny you are," sneered the Turk.

"Give me my armor, demons! I swear you are going to hell!" And without thinking about the consequences, the captive kept condemning the souls of his captors, while the men enchained nearby watched their leader, skeptical but impressed by his courage.

A Turk approached him carrying huge tongs and wearing a sharp sword at his waist. "You who are the helper of your god—ask him what we are going to do to you." As he spoke he was waving the tongs slowly and threateningly.

"You cannot do anything to me because my God protects me!"

Several men grabbed him violently and immobilized him, and the joker with the tongs asked him again, "If I am not going to pull out your teeth, guess what I am going to cut from you?"

"You are going to condemn yourselves!"

That was the cardinal's last scream.

With a great display of violence and mockery, the infidels held him back, cut off his tongue, and then took out his eyes. "Identify your enemies now," their leader said. "You can leave . . . you are as free as a bird!"

23

When Dracul received the news that the Crusade of Varna had been a complete disaster, he took his guard and part of his army and headed to the castle of Hunedoara, the residence of Janos Hunyadi. He walked in without greeting the White Knight, shouting, "I told you it was insane, that stupid crusade!"

Hunyadi answered with difficulty due his battle wounds. "Everything was going well; victory was ours," he said. "But because of the wet ground, King Ladislas's horse slipped, and as I was helping him back onto his horse, an Ottoman decapitated him. From there on, everything was chaos. Our men fled. With a little more help we surely would have won. We needed you! You are a coward!"

"You are the coward!" Dracul yelled. "Instead of defending your last man, you ran away like a hare!"

"The battle was over and lost! Why should I stay just to be murdered?" Hunyadi raised his voice more. "Your son Mircea is another coward! He placed himself in the rear guard of the army and sent the brave ones up front—like father, like son! A couple of chickens! If you had had the courage to carry your banner of the Order of the Dragon and lead all your army, I am sure we would be celebrating our victory!"

"My children must be dead by now, thanks to you. You are responsible for the defeat of the Crusade of Varna—and, now, for the death of my children!"

"You and Mircea are responsible, because you are cowards! You did not go to battle, and your son ran away!" By now Hunyadi was screaming.

They were about to draw their weapons and use them, but Hunyadi was seriously injured and Dracul was not going to take advantage. So, Dracul left, escorted by his boyars. As he rode away, the memory of his children was fixed in his mind. He traveled in silence, his hardened face coursed by tears. How badly did the torturer hurt them? Were they still with the executioner? Were their bodies going to be buried? These and more questions kept coming to his head. There was no comfort for his anguish.

24

The Ottoman sultan set off for his empire, where he would be received as a hero for having won the important battle. During a break in the journey he told his smart and brave son, Mehemed II, "I am going to kill the prisoners."

Anguished by the possible death of his lover, Mehemed said, "First we have to see if their father has betrayed us. I agree with your earlier plan of placing them in Wallachia. If you watch them closely, you'll see that they are as Ottoman as anyone. If we kill them without confirming our suspicions, it will be a waste."

Murad met with his chief falconers and spies to evaluate Dracul's attitude. "I want to know if our ally Dracul joined our enemies," he told them.

"I have been informed that banners of the Order of the Dragon were seen during the advance of our enemy," one spy said.

Another added, "My informants told me that Dracul was in Wallachia during the whole crusade and willingly gave asylum to Ottomans and Bulgarians."

The sultan had a doubt about Dracul. Was he an ally or an enemy? Since his doubts were not resolved, he said decidedly, "I am going to kill Dracul's sons, but don't say anything to them. I want to see their faces when I give them the news."

<hr/>

In a secret hideout, Dracula knelt in front of the crucifix he kept hidden along with his dagger. *Holy God, give me the strength not to baptize my dagger with Murad's blood! I need to get out of here and defend your faith! I ask you for the soul of my father and my brother Mircea, who at this moment must be with you in your kingdom.* Dracula stood up, wiped his tears, and prepared to face his enemy. Now, more than ever, he needed to wear the chameleon's skin.

When he met the returning infidel, Dracula gave him his best smile and a warm hug, saying in an especially loud and emotional way, "Thanks to Allah you are alive and well, Father!" Feeling his enemy's closeness, the boy wanted to take out his dagger and pierce the man through, but that would have been stupid; another Ottoman would come to take his place, and he would die without getting any benefit. That demon had surely killed his loved ones; when he thought of it he could not hold back his tears. Breathing deeply so as not to kill the sultan, he said in a soft, sweet voice, "I am so happy. You have come back alive, Daddy!"

Murad II was confused. He wanted to kill these poor devils, who loved him like a father? Mehemed II was right: it would be better to plant them in Wallachia. That way he could take the place without bloodshed.

There was a big party for the sultan and his victory. The celebration lasted seven days, and everybody was happy. Even Dracula was laughing, although inside he felt destroyed.

When the celebration was over and everything returned to normal, the sultan asked Dracula, "How is your training going?"

The boy had a black eye and was favoring his left leg. "I think I am doing well," he said, "but what I think does not concern me. I am making my best effort to please you, Father."

The sultan sent for one of his trainers and asked him, "How is Dracula's performance?"

The trainer brightened as he regarded the boy. "We've never had such a dedicated and talented student as this one. He is persistent, quick, and highly skilled, and he has a marked tendency toward perfectionism. Without a doubt he is going to be the our best soldier."

Turning to Dracula, the sultan said, "Didn't you tell me Mehemed was the best student?" Then, leaning close to the boy's ear, the sultan said in a low voice, "Thanks for convincing me not to kill him. That saved your life, too."

Then Murad started talking with Dracula in some other languages that were spoken in the empire, and the sultan was amazed and pleased by the way the prisoner had mastered them.

Murad II was happy with his apprentice—so happy that he named him chief falconer and placed him in charge of a small army, which under his leadership conquered a place near the empire and subdued the inhabitants. The most beautiful women and young ladies were taken to the harem of the sultan; the other women were taken to brothels; the children and young men were taken to join the Janissaries; the docile and strong were sold as slaves; and the old, uncontrollable, and rebellious were decapitated.

An Oman who had accompanied Dracula and his army informed the sultan, "I am impressed by the devotion your son professes to Allah. He faithfully fulfilled all our religious ceremonies."

"Did you see him make the sign of the cross at any time?" the sultan asked.

"No," the Oman said, smiling. "Dracula is as Ottoman as you and me, you can be sure of that!"

The sultan nodded, satisfied. "So I wasn't wrong! As soon as he turns eighteen, I am going to place him on Wallachia's throne. That entire place will be converted to Islam without my shedding a single drop of my army's blood.

25

"I am furious at the Ottomans!" Mircea told his father. "My brothers surely died in unthinkable pain. But I promise you, this situation won't last!"

"What do you want to do, Son?" asked Dracul.

"I am going to make a campaign against the Turks; we'll go in galleys through the Danube. We will also look for the remains of King Ladislas. I am going to invite Jean of Warvrin, lord of Forestel."

"While you do that, I am going to attack the Giurgiu Fortress," said Dracul, his rage rising with Mircea's.

"They are attacking us!"

The inhabitants of Nicopolis were screaming, terrified, as they ran away to protect their lives and their children. Then their grain and homes were plundered by the enemies. An enraged Mircea led the charge, screaming, "Kill them all!" After doing all the damage they could, his soldiers took Turtucaia and repeated the scene.

Meanwhile Dracul, thinking his sons were dead, took the Fortress of Giurgiu. The Ottoman defense could not hold against the fury of the crusader.

Vladislav II begged Hunyadi, "Give me your authorization to eliminate Dracul and Mircea!"

Hunyadi considered the thought but then shook his head. "It doesn't seem like a bad idea," he said, "but although I've had big problems with Dracul, since the sultan killed his children he has attacked him with all the strength of his army. A Christian man who fights for his faith must be respected." After a while, the coward again asked Hunyadi for permission to eliminate his enemies, but the White Knight again wouldn't allow it.

Dracul and Mircea's sorrow at the loss of Dracula and Radu was even worse than usual one gloomy afternoon, when, at the distance, Dracul saw a retinue of Ottomans carrying a white flag. *They are coming in peace,* he thought. His first reaction was to attack the enemy and destroy them; however, that was not the way a Christian knight behaved. The retinue passed through toward the palace, and after greeting each other coldly, the chief falconer gave them news that fell like a bombshell: "Your children are alive and well."

Dracul and Mircea looked at each other, their eyes full of tears, and they hugged each other tightly. It wasn't possible! They wanted to burst from happiness.

When they had assimilated the news, the chief falconer said, "Our sultan asks that you give us back the Fortress of Giurgiu and the thousands of Ottomans in your lands. He offers to return your children and to respect Wallachia's independence. To make the agreement official, we have brought a standard written treaty."

Dracul beamed. "I never imagined that our beloved sultan was so magnanimous! Give me that treaty—I will sign it gladly!" He printed his signature and kept a copy for himself, and the Ottomans returned to the empire, having fulfilled their mission successfully.

On November 6, 1447, Vladislav II informed Hunyadi, "Dracul and Mircea made a pact with the Ottomans. They have returned the Fortress of Giurgiu and the Ottomans they held captive."

Hunyadi leapt to his feet. "This is treason! I give you my authorization to attack them!"

That was the order Vladislav II had so long expected. He organized the offensive and sent his reliable boyars to attack them without warning.

Dracul, Mircea, and their boyars, including the faithful Ivan, were surprised and apprehended. They were taken to a place near the church of

Snagov, where the boyars were systematically murdered; Ivan received a wound in his left side and was given up for dead. Dracul and Mircea were savagely beaten, and then Vladislav's boyars continued the lesson, torturing father and son, one in front of the other.

One boyar had a great idea: he put an iron bar in the bonfire, and when it began to glow red he took it out and showed it to Dracul. "You're going to die today! But there is no hurry . . . we have time to have fun. The night is still young, and it is deliciously fresh because of the snow. So what do you prefer—hot or cold?" Like men most of his sort, he enjoyed seeing his enemy's fear.

But Dracul held his torturer's gaze in silence.

The sadist torturer smiled and said, "For being a despot and not answering me, I am going to be generous and give you both." And he stuck the hot iron in Dracul's eye, provoking a heart-rending scream.

"Coward!" Mircea yelled.

The boyar turned around. "Did you bray?" he asked, and he stuck the hot iron in the son's eye.

The concert of horror had started: the previous beating was child's play compared to what was coming. The boyars took the prisoners out into the snow. "Did you get burned?" one boyar asked. "Poor things—let's refresh you!" And the sadists put ice in their burned eyes.

Then another boyar addressed the tormented men. "This party is to celebrate the ascent to the throne of Vladislav II!—and you are the main guests. Without you, this party wouldn't have meaning!"

Another drunken boyar agreed and opened another bottle of wine, screaming, "It is true! You are the life and soul of this party!" Dracul and Mircea were lying frozen in the snow, hearing everything.

So as not to ruin the festive atmosphere, whenever they pleased, the partygoers would go out and beat the Draculesti, making fun of their pain, while the others kept on with the party. When the prisoners were almost frozen, one of the boyars said, "We're forgetting about our guests! Maybe they are uncomfortable and cold." And he went out and asked them sarcastically, "Wouldn't you like to be in a warm place?" And without waiting for an answer, the group took the men and put them in front of a fire saying, "Do not die so soon!"

Those extreme changes of temperature surely would cause serious health problems in the future . . . but who was thinking about the future? There was no tomorrow for these men.

As the two huddled by the fire, they heard an authoritarian voice: "Dig your grave!"

Mircea arose and fulfilled the order with difficulty. When he finished digging, a boyar burned his other eye with the hot iron and the others beat him, and then they threw him in the snow so they could attend to his father.

Completely blind now and trembling, Mircea said, "I am cold."

One of the boyars, taking pity on him, said, "Poor little thing . . . I am going to put you in a warm place"—and pushed him abruptly into a wooden coffin. Then he added in a kind tone, "I am going to make you a promise: I will protect you and won't let anyone else beat you again or hurt you for the rest of your life. Just let me give you one last lesson." Looking at his friends, he said, "Don't be rude! Let's say good-bye to Mircea as he deserves." Together they gave him his last savage beating, after which the kind boyar added, "I am going to nail on the cover for your best protection!"

Dracul witnessed the grisly destiny of his son, praying he would die quickly. He watched them close the coffin amidst a concert of sinister laughs, tears streaming from his only eye. Then the executioners looked at him and said, "Bury him!"

"He is alive!" Dracul protested.

"Do you want us to kill your lover and your bastard? If you don't do it, they will die this same way . . . and you will bury them!"

Dracul had no choice: he took the shovel and started carrying out the macabre order.

Mircea, hearing everything from his cloistered place, began screaming, "Help me, Father!" He knew his father; he knew that if he was doing this thing, it was against his will. Trapped in a nightmare, Mircea fought with the only thing he had: his hands. With his fingers he was making superhuman efforts to open the coffin, not noticing that he was tearing off his own nails. He had long imagined dying pierced by the sword of his enemy in the middle of a glorious battle, defending Jesus Christ—not this death, which was humiliating.

With every shovelful of soil Dracul threw on the coffin, he felt his soul was dying, and he started to pray, asking God's forgiveness for the thing he was doing. By the time he finished, the boyars were almost too drunk to stand. Taking advantage of their drunkenness, Dracul ran away, got on his horse, and went to find his Ottoman ally.

But with his wounds, he couldn't ride quickly. His punishers reached him in the swamps of Balteni, near Bucharest, and one of them told him mockingly, "I can hardly believe it! We considered you the life and soul of the party, and you abandoned us!" Looking at his partners, he asked, "Did we give Dracul permission to leave?"

"No way!" came the chorus, and the boyars started to beat him anew. When they saw that he did not complain or resist their blows, one of them said, "Either you ask for forgiveness . . . or I'll cut your head off!" The silence of the tortured man enraged him. "You asked for it!" he said as he cut off Dracul's head.

Knowing the great devotion of the governor, the monks took his valuable remains and buried them solemnly in an elaborate Orthodox ritual at the Dealul monastery.

26

Hunyadi, commanding an army of eight thousand Hungarian, Wallachian, and Transylvanian soldiers, crossed the Danube and took Turkin.

Skanderbeg the Albanian lord, joined them with part of his war forces, and others were due to arrive with new armaments. Together they would take Serbia. On their way they committed the same atrocities as the crusader knights: they robbed, killed, set homes on fire, and raped women regardless of their age.

This army had a confrontation in Serbia, a battle that lasted from October 17 to 19, 1448. By then the Christian retinue had grown, with twenty thousand military men counted against forty thousand Turks commanded by the despot George Brankovic. As the fight raged, the Turks' numeric superiority became obvious; the scale leaned toward the Ottomans.

On October 18, Christian reinforcements arrived. They brought new muskets with gunpowder, provoking horror among the Ottoman ranks. After unloading their artillery until their ammunition ran out, the Turks attacked with such fierceness that they subdued the Christians; Janos Hunyadi, together with his subordinate Vladislav II, were taken prisoners.

Brankovic furiously confronted Hunyadi. "Explain to me why you allowed your army to commit the atrocities it did on its way through my towns and villages!"

Hunyadi did not know how to answer. In fact, he was responsible for the behavior of his army; he allowed those excesses in order to boost the soldiers' morale so they would not abandon the campaign. But because he couldn't say that to his enemy, he remained silent.

"Your damned silence will not return peace to my people!" Brankovic shouted. "You are a beast! Your soldiers are all animals!" He kept unloading his rage, and then he called to his guards. "Beat these bastards savagely, but do not let them die. Give them only bread and water."

Hunyadi was desperate. With the exception of the Crusade of Varna, he was accustomed to the taste of victory. Now he was tasting bitter defeat, and in a dank cell—hungry, thirsty, and cold, and fighting an army of insects that did not let him sleep with their voracious bites. This end did not agree with the one he had expected; this death was a humiliation! When the jailers arrived, Hunyadi tried to provoke them into killing him, saying, "You are not men—you don't know how to kill Christians!"

The jailers wisely kept silent. Their only response was a generous—but nonfatal—beating.

27

The sultan received information from his military intelligence that Dracul and Mircea had not been seen anywhere, despite the fact that Hunyadi and Vladislav were prisoners at the Fort of Smederevo. Suspecting that his allies, the Draculesti, had problems, he said to Dracula, "Son, I promised that when you turned eighteen I would put you on Wallachia's throne. You are only seventeen, but unfortunately for us, your father and your brother have disappeared. If we don't hurry, our enemies will kill them. My spies have informed me that Vladislav II dispatched the Danesti clan, who are furiously looking for them. If they find them . . . you can imagine what they are going to do. Besides, your enemies are now prisoners. Your time has come!"

Adrenaline surged through Dracula's strong body. His beloved father and brother were in danger; he was not just going to stand there with his arms crossed. "Father," he said, "Thank you for the education. Thank you for caring for me and making me a warrior. I am going to take the throne in Wallachia. You'll have news from me soon."

Dracula went to his brother Radu and hugged him. "Brother, I love you. Soon we will be together in Wallachia with our family."

Radu's beautiful eyes showed no emotion. In fact he preferred to stay with Mehemed II, and he answered Dracula's warm farewell coldly, saying, "Say hello to our father and mother and to Mircea."

Dracula got on his horse and headed to Tirgoviste, escorted by part of the Ottoman army.

They arrived in Tirgoviste in October 1448, and Dracula took the throne there without any opposition. The Saxons of the town council received him with joy. Dracula was the son of Dracul, the nephew of Alexandru Aldea and the grandson of Mircea the Great, all puppets of the council. Certainly this new ruler would be no different.

Dracula greeted the councilmen with warmth and respect. Moses approached him and hugged him solemnly, saying, "We are really sorry!"

"What?" Dracula asked, startled. "Are my father and Mircea dead?"

"No . . . it was your mother," the Saxon answered with an inexpressive face.

Dracula's eyes filled with tears, and assimilating the sad news, he decided to look for his father and his brother immediately.

The Saxon vice-governor, greatly concerned by the rumor that Hunyadi was dead, demanded that Dracula clarify the facts. Dracula answered him with the following letter:

> To Nicolas Ocna of Sibiu:
>
> You wrote and asked us to be so kind as to return to you the real governor of Hungary, who was coming back from war. We cannot do that. An emissary of Nicopolis came to us this Tuesday, October 29, and said with certainty that Murad II, the Turkish sultan, made a three-day war against Hunyadi the governor, and that on the last day Hunyadi formed a circle with his caravans, Hussite style, and the sultan went down with his emissaries, broke the line, and killed him. If we follow them, the Turks are going to kill us. That is why I ask you for patience until we know what happened to Hunyadi. We do not know if he is alive. *If he comes back from the war, we will make peace with him.* But you are our enemies today, and if something happens to us, you will be responsible before God.
>
> Written in Tirgoviste the day before the day of All Saints, the year of our Lord 1448
>
> Signed,
> Wladislaus III, Dragwlya

Dracula said to one of his commanding officers, "I am sure that if Janos is alive, he will read this letter, and when he does he will realize that I respect him and that my fight is also for the defense of Christianity."

On November 1, 1448, Dracula gave a joyful shout: "Ivan!" And he jumped from his chair to hug the faithful boyar like a brother.

Without breaking the young man's embrace, and with a faltering voice, Ivan Stokovich said, "I am really sorry!"

Guessing the bad news before he heard it, Dracula sat down abruptly. "Are they both dead?"

"Unfortunately," Ivan said. He was silent for a moment and then he added, "I know who the murderers were. The one who ordered everything was Vladislav II, and I will never forget his boyar assassins . . . I remember their faces as if their images were engraved in my mind. Look at my back! They cut me like a pumpkin and left me for dead, but I have more lives than a cat!"

"Thank God!" Dracula said.

Dracula felt the weight of the world on his shoulders. What was he going to do without his brother? He had always dreamed of collaborating with him, together being the best rulers of Wallachia: the powerful Mircea with his brother Dracula as his right-hand man.

His eyes got cloudy; his tears betrayed him. He rose, feeling dizzy, and looking for a crucifix knelt down before it and said, "My God! I swear before you, the most sacred one, that I will not rest until I find those executioners and punish them in the most horrible way there is on earth."

Then, to corroborate Ivan's story, Dracula headed toward the place the faithful boyar had described. He had the terrible feeling that everything the survivor had told him was true, although he kept hoping he was in the middle of a nightmare.

Ivan led him to the exact place, telling the exhumers where to dig.

When they lifted the wooden coffin out of the earth and opened it, Dracula felt his world come apart. The body was face-down: the man had been buried alive! Dracula checked the lid; it was covered with scratches. Then he checked the hands, which had no fingernails. That is how he knew that the deceased had fought until the very end. They saw that his face had been burned and broken; he had no eyes. Dracula then looked in the deceased's clothes. When he found the round stone, there was no doubt. It was his brother.

Dracula was caught in an emotional turmoil. Rage, hate, revenge, impatience? They were mere words. There was no name for the feeling that ran through his veins. Wracked with pain, his face bathed in tears, he lifted his eyes toward the sky and implored, "My Lord, put the soul of my brother at peace. I offer him to you in exchange for defending your faith as no one else has. I will be your most faithful and ferocious soldier. Put at peace, also, the soul of my father. Although I hope to see him alive, I accept your will with resignation."

He had put into the hands of his God the soul of Mircea—and surely his father's, as well. As Dracula came back to reality, his new character already had begun to form itself: hardened, strong, implacable, but fair. He thought about the death he would give those damned executioners. Beheading them would be too kind; he needed to mutilate them while they were still alive, to torture them and then kill them . . . but how? Suddenly he had a spark of inspiration: impale them! That's what he was going to do with those bastards—he was going to impale them!

Together with his boyars, Dracula searched for the body of his father without success. The monks who had buried the body in the Dealul monastery were cloistered and did not see him searching.

———◆◆◆———

Dracula's exhaustive search led him to the monk Barbat in a monastery in Bucharest. When the monk saw the young man dressed like an Ottoman, he stared at him in silence. Dracula answered his stare by kneeling down before him. "Father, give me your blessing."

Barbat was taken aback when he saw that the Ottoman was a fervent Christian. "Why do you dress like that?" he asked, intrigued.

"Because these are the clothes I like the most. I'm comfortable in them. But I wish to talk about our God."

Dracula spent praying a quietest evening in that monastery, at the side of the monks. At his departure, Barbat said, "You are our beloved son. And if one day you are in trouble, remember that this is your home and we will be like your brothers. Now kneel down so we may give you our blessing." Dracula humbly knelt to receive the blessing of those good and selfless monks. Then he left to continue his search.

When he arrived back in Tirgoviste, he met with the Saxons of the town council, telling them, "I wish to establish a new law of justice, so that the one who steals, rapes, or kills, or who betrays our king or the vovoid, must pay for his crime by dying impaled and the lazy man should be decapitated

Moses, the leader of the group, said, "Since before the time of your grandfather Mircea, justice has been administered by the town council, which dictates the rules and imposes the sentences and fines for each crime. It would be unfair to make changes."

"Unfair to whom?" Dracula asked angrily.

"To Wallachia," the Saxon replied.

To that Dracula replied firmly, "You will now begin deliberating the application of this new law. True, the town council will no longer profit from crime, but the townspeople will be happy to know there is real justice in Wallachia. I declare this meeting closed, and I hope my law will be approved for the next meeting." He rose from his seat. "Have an excellent night, gentlemen!" And with those words, he left.

The Saxons stayed to deliberate. One councilman, Jacob, said angrily, "If we do justice like this madman wants, our income will diminish drastically."

Ruben said, "Something tells me this Dracula won't be docile. I propose that we approve the law, since we have no other choice. Then once his Ottoman soldiers have gone, we will overthrow him and put in place another one who respects us."

Ruben's proposition was accepted unanimously, and the Saxons started hiring mercenaries and contacting Dracula's rivals. Nobody was going to affect their interests!

"Two months have passed and everything is in order," said the chief falconer, who commanded the sultan's army

"It is time for you to go back to the empire," Dracula said. "Tell my father that the necessary actions will be taken to achieve his objectives. Thank you for your support, and may Allah guide you!"

The army left, and Dracula stayed behind, supported by the power of his boyars, some of whom were mercenaries Ivan had selected.

28

Zapolva was a widow with two daughters; life was difficult for her. But she was a pretty woman, and a sturdy and strong man approached her with a proposal of marriage. Soon they were a family, living in a small hut.

Logofat was a hard-working man, his athletic body the result of his demanding labor. No one doubted his physical strength.

Caplea, Zapolva's oldest daughter, was like any other girl, helping at home and playing when she could. At just eight years of age, she did not know evil; she thought the world was as pure as her own white heart.

One day Caplea was playing hide-and-seek when her stepfather quietly called her aside. "Come, my girl, I am going to show you a place where they cannot find you!" He took her by the hand and went deep into the forest and he rapes her. When he finished the violation, he threats her: "If you tell your mother or anyone what I did to you, I will kill you all!"

And with that, Caplea's dreams and illusions died. She had hoped someday to marry a good man, but now she could offer only dishonor and shame. The bastard had stolen her virtue, her future, her honor, her dreams and hopes.

That Saturday, like every Saturday of his life, Logofat headed to the confessional. He was a pious Christian who wanted his soul always to be in God's good graces. When he arrived, he knelt down and waited patiently for his turn to confess. Then the window slid open and a familiar voice intoned, "Hail Mary, full of grace . . ."

"Forgive me, Father, for I have sinned."

The priest immediately recognized the voice and scolded him: "I thought you were not going to come back today, Logofat! And now you come in late—I have almost finished hearing confessions. You don't need to tell me your sins; I know them by heart. Which girl did you sully now?"

"Father, the strength of the devil is too great!" Logofat said. "How can I resist his attack?"

"I've told you a thousand times! Ask strength from our God Jesus Christ when you are about to sin, and he will give it to you. Only that way can you resist temptation."

"I do that, Father, but the devil is too powerful. He drags me to the dominions of lust, and I lose my mind."

"Whom did you rape now?"

"My stepdaughter Caplea, again, and Ryngalia, and I took Stana's virtue. This time I am truly repentant! Do you think the blood of my Christ could forgive again my indescribable sins?"

To the priest, that challenge was blasphemy. "Are you a heretic?" he said. "There is no sin, no matter how big, that the infinite mercy of Christ could not forgive if there is repentance."

"That is why I am here, Father," Logofat said in an anguished voice. "I have truly repented."

The priest knew that the man everyone described as a monster was nothing more than an innocent victim of Satan, and he deserved another opportunity. He had shown his regret, and that was enough. With the power that had been invested in him, the priest summoned the strength of the precious blood of Christ and forgave again Logofat's sins—but not without imposing a severe penance. So that Logofat would remember not to sin again, he had to say the Lord's Prayer three hundred times.

Satan's victim fulfilled the penance, and the next morning at Sunday Mass, he received the sacred Body of Christ through Holy Communion, and gave generous alms . . . as usual.

Caplea watched from her pew and understood that the monster had a protective shield that prevented anyone from hurting him. Seeing him so powerful and untouchable, she made a desperate appeal to the Christ of the temple. *My God, who is protecting that cruel and diabolical beast? Why is he having communion if he hurts me so much?* Her nightmare resumed a few days later, when the innocent victim of Satan again fell into the clutches of sin, and he raped Caplea and then another girl. Another confession would come, and another repentance and another penance, and another Holy Communion, and another alms, and then another victim. Fortunately for Logofat, the powerful blood of Christ was benign and precious, so precious that it could forgive even seventy times seven! Meanwhile, the letch boasted about his crimes to his friends, as if his actions were a reason to be proud.

This story repeated itself in different ways throughout all Wallachia, as fathers, stepfathers, uncles, grandfathers, friends of the family, and neighbors seized the opportunity when they could, raping the females without caring whether they were their relatives or even little girls.

29

On November 14, 1448, in the Fort of Smederevo, as the White Knight and Vladislav II prepared to be transferred, Hunyadi analyzed the situation and said Vladislav, "Be ready! The worshipers of Allah mourn their dead for three days. As soon as we see the mourning start, we are going to escape. I am sure we will make it!"

Vladislav was willing to do anything to escape that hell. He had never been so cold, had never felt such hunger or thirst or such intense anguish. He agreed to the White Knight's plan, and when mourning period began, they fled to Hungary.

They arrived at the castle on two weak and tired horses. A guard stopped them, commanding, "In the name of the king, identify yourselves!"

Hunyadi dismounted and, assuming the stance of a great lord, said loudly, "I am Janos Hunyadi, the governor of Hungary and Transylvania!"

The guard laughed out loud. "That's a good joke!" he said, and then, making a great effort to control himself, he said, "Do you think I am going to believe that a filthy, skinny beggar, a hairy and ragged tramp, is the governor of Hungary and Transylvania?" He chuckled again, adding, "If you are the governor, I am the king!" He smiled cynically and said, "Stay back. You are not going to enter!"

A fellow guard, who never forgot a face but also knew the governor had been given up for dead, immediately stepped forward and said, "Welcome, my lord!"

"Have you gone crazy?" his companion yelled. "Governor? This beggar?"

The guard drew his sword and ceremoniously placed it on the ground. Then, with one knee on the ground and his hand on his chest, he cried, "Our governor has arrived!" Recognizing that Hunyadi was weak and ill from lack of food and water, as well as the long trip, he offered the governor his arm, saying, "My lord, grant me the honor of being your support at this moment!"

Hunyadi was confused. One guard had received and treated him like a beggar, and the other like what he was, a great ruler. He wanted to punish the forgetful one, but he would have time later to attend to such unimportant matters. The first thing he asked for was a long, delicious bath to try to clean away his memories. Then, clean and dressed in his military uniform, he went to the king's court and summoned Vladislav to design the military action that would come.

"What is your name?" Hunyadi asked the guard who recognized him.

".Sweryge"

"From now on, Sweryge, you will be part of my personal guard."

Sweryge stood at attention before his new leader, never having imagined he would enjoy such an honor. No matter how hard he tried, he could not erase the smile from his face.

Without wasting a moment, Hunyadi issued an order to Vladislav II: "You must to take Wallachia immediately!"

So Vladislav held a secret meeting with the members of the town council. Moses received him euphorically. "Welcome! You arrived at the right time in a moment of need."

"I have come to overthrow Dracula," Vladislav said.

Moses gave him a pat on the shoulder and replied, "And we need you to overthrow him. We have a group of boyars and soldiers ready to receive your orders, and from now on, you have all our military support—and our economic support, as well. As we told you before, you have our full consent to be the next vovoid. So that you do not fail in your attempt, here are two bags of gold coins to negotiate with Dracula's mercenaries."

Vladislav II met with Lobzuowo, the chief of Dracula's mercenary boyars, and said, "Let's us talk in a more eloquent language: how much it will cost me to overthrow Dracula?"

"Two hundred gold coins," Lobzuowo said firmly.

"Here they are!" Vladislav said, pushing the bags toward him. "Now bring me Dracula's head."

"You paid to overthrow him. If you want us to deliver his head, it will cost you two hundred coins more."

Vladislav considered the deal and then shook his head, smiling. "That's a lot of money. I will catch him myself," he said. "It was a pleasure doing business with you!"

Lobzuowo gathered his soldiers, organized a plan, and without saying a word took Dracula by surprise. They aimed their swords at Dracula's chest, disarming him, and then said, "We are war merchants. We work for the one who pays the most. If one day you have enough money, we will be at your service. But today, Vladislav II has paid us to overthrow you; he did not want to pay the two hundred gold coins I asked of him to deliver your head."

"Why did you betray me?" Dracula asked.

"I don't betray!" Lobzuowo protested. "I just make business with my weapons. And if now I am warning you, it is not because I want to do you a favor; it's because I know that maybe tomorrow you will have money to hire my services." Then, looking Dracula in the eye, he said, "Run while you can!"

Lobzuowo and his soldiers had betrayed Dracula, but he did not consider them his enemies. Still, they had shown they would kill him for money, and so without delay he prepared to take the advice of the mercenary.

"We have to run, quickly!" Dracula said to Ivan. "Go tell the others to flee in diaspora. I will see you again when I recover the throne."

The faithful Ivan hugged his vovoid, and when he spoke, it was from the heart. "Royal blood does not run through my veins, but I love you like a brother. God bless you!"

Vladislav II made an offer to his boyars and soldiers: "Whoever brings me Dracula's head will receive fifty gold coins!"

The military men went searching in every direction, each one desperate to earn his fortune and look good before their lord.

———◆◈◆———

Dracula knew that he would lack nothing if he went to the sultan. He would have military support, money, power, wealth, and even his brother Radu. But he would also have to renounce his faith in Christ and worship Allah. His love for Christ was so great that he preferred to be a fugitive who might at any moment die an unexpected death, rather than live in opulence away from his God.

The first thing he had to do was get rid of the expensive, Ottoman-style clothes that marked him as ruler. So he found a beggar about his size and offered to exchange clothes with him.

The beggar thought it was a prank. Why would such an elegant man ask him something like that? It was ridiculous. Pushing Dracula aside, he said, "Don't mock me. Let me go on my way."

But Dracula insisted. "It is critical that I have your clothes—I am not joking. I'll exchange mine for yours."

The beggar could not believe it: that crazy man started to take off his clothes. The beggar was not going to miss an opportunity like that. When he saw the proposal was serious, he imagined himself dressed in that elegant attire and felt very happy.

While the exchange was being made, the beggar asked him, "Why do you want my clothes? They are old, threadbare, and dirty. Yours, on the other hand, are elegant and expensive."

Dracula did not want to socialize with the man; he just needed his clothes. "Hurry up and don't talk so much," he said. "If you don't want to do it, I am not going to force you."

The beggar quickly took off his clothes and gave them to him, saying, "You have already gotten me excited about the idea, and you gave your word . . . don't change your mind!"

After making a successful exchange, Dracula hurried away toward Brasov.

The beggar went on his way, turned into an elegant Ottoman prince. His fine new fur coat was really warm—there was no comparison to the thin fur he had been wearing. He glowed with happiness, suddenly feeling handsome and interesting.

Late that night some boyars approached a bonfire, and when they saw Dracula's figure they surrounded the area immediately. They decided to take every precaution; after all, there was no rush—they had him! And so they sat patiently, like animals stalking their prey, waiting for him to fall asleep so they could capture him.

The beggar before long he fell fast asleep. He was awaken by violent blows to his head and body. He was frightened and confused; he had no issues with anyone. He kept screaming, "Why are you beating me?" Then he was surrounded by swords, and he was overcome by fear. With a trembling voice he implored his aggressors again, "Why are you beating me?"

"Let me cut his head!" one of the men said.

"You are insane!" the beggar cried. "What did I do to you?"

"And still you dare to ask, Dracula? You are a coward, even in death!"

"I am Lactuzher, not Dracula! You are making a mistake!"

The darkness of the night did not allow them to distinguish his face; they had identified him only by his elegant clothes. But some of the mercenaries had also served the fugitive and knew him perfectly well, and when they saw the face of the beaten man, they said, "This is not him!"

One of the boyars grabbed the beggar by the throat and said, "You are not Dracula, but you know where he is. Why do you have his clothes?"

The beggar was terrified. He had never imagined that the cost of that elegant attire would be so high: first a severe beating, and then the accusation of being the accomplice of a political fugitive he did not even know. His life was hanging by a thread! With a trembling voice he replied, "He gave them to me in exchange for my clothes."

The boyars were surprised by the fugitive's cunning. "What did your clothes look like?" one of them asked.

"Black rags and a dark-brown fur."

"And where did he head to?"

"He was going toward Brasov," the beggar stammered.

"This is just an idiot!" said a boyar, kicking him in the bottom.

Another boyar said, "Get lost, you moron! And if you see him, don't forget to notify us. If you don't, you'll be considered his accomplice."

The beggar stumbled away, his body aching from the beating they had given him. Now he would look for another beggar so he could get rid of that beautiful suit, the reason of so much misfortune.

30

Meanwhile Dracula arrived on the outskirts of Brasov. Feeling for the first time hungry, thirsty, and cold, and dressed in his new attire, he walked to a humble hut and cautiously knocked on the door.

A man opened it a few inches. "What the hell do you want?"

Dracula immediately remembered that face. He was eight years old when that man knelt in front of him, pleading for mercy for not having paid the tribute. However, that was about nine years ago; surely the man didn't recognize him. "I am freezing," Dracula said, "and I am very hungry and thirsty. Can you give me something to eat and some water?"

The man watched the poor beggar trembling without a coat. "Come in," he said. When he realized that the beggar was almost frozen, the good Christian lit the fireplace in his little hut and added, "Get close, my friend. The heat will help you recover sensibility and movement." Then he gave him a cup of warm water and a little piece of bread, saying, "I wish I could offer you something else to eat; but we are poor and barely have enough for ourselves. We have to ration our food, as we often live hand to mouth."

At some point during his escape, Dracula had lost the thin fur that covered him, and so now his host asked, "How come you are outside in this damned cold without something to protect you?"

Dracula could not tell him the truth. "I fell asleep and someone stole my fur."

They kept on talking about trivial things, and as the fire started to warm his body, the refugee wanted to thank the good man for his kindness, but he could not find the words. Meanwhile the man's big family gathered around the strange visitor, looking at him as if he were a freak, asking themselves, *Why does this beggar have the bearing of a great lord?*

"My name is Kardotas," the host said. "And yours?"

Saying his real name would be like putting his head on a silver platter. "Dragomyr," Dracula said.

"Those damned rulers of ours are going to drive us mad with their damned tribute," Kardotas said. "We work all day, they take the bread from our mouths to gather that damned payment, and we live in fear that they will take one of our children to the damned sultan."

Although Dracula knew well the consequences for not paying, he wanted to make sure he didn't give himself away. "What if you tell them you don't have the money?"

An anguished expression crossed Kardotas' face, and he started to speak in a soft voice. "Many years ago, a very evil ruler named Vlad II—the one they call the demon—came here joined by some damned Turks to charge us the tribute. We barely had enough to eat. We did not pay because we spent the tribute trying to save my sick daughter, who later died. Those bastards did not understand, and they became furious. They beat me savagely and raped my wife and daughters in my presence. Fortunately my sons were too small to be taken for the damned conscription. The men said they respected our lives, that they were not going to enslave us, but that the next year they would come back, and if we didn't pay, the same thing would happen. Then they burned our shack. Consequently we haven't eaten properly since then, just to gather enough for that damned tribute!" As he spoke his eyes filled with tears, and then he added, "They say we are not their damned slaves, but maybe it would be better if we were. Then they would have to feed us and protect us. Now they just rob us!"

Dracula did not know what to say. He did not know how to comfort this man who had been harmed by his father just to fulfill the yearning for conquest and thirst for wealth of the Ottoman sultan. Feeling rage, desperation, and helplessness, he wanted to explain that his father suffered greatly when he charged that tribute, that he cried over his own lack of strength to face the enemy; however, to say that would be to turn himself in. Instead, Dracula tried to console Kardotas. "Seek refuge in our God," he said. "He marks the way and helps us in our most desperate moments."

Kardotas was quiet for a moment, studying his gnarled hands. "That damned day about nine years ago, I was pleading, crying to God to help me defend my family . . . and where was he? On the side of those damned powerful men. They love and respect God because he loves and respects them—but what do we have? Damned hunger, cold, anxiety because at any moment the town council might take our land. You are a beggar; you know about the damned pain we all feel. But if you were a member of the damned Draculesti or Danesti, you would think differently . . . and maybe you will be more religious."

Somewhere amidst the conversation and curses, the time to sleep came, and the host offered his hut to the beggar, giving him firewood and saying, "Don't let the fire go out during the night; you'll get cold."

Dracula could not find the words to tell that foul-mouthed and good man thank you for what he had done for him. In that hut, among those poor people, he felt a sense of warmth and protection he had not felt in years. He slept like he had not done in a long time, and then very early in the morning he bid farewell to those strangers who had behaved as if they were his relatives. "Do not ask me anything," he said to Kardotas. "Just trust me. And forgive us!" With that he put a gold coin in the old man's hand.

"Who are you?" Kardotas asked, suddenly frightened.

"You gave me warmth and a bite of food when I needed it most. I am never going to forget you, and someday you will hear from me. Trust me," he said again, "and forgive us." Then he said another grateful good-bye.

Kardotas watched, intrigued, the bearing and confidence of that . . . beggar? *Who is he? Why did he give me a fortune? Why is he so enigmatic and polite? Why is he asking me for forgiveness?* Kardotas was an intelligent man; he knew something very strange was happening. He decided to walk Dracula to the door, and when they opened it they saw that the town was surrounded by soldiers. Dracula blanched, and Kardotas noticed immediately. He closed the door again and asked, "Do you have issues with those damned bastards?"

"Yes," answered his visitor. "They are chasing me to kill me."

If these are his enemies, then he is my friend, Kardotas thought. "I am no one to judge you," he said. "I have a damned plan." He shouted for his family, who surrounded them right away. Addressing his two oldest daughters, he said, "You two—bring damned water, quickly!" Without asking questions, the young women took two buckets each and went to the well. To his wife he said, "Take out my formal clothes and prepare them," and she ran to fulfill the order. Then he turned to his sons. "Saddle up the horse, give it food and water, and fill the damned saddlebags with the food we have stored." Like their sisters, the boys went running to fulfill their father's orders. "Watch the windows," he commanded his two remaining daughters. "If those damned riders come, let me know!"

Then he turned to Dracula. "And you, Dragomyr—bathe yourself immediately with this damned water. Use these herbs. They cleanse really well."

Dracula was impressed by the mental dexterity of his new ally. For the first time in his life, someone from a lower level was making decisions for him, even giving him orders. That was incredible, but Dracula also understood the plan perfectly well. He bathed and put on the clean clothes that were given to him: he was a new man! Now he bid them farewell in earnest, telling them, "Someday you will hear from me."

Kardotas smiled. "I know; I have to trust you, and we forgive you . . . but go now with God! And I hope you get out alive. Who the hell are you?"

Dracula returned his smile. "Whoever I am, today you have made a true friend for life—trust me! And thank you for your forgiveness." He pressed another gold coin into Kardotas' hand, saying again, "Thank you very much!" Then he went out the door looking cool and unhurried, mounted the horse the boys had prepared, and headed straight toward the very soldiers who were looking for him. He passed very close to them, eyeing them curiously. The soldiers paid no attention to the gentleman who rode by; they were looking for a man in black rags with a dark fur coat, and they already had a group of suspects who matched that description. So Dracula went on his way, and as he rode he thought about all the things Kardotas had told him. He was starting to understand his people's needs.

Some soldiers arrived at Kardotas' hut, asking if he'd seen a young man with green eyes, dressed in black rags and a dark-brown fur. Kardotas had burned the rags in his fireplace, and he'd never seen the fur, so he answered, "No, I haven't seen anyone with that description." Then, out of curiosity, he asked, "Who are you looking for?"

"Vlad III, known as Dracula, son of Vlad II," a soldier told him. "The son of the demon."

Kardotas felt his blood run cold. He felt like he was about to faint. Who the hell had he helped? The son of the man who had hurt him so much! His first reaction was to tell everything he knew, but when he remembered the fugitive's humble and generous attitude, something stopped him. He was petrified.

The soldiers interpreted his apparent bewilderment as the typical answer from a stupid peasant, and they left to continue with their inquiry. In the distance could be heard the screams of unfortunate men suspected of harboring the fugitive.

31

Dracula did not continue to travel on the roads. Instead he went deep into the forest, and with the food his new friends had given him he was able to disappear from his enemies' sight. Solitude gave him the opportunity to be with his favorite friend, Christ, who always joined him everywhere.

He wandered around without a destination in mind until he finished his provisions. Then, arriving at a village, he went up to a house and knocked on the door. A kind-looking old lady came outside, asking, "How can I help you, Son?"

"I am hungry," he said simply. "Can you give me something to eat?"

"Yes," she said, and she gestured to a small pile of logs by the house. "While I make some soup, you cut that wood."

Me, cut wood? The idea was inconceivable. *How does this woman dare to think I am going to do that job?* But his hunger prevailed and he asked, "Where is the ax?"

"There," she said, pointing at the tool, which was leaning against a tree. "Why aren't you at Mass?"

Thanks to that question he learned it was Sunday. "I have been lost for a while and I lost track of time," he said. "You can't imagine how I wish to go to Mass . . . but first I want to eat!"

His body was accustomed to heavy exercise; he carried and fought with a sword heavier than this light ax. He was almost finished with his task when he heard the old lady call, "Son, the food is ready!"

"I am so hungry I could eat a whole elephant!" he said.

"I have made you a rabbit with vegetables and salt," she said warmly. "I hope you like it."

Dracula took a single spoonful and declared it the most delicious stew he'd ever tasted.

"Do not exaggerate, Son," she said. "It tastes good to you because you are eating it with the best condiment: hunger."

Just as he finished eating, the honorable family who lived there arrived. The head of the family asked, "Who is this young man, mom?"

"I don't know his name," she said, "but he had not eaten, and I gave him some food." And then turning to her grandchildren she took them by the ears and said, "Learn from him, you lazy boys! This young man cut in just a little while more wood than you cut in three days."

The man turned to Dracula. "My name is Kestywz. What's yours?"

"Dragomyr."

Kestywz introduced the rest of the family. "This is my wife, Ringalya; you already know my mother, Mazurka; this is my daughter, Zalesha; and these are my sons, Vajk, Istvan and Gyula."

Dracula was so dazzled by Zalesha's beauty that he might have been staring into the sun. Her eyes were green like his, and in an instant he felt bathed by celestial glory, as if he were standing in front of the most beautiful angel from heaven. He loved her immediately although he hadn't spoken a single word to her.

Zalesha was equally impressed. The stranger was the most handsome man she had ever seen, and he seemed so polite and learned that she was embarrassed to speak.

Dracula needed a place to stay, and so he asked Kestywz, "Can you give me a job?"

"A job doing what?" Kestywz answered. ". You can sleep in the stable as long as you want, but if you want a job you'll have to get it in town. Or if you want, you can help me sow, and we can share our bread with you."

"I would like to help you sow, but you are going to have to teach me how."

"Let's see if you can take hard work!" Kestywz challenged him. "We'll begin tomorrow before dawn."

The next day Kestywz gave Dracula his first lesson in farming, showing him how to steer the oxen to make precise, curved furrows.

Over time, a warm affection developed between Dracula and Kestywz, and soon that affection turned into a great friendship. Kestywz's family were good Orthodox Christians; Zalesha was virtuous but very shy, hardly ever speaking.

Kestywz quickly learned to trust his hard-working farmhand, who seemed unusually well-bred. "Have you noticed how polite Dragomyr is?" he asked his wife.

"He has the bearing of a prince," Ringalya agreed. "He knows a lot about religion, and he's an industrious young man, too."

As he plowed the hilly land, Dracula started to consider the design of the tool and the furrows he dug. One day, while Kestywz was in town, he decided to change the pattern of the new furrows and made them straight, running from top to bottom, "Now they are perfect!" he said to himself, pleased.

When Kestywz arrived and saw what he had done, he approached him, put a hand on his shoulder, and said, "Oh my,. Dragomyr You have a strong will, don't you? I can see that you are an intelligent and diligent young man with great initiative." Then, smiling from ear to ear, he added, "But you still have a long way to go to master the techniques of farming."

"If we make the furrows straight and from top to bottom, it will be a lot easier to sow and to remove weeds and to harvest," Dracula explained. "Besides, more plants fit that way."

Still smiling, Kestywz asked kindly, "What about rain and erosion?"

Until that moment, Dracula had not understood why the furrows had to run in curves from side to side: that way when the rain came, the water would not drain away, and consequently the soil stayed damp and erosion was avoided.

Dracula felt his face grow warm. "I made a big mistake," he said.

Kestywz hugged him affectionately and said, "Any man would give anything to have a son like you. You make mistakes because you work hard and are always thinking of new ways to make things better. I congratulate you—keep on making mistakes!"

For the first time in years, Dracula felt truly happy. He was being treated like a son. He had found a family.

Every time Dracula's eyes met Zalesha's, the young people felt the love around. Their encounters were always silent, but they became more and more frequent; somehow, without them knowing how it happened, love touched their hearts. One day when the two found themselves alone together, Dracula gathered his courage and broke the silence. "I love you," he said, and a timid, tender kiss followed the declaration.

"Will you marry me?" Dracula asked.

"Yes," she said, smiling, and a tear ran down her beautiful face.

"Those two must be a couple by now," Kestywz told his wife. "They look at each other constantly, and when I ask Zalesha if she likes Dragomyr, she is silent and turns red."

Ringalya frowned at him. "You are so indiscreet! They are of marriageable age, Kestywz, and besides, Dragomyr is a good, hard-working boy, a good Christian. Honestly, I think he would be the perfect suitor for our girl. I would like for them to marry!"

"I would, too," Kestywz said, "but let's not rush things. Let life take its course."

The months went by, and one day Dracula walked into the house and found Kestywz deep in thought. "What's wrong, Kestywz?" he asked.

Kestywz answered worriedly, "They saw I was doing well with the sowing—thanks to your help—and now the town council has summoned me. They are probably going to charge me an extra tribute, and if I don't pay it they are going to take away my property."

Dracula put an arm around his shoulder. "Don't you worry," he said. "God is going to help us."

The day of the appointment arrived, and Isaac the Saxon, now leading the town council, began by congratulating Kestywz. "You have had a good year, although I don't know how you did it," he said. "But you are going to harvest more than the other peasants, so it is essential that you pay us another twenty-five silver coins."

Kestywz looked stricken. "That is a lot of money!" he said. "Remember that my family has to eat! Please reconsider that tax!"

"If you don't pay it by selling your crops, then you must vacate the land. That is our final decision."

When Kestywz arrived home he was on the verge of tears. "Say good-bye to the cows we were going to buy with the profit from this year's harvest," he announced to the family. "Those damned Saxons have stolen everything from us." Then he told them how he was being dispossessed of the fruits of his work.

Dracula considered Saxons' greedy and unscrupulous actions, which he would never forget.

Many months passed, and one day Kestywz called to Dracula. "Son, you are honest and industrious," he said. "We want you to come live in our house. We've made a little room for you so you will have the privacy you need." Dracula smiled and thanked Kestywz, who hugged him effusively in return, saying, "What would I have done without your help? You remind me of the beloved son I lost."

Dracula wanted to know about that lost son, but no one in the family had ever spoken of him before, and Dracula preferred to wait for them to tell him.

Things went well for the family with Dracula there to help. Still, he could see that Kestywz was distracted. Finally Dracula asked him, "Why are you so worried?"

"It's time for them to come and collect the tribute," Kestywz said. "The harvest has been good—we have the money to pay it—but I am still afraid. Eight years ago they took one of my sons for conscription to the sultan." Kestywz's voice quavered and he stopped talking for a moment. "We never heard from him again. Every time this month arrives, Ringalya and I cannot sleep for fear that they will come and steal another son from us."

Dracula remained silent. Now he was seeing up-close the anguish his people suffered as a result of the excessive ambition of the sultan. He could not find the words to calm that poor father. Two of his children were of conscription age, and his anguish grew as the time of the tribute neared.

"All our governors are the same," he said. "They only charge the poor, never the Saxons. It's unfair! I wish that for one day—just one day!—one of them could live like we do."

Dracula was drawing his silent conclusions.

As it did every year, the town filled with military men, and as usual, a group of them arrived at Kestywz's house to collect the tribute. The soldiers then began organizing the children for conscription.

"Any boys between the ages of seven and fourteen must stand in line here," one soldier ordered. The order was carried out, and the soldier began walking up and down the line. "These three—chain them!" he said. Among them was Gyula.

Ringalya let out a heart-rending scream. "No! You've already stolen one of my boys eight years ago! For the love of God, don't take another one!"

Kestywz walked toward the boyar in charge and knelt down before him with tears in his eyes. "Eight years ago you took one of my children! We have already done our part for the sultan! Please, I beg you, let my boy go!"

But the boyar was used to tears and arguments, and he was deaf to the father's pleas.

Gyula was chained.

In a flash of inspiration, Dracula took a gold coin from his pocket and held it up for the boyar to see. "Wait!" he said. "One day I found this treasure and I hid it for when I was older, so I could go live in Tirgoviste and be a great boyar. I will give it to you if you free my brother!"

The boyar stared at him and said, "Wait a moment . . . I know you. I know I have seen you somewhere."

Dracula shrugged, feigning ignorance. "I live here, and I am at your service," he said. "Do you want me to go with you to be a boyar?"

The boyar sneered. "In your dreams! Everyone wants to be powerful. The most you would achieve is to be a soldier—and even that may be in your dreams. Give me that money!" He snatched the coin from Dracula's hand, shouting over his shoulder, "Release that boy! Now bring the others, and let's go!"

When that retinue left, Kestywz approached Dracula and with a faltering voice said, "Bless you—you have brought me back to life! I will always be indebted to you!" He went to kiss the young man's hands, but Dracula, confused, pulled them away abruptly.

Ringalya and her son, who had been crying inconsolably, rushed over to him when they realized there was no danger. "Bless you!"

Dracula looked sadly at the man and woman who had been like parents to him. "It was a pleasure to meet you and to be able to help you," he said. "Thank you for treating me likes a son—but I have to go."

Zalesha who was also in tears, widened her eyes and let out a stifled scream. "No!"

"Of course you are not leaving!" Kestywz said vigorously. "You'll stop being our honored guest . . . to become our beloved son." He hugged Dracula. "Thank you! Thank you very much, and may God always bless you! We have noticed that there is a relationship between you and Zalesha that goes beyond friendship. Nothing would make us happier than to see you marry her."

Dracula was beaming. "I love your daughter with all my heart, and marrying her is my greatest dream. I've been really happy with you—you are good people—but if you know who I am, you'll surely hate me."

"You are crazy!" Kestywz said, patting him on the back with a chuckle. "I would kiss your feet with respect if you were the devil himself. You are the kindest angel my Christ has ever put in our path. Now, whether you want it or not, you are going to be our beloved son!"

Zalesha was still crying as she held the hands of her beloved. She was going to marry the love of her life, and she was drunk with happiness.

Dracula looked around at the humble people he now considered his family. "I am not Dragomyr he said softly. "I am Dracula, the son of Vlad II, and I am fleeing Vladislav II because he wants to kill me."

Kestywz stood speechless when he heard that confession. There at his service was a member of the Draculesti family, a powerful man with royal blood. He stared at the young man, clearly petrified, as his wife beside him covered her face with her hands.

Zalesha, confused, asked Dracula, "Why did you never tell me you were a prince?"

"Whether I'm a prince or a beggar, my heart beats only for you," he said. "Promise me you will wait for me."

"My heart is all yours," she said.

"I have to go because that boyar almost recognized me," Dracula explained to his new family. "It might take him some time to realize who I am, but when he does he will come looking for me, and if he finds me here they will take me away and all of you will be punished for harboring me." Addressing Kestywz he added, "I am sure he will come back, and you must tell him that I am your son, and that I went to Tirgoviste to look for him, hoping to become one of his soldiers."

Eyes downcast, Kestywz said, "My lord, we will prepare a horse and food for your trip."

"Am I not your son anymore? Why do you call me lord? I am going to fight to regain my power, and one day I'll send for you!" He turned to Zalesha. "You have not answered me . . . will you wait for me?"

Zalesha smiled shyly. "All my life," she said, and she threw herself into his arms and they kissed each other passionately, with the entire family as their witness.

Dracula knew he was making a commitment with that kiss. When they drew apart he made a solemn promise. "Before my Christ, who is here with us, I promise to be faithful to you and to send for you when the time comes."

Kestywz took the little money they had and gave it to Dracula, saying, "I will not accept any excuse for you to reject this money. It is not much, but it is all we have. After all, we have paid the tribute and we have enough food, God will provide more next year."

More than the money, Dracula appreciated the love Kestywz and his humble family had shown him with this action. He also knew that that small amount was all the fortune they possessed. He had plenty of gold with him, but he had hidden it away and hadn't told anyone about it. So looking Kestywz in the eye he said, "Don't worry—I don't need it," and he pressed the coins back into Kestywz's hand. Then he bid farewell to everyone, and without anyone noticing, slipped five gold coins into his lover's bag.

The grandmother asked him to kneel down to receive her blessing, which he accepted gladly and respectfully. Then he hugged Zalesha's brothers. Kestywz and Ringalya said their good-byes with eyes wet, blessing the angel that God had sent them. Zalesha was crying inconsolably, yet she trusted her lover and knew he would come back someday.

Dracula mounted his horse and soon was lost in the dense forest. But already his heart ached; blessed love was now his greatest pain.

32

Dracula kept riding without a destination, moving from one place to another; he was the most wanted fugitive in Wallachia. Along the way he was aided by very poor but reliable and virtuous people. Finally he made his way to Moldavia, where his uncle Bogdan lived and ruled.

When he arrived in Sucaeva, he was relieved to learn that he was not wanted there. He bought a beautiful thoroughbred horse, using the plow horse Kardotas had given him as a partial payment. Two days later, the merchant, who was an honest man, found Dracula and gave him a little sack, saying, "Lord, you don't know how much trouble I went to find you! You left this money in your horse's saddlebag."

"What is your name?" Dracula asked.

"Luga," the merchant replied.

Poor Kestywz, Dracula thought. *He gave me all his savings, thinking I did not have money.* Looking at Luga he said with authority, "What you did today had consequences! The money is yours. It was more than a pleasure to meet you."

Luga smiled broadly. "Thank you, lord," he said. "My parents taught me to be honest, and I've learned I am happy this way." He said good-bye and left, pleased that he had earned that money in an honest way, thanks to his decency.

33

On December 28, 1449, Dracula bought elegant, Turkish-style clothes that would indicate his high social status, and with the bearing of a great prince he appeared at the court of his uncle. The court crier announced him by knocking his cane three times on the floor and saying in a strong voice, "Coming before you, your highness, is Dracula, son of Vlad II!"

The visitor walked toward his uncle and greeted him with the respect a great king deserves. Bogdan II, who knew of his nephew's misfortunes, said admiringly, "Tell me, nephew, how did you get out of Wallachia with an army chasing you? Are you a magician?"

Dracula recounted in great detail his odyssey, and the uncle listened attentively. Certainly it was the most interesting story he'd ever heard, as Dracula related the details and described the scenes with great dramatic effect. The king cancelled his audiences for the rest of the day, and the two men talked for hours until nighttime. Finally they went to sleep, leaving the rest of Dracula's tale to be taken up the next day.

Dracula was in his element. He had arrived at a real court, with servants, bountiful food, and many luxuries. He was treated like a prince! However, he missed the woman who had stolen his heart, the virtuous Zalesha. He never imagined that love could bring so much pain to the loved one.

On his second day there, he saw his cousin Stephen and said, "Oh my, how you've grown! The last time I saw you, you were two, and now—look at you! You're a man!"

Stephen, of course, didn't remember having met Dracula before. But the two began talking, and Dracula told Stephen the same stories he had told his uncle. When Dracula started talking about Zalesha, he feared that his tears would betray him, and so, seeking an escape from that painful subject, he changed it to religion. That's how they realized that they shared the same Orthodox upbringing. Dracula told him, "If royal blood didn't run through my veins, I would be a humble and pious monk."

Stephen nodded eagerly. "Me, too!" he said. "I have always thought the same thing. But I have to fulfill my destiny and be my father's successor to the throne."

They studied theology together under the strict supervision of the Orthodox monk Urbano, who insisted that the Jews were ultimately responsible for Christ's death. "They don't accept Christ as their God," he said, "and they say he is only a prophet! It was a miserable Jew who sold our Lord for thirty pieces of silver!"

With Urbano's words, Dracula found anger rising within him. His father had long ago planted in Dracula the seed of hatred toward the Jews, and now, thanks to Saint Augustine's writings and Urbano's lessons, that hatred turned to rage. Dracula would become a ferocious anti-Semite.

Dracul taught his cousin some of the war techniques he had learned from the Ottomans. They went to the training field together, always looking for something new to learn. Whenever Stephen mastered a skill, he wanted more.

Also living in the court was Dracula's uncle Petru Aron, brother of Bogdan II. Dracula saw in his uncle's gaze a strange, dull glow, and his instinct warned him of imminent danger. He decided to spend some time with the man to study his personality and try to discern his hidden intentions. Seeking an ally to help him investigate his suspicions, he remarked to Stephen, "I feel Uncle Petru Aron is evil. Something tells me he can't be trusted."

Stephen looked upset. "You are paranoid," he said. "How can you believe that? He is my father's most beloved brother and my favorite uncle!"

"Look, Stephen, I am never wrong in my judgments about people," Dracula said. "You can say whatever you want, but I feel certain that we are going to have serious problems with him. I know what it means to be on the run, and I assure you it is terrible having to do it without money. Fortunately I am cautious, and I always have plenty of gold with me, just in case . . . I would recommend that you do the same."

Stephen shook his head in wonder. "You are paranoid," he repeated. "You see enemies where your friends are! What do you think of me? Do you think I'm your enemy, too?"

Dracula stared at him steadily and said, "If I told you that someday you would disown me, you wouldn't believe it."

"You are insane!" Stephen protested.

"Insane, maybe, but Petru Aron is up to something, and I am going to find out what it is."

Dracula began following Petru, trying to study his routines. He learned that Petru had three lovers, and that he frequently met in secret with a group of boyars. After Dracula had gathered enough information, he waited for the right moment and then, when he and Petru were alone, asked him, "Uncle, do you think a Christian man should be unfaithful to his wife?"

Petru furrowed his brow. "No . . . a man must be upright!" he said. Dracula watched him closely. As he answered, he shifted his gaze to the left and he slightly closed his right hand.

A little while later, Dracula took him aside and asked him conspiratorially, "Uncle, do you have a lover?"

"Of course not!" Petru snapped. And he looked to the left and slightly closed his right hand again.

Then Dracula asked, "Do you believe in the divinity of Christ?"

"Without a doubt!" This time Petru held his nephew's gaze and his right hand stayed firm.

Dracula had drawn his conclusions. Now that he knew when Petru was lying and when he was telling the truth, he was going to find out what his uncle was up to.

34

On February 3, 1451, the Islamic world was shaken when Sultan Murad II died and was succeeded by his son, Mehemed II. The new sultan was a very active and ambitious man. Even before taking the throne, he had already planned a strategy to take Constantinople, then Rome and Europe. In order to succeed, he needed Wallachia on his side, so he invited Prince Vladislav II to the empire, where the prince and his retinue were treated like honored allies. They were given women, wine, food, and many other gifts during a three-day-long party. Then Mehemed invited Vladislav to inspect the troops.

"So, what do you think of my soldiers?" Mehemed asked.

"What a large, well-equipped army!" Vladislav said, obviously impressed.

"That is only a small part of my army," answered the proud sultan.

After they inspected the troops, Mehemed invited the prince to his trophy room and said, "These are the heads of the ones who were once our enemies. I have reserved a place of honor for Constantine XI."

"The emperor of Constantinople?" asked the guest, appalled.

"His head will be here one day—just give me time," said Mehemed, smiling. "I summoned you here to invite you to make a pact with me. Do you want Wallachia to belong to the powerful Ottoman Empire? I would be your only master! You would have my army's protection, and in exchange you would absolutely obey me, and no one else. What do you think? Are you with us . . . or against us?"

Vladislav II was euphoric—why wouldn't he be? With the sultan's support, he would become practically invincible . . . although he would also be enslaving his people.

His host immediately began issuing orders. "Here are the rules of the pact: The army is yours, but you also have to help support it. You will pay ten thousand gold coins and contribute one thousand children of conscription per year so our army will continue to grow more powerful.

From now on, you are part of the great Ottoman-Turk alliance! No king or ruler can give you orders or dethrone you! And if someone does, he shall face our powerful army, and without a doubt you will be restored to your throne."

Vladislav II was exuberant and signed the treaty immediately. He did not need the holy Roman emperor, nor did he need to be a subject of the king of Hungary. He did not need to obey the pope or Janos Hunyadi or anyone! The powerful Ottoman sultan was his only master.

35

On May 6, 1451, Bogdan, his brother Petru Aron, Stephen, and Dracula were having some wine, and Dracula said to Petru, "Uncle, you are one of the most upright men I know. Would you be capable of stealing?"

Petru held Dracula's gaze. Keeping his hands open, he answered firmly, "Never!"

"Integrity and honesty are common qualities throughout our family," Dracula remarked. "Uncle Bogdan works like crazy, but he also enjoys being entertained. I remember how, on the day I arrived, he enjoyed hearing about all my adventures when I was a fugitive. You should invite him along when you meet with your friends. I'm sure he would enjoy the diversion."

Petru Aron flushed and took a quick sip of wine, but remained silent. Dracula, who watched everything, immediately put two and two together. He also took a little sip and then added, "I think my brother Radu is going to turn into an authentic Turk and someday betray me," he said. Turning to Petru, he asked, "Would you be capable of betraying your brother?"

"No! Never!" was his immediate answer. His gaze fell to the left, and he slightly closed his right hand.

Fear struck Dracula's heart: Petru was going to betray his uncle Bogdan! But he kept on talking and drinking, turning to more cheerful conversation, until Petru briefly excused himself. As soon as Petru left the room, Dracula said quietly, "I know this may seem crazy, but I suspect your brother is going to betray you."

Bogdan burst out laughing. "How can you think my beloved brother would be capable of something like that? You're crazy!"

Stephen joined in, saying, "I know—I can barely believe the wild ideas you come up with. Only you would think of something so absurd."

"Please do not tell my uncle about my suspicions," Dracula said. "I am going to prove to you that I'm right." At that moment Petru returned, and the men continued talking and drinking with no further mention of Dracula's suspicions.

When the gathering was over, Dracula took Bogdan aside and said, "I spent time as a fugitive, and the only way I survived was by having enough gold and resources with me. Believe me, it is less risky to escape as a fugitive than to wait here for Petru to betray you. I have asked Stephen to make it a habit to carry a good amount of money, but he refuses to listen to me. Please give me some money, and if one day your son is in trouble, I will deliver it to him. You know I am honest; I would never steal."

The king felt Dracula's distrust of his brother was insulting, but he loved his son above all else, and so he gave Dracula two bags of gold coins, saying, "I know you will be accountable for this money. I do not doubt your honesty in the least, and although I do not want to believe your suspicions, I agree that it's better to be cautious today and avoid any regrets tomorrow."

Dracula left and went to a nearby cave, where he buried the two bags. Then he went back to Sucaeva.

That night, as always, Dracula and Stephen prepared for sleep by kneeling down together and saying their prayers. It was a strange connection, uniting them by faith.

On October 7, 1451, Petru Aron met with his trusted boyars, those who would help him with his coup d'état, and told them, "I have a nephew who is really clever, and my brother told me about his suspicions concerning our plan. We have to rush our actions . . . I am starting to get worried."

"Let's kill him!" one of the boyars proposed. "It would be ease. We could feign an attack—we'd have someone fight with him, and then I'd stab him in the back."

"No!" Petru said. "They would suspect me! And with Bogdan on alert, we might fail. We'd better act quickly and put our plan into action in the next battle against the Turks."

On October 17, 1451, as King Bogdan fought in the middle of a battle against the Ottoman Turks, he felt a sword pierce him through the back and heart. His last lucid thoughts were of Dracula's warnings. If only he had listened, his destiny would have been different. Now his turn for final judgment had arrived. He had found death in a battle defending the faith of their God, but it came as a cowardly murder, ordered by his treacherous brother.

When Dracula learned how his uncle had died, he drew his conclusions and said to his grieving cousin, "Do not trust Petru; I am sure he is responsible for the death of your father. Please, take the power of the throne immediately and apprehend him—don't wait for him to get stronger. This is the right time declare yourself king!"

Stephen, devastated, was incapable of carrying out actions of any sort. After Bogdan's funeral he fell into a deep depression and hid in the refuge where he used to pray. Taking advantage of his nephew's emotional turmoil, Petru Aron assumed power after the funeral and issued his first order: "Bring me Stephen, dead or alive. Fifty gold coins to the one who brings him to me."

When Dracula could not convince his cousin to act against the traitor, he went to the training field, where he was apprehended and interrogated by a powerful boyar whom he immediately recognized as one of Petru Aron's close friends. Knowing that Dracula and Stephen were always together, the boyar demanded to know where his cousin was.

Given the boyar's aggressive tone and arbitrary question, and knowing that he was a friend of the traitor, Dracula knew he was looking for his cousin with very bad intentions. "I would like to know that too," Dracula said. "That miserable worm is a heretic! When he found out about his father's death, he renounced his faith! The last time I saw him was by the river. We had a fight."

The boyar was dumbfounded. "What did you fight about?"

"That idiot told me that God had gone mad by ordering his father to die, and then he said that the Holy Spirit came from the Father and the Son and so the Son had also given that absurd order. He defended his point of view so strongly that we ended up beating each other. He is a heretic and a traitor to the Orthodox Church! If you find him, beat him up!"

"Petru Aron just took power and has declared him a traitor," the boyar said. "He has to die—there's a reward of fifty gold coins on his head, dead or alive. If you see him, cut off his head. You'll earn a fortune!"

Dracula was shocked by the news. Having successfully deceived the murderer's accomplices, he continued training so as not to arouse suspicions, and he noticed that despite of his declaration he was being discreetly watched. After he finished training he left the field and, managing to evade the boyars, headed to Stephen's hideout. He prayed that his cousin hadn't left yet to attend afternoon Mass.

Stephen did not know about the profitable reward upon his head, so when he saw Dracula arrive unexpectedly he asked nervously, "What is it, Cousin? Why are you so agitated?"

"Our uncle Petru Aron just took over power. He wants to kill you! Your head is now worth fifty gold coins!"

The color drained from Stephen's face. That amount was enough to tempt even a saint! His voice faltering from fear, he exclaimed, "Why didn't I listen to you and carry some gold? I have to get out of here immediately. Good-bye . . . and thank you for saving my life!"

Dracula knew Stephen wouldn't survive on his own; he was as overconfident as his father. Besides, he would surely die without money. "I am going with you," Dracula said.

"But you are not in trouble," Stephen protested. "I'll escape on my own. I know I am not going to get far with that reward, but I am going to make my best effort."

"You are not going to survive alone," Dracula said firmly. "I am going with you."

They saddled their horses and rode a good distance until, at the outskirts of the city, they saw some soldiers blocking the road.

All hope was lost.

"Don't ask questions," Dracula said, tying a rope loosely around Stephen's hands and hiding a sword among his belongings. "Trust me," he whispered. "I am going to turn you in, and when the action starts, attack!" Dracula approached the soldiers with his prisoner in tow, saying, "I captured this miserable traitor! Help me turn him in and I will give you part of my reward, on one condition: that we give all give him a good beating!"

Before the soldiers could register his words, Dracula drew his sword and cut the throat of one of them. When Stephen saw that, he grabbed his sword from among his clothes and did the same to the soldier nearest him before the man could finish drawing his weapon. The fight against the remaining soldiers was more difficult; however, Dracula was an energetic young man, and he quickly dispatched his enemy. Then he prepared to have some fun watching the combat between his cousin and the only soldier left.

The fight was to the death, and while Dracula trusted his cousin's military skill, the soldier he was fighting was obviously strong and experienced. Just as Stephen appeared to gain the upper hand, he lost his footing and the attacker raised his sword, ready to pierce him through. Just then a dagger flew through the air with extreme speed and the accuracy only practice can give, plunging into the attacker's throat. The soldier immediately let go of his own weapon to grasp the dagger that was taking his life from him.

Stephen watched, breathless and terrified. His cousin had been right not to leave him alone. Dracula had saved his life twice in just a few hours.

The Dragon went to recover his dagger, the one his father had given him. Again he had honored the weapon by bathing it with the enemy's blood; he pulled it from the soldier's throat and put it away without cleaning it.

Soon they were on their way again, and they arrived at the cave where Dracula had hidden the two bags of gold. He unearthed them and gave them to Stephen, saying, "I would like to have been wrong and looked like a madman to you and your father, but look where have we ended up for trusting that traitor!"

"You thought of everything, Cousin," Stephen said enthusiastically. Thank you, Cousin!" Then he gave Dracula one of the bags and said, "Take this. Money was never earned more honestly. It's yours!"

"I have my own money," Dracula said. "Take care of yours; you are going to need it."

Stephen insisted, "If you have it, it will be as if I had it. Besides, I feel safe knowing you are watching part of the money. Do with it as you please. I'm giving it to you to thank you!"

They left Moldavia knowing that all the roads were being watched, so they got rid of their fine horses and their elegant clothes and walked without a destination in mind. By passing themselves off as peasants they went unnoticed, hiding from the patrols that were diligently looking for them. And every night before they slept, they prayed together—the one tradition that was still part of their lives.

36

Dracula had just one idea fixed in his mind: Zalesha. In silence he remembered her first kiss. Meanwhile, his beloved was thinking only of him, and the strength of those mutual thoughts guided his steps until November 6, 1451, when he ended up at her front door. The sun was about to set, and considering himself a member of her family, he entered the house without knocking, as he had always done.

When a man suddenly walked into their house, the family was petrified. Then they recognized him, and everyone let out a happy cry. Zalesha jumped up and threw herself into his arms, crying and saying his name over and over again. Dracula felt her body shaking, and he closed his eyes and held onto the heaven he could not believe he was living.

Then Zalesha knelt down before a crucifix on the wall, silently praying and still crying. As she did so, the family surrounded him, greeting him lovingly and effusively. Kestywz hugged him, saying, "Son! I'm so happy to see you again!" Then Ringalya hugged him. She was crying and shaking, too. Then Zalesha got up and hugged him again. The joy was spontaneous and noisy. Even the grandmother was caught up in the excitement and could not stop blessing him.

Stephen was not used to such effusive behavior; he was watching in silence, amused by that incredible and strange welcome.

Kestywz grabbed Dracula by both shoulders. "They are desperately looking for you two!" he said.

Dracula looked at him skeptically. "How do you know? Are you clairvoyant?"

"When you left, some soldiers arrived, and the one who received the coin from you asked me for Dracula. I told him I didn't know him, and then he assured me that was the young man who had given him the gold coin. I explained to him that the young man was my son, and that you had gone on to Tirgoviste to look for him to beg him to accept you as a soldier. They believed me, but they told me that if a young man who looked like my son arrived, they would give me ten gold coins. Then two days ago, some different soldiers came and said there were two important fugitives—they matched your description—and they offered us twenty gold coins if we turned you in!" Kestywz paused, breathless.

When Stephen heard that, he got scared; he knew a fortune that big would be an irresistible temptation to any humble peasant.

With the shrewdness and distrust that characterized him, Dracula seemed to hear his cousin's thoughts. "Don't think what you are thinking," he said. "These people are my family." Then, addressing Kestywz, he said, "In Moldavia alone there is a reward of fifty gold coins for the head of my cousin."

Stephen was astonished. Why was Dracula revealing that to this needy man? What had these humble peasants done to earn the trust of the most distrustful man he knew? Intrigued, he kept watching in silence, seriously wondering whether his cousin had gone insane.

Then Dracula offered an embarrassed apology. "In all the excitement of seeing you again, I forgot something very important. I would like to introduce you to my beloved cousin Stephen, prince of Moldavia."

The peasants bowed respectfully, never having imagined that one day they would host two princes in their humble house. Stephen responded with a slight bow of his head. Dracula watched, amused by his stiff manner.

"The patrol that came two days ago searched the entire house— the barn, the crops, and even inside the well," Kestywz said. "They are desperately looking for you. They know you are around this place, and those bastards might come back any minute now. The best thing for you is to leave as soon as possible."

"May I speak to Zalesha for a moment?" Dracula asked him.

"Of course, Son," was the immediate answer.

They went out of the little house and sat at the edge of the well, moonlight illuminating the face of the most beautiful angel heaven would possess someday. Dracula could not stop staring at such beauty. Their hearts seemed to want to leave their chests, and without thinking about it they came together with a long, passionate kiss. Finally the young man had to interrupt that dream to ask his lover, "Would you marry me tomorrow?"

The answer to that question was another kiss, joined by tears of excitement. Then Zalesha took a deep breath and said with difficulty because of the crying, "I am very happy."

Dracula corrected her. "You realize, don't you, that I am not a prince charming? I am just a fugitive with an uncertain future. My head has a price, my life is in extreme danger, and if you decide to join your destiny to mine, your life could be as bitter as a lemon."

"I don't care if you are the poorest man or Wallachia's most wanted," she said. "I love you with all my soul, and my greatest desire is to be your wife. Tomorrow we will get married; we will consummate our marriage later. I just want to know that you are my husband before God."

Dracula smiled. "My Christ, is here with us, and before him as the most valuable witness, I give you my love and my soul. From now on I accept you as my wife, and I promise to be faithful until death do us part."

Zalesha searched in vain for the words to express her strong feelings. I do, too . . . the same," she said.

They sealed the commitment with another lingering kiss, considering themselves joined before God as husband and wife. Now they would have a humble and secret ceremony with all their loved ones at the church, with the blessing of the town's patriarch to formalize their union. They entered the little house, Dracula ready to inform the family that he and Zalesha were getting married in the morning, but before he could speak Ringalya announced, "Dinner is served!"

"You have to eat and leave immediately," Kestywz said.

Taking Zalesha by the hands, Dracula addressed Kestywz and Ringalya, with the whole humble family and Prince Stephen as witnesses. "I am a fugitive, and my destiny is uncertain," he said, "but we want to get married tomorrow." Looking at Kestywz he added, "You have already given me Zalesha's hand in matrimony!"

Kestywz smiled and hugged the suitor, saying, "You've made me very happy. Now you are going to be my real son." Ringalya stood by her husband and beamed her complete approval.

Stephen was understanding less and less about his cousin. Dracula was going to marry that humble peasant? If he was going to fight to recover his power, he could have married any princess worthy of his lineage, or any rich and powerful woman, for that matter. Everything he'd seen here was incomprehensible. There was no doubt about it: his beloved cousin had lost his mind! *When and how did he become crazy?* Stephen wondered.

———————◆———————

The joy of the next day's event made them forget the danger that threatened them. As they ate and talked, Dracula asked Kestywz, "Why did you hide your money in my saddlebag?"

"Because you were going to an uncertain destiny, and I think of you as my son," the man said. "We would have given you more, if we'd had it. And what about you? What a rogue you are! Why didn't you tell me you had so much money? The five gold coins you gave to Zalesha were very useful to us."

Dracula took the bag his cousin had given him and opened it, showing Kestywz the gold coins. "We have plenty," he said. "You won't need to worry any longer."

Kestywz gasped. "That is a fortune!"

"And we have a lot more," Dracula said, closing the bag. "But remember, it's only money!" Now Stephen was really worried about Dracula's strange attitude. There was no doubt about it: love had made him completely insane.

Without letting go of the hand of his beloved, Dracula said, "Tomorrow we will get married very early, and then Stephen and I will follow our plan immediately. We are going to recover our power."

Kestywz put a broad hand on his arm. "Son, if you fail, your family will always be here waiting for you with our arms wide open. You are not powerful here, but you are a beloved son of our hearts." He stood up and gave the young man a warm hug, saying, "I love you, Son!"

Stephen watched, bewildered. *What strange values poor people have*, he thought.

The family kept talking, and Dracula said, "The love we have is the greatest and most blessed gift God gave us. I am sure that with God's help I will recover my throne. Then I will fight to defend the faith, make Zalesha happy, and one day free Wallachia from all oppressors." Inspired by his courage, the family felt proud of their newest son. They loved him so deeply that they felt privileged to risk their lives so that he might accomplish his objectives.

The grandmother slept fitfully due to her advanced age, and the next day she got up before dawn to heat up tea and make breakfast. It was a very special day.

When Zalesha heard her grandmother in the kitchen, she jumped out of bed to get ready for the important event. Dracula did the same. In fact, the entire family was very excited—all but Prince Stephen, who remained in bed. He did not condone this crazy marriage and kept trying to sleep, as he cared only about his own rest. When he finally got up to wash himself, he looked out the window to see a patrol of five soldiers approaching. He let out a warning shout: "We are doomed! They have found us!"

When Dracula saw the patrol he knew there was no saving them. Perhaps they could fight off these soldiers, but then others would come looking for them, and when they found out the family were accomplices, they would massacre them. He had to turn himself in to save his family.

But what about Stephen? His cousin was also his responsibility; he had to keep Stephen safe to ensure that Moldavia would remain faithful to Christianity. He was confuse, and time was short. Then, with the shrewdness and speed that characterized him, he said, "Everyone stand up here!" Without asking questions, the family went where he told them to go. He got a rope and began tying them together.

Kestywz did not understand, but he knew he could trust his soul to his son, who would never betray him.

When they were all bound, Dracula said to his cousin, "Prepare for the attack!" And he said to the ones tied up, "You will say that Dracula and Stephen arrived, tied you up, and beat you savagely. Make them believe that we are monsters, that we were going to kill you. Then thank them and tell them that they are your saviors. That's the only way we will be able to rescue you." He turned to Kestywz. "Father, I love you!" he said, and he gave him a strong blow to the eye, leaving it bruised. He moved over to one of his brothers-in-law and said, "Trust me!"—again accompanying his words with a powerful blow to the face. The blood gushed out abundantly. When he stood before Zalesha he said, "Believe me, in my heart you are now my wife, because at this moment, before my Christ who is here with us, I reconfirm that I take you as my wife. And I will be faithful until death do us part!'"

"I do, too," Zalesha whispered, and he leaned down to give her a quick kiss on the mouth. Then he drew his hand back and gave her a slap on the face so hard that her mouth bled, staining her dress. Dracula looked more pained than she did. "I love you more than my own life," he said.

By the time the soldiers were near the house, the family looked terrorized. Everyone was bleeding except the grandmother, who looked petrified. "You are the people I love the most," Dracula told them. "I hope that one day you can forgive me. I have hurt you to save your lives, and I will fight with all my heart not to fail you. Now I have a new reason to recover my power." Then, slipping five gold coins in a crack in the wood wall, he left the house with Stephen.

Kestywz and his family understood the plan, but they wept from the pain.

The soldiers arrived and, as usual, entered the house without knocking. When they saw the family bound and beaten, they realized they had found the fugitives.

"Where are they?" one soldier demanded.

Kestywz began to speak, but before he could form his first word, the soldier gave a loud gasp. At that moment two swords pierced the backs of two of the soldiers, and as their souls escaped their bodies, the battle started, with Stephen fighting one soldier and Dracula two, and the family acting as astonished witnesses of the fierceness and skill of their relative. In mere moments Dracula had disarmed and wounded his opponents, while Stephen killed his.

Dracula made sure his soldiers were badly injured but alive, so they could tell other soldiers what had happened. Then, knowing that it would be practically impossible to escape the place, he and Stephen dressed in the dead soldiers' clothes. Before he left, Dracula glanced at his lover; it was his good-bye, as he dared not say a word to her for fear of being heard by one of the soldiers who were still wounded. He and Stephen took their enemies' horses and shrewdly managed to escape by riding boldly past the other patrols.

37

The men wandered aimlessly for a weeks until they reached a safe place. A joyful shout broke the silence in the monastery of Bucharest. "Dracula!" the monk Barbat yelled. "I cannot believe it!"

Dracula gladly received the monks' blessing and gestured to his fellow refugee. "I introduce you to my cousin, Stephen of Moldavia."

Barbat looked frightened. "They are desperately looking for you," he said. "It is a good thing that you came to us." After Dracula told them in great detail what had happened, the monk said, "We told you that this would always be your home, and that here you would be received as a son. This is the time to prove it. You are welcome. You can feel safe here."

The sun had set, and the two fugitives said their last prayers of the day. When they had finished and were about to put out the torch, they felt a strange energy in the room. Dracula said to Stephen, "Cousin, I feel the presence of the Holy Spirit among us."

"I do, too."

There was, in fact, something in the atmosphere that made the two cousins want to talk. "I remember like it was yesterday the day I arrived at your father's court. He received me with joy, and you quickly became my best friend."

Stephen nodded. "When I saw you, I felt sorry that you had suffered so much. I knew that they had killed your father and part of your family, and that your brother Radu was still prisoner of the Ottomans. What amazed me about you was the flame of your faith and your passion for Christ. When you came into my life, my faith in God revived until it burned like a bonfire. How could I have known then that destiny would treat me worse than it treated you?"

"Cousin, only our faith in our God makes us worthy, and that's all we have right now," Dracula said. "Through our veins runs royal blood, and I am sure that one of us is going to succeed in our mission. I propose that the first of us to recover his throne help the other do the same. If we always help each other, there will never be enmity between us."

Stephen smiled excitedly. "I think that is an excellent idea!"

"We will seal our pact with blood," Dracula said. And taking out his dagger, his most valuable treasure, he cut a cross on his right palm, just until he started to bleed. Then he passed the dagger to his cousin, who did the same. They joined hands and Dracula said solemnly, "I swear by my Lord and God Jesus Christ that there will never be rivalry between us, that I will always help you, and that if I recover my throne first, I will help you recover yours."

Stephen then said, "I swear by my Lord and God Jesus Christ that there will never be rivalry between us, that I will always help you, and that if I recover my throne first, I will help you recover yours." They then prayed three Lord's Prayers together.

Stephen said solemnly, "Whenever I see the scar on my hand, I will remember our oath."

"As will I."

Then the young men knelt together on the bed and said their last prayers of the day.

It was November 4, 1453, and Hunyadi was thoughtful. It had been awhile since he had received a copy of the letter Dracula had sent to the Saxons of Brasov, offering to reconcile with him. His intuition told him that the man was being honest, and his hunches never failed him. His spies had learned that Dracula was in the monastery of Bucharest, so Hunyadi sent a retinue to summon him.

When the soldiers arrived and pounded on the monastery door, Brother Barbat rushed to answer, muttering, "Who is knocking in that way? This is a house of prayer!" Dracula and Stephen were standing hidden a short distance away.

The voice of the commanding officer was strong: "We have come for Dracula!"

Stepping outside and closing the door behind him, the monk answered bravely, "He will not leave the house of the Lord!"

"We come on behalf of Janos Hunyadi," the soldier's voice boomed. "Turn him in! We have a reward of twenty gold coins for your service!"

When Stephen heard that offer, he knew it was the end for his cousin; few people would have rejected such a bribe. Instead, something unbelievable happened. Brother Barbat replied, "We are in great need, but we will not give up the refugee for any amount." The monk crossed his arms and squared his body in front of the door. "Over our dead bodies!"

The commanding officer had two choices: knock down the door and fulfill the order, or to go back without Dracula. He chose the second, knowing that if he used violence in the house of God, Hunyadi would never forgive him.

Then Dracula emerged from a window overhead, announcing, "I am going with them!" Speaking to the commanding officer, he said, "First deliver the coins!"

But when the boyar in charge tried to give the coins to Brother Barbat, he exclaimed, "We will never take them—our hands would be burned just holding them!"

Dracula turned to the monk. "Receive them," he said firmly. "I have the feeling that everything is going to be fine." Barbat accepted the coins reluctantly. "I am coming down," Dracula called.

From inside the room where they hid, Stephen tried to stop him, saying, "I don't think you should go . . . I have the feeling you are going to die."

Dracula held out a hand to calm him. "There is something I have that makes me worthy: it is my faith in my Christ. If I die it will be in his defense, and I will die happy."

Stephen was scared to take the risk. "I am sorry, but I can't go with you. You are too brave for your own good—in fact, you are a reckless fool. But they have not asked about me, so I'm staying here."

Dracula gazed at his cousin with his deep-green eyes and handed back the bag of gold Stephen had given him to hold. Then he hugged Stephen, saying, "I am going to carry out the will of Christ."

Stephen had no words to say. He was sure it was the last time he would see his cousin, so he just hugged him tight and then watched the guards escort the refugee to his destiny.

38

Now Janos Hunyadi, powerful governor of Transylvania and Hungary, stood face-to-face with the fugitive. All Dracula carried with him were the royal blood in his veins and his father's dagger.

When he saw Dracula, Hunyadi was puzzled: he had heard that Dracula was a staunch Christian, but his clothes were Ottoman. For his part, Dracula knew the history of the Christian warrior before him, and so, breaking the silence, he said, "To be in your presence is a gift my s Christ has granted me. I very much admire your hatred of the Turks and the Jews."

Ignoring that affirmation, Hunyadi asked, "Do you worship Allah?"

"When I was among my enemies and torturers, I worshiped him like a parrot worships God, only without the beak!" Dracula said. "But my heart has always belonged to and venerated Christ."

Still Hunyadi was skeptical. He eyed Dracula's elegant and expensive Turkish outfit. "What proof do you have of what you say? How do I know you are not Ottoman? You dress like one of them."

Dracula was thoughtful; he knew his sharp wit was being tested. With a slow and relaxed manner, he answered, "Of all the things the Turks have, what I like the most is the way they dress, and so I dress like this because I want to. When my father was forced to leave me as collateral with our enemies, he told me clearly that I had to behave like a chameleon: I had to deceive them and make them believe I was one of them. I had to learn their language, their customs, their religion, the way they made war, and everything they knew. Then, when I had the opportunity, I could change my skin and turn into the most ferocious defender of Christ.

"And so I did: I deceived the sultan and he placed me on Wallachia's throne! When Vladislav II took it away from me, do you think it was my first reaction to try to recover it? To go back to the Ottoman Empire and ask the sultan to help me? No! I did not do that, and I never will! And do you know how the sultan treated me? Like a son! Do you know what I called him? Father! And he considered himself my father. Recovering my throne would have been the easiest thing. Even now, Mehemed is like a brother to me; in fact, he owes his life to me.

"You don't know the military power of the sultan. If I had sought his protection, I would be Wallachia's ruler again, and my God, would be a burden to me. But no, I choose to be a poor fugitive, being pursued with a reward upon my head, but with a heart that fights to defend the Christian faith. I would rather that than be a wealthy slave to Mehemed and his god Allah. I may betray the sultan. I may betray you! But betray my Christ? Never!"

When Dracula finished, Hunyadi was deeply impressed. He did not know if Dracula was seeing a monk or a saint; certainly he was a sacred warrior of Christianity. From that moment on, the two men identified with one another. Certainly Hunyadi would seek the friendship of that fugitive, as they shared a deep hatred of their enemies, the Ottomans and the Jews, as well as a solid faith in the same God—although one was a Catholic and the other an Orthodox.

When he saw there was no danger, Dracula went back to get his cousin, but he had fled from the monastery. Dracula shared his great knowledge of Ottoman military tactics to empower the army of his new ally, Janos Hunyadi. With everyday coexistence, their mutual trust grew, and this, in turn, became an indestructible friendship and then brotherhood. Their solid relationship would last until God summoned one of them to his celestial glory.

Mathias Hunyadi, son of Janos Hunyadi, saw Dracula and wanted to be like him, as his father spoke of him only to praise him. The future king of Hungary could not avoid the incipient jealousy he felt. Laszlo, Hunyadi's other son, also watched Dracula. Meditative and reasoned, he was very intelligent, smart, and skilful, and like Dracula's brother Radu, he was known as the Beautiful.

39

In March 1453, a humble peasant named Stanyzkwl said to his wife, "I'm so happy! The crop was abundant this year, and we'll have the cash to pay the tribute in two months."

Gjon was a lazy man, known as the town leech. He'd realized that it was easier to live by theft than from work; he was so cynical, in fact, that he openly declared, "If they take me to jail, at least they'll have to feed me there!" For him the word *work* was a synonym for *torture*; he refused to work for any reason, as work was only for oxen and fools. He had noticed that Stanyzkwl always worked hard, and he had no doubt that Stanyzkwl had his tribute ready to be paid to the Ottomans. That's why he decided to pay Stanyzkwl a visit. For weeks Gjon sat at a prudent distance, watching that family's routine. According to his observations, Sunday seemed the right day to carry out his vile action.

Sunday arrived, and Stanyzkwl and his family prepared to go to church and thank God for the product of their labor and for the luck of having gathered the tribute ahead of time. That was reason enough to be happy. After they left for Mass, Gjon entered the house and searched in vain for the victims' savings, desperately asking himself, *Where the hell did they hide it?* Just as he found it, Stanyzkwl arrived home and, seeing Gjon, yelled, "Give me my money!" But the bastard thief ran off with the product of the work of those industrious peasants.

Stanyzkwl and his family looked everywhere for Gjon, but it seemed he had fallen off the face of the earth. The family was frightened; they knew they would be punished if they did not pay the tribute. Stanyzkwl decided he would ask for a deferment. Witnesses to the event were willing testify about what had happened, and they could identify the criminal. His name was Gjon.

———◆———

"Your tribute!"

Stanyzkwl heard the familiar words of the soldier in charge of the collection. Anxiously he began explaining: "A thief named Gjon stole it from me! All these neighbors are witnesses—I am telling the truth! The next year I promise I'll pay you double!"

The soldier stared at him in silence and then repeated more forcefully, "Your tribute!"

Stanyzkwl said again, "Gjon stole it! And my neighbors are all witnesses; they can tell you that what I am saying is true!" As Stanyzkwl spoke, the neighbors gathered close, confirming aloud Stanyzkwl's declaration.

An imperative shout came from the Ottoman's throat: "For the last time! Your tribute!"

Knowing the punishment he could receive, Stanyzkwl knelt down with tears on his cheeks and said, "Please . . . it was stolen from me! Next year, I swear, I will pay double!"

The man in charge looked at his soldiers and gave the simple and emphatic order: "You know what to do!"

His wife and daughters were savagely raped; his little children, aged three, four, and five, were not sent to the sultan as children of conscription but were beaten savagely. And his neighbors saw what happened to those who did not pay the tribute.

Stanyzkwl wept at his own impotence. Even as he was being severely beaten, he was hearing his own flesh and blood asking for help, and he could do nothing. His eyes were witness to the greatest brutality he had ever seen, in his heart a deadly hate sprouted. He hated Vladislav II and the Turks, and most of all, he hated with every cell in his body that damned thief, Gjon.

Stanyzkwl had to start from scratch, determined that from now on he would be more careful with his money. But just as he was about to rebuild his house, he received a visit from a Saxon named Josue, a member of the honorable town council. "Empty your land and leave this house!" Josue demanded.

"Where am I going to go?" Stanyzkwl asked, anguished. "What about my family?"

"That is not our problem. Empty your land or you will go to jail!"

"And what am I going to do for a living?" cried the desperate peasant.

"You have until tomorrow to fulfill the order," the Saxon stated, and then he turned around and left.

Life changed completely for Stanyzkwl. He found a job as a helper on another peasant's farm, and his poverty increased in proportion to the hatred that was depleting his tranquility.

In a church far away, the thief Gjon, fearing his soul would go to hell, confessed, repented, and received forgiveness for his sins thanks to the infinite kindness and precious blood of Christ. As he left, he gave generous alms, part of the product of his criminal activity; but this dirty money, once in the hands of the Holy Church, turned white as snow. The next day Gjon received the sacred body of Christ. Over time and with a clear conscience, the sinner continued his usual ways: running out of money, getting hungry, and stealing again; feeling regretful, confessing, and giving alms that were a product of his professional work; receiving the grace of God through Holy Communion; and then, having spent what he stole, again stealing to feed himself. The story would stop only when God took Gjon's precious soul and placed him in heaven next to his God Jesus Christ. At least that was Gjon thinking; he cynically believed that God had sacrificed his son precisely to save sinners like him, and that with his sins he was giving meaning to that sacrifice. Gjon believed that Christ existed because of the bad behavior of people like him; otherwise he would not have a reason to exist!

40

The gunsmiths in the Ottoman Empire were struggling with the same problem as those in Wallachia: they could not find the way to use strong gunpowder in their cannons without cracking them. Like their enemy counterparts, they had done hundreds of experiments with various alloys, and they still did not have a solution.

Jared, the Saxon gunsmith, was experimenting with yet another alloy to try to solve the problem, although Cainan, his helper, argued against it. "I don't think it is logical," he said. "We're just going to waste more materials."

"Perhaps," Jared said. "Still, we have to try." With that he lit a fuse and the great cannon roared. The gunsmiths approached the weapon to check it.

Cainan's joyful shouts reached the ears of everybody in town: "It didn't crack! It didn't crack!"

"It didn't crack!" Those seemed to be the only words spoken in Sibiu; even the children told each other the exciting news.

Jared, the master gunsmith, was more reserved, meticulously examining the cannon, looking for the least crack. At last he could no longer hold in his excitement, exclaiming almost without believing it, "We finally did it!" The secret to making the most powerful gun on earth was theirs.

———✦———

The Saxons gathered to discuss how best to benefit from their secret. Master Jared spoke: "The Draculesti family gave us the money to develop this weapon; it belongs to them."

"They are no longer in power," a councilman named Neri explained. "Therefore the secret is ours. We are not going to be fools and share it."

Another councilman, Samuel, proposed, "What if we make the cannon and sell it to the king of Hungary?"

Hans, to his right, spoke up: "I think we would get more money from it if we built it and auctioned it to the highest bidder: the sultan, the king of Hungary, or the Roman emperor."

Samuel shook his head vigorously. "The Ottoman sultan is an enemy of the Cross. He must not be included in our plans."

Some of his fellow councilmen looked at him skeptically. "We are Jews!" argued Abraham. "We do not believe in the divinity of Christ. We do not have to be faithful to the king of Hungary—he is a Catholic."

Now defensive, Samuel replied, "So what's been the purpose of everything we have invested in the Catholic Church?"

"We have paid a tithe because it was convenient for our interests," Isaac explained. "If the vovoid finds out that we are Jews, he might inform the pope, who could establish an inquisition here—and then we might end up in a bonfire! The Jews who established themselves in the Ottoman Empire live in peace; they can practice our religion without being persecuted. If we sell the cannon to the sultan and he conquers this land, we will be contributing to the peace, and we will be able to say freely that we are Jewish, that we worship Yahweh. We will be safe from the hateful Catholic Church—we will win in the end."

Samuel and several other councilmen shared Isaac's dilemma: they professed the Catholic faith for fear of being treated like the Jews were treated in Europe. When they understood the benefit of having the Ottoman sultan as their governor—the liberty of professing their true faith—they agreed they should sell the cannon to the sultan.

Then Joshua made an important observation. "But what would happen if Christianity prevailed here?" he asked. "The Saxons would be seen as traitors."

The councilmen looked at each other, waiting for someone to propose a plan to avoid that possibility. Finally Isaiah said, "What if we only sold the secret of the alloy, and let Ottoman gunsmiths manufacture the cannon under our supervision?"

So they voted and passed the proposal by an overwhelming majority: they would sell the secret to the sultan, whose gunsmiths would fabricate the cannon. The Saxons would only supervise the process and therefore remain completely anonymous.

A retinue of Saxons stood before the powerful sultan. Because their negotiations were very delicate and important, they had decided to attend to them in person.

Jarred spoke first: "Lord, we have fixed the problem of the gunpowder cracking the great cannon."

The sultan did not want to socialize with these foreigners; he just cared about their findings. "How much do you want for your secret?" he asked them drily.

"Thirty thousand gold coins," the gunsmith said. "This includes our supervision of your gunsmiths until the cannon passes the tests satisfactorily. You will give us half the money now and the other half when the cannon has passed all the tests your gunsmiths deem necessary and when you are completely satisfied with it."

The sultan looked astonished. "That is three times the yearly salary of my Janissaries!" he exclaimed. "However, the secret is worth it. We have a deal."

41

On March 9, 1453, the cannon was ready to lead the siege, having passed every test to which it was subjected. It was a metal monster: almost eleven yards long, with the strength of hundreds of oxen. It took at least one hundred men to move it.

"We have the right weapon to take Constantinople," Mehemed II told his counselors. "Only the strength of Allah can stop our attack."

Roman Emperor Constantine XI Palaiologos was getting nervous. His spies had informed him that his enemy's new weapon was a huge cannon that could bring down a mountain. He addressed his men, trying to lift their spirits, "Christ has never abandoned us! He has always fought by our side! The proof of that is this city, which throughout the centuries has survived thirty-two sieges. This is just one more!"

His excited soldiers shouted their support: "Our God Jesus Christ is with us! No one is going to defeat us!"

A few days later, the emperor saw in the distance what looked like little ants struggling to carry something very heavy and bulky. He felt a flash a fear. *Is this the weapon they were talking about? It is! It's the cannon!* He headed for the church of Saint Sophia and ordered the priest there to toll the bells. When the population gathered, the emperor declared, "We are under siege again! Again we are going to defend the city of our God! This time we are facing a new weapon—they say it is really powerful. But we have the protection of our God, and with that shield not even a thousand armies can conquer us! Soldiers, women, elderly, children . . . everyone is going to defend the city of God."

With that, each citizen went to participate in the city's defense, boiling oil or preparing the weapons as builders brought in sacks of sand. Everyone helped diligently to repel the new invasion. The women, children, and old people gathered in the church to ask Christ for protection, and not to let the other god be more powerful than he was. Their prayers and petitions were desperate and usually accompanied by tears, and cries.

April 6, 1453, would turn out to be one of the most significant days in the history of Christianity and Islam. It marked the beginning of the end, as 120,000 men—part of the sultan's army, comprised of Ottoman soldiers and mercenaries attracted by the lure of fame and fortune—prepared to besiege the city of Constantinople by land and sea. With each man in position, the army awaited the order to start the action.

The huge cannon advanced slowly to the front lines. The gunpowder and heavy ammunitions were transported separately, in carts pulled by oxen.

Before the attack began, the powerful sultan, Mehemed II, spoke to his soldiers. "Today we are going to fight for our faith," he said. "Indubitably, Allah will protect us, and so we have nothing to be afraid of. We are soldiers fighting for our God, and only victory will stop us! The first brave man who gets up and conquers the wall will be appointed governor of a village!"

The Roman pope sent a ship with supplies, weapons, and three hundred skilled archers equipped with new and precise crossbows. This military retinue was commanded by the papal legacy, Cardinal Isidro, who looked ravishing in his expensive armor.

This siege was not like the others. Both the emperor and the empire's inhabitants felt fear.

The racket of enemy drums livened up the action, encouraging the attackers and intimidating the attacked. The drumbeat kept getting stronger until it stabilized into an annoying, discordant concert. Suddenly there was a roar of a potent thunder and the earth was shaken to its core. The powerful cannon had blasted its deadly ammunition against one of the city walls. And with that, the order to attack was given.

When Mehemed II saw his new weapon in action and imagined his enemy's panic, he felt pleased and powerful. *If my father could see me right now,* he thought, *he would forget about my deviance. He would fell very proud.*

Emperor Constantine was speechless. *What was that?* To bolster his soldier's morale, he bravely went to the front, shouting, "Do not let them destroy our faith in Christ!" That encouraged his men, who fought with renewed spirit.

The heavy cannon was slow to reload. It took hours to place and press the sacks of gunpowder, insert the thirteen-hundred-pound marble bullet, aim the giant weapon, and then shoot it. Although its accuracy was terrible, the damage it caused when it hit was so great that all the work was worth it.

The city walls were built by intelligent engineers who had thought of everything but gunpowder and artillery, because they'd never imagined such things. Within less than a week of constant attacks, the walls began to crack. At night its defenders sent out builders who used sand and stone to patch them, protecting themselves from the enemy's arrows with wooden shields.

It was an all-out war. From behind the walls the city's defenders also sent arrows, causing many enemy casualties. Also protecting the walls was a moat varying in depth from 100 to 230 feet, which stole the courage from the bravest daredevil.

On May 24, 1453, the moon disappeared from the sky. The city's inhabitants were horrified when they remembered the ancient prophecy: "Byzantine will resist any siege . . . as long as the moon shines in the sky."

The bells of the church of Saint Sophia pealed, and the religious men immediately instructed those praying to process through the main streets holding the statue of the Virgin Mary. And so it was done, and the mere presence of the sacred statue seemed to protect the city, offering peace and security to its citizens.

Suddenly a torrential rain started, and the inhabitants immediately attributed it to their plea for divine help. The Mother of God had not failed them! She had sent that water to ruin the gunpowder and stop the damage that damned cannon was making to the city walls. The people's hymns got louder; their faith burned in their hearts. If anyone still doubted the power of the Virgin, he could look at the facts.

But the rain also made the ground wet and slippery, making things treacherous for the sixteen people who were carrying the holy statue through the streets. The statue was very heavy, and the stakes that served as its supports became slippery, as well. When two carriers from the same side fell, the weight became unbalanced. The holy statue fell and was smashed to smithereens.

The townspeople were terrified: the holy Mother of God had fallen. As people quickly began picking up the pieces to take them to the church of Saint Sophia, the new spread like wildfire until it arrived at the ears of the brave defenders of the walls, who felt defenseless. The beginning of the end had started!

Mehemed II interrupted the assault due to the rain.

To raise the spirits of his soldiers and give them a feeling of security, the Byzantines claimed that the siege had ended because the Mother of God had sacrificed herself for them. The church bells did not stop pealing, and the churches were packed as the people gave thanks to God and his Holy Mother, whom they considered at that moment their greatest heroine, a martyr for and defender of the empire. The rain continued, but Emperor Constantine saw that the enemy's army was not leaving. Something told him that the siege was not over, and so he sent his soldiers to their positions.

On May 29, 1453, the battlefield was finally dry. The dawn silence was broken by a familiar roar that made the townspeople tremble in fear. Everyone took his position, and the siege started again.

The attack was focused on the Valley of Lico. Some masons who repaired the wall had left the door of the west wall, the Kernaporta, half-open, and the enemies entered. Everything was chaos from there.

Emperor Constantine XI lost his life fighting. He battled furiously until the last moment and had the death every Christian warrior yearns for: he gave his life to defend his faith with Christ's name on his lips.

The city had been taken! When the victors remembered that the inhabitants were theirs for three days, they committed the typical atrocities of human nature: plundering, robbing, raping, and, when there was nothing left to steal, taking prisoners to sell as slaves.

Constantine was decapitated and taken to Mehemed II, who proudly showed the head to both his army and his enemies. Then he put it in the place of honor in his macabre collection.

The news of the fall of Constantinople spread around the world, with everyone expressing his own opinion depending on how it affected his interests.

In the Vatican, Pope Nicholas V said with great pain in his heart, "The light of Christendom has been extinguished."

Vladislav II was happy—so happy he thought he might burst from joy. He considered his ally, the sultan Mehemed II, to be a hero. The sultan had managed to take the unconquerable city, and Vladislav would always be willing to help him.

42

The next years were hard work for Hunyadi and Dracula.

The night of May 18, 1455, Dracula told Hunyadi, "I am as sure of something as I am of the divinity of Jesus Christ."

When Hunyadi heard his friend's solemn tone, he asked, "What is that?"

"I am sure of your solid faith in our Christ, and of your hatred of the Ottomans and Jews."

Hunyadi answered, smiling, "The same as yours."

Dracula nodded. "That is why we are allies," he said. "I can honestly say that you are the bravest, holiest Christian warrior I know. But why don't you get Matthias and Laszlo involved in your interests? Remember, we won't be here forever. Someday we must account to God during our final judgment. Get your children more involved."

Hunyadi raised his eyebrows. "They are just kids! Matthias is barely fourteen, and Laszlo is fifteen."

"Your children are of age," Dracula said. "My father admired Pepin the Brief. That Christian warrior took his son Charlemagne along to battle from the time he was a little boy and instructed him in the teachings of Saint Augustine of Hippo. Following his example, my father did the same with us. He made me a knight of the Order of the Dragon when I was an adolescent."

Hunyadi looked at him, puzzled. "How did that happen? When? Who were the witnesses?"

So Dracula told him in great detail about the special way he was ordained, and the reason why his only witness was their Lord. Then, unsheathing the dagger of the Order of the Dragon, he added, "My father gave me this dagger when he ordained me. He had baptized it with the blood of his unfaithful brother, Alexandru, and I have honored it with more heretic and infidel blood."

Hunyadi stood in front of Dracula. "Stand up!" he said. Dracula complied, and Hunyadi took a similar dagger from his own belt and said, "I was witness to your father's ordination. Now we are brothers from the same order!" And he hugged Dracula warmly.

Dracula smiled. "Get close to your children," he said. "Look out for them. Get them interested in our faith . . . they are very good boys."

"I have given them the best Christian education I could," he said. "I have given them the best teachers and the best religious instructors. They speak several languages, they are cultured, and they have a strong working and theoretical knowledge of government. What more do you want?"

"I am still not a father," Dracula said, "but I was a son. And I assure you that one word from my father was more valuable to me than a thousand words from my best instructor. Give time to your children. Talk to them about our Lord. Instill in them hatred of our enemies and also of the damned Jews."

"I promise you I will do what I can to have more communication with them."

<hr>

As they spoke, Dracula was becoming nostalgic. "My dream was to support my brother Mircea and be his right-hand man, but Vladislav II killed him." Dracula looked up at Hunyadi. "You are like my older brother," he said. "Allow me to fight by your side and support you in all your actions. My greatest desire is to die defending the Christian faith with God's holy name on my lips."

When Hunyadi saw the honest, trusting expression on the face of his brother Dragon, his conscience screamed so loudly that he could not remain silent anymore. With great effort, he forced himself to speak. "There is something I have to confess," he said quietly. "Please . . . sit down." Dracula obliged, looking perplexed.

Hunyadi was quiet for a moment and then began. "When your father and brother returned the Fortress of Giurgiu and the Ottoman prisoners, Vladislav II deceived me. He made me believe that your father and brother were traitors to Christianity. That is why . . . I authorized an attack upon them." Dracula started from his chair, but Hunyadi raised a gentle hand. "Please . . . my conscience keeps me awake. I regret not having investigated

Vladislav's claim before making that quick, decision. I swear to you that I only did it thinking about the defense of our Lord. I know that it is a lot to ask of you . . . but I swear by my God that I am really sorry." Hunyadi unsheathed his dagger and placed it in Dracula's hand. "I ask you for your forgiveness," he said softly, "but justice is yours." Then he opened his coat and bared his chest, awaiting the decision of his brother Dragon.

Dracula grasped the dagger in his hand. His first impulse was to plunge it into Hunyadi's heart. Hunyadi remained motionless, bravely waiting to pay with his life for his mistake. Dracula too, was still, now considering the facts. His brother Dragon was human; if he had made that bad decision, it was because he had been deceived. If Dracula's God had forgiven Hunyadi—had given his life to forgive this man's sin—then why shouldn't Dracula forgive him, too? Returning Hunyadi's dagger, Dracula said, "The example we have from our God is forgiveness. I will forgive you on one condition: that we fight until the end to defend our Christian faith!"

Hunyadi hugged him, saying quietly, "I swear to defend our faith until the last day of my life."

Dracula returned the hug with difficulty. "Time will cure this bitterness," he said. "Whatever happens between us is far less important than our real fight for the defense of our God."

43

On June 28, 1456, Hunyadi received troubling information from one of his spies: "My lord, Vladislav II has just collected and paid the tribute to the Ottomans."

Hunyadi felt his blood boiling in his veins. His ally had betrayed him and made an alliance with his bitter enemies. Without wasting a moment, Hunyadi dispatched emissaries to bring Vladislav to his presence.

———◆———

The soldiers traveled to Tirgoviste, appeared before Vladislav II, and gave him a mandatory invitation to appear before Hunyadi. Vladislav took and read the letter; then he wrote his own letter and gave it to the emissaries, saying, "Put this letter in the hands of your governor. I am not going with you!"

The soldier in charge straightened up. "It is essential that you come with us!" he said. "That is an order from our governor!"

"I won't go unless you take me by force," Vladislav answered defiantly.

When the soldier assessed the strength of his retinue, knew that he could not force the issue. So he took the letter that was given to him and, without saying a word to Vladislav, turned around and told his commander officer, "Give the order to go back."

Hunyadi received the letter and read it with hands shaking from fury.

Janos:

In the name of Allah almighty, I inform you that we are no longer allies. My new master is the Sultan Mehemed II. All I require from you is never to find you in my way again.

Signed,
Vladislav II, Prince of all Wallachia

By the time Hunyadi talked to Dracula, he was spitting fire. "He signed it 'Prince of all Wallachia'! Who could have imagined that this man, a Dragon knight who was like a brother to me, a man I helped rise to power—has now made an alliance with our enemy, despising our God!"

"There is just one way to treat traitors," Dracula replied. "He is responsible for the death of my father and my brother. I won't rest until I see him impaled!"

A strange combination of feelings filled Hunyadi: a sense of justice and honor mixed with horror at his own desire for revenge. He got goose bumps hearing the gruesome intentions of his brother Dragon; the plan was drastic, yes, but without a doubt it would be effective.

Months went by, and Hunyadi learned that now that Vladislav II had appointed himself Prince of all Wallachia as well as the surrounding frontiers of Amlas and Fagaras. He was enraged—*Who gave him that title?*— and he sent some emissaries with a letter.

In Wallachia, the vovoid received and read it:

Vladislav II:

Together we have defended the Cross of our Lord Jesus Christ. I know your heart, and I know inside it the flame of passion has not been extinguished. It is my desire to come together to take the necessary actions to fight our enemies. I trust my Christ that you will accept my cordial invitation.

Signed,

Janos Hunyadi, Your Governor

After reading it Vladislav II immediately sent a reply:

Janos:

As I made clear in my previous letter, we are no longer allies. My new lord is Sultan Mehemed II. I answer only to him. You are no longer my governor; you are simply my enemy. And my new God, Allah, has substituted your wild god, Jesus Christ.

I hope to hear from you next when we meet on the field of honor.

Signed,
Vladislav II
Prince of all Wallachia and
surrounding frontiers of Amlas and Fagaras

When Hunyadi received that answer he made new plans. He followed Dracula's advice and involved his children in his military and religious interests. Before long, father and sons were always together, and Hunyadi said to Dracula, "Why didn't you talk to me about this before? I missed so many years when I could have been enjoying my children." He smiled proudly, adding, "I appointed Matthias and Laszlo commanding officers of Hungary's army."

"I am happy for you!" Dracula exclaimed.

"It is time to take back power in Wallachia and make a solid front against our enemy," Hunyadi said.

Dracula thought for a moment. "I want to suggest a strategy for retaking Wallachia," he said. "It's very risky."

He laid out his plan, and after analyzing it closely, Hunyadi said quietly, "It is certainly very risky, but it is also clever and well-structured. I give you my authorization to carry it out."

And so Dracula began making preparations to fulfill the order of his commanding officer.

A spy stood before the White Knight and said, "The sultan will attack Belgrade."

Hunyadi summoned Dracula, Brankovic, and Mikhail Szilagyi. "We are going to fight a really important battle against our enemy," he said. "We need to use new muskets—and we have to think of a way to get better results from our weapons."

The four warriors developed a new military formation, which was then studied and practiced by the soldiers who would have the privilege of using them for the first time in a formal battle.

The Battle of Belgrade started with the firing of the small Ottoman cannons, which was a serious blow to the morale of the defending soldiers. They knew they were being attacked by the most powerful army in the world, personally led by the feared and hated Mehemed II. Meanwhile they were fighting blind, following the orders of their military leaders.

However, the fortress resisted the Ottoman's fierce attacks. No matter how hard they tried, the enemy could not get in! Then something happened that the aggressive Ottomans found inconceivable, even absurd: the city's five bridges began to open! Had their enemy gone crazy?

A large group of Christian soldiers appeared, armed with pieces of wood, further puzzling the attackers. The soldiers assumed a strange formation just as the Ottoman soldiers were given the order to kill them.

Just as the Ottomans attacked, their terrifying screams heightening the ferocity of the battle, the defenders' muskets spit fire. A wave of attackers fell to the ground.

When their comrades saw that they fell without having had physical contact with the enemy, they attacked all the more fiercely, but they were stopped in their tracks by another deadly discharge. Still the Ottoman soldiers kept advancing, and another deadly discharge stopped them. While some defenders were shooting, others were preparing their deadly weapons. Terrified by so many deaths, the Ottomans asked themselves, *What kind of devilish weapon is that?* Then there were more shots, and more Ottomans fell, and with that they started to run away, while the Christian cavalry ravaged their ranks.

At the end of the battle there was a clear loser: Mehemed II. Looking with contempt at the ones who had run from the field of honor, the sultan screamed, "You were given the honor of dying in the fight for the glory of Allah! Instead you will die for your cowardice, as you deserve!" Trembling with rage, he turned to the Janissaries. "Cut them like pumpkins!" he said.

After that important victory, the city of Belgrade was reinforced, and Hunyadi and Dracula headed to the castle of Hunedoara.

Hunyadi was feeling terribly sick, although he had suffered no wounds. When he continued to worsen, he consulted with the best doctors available, who administered the most sophisticated medicine of that time to try to cure him of his mysterious illness.

On August 11, 1456, Hunyadi lay in his bed. "This is odd," he said to Dracula. "I have had many wounds, some of them really serious, and I have never felt as bad as I do today. I think I am dying." Hunyadi's sons, Matthias and Laszlo, were now sixteen and seventeen years old. They were desperately worried because no doctor could seem to cure their father.

Trying to cheer up his friend, Dracula said, "You have come out of worse troubles, Janos! Trust in Christ. I am sure that with his help you will emerge victorious from this convalescence."

"You are optimistic," Hunyadi said. "I feel my God is calling me. I would have preferred to die in battle with the name of Christ on my lips, but I have to settle with the destiny he has chosen for me."

Dracula leaned down and whispered in his ear: "When I was a boy, I found out by accident that you were the son Sigismund. Don't you think it is time for your sons to know the truth?"

"I do not want to stain my father's memory to benefit my children," the knight answered. "Promise me you will keep the secret."

Dracula nodded solemnly. "I swear by my God, that this secret will join me in the grave."

Then calling his children to join Dracula at his bedside, Hunyadi said, "I want to say my last will. Take Wallachia as we had planned it, and let my brother Dracula establish the government and defend it from our enemies. Please, always seek the defense of Christianity and the welfare of our people. Think of each other as brothers; do not waste your time and resources fighting among you." He looked at Dracula and said, "Take care of my children." Then he looked up and said, "Blessed is my God, Jesus Christ!" At that moment, his eyes became fixed.

In his last battle, Janos Hunyadi had stopped the invasion of the powerful Turkish army. This battle was written in gold letters in the universal history of Christianity, giving its commander the honorable title of "Sacred Warrior of Christianity."

And so Hunyadi was received by God, a victim of a strange epidemic. This colossus, this tireless defender of the Christian faith, finally would rest in peace, with the spiritual assistance of the Holy Communion he had received several times before he died. His memory would remain in the mind of every good Christian.

Dracula's eyes filled with tears, and a strange pain pierced his chest; he could not escape his terrible grief. Matthias and Laszlo also cried inconsolably for their irreparable loss.

When Mehemed II heard about the death of the great warrior, he felt both relief and admiration. "Although Janos was my most shrewd and bitter enemy, I feel a pain for his death, because the world will never again have a warrior like that," the sultan said.

Pope Callixtus III also expressed great sorrow over Hunyadi's his death, remembering him as the greatest defender of the faith and giving him the honorable title of the Shield of Christendom. He ordered all Catholic churches to toll their bells at midday to commemorate the warrior's last great victory.

In time, many Christian historians would compare Hunyadi with the legendary Greek warrior, Achilles.

44

Under Dracula's orders, Matthias and Laszlo dispatched part of their army to fulfill the last will of their father and retake Wallachia. Following his own plan, which Hunyadi had authorized, Dracula left part of the army in Karpathos to protect it from a possible attack by Ottoman reinforcements. Then he sent soldiers dressed as merchants into Tirgoviste. One by one the soldiers killed their enemies, whose bodies were placed in carts disguised as merchandise. As some Ottoman guards were being eliminated, other Christian soldiers arrived dressed as bread or rug sellers, peasants or beggars. Finally Dracula's army entered the city, and when the remaining soldiers tried to defend themselves, it was too late. There were very few casualties in the attacking army. When Tirgoviste was taken, Vladislav's boyars, seeing the square was lost, escaped, leaving their leader alone.

Finally Vladislav II and Dracula were face-to-face. Knowing he had nothing to lose, Vladislav challenged his enemy to a duel: "If you are a brave Christian, you will not be afraid to fight to the death!"

Dracula accepted, they drew their swords, and the battle started. Dracula's superiority was immediately clear; his technique was perfect and his strength was evident. With a quick move, Dracula sliced the hand with which Vladislav was defending himself; then he put the tip of his sword to Vladislav's heart.

Bleeding profusely, Vladislav threw out his chest, shouting, "Pierce me if you have the courage!"

Dracula did not answer; his opponent did not even deserve his contempt. But the hate he felt toward the murderer of his loved ones was so great that Vladislav betrayed the law of his God. Without letting go of the sword, he said, "Take him and torture him in the dungeon—but do not kill or blind him."

Vladislav II was taken to the dungeon to fulfill his destiny, not realizing that the short trip would comprise his last tranquil moments. He was sure his powerful Ottoman master would soon rescue him and restore his power.

In the meantime, he trusted in the immediate action of his accomplices, the Saxons, who certainly would rescue him at any moment. He just had to endure this situation a little longer, he thought, never imagining what Dracula had in store for him.

When the soldiers imprisoned the traitor, they found several unfortunate men locked up and took them to Dracula. *If these men are Vladislav's enemies, then they are my friends,* Dracula thought. "You are free," he told them.

A few left, thanking their liberator, while others stayed, begging to be his soldiers. One of them, however, simply stared at him.

"Do you know me?" the man asked.

The man was unrecognizable: thin, dirty, and hairy. But the voice he knew without a doubt: it was his faithful boyar, Ivan Stokovich. Without caring about the looks and stench of the prisoner, Dracula hugged him like a brother. "I never imagined that in just one day my God would give me so much happiness!" he exclaimed. Then he added, "And, as usual, wherever I go, you'll go too." Dracula called to his solders, "I want to be alone with Ivan." The soldiers immediately left. Dracula looked at his old friend, saying, "It is a blessing that you are even alive . . . look how thin you are!"

To prove Dracula true, Ivan displayed his fingers, which had no nails. "You freed me just in time," he said hoarsely. "They were torturing me horribly! They promised me a more painful death than the one your father and brother endured. I am beaten to a pulp. Thank you for rescuing me!"

"It is not me whom you should thank; it is Christ who allowed it. Now we have to find the murderers of my brother and father."

"I know where they are!" Ivan said. "And if we want to catch them, we must hurry before they escape."

Taking a group of boyars and soldiers with them, Dracula and Ivan left to apprehend the murderers.

When Wallachia fell, they hid in a secret refuge. Knowing it was too risky to attempt an escape during the day, they decided to do it that night. Then, under the moonlight, they would search the enemies of Dracula: Dan III, Basarab Laiota, and Dracula's half-brother, Vlad Calugarul the Monk.

As he led the group to the refuge to apprehend the traitors, Ivan told Dracula, "They thought I was dead and talked about everything in my presence—even where they had their secret hideout. They never thought I was going to get out of there alive."

When they arrived at the hideout, Ivan asked for the privilege of arresting them. "Surrender!" he shouted. "You are surrounded!"

Lobzuowo, the chief of the mercenaries, said to his men, "If we turn ourselves in now, they will put us in jail, but the Saxons and the Ottomans won't take long to rescue us. They won't really do anything to us. Let's turn ourselves in!"

But the boyars faithful to Vladislav II were afraid of retribution. "Can you say that we are your mercenaries?" one of them asked Lobzuowo.

Lobzuowo, who'd never lost his touch for negotiation with anything related to war, said, "For ten gold coins, it will be a pleasure!" The money was delivered, and Lobzuowo shouted, "My mercenaries and I surrender! We are unarmed!" The sixty-eight men went out with their hands up and were summarily chained.

Ivan examined the supposed mercenaries and identified the nineteen murderers who participated in the deaths of Dracul and Mircea. "Put those bastards aside," he told the soldiers. "And don't take your eyes off them for a minute." Looking at Lobzuowo, he said, "These are not your mercenaries—they are Vladislav's thugs! You are a liar!"

Lobzuowo offered a cynical shrug. "I am just a war merchant."

Ivan walked over to Dracula. "I found the murderers and separated them from the rest," he reported. "I sent them to the most secure dungeon."

"Ivan," Dracula said, "I want you to remember, step-by-step, how those bastards tortured you. Don't forget the night when they thought you were dead, leaving you with that painful wound in your gut. Remember how my brother and father died, and keep in mind the destiny these scoundrels had prepared for you. Look at your fingers without nails. You are going to make them suffer like they made you and my loved ones suffer. Give them bread and water, torture them however you wish, but please don't let them die . . . and do not touch their eyes."

Dracula had dreamed of impaling those bastards, but he wanted to make them suffer even more. He had learned and perfected the impalement technique under the Ottomans, who had taught him how to make the pain last longer. In a typical impalement, the pointed stake that entered the testicles tore through the internal organs, so that in some cases the impaled lasted very little time, diminishing the time of pain. To fix this problem, Dracula removed the point, making the end of the stick round, and then used grease to introduce it slowly through the anus. As the greased stake was inserted further, it pushed aside the internal organs without hurting them, finally exiting through the back. At that point the executioner would fix the stake with a nail that preferably would grab bone.

"Instruct some soldiers to take immediate action," Dracula ordered. Then, one by one, he looked into the eyes of the murderers of his brother and father. He wanted to see the faces of the ones who had filled him with pain. He would never forget those faces, but he didn't curse them or shout at them, because showing them his pain and rage would only make them feel powerful. He just stared at them . . . and said nothing.

When the murderers saw Dracula's face, they were stunned and terrified, reading in his silence unspeakable violence and aggression. They saw the flames of hate and rage in his eyes. Still, while they feared their immediate destiny at the hands of Ivan, they trusted that they would soon be rescued.

Dracula visited Vladislav II and saw that his soldiers had done an excellent job generating pain without causing death. The traitor did not have fingernails, teeth, or testicles, and he was begging for death. Dracula looked him in the eyes without saying a word.

"For the love of God, kill me!" Vladislav screamed.

Dracula looked at him mildly, made more terrifying by his silence. He turned and left that wicked traitor in excellent company. As he walked away, he could hear the screams of the murderer. "May your soul go to hell! Damn you, son of the devil!"

Dracula went straight to his construction engineer. "I want you to build a dungeon whose walls are solid stone," he said. "It must have only one entrance, and the prisoners must be in vaults—four huge cells with special locks—twelve yards under the palace floor. I want this mousetrap finished yesterday."

"It is impossible to finish it by yesterday, my lord!" exclaimed the frightened engineer.

Dracula give him a joking pat. "I know!" he said. "Not by yesterday. But what about today? The construction must start right now and not stop for one minute. I'm holding you responsible for it."

———◆◇◆———

Dracula planned to give a public lesson to Vladislav II in the main square of Tirgoviste the next Sunday after Mass. Meanwhile, in the dungeon, the traitor's intense pain made the time go by so slowly that he was convinced that it had stopped. But Sunday arrived, and after Mass the church bells pealed incessantly, calling the townspeople to the place of execution. The sharp noise of a drum also guided the curious, who knew by the sound that an extraordinary event was going to take place.

Chained and escorted by soldiers, the condemned man was brought to the square. The spectators hushed expectantly. When Dracula appeared, the drum fell silent. The vovoid declared, "I defeated my enemy by the grace of my God." Looking at Vladislav, he sentenced him: "For betraying the trust of King Ladislaus Posthumus, for making alliances with the enemy, and for worshiping Allah, I, vovoid of Wallachia, by the grace of my Christ, condemn you to death by impalement!"

The crowd was confused at the unfamiliar word. "What punishment is that?" they whispered. "Will it hurt?"

Vladislav, on the other hand, began screaming curses at the judge, until a soldier stepped forward and hit him hard in the stomach with the handle of a mallet. The condemned man felt all the air leave his lungs; he wanted to breathe but couldn't. When he finally took a gasping breath, he received another potent blow with a huge rock to his mouth and nose, making him see stars. Without the protection of teeth, his gums split; he could feel the pieces with his tongue. Again he felt like he was suffocating; when he finally caught his breath, he inhaled blood and pieces of tissue along with the air. Now he regretted having offended his enemy. He felt like he was dying, but his torment was barely beginning.

The people watched the proceedings, shocked. What an aggressive way to punish a criminal! They were scared and began whispering to each other, "The impalement is really painful!" They believed that the criminal had just received his punishment; in a moment, however, everything was going to become clear.

The soldiers took Vladislav II and tore off his clothes, leaving him covered only in blood. He, the almighty master of Wallachia, was being vilely humiliated, and even with his pain, the shame made him to want to hide. Now everyone could see his naked body—and even worse, they were seeing him without testicles! Next he was tied with four harnesses, one for each limb, and unceremoniously kicked to the ground, face—down. Then each harness was tied to a horse, and in that uncomfortable position he suffered terrible humiliation in front of his people.

A soldier took a stake and generously greased it.

The convicted man began screaming when he saw the stake, but he was quieted by a soldier's kick. Then the horses started to pull his legs and arms; no matter how hard he tried to minimize the strength of the animals, he couldn't achieve his objective. When he felt the stake enter his anus, he began screaming with all the strength of his being. The horses, oblivious to his pain, blindly followed the soldiers' orders, and, slowly, the stake kept entering the traitor. The grease made the stake gently slip by the internal organs without hurting them, yet the miserable man could feel the stake piercing him, hurting him beyond what anyone could imagine. When it finally came out through his back, the soldiers used a huge nail to grab the bone so the traitor would be well fixed and not fall. He wanted to talk, but he couldn't. He wanted to moan, but when he did it hurt him deeply. He was immobilized; the only things he could move without pain were his eyes. Then he was lifted up high, naked and fixed there, immobile. He looked out at the crowd and felt humiliated to be seen like that after having been their master. So he fixed his gaze instead on the monster who was watching him in silence, with an inexpressive face that scared the impaled man. But what else could happen to him? All he had to do now was wait for death.

But he was wrong. He had suffered only the first part of his impalement. Now, in the sky, hungry birds and vultures were flying in circles, waiting to eat.

The town's inhabitants were horrified. Some had even fainted at what they'd seen. They stood in stunned silence, not knowing what to do, what to say, what to think. They were motionless and terrified.

A vulture was forced by its great hunger to land on the head of the traitor, who felt the animal's powerful talons grip his cranium. Suddenly it stuck its beak into one of his eyes and swallowed it at once; then it changed its position. Vladislav looked at the monster—and that would be the last image his brain would receive. The bird left him completely blind.

Vladislav needed to move to scare the damned bird that was eating him alive, but the pain wouldn't let him. Then other birds arrived and start pecking at him. It was a living hell.

Was it night or day? Who knew! He was beyond noticing hunger and thirst, but he felt the cold. He knew it must be night because everything was quiet, and he wanted to sleep, but how could he? Nobody could go to sleep with that much pain! The seconds seemed like years, the minutes centuries, the hours an eternity—and without spiritual assistance he knew he would end up in hell and his torment would continue even after he died. His anguish and desperation increased. His body had become a victim of nocturnal vampires—insects that sucked his blood without mercy. After an eternity of eternities, he heard the murmur of people again. Then the sun began to burn his body and he felt a heat from hell. His thirst was suddenly unbearable—what he would have given for a sip of water!—and then the hunger appeared, too. He did not know it had been just one day of punishment. Now his body seemed to be invaded by daytime bugs that were biting him, taking advantage of the fact that he could not move. They seemed to be eating him alive. The immobility of his body was painful, too; he wanted to move to another position to get some rest, but just the thought of moving terrified him. His pain increased every moment, as did his desperation. His hunger and thirst, the cold, the heat, and other pains he could not even identify were taking him through hell on earth. On the fourth day he prepared for the last judgment of his soul. There Dracula could not interfere—he just did not allow Vladislav to have his last rites . . . and that was the most important part of the punishment.

45

On August 22, 1456, in the cathedral of Tirgoviste, very important public figures gathered to witness Dracula's ascent to power a second time, at the age of twenty-five. In the place of honor, representing the king of Hungary, Ladislaus Posthumous, was Count Ulich Cilli. Testifying to the important event were the commanding officers of the army of Hungary, Matthias Hunyadi (who would later become the king of Hungary, Matthias Corvinus) and his brother Laszlo Hunyadi. Dracula's beloved brother Dragon Mikhail Szilagyi also joined him, and many other important public figures honored the event with their presence. Accompanied by a solemn Te Deum, Dracula was appointed vovoid of Hungary-Wallachia and the dukedoms of Amlas and Fagaras, subject of the King Ladislaus Posthumous In the midst of so much joy, the vovoid eulogized his best friend, honoring his memory by nostalgically remembering him as the most important Christian he knew. His brother Dragon Janos Hunyadi—had died eleven days ago, and Dracula was happy to have fulfilled his last will.

Almost all Tirgoviste threw itself into the festivities marking Dracula's ascent to the throne. To celebrate the special occasion, a huge communal party was held outside the governor's residence. Inside, Dracula celebrated in private with his highly esteemed guests. As a mute witness to the change of power, the corpse of Vladislav II remained high on a stake. His body had been left there as a reminder to anyone who would try to betray the king and the new vovoid.

The only activity that did not stop for the celebration was the construction of the mousetrap. That work went on full-time, with not a moment of rest for the workers, as it had to be finished as soon as possible.

The workers building the claustrophobic place were horrified to think it would give shelter to the enemies of the vovoid.

Every night that month and part of the next, for a total of seven weeks, a comet with two tails appeared in the night sky. Everyone saw them as omens, though their meanings depended upon the interests of the interpreter. To Dracula's enemies they meant change of government, hunger, misery, pain, invasion, earthquakes, disease, war, and all the bad things in the world. To his supporters they meant a change of power resulting in more prosperity, wealth, justice, peace, and all the other good things in the world.

The sultan burst out laughing when he read a proclamation by the Holy Father in the Vatican condemning to hell the demon, the Turk, and the comet. When he tired of laughing at the crazy remark, he said, "What a bizarre knowledge have the spiritual leaders of the Catholics. If these are the shepherds, I cannot imagine the sheep!"

King Ladislaus Posthumous professed Catholicism, and also to that faith belonged the Order of the Dragon, of which Dracula was member, and the church of Tirgoviste, where power was given to the new vovoid. Therefore, according to the custom and the law in those times, all the inhabitants of Wallachia had to be Catholics.

In Dracula's heart, however, the flame of the Orthodox faith still burned; his father had made sure to give him a good religious foundation. Three years had passed since Constantinople had disappeared; there was no one to lead the Orthodox Church there. But Dracula was there—and of course he would do it. He was not going to disappoint his father. So he issued a proclamation: "By order of our King Ladislaus Posthumous in Wallachia, the Catholic religion will be professed there, and as the Orthodox faith is professed by many of our inhabitants, and this faith reveres, venerates, and worships with all the sacraments our God and his Holy Mother the Virgin Mary, the inhabitants of Wallachia will have the freedom to profess the religion they desire: the religions will coexist, with the government respecting the personal choice of each habitant, and there will be no quarrel between the two Churches." He then appointed himself the highest pontiff of the Orthodox Church in Wallachia.

Dracula's proclamation clarified the relationship between the churches and gave him the authority to name the metropolitan leader and bishops of the Orthodox Church in Wallachia.

Dracula summoned the town council and told them, "It is my intention to have good relations with you; we are going to work together to have a better Wallachia."

"If you wish to have good relations," Moses said, "show us a gesture of your good will and free the soldiers you are holding as prisoners. They are mercenaries and were just following orders."

"Not without investigating them first," Dracula said.

"Who are you to investigate them?" Moses exclaimed. "We are the law!"

"I have given you my final word. I will free them after I investigate!" Dracula turned around and walked out

The councilmen were furious. "This governor is not like the others," Isaac said. "Remember that the first time he took the power, we had to overthrow him."

Moses looked around at his fellow councilmen. "We have no other choice," he said. "We have to overthrow him again!" And they started to conspire.

The next day Dracula went to the jail and separated the murderers and rapists from the rest of the prisoners. "When you committed your crime, you did not know the new law," he said. "I am going to show mercy in my punishment. You will die decapitated."

The prisoners' pleas did not make him change his verdict.

The pealing of the bells called to the people, who, guided by the loud beating of the drum, gathered in the main square. Then the bells stopped, and when Dracula appeared, the drum fell silent. He climbed the platform, and with strong, clear voice, he addressed the men in charge of the towns, saying, "You will represent me in the most important places in Wallachia!" Then, speaking to his boyars, he said, "You are my arms, the manifestation of my power!" Finally he addressed the people. "And you I have left for last, because the last shall be first, and the first"—he looked at the town representatives—"shall be the last. I am going to announce the new law in Wallachia. From now on, it is forbidden to steal, rape, or kill, or to betray me or our king. The ones who do any of these things will receive the same punishment: death by impalement. And all the inhabitants of Wallachia must work. The one-handed, one-legged, blind, or lame will get a job according to his skills. Those who cannot get work will go to build a castle in Poenari and will be paid fair wages. Those who refuse to work, preferring to be leeches on society, will get death by decapitation. This is the new law in Wallachia. Therefore do not steal, rape, or kill, do not betray me—and work. Those who break the law will end up high on a stake—naked, humiliated, aching, and ashamed—and the parasites will be decapitated. Their souls will have no rest because their bodies won't have a Christian burial. Don't accuse me of being evil: I am just the judge who applies the same law to all. You condemn yourselves with your actions; they are your real executioner!"

There, next to the platform, were some lowly thieves. Dracula addressed them, saying, "You, who love the things that do not belong to you, I am going to make you a promise: you will not steal again. And I am going to keep my promise! By my Lord Jesus Christ, this will be your last chance to be honest, hard-working men."

Then he addressed the people again: "The murderers and rapists who were in jail will not commit their crimes again. I decapitated them. I showed them mercy because they did not know the new law."

That news fell like a bombshell on the inhabitants, each of whom expressed an opinion of the new law from his personal point of view. The honest and hardworking people—who were the vast majority—received it with pleasure, although some criticized him, saying, "All the governors promise a lot. They arrive full of energy, and then they turn into servants of the Saxons."

After announcing the new law, Dracula encouraged them to go back to work to continue building a strong Wallachia, and to fight until they achieved their freedom.

The Saxons of the town council were confused. What about them and their authority, and their request that Dracula show his respect by releasing the prisoners? They met again to further their conspiracy against him.

Gjon, the thief who had stolen from Stanyzkwl, among many others, had a huge smile on his face as he left the square. *I never imagined I would get out of prison so easily and so soon,* he thought. *These rulers are getting worse. Instead of punishing us, they look for excuses not to feed us in jail, instead rewarding us with freedom.*

46

Caplea was a shy young lady—pretty, quiet, and, most of all, terrified. Her stepfather continued to rape her despite Dracula's law. He felt so strong and superior that he was not afraid of the devil himself. On the day Logofat was caught raping Neagoe, her little sister, the townspeople whose attempt to hang him had been frustrated by the soldiers were encouraged by Dracula's sentence. Logofat would die impaled. It would be the first trial involving the new law.

The next day the Saxon members of the town council appeared before Dracula. "We have set the amount of twenty silver coins for the criminal's release," Moses said.

Dracula, unsurprised by the mercenary attitude of the leeches, looked Moses in the eye and said, "We'd be better to charge thirty, the amount for which Judas sold our Christ!"

The sarcasm upset him, but Moses didn't want to offend the new vovoid. So, taking a deep breath, he replied, "Fine. Let it be thirty."

Dracula was furious. "There are human beings who were hurt!" he shouted. "They are suffering and crying out for justice. Is this the way to give it to them? All of this is going to change. Nobody and nothing can save that damned rapist from his punishment! He will die impaled on Sunday, and no one can stop that!"

Moses' answer was categorical and authoritative. "Not if he pays his fine!" he said. "Is that so difficult for you to understand? We are the authority! We determine and apply the law! Besides, you must free the boyars you are holding prisoner. They are innocent; they were just following orders!"

"Then *you* were the ones who ordered them to torture Ivan and to kill my father and my brother?" Dracula asked, enraged.

"We don't know what you are talking about!" said the Saxon, "But we do know that the boyars must be set free. They didn't do anything!"

Dracula walked over to Ivan, who was seated nearby, listening attentively. "And this?" He held up Ivan's mutilated right hand. "Look what they did to him!"

Moses merely shrugged. "Regardless of your opinion, I am a representative of the town council, and I demand the immediate release of the arrested boyars. We are the law!"

"What law?" Dracula hissed. "Do you think I am so stupid that I don't know where your wealth comes from?"

"From our work!" the councilman Abraham protested energetically.

"Liars!" The vovoid screamed. "You are rich because you sell justice! Because you extort money from the peasants! Because you take bribes for boyar positions! Because your Saxon henchmen pay you not to make them pay taxes and to keep others from competing with them! You are scroungers! You are good for nothing! From now on, your future is going to change. All your wealth will be confiscated for the benefit of Wallachia. This clique called the town council is now dissolved—you are no different than any other Wallachians. And you should give thanks to God that I am not impaling you for theft! From now on, you must work for your money. If you do not find a job, I will give you a decent one in the castle I am going to build in Poenari. That way you will earn your bread with the sweat of your brow, as our God orders it." Then, without waiting for a response, Dracula bid them a contemptuous farewell: "Parasites!"

The councilmen were astonished. That demon had not asked their authorization to rule Wallachia, and he dared to dissolve the town council! What was happening? Who would protect them from that damned demon? What were they going to do now? The boyars who protected their authority were prisoners; their only hope now was in their allies: Dan III (brother of Dan II), Basarab Laiota, and Vlad Calugarul—but where were they? Thousands of questions came into their confused heads, and they felt powerless. The councilmen had come to hate Dracula with every miserable cell in their bodies.

Dracula left angry but satisfied. Only he knew what was happening now, and he enjoyed defeating his enemies. He thought of his brother, his father, and his grandfather: if they could see what he had done, they would be pleased. Now he was accountable to no one, and no authority was going to put his personal interest before the interest of Dracula's beloved Wallachia. But he had declared war on the most powerful group in the region, the Saxons, and he knew that from that moment on, he could not trust them, even if they called themselves his brothers.

When Dracula left, Moses said, "Who does that moron think he is? Without our support he will be no one." And at that moment they began working with renewed energy to overthrow him. With his actions Dracula had guaranteed that the Saxons would be his enemies even after God had taken him to his kingdom.

Meanwhile Dracula, a man of action, gave firm instructions to one of his secretaries: "The wealth of the members of the town council must be expropriated. Make sure this order is carried out immediately."

The news spread like wildfire in Wallachia: the feared and arbitrary town council had been abolished! In its place there was a new system of justice that was giving hope to the people. Everyone was happy.

The time of truth had come. Sunday Mass had ended, and a drum began to beat in the main square, inviting the town's inhabitants to witness the new justice Dracula was establishing in Wallachia.

Little Neagoe wanted to leave the place of the impalement. Her stepfather terrified her, and she still could not believe that, finally, somebody was giving him what he deserved. When she saw the letch's cynical smile, she wanted to run away and seek refuge—but where? She was more frightened than ever, and her fear puzzled her. Something inside her was telling her that the bastard was going to get forgiveness from the new ruler. She sought refuge in her mother's arms. "Mommy, I have a horrible feeling, I don't know why, but I think they're going to let Logofat go free."

Her mother secretly agreed, but she tried to calm her daughter, reminding her that when they had gone to Dracula to demand justice, he had promised to impale Logofat—had sworn to it, in fact.

The drum and the crowd fell silent when Dracula appeared; everyone was anxiously waiting for him to reconfirm his fair sentence. With a look of contempt in his deep-green eyes, Dracula gazed at the rapist and, with a clear, determined voice, repeated, "You know my law—it is clear. The ones who steal, kill, rape, or betray me will die impaled! You raped—therefore you will die impaled, immediately!" He turned to his soldiers. "Impale him!" he shouted.

The condemned man received the sentence without fear, the cynical, tight smile not leaving his face. Then he raised his head. "I want to say my last words!" he shouted. Then, with a challenging tone, he addressed Dracula, "You are the highest ecclesiastical authority in Wallachia! You are the defender of our God, of his law and his faith! And it is him you have to obey! Your law is very clear: the ones who steal, kill, rape, and betray you will die impaled. But that is your law. I tell you that there is another law that is above yours: the law of God. And it says any sinner will receive forgiveness if there is repentance, because our Christ died on the cross and shed his blood for that forgiveness. I am very repentant, and there isn't a sin, no matter how monstrous, that is worth more than one drop of the savior's precious blood. By the blood of Christ, you have to forgive me! Real justice comes only from our God, and our sins are judged in the final judgment, in front of our real and only judge, our God Jesus Christ!"

Dracula was prepared for everything except an argument so solidly supported. The crowd stood in dead silence, stunned by that brilliant defense.

The letch felt victory within his grasp. He waited, not doubting his imminent release.

Dracula faced a real big problem an insignificant and simple trial had turned into a dilemma of moral values. On the one hand there was the rapist, who wanted divine justice and his freedom; on the other there were the people, who wanted real justice and the impalement of a beast. Dracula felt the collective gaze of his subjects; his prestige and the future of justice in Wallachia depended on his decision. What was he going to do? If he applied his law, he would be stepping on the law of God, and the sacrifice of his Christ would be worthless—and Dracula wished with all his might to be its greatest defender. He concluded that it must be his God whom he would serve, even if he had to change his name to 'Dog' and the world turned against him.

Everything was clear now to the judge. He raised his right hand and prepared to announce his verdict, which the townspeople craved as a thirsty man craves water.

When Dracula began speaking, it was quietly and with difficulty. "Our heavenly Father made a sacrifice that only a God can make: he sent his most valuable treasure, his only child, to be sacrificed on the cross, in indescribable pain, to shed his precious blood for the forgiveness of our sins. Although it is too difficult for us to understand, what this miserable rapist says is true: Christ paid with his pain and with his blood for our sins to be forgiven! It does not matter how great the sins are, there is no sin in this world that is more valuable than a single a drop of the precious blood of our God! I am the highest representative of the Orthodox Church in Wallachia, the defender of the Christian faith. My decision is that his will must be respected, and the—"

Little Neagoe did not need to hear any more. That beast was going to get his freedom! She felt herself getting dizzy, and with a pitiful scream, she fainted. There was a commotion in the crowd, and someone ran to get her water. The townspeople were upset that Logofat was going to be liberated, upset by the attitude of their vovoid before the skilled defense of a rapist. They looked at each other, outraged: this was not the justice they had been promised!

When Dracula saw the innocent victim lying on the ground, he felt as if he'd been struck by lightning. *What am I doing? I'm about to set free a monster who was protecting himself with the mercy of my God!* With a voice as loud as thunder, he looked at the criminal and said, "Your actions are your executioner! Do not cry like a woman if you are not man enough to control your instincts! That regret you are showing? Show it instead to our God. He will judge your soul and give you forgiveness in heaven or damnation in hell. But on earth, justice is mine, and your body will be treated according to my justice!" Again he turned to his soldiers, shouting, "Impale him!"

That sentence left the letch dumbfounded, and he was undressed before the astonished eyes of the people. Those who had wanted to lynch him were happy because they knew something even more painful would be done to him. Then he was tied at the feet and arms as he screamed, "Jesus Christ! Savior! Forgive my soul—I am repented!" A soldier arrived with a stake that was even thicker than usual and started pushing it into his body.

The letch felt the greatest pain he had ever felt as the stake made its way through, slowly tearing his entrails, and he quickly forgot the shame of being naked and humiliated. Nothing stopped its advance until it came out through his back. He wanted to scream, to curse the devil, but the pain left him unable to speak. Now defenseless, he felt his eyes fill with tears.

Caplea, a silent victim of the monster for so many years, remembered how she felt the first time the bastard tortured her; it gave her pleasure to see him howl with pain. She wanted to shout, "How does it feel to be raped, you devil?" But instead she hugged her little sister, who had recovered her senses and was happy with Dracula's justice. Finally she knew that the demon would no longer disturb her, that she could sleep and play in peace without the letch prowling around, waiting to attack her. Bravely, the little girl stood before her tormentor to look him in the eye.

The process followed its usual course, and from the height of the stake, the letch looked down at Neagoe and Caplea, but he also found among the crowd Calinica, Margit, Rada, Ruxandra, Serpega, Marie, Stana, Palaiagongia, Ryngalia, and many others—some young women, others little girls, and all of them watching him with looks of solemn approval or even great smiles on their faces. Finally, the rapist had received his rightful punishment . . . and now they could begin to live in peace!

All the fathers, uncles, brothers, grandfathers, stepfathers, and neighbors who were secret rapists now understood the lesson, because in front of them was reflected their destiny if they continued their actions and were given away. After that they stopped committing their crimes.

A new age had arrived for the girls and women of Wallachia. Now they could play, work, walk, and live in peace, and in their nightly prayers, they thanked God for their beloved guardian angel, Dracula.

47

After furious, nonstop work, the mousetrap was finished. That dark, quiet, cramped hole was like the threshold to hell. The only one who could get in and out of there at will was Death. When they learned they were going there, the traitorous boyars were terrified.

Lobzuowo, who was claustrophobic, protested desperately. "I am scared to be locked in this place!" he screamed to Ivan from his cell. "For the love of God, I cannot breathe—I need a window! Tell your master I want to make a deal with him . . . but he has to get me out of this hole!" His voice was choked with anguish and desperation.

Ivan obliged and went to Dracula. "Lobzuowo and his men are scared and miserable in the mousetrap. They've asked to speak to you to offer you a deal."

Dracula smiled slightly. "Follow me with the guard," he said. The two men descended the stone steps into the gloom until they arrived at the cells where the enemies were imprisoned. "What deal do you want to make?" Dracula asked Lobzuowo.

The prisoner was sweating and shaking as he offered his proposition. "We want to join your cause! I swear to be faithful to you until death—and we won't charge you a coin! Our payment will be to get out of this hell. Remember, I gave you the opportunity to escape—now you have to return the courtesy!"

Dracula frowned. "At that time you were working for me, and you betrayed me because you received money from my enemies. If you freed me—and you said this yourself—it was because doing so was in your own interest, not because you wanted to do me a favor. You are a traitor, and I owe you nothing. And like all traitors, you are going to die impaled."

When Lobzuowo heard the sentence he almost lost his mind. He knew that punishment perfectly well, and he certainly didn't want to die that way. Trying another tactic to free himself, he said, "What do you think of this plan? I join the rest of Vladislav's boyars that escaped, and then I kill them and bring you their heads."

The vovoid looked at him and thought, *He is not even out of prison yet and he is already betraying his friends. If I give him any opportunity, he will betray me, too. He has no fidelity but to his own interests.* He beckoned to Ivan and left without giving an answer. He did not have to: they were miserable opportunists who did not even deserve his contempt.

As they walked away they could hear the mercenary screaming, "Get me out! I cannot take being locked up without windows! Give me another chance! I swear I will be faithful—I will never betray you!"

"I think they don't look well—start giving them more food," Dracula said to Ivan. "I want them sturdy and strong for Easter so they will endure the final torture."

The men then visited the murderers of Dracula's father and brother. The vovoid was pleased: the prisoners were howling in pain, and parts of their bodies were missing. *I would love for my father and brother to see this,* Dracula thought. Turning to Ivan and the soldiers in charge, he said, "I congratulate you! You are doing an excellent job. I will just remind you not to kill them or blind them."

The traitor boyars were counting the excruciating minutes, wondering, *Why have they not rescued us?* Cut off from all communication, they did not know that Vladislav's Saxon friends no longer had power, and in fact since Vladislav was dead, the sultan had lost interest in the place. The traitors, however, still had hope, trusting blindly that their allies would not let them die.

48

Dracula had lived among powerful kings. He had also lived among humble peasants, beggars, and fugitives—in fact, he had been one of them, and he knew their nature, their needs, their dreams and ambitions. He wanted to be a good ruler, and he knew his people needed jobs so they could share the wealth. So with this idea in mind, he established a structure in his government like the one he had seen in the Ottoman Empire: he had servants in charge of the clothes, the house, the horses, the taxes, and the food; he had tasters, personal guards, and other servants with even more specialized jobs. And they all did their job with extreme care and effort, because although their lord was kind, he was also a perfectionist. He did not like mess or idleness, and the idea of stealing was inconceivable to him. Since he had never stolen anything, he did not tolerate thieves.

One day Dracula approached Kazymiers, one of his boyars. "I want you to go to Sucaeva," he said. "There is an honest horse salesman there named Luga. Bring him here with his family. Do not come back without him for any reason. I need him."

Kazymiers traveled to Sucaeva and found Luga, saying, "Our vovoid wants you to go to Wallachia with your family."

"But I have my business here," the salesman said. "I am poor but happy."

"I do not know what you did, but our vovoid is very pleased with your honesty," Kazymiers said. "He told me to remind you of the money you found in his horse's saddlebags—the money you returned."

"Oh yes!" Luga said. "Now I remember him! I can leave my brother in charge of the business, but before I take my family, I wish to know what your lord wants from me."

When Luga arrived in Tirgoviste, he was impressed by the sense of security, order, and formality in the place. When he was in front of the vovoid, he greeted him respectfully.

"I know you by your actions," Dracula said. "You are an honest man. I summoned you to be my treasurer and to handle our economic resources. I will pay you what you deserve, and you will live happily among us, joined by your honorable family. What do you say . . . do you accept?"

Luga could not believe it: the job he was being offered surpassed his most ambitious dreams. He was speechless.

Dracula took his silence as a refusal and said, "Fine, I cannot force you. I would have liked for you to work for Wallachia, but it was a pleasure to see you again, anyway, and if one day you decide to work with me, I will always have a special place for you."

Luga was a sentimental man. He had to wipe away his tears as he exclaimed with difficulty, "I promise to be the most honest of your servants."

Dracula smiled broadly and said, "From now on you are the treasurer." He rose from his chair and gave the surprised man an effusive hug. "Welcome to Wallachia!"

The treasurer sent his collectors to all 225 villas and towns of Wallachia. Under his supervision, the tax was gathered and carefully registered.

49

In the square of Tirgoviste was a gold cup, placed there so the people could drink water with dignity. For a while it was watched from a distance by a guard, but eventually even that measure was not necessary. While Dracula was governor, no one dared to steal it.

Another fight for power clouded the peace among Christians, allowing Islam to strengthen: Matthias Hunyadi was trying to overthrow the young King Ladislaus V of Bohemia. It was time to make alliances and take sides.

The power, money, and prestige belonged to the dynasty of Habsburg, Emperor Frederick III, and the powerful Count Cilli, a relative of Dracula. These were the allies of Ladislaus V.

On the other side was the weak Matthias Hunyadi, son of Dracula's late friend and brother Dragon Janos Hunyadi. But Matthias did not have the resources that his opponents had. His allies were his mother, Erzsebet Szilagyi; his uncle, Mikhail Szilagyi; and his brother, Laszlo.

When Count Ulrich Cilli was murdered, Matthias and his brother Laszlo were accused of the crime. King Ladislaus V arrested them and locked them up in a dark dungeon. He had Laszlo decapitated in March 1457, and he promised to do the same to Matthias at the beginning of Easter.

Dracula had to take sides. He is indecisive. He had sworn loyalty to the holy Roman emperor when his father appointed him Dragon knight, and with this allegiance he would, in fact, have everything he needed to defend his territory, as well as certain sovereignty. But he also would have to become a Catholic, and that was not part of his plan; he wished to be Orthodox, like his people. There was not much time to think about it. Janos Hunyadi was dead, and no one was going to demand that Dracula support the sure loser in this power struggle, and a prisoner at that. But his noble heart and his fidelity toward the Orthodox Church and his late friend and brother Dragon made him make a strange and absurd decision: he would support the convict.

He met with Matthias's weak allies, Erzsebet and Mikhail Szilagyi, who trusted in his skill, intelligence, shrewdness, and boldness. He proposed a plan; then they rescued the prisoner, who continued his campaign against King Ladislaus V.

Dracula's bitter enemies, the wicked Saxons, organized and sent a retinue to the king. "Dracula is our worst enemy and Matthias Hunyadi is yours, and they both allied against you," said Moses, the leader of the retinue. "We came to ask for your support and to offer you ours."

Ladislaus knew about the Saxons' great economic power. "What is your plan?" he asked them.

"Dracula dissolved our town council in Wallachia, an action that has affected us considerably," Moses said. "He is now the one who applies justice and dictates the laws, and he imprisoned the boyars who gave us military strength. We want you to order him to reinstate the council and set free those boyars. That way we will be able to overthrow our enemy and weaken yours."

Ladislaus thought for a moment and then summoned his scribe. "I need you to write a letter for me."

Wladislaus III, Dragwlya:

You shall immediately reinstate the Town Council of Wallachia and release the boyars you have in prison. This is an order from your king. The boyars are mercenaries paid by the Town Council. I trust you will obey my orders immediately.

Signed,

Your King, Ladislaus V

Moses returned to Tirgoviste and delivered the order to Dracula, who upon reading it immediately sensed that it was a childish plan of his enemies. He kept silent, however, and taking a deep breath, he said simply, "I will consider this order."

"Aren't you going to reinstate the town council?" asked Moses. "And free the innocent boyars immediately? You cannot 'consider' the king's orders—you must obey them! And this is an order from our king!"

Dracula stared at him steadily and, after a long silence, repeated, "I am going to *consider* this order. Now please let me work!"

The Saxons had been practically thrown out. Furious, they kept conspiring against Dracula.

Dracula's intelligence became evident when he checked the appointments made by the abolished town council: they corresponded with the names of the prisoners he had in the mousetrap. There were also some he did not have in prison, but now he had confirmation that they were his active enemies: Dan III, Basarab Laiota, and Vlad Calugarul, his half-brother.

50

On April 17, 1457, the first Easter of Dracula's new rule as governor, the sixty-eight men who fought at the side of the traitor Vladislav II went to meet their destiny.

After Mass, the church bells pealed and the drumbeat echoed, guiding the town's inhabitants to the place of the event. When Dracula appeared the drum fell silent, and he said with loud voice, "Today I will apply the law that is meant for everybody. Do not betray your vovoid! The one who does will earn death by impalement." With this he turned to the prisoners, saying, "I am only your judge. You"—he pointed a finger at the condemned men—"you are your own executioners, with your actions! Do not cry like children about the outcome of your decisions." He settled onto a stool and gave the order to his soldiers. "Let the impalements begin!"

The traitors were shaking. Until now, they had never imagined that someone could even touch a hair on their heads, not to mention put them to death. They were used to serving Vladislav and their lords, the Saxons, on their knees, and abusing everyone else. They fought against their chains, screaming curses at Dracula.

Everything was ready: the stakes, the grease, the horses . . . and the vultures would surely arrive soon.

Dracula was watching the process with his cold stare. First they undressed the traitors in front of the people, exhibiting the murderers, who no longer had reproductive organs. Their protests were energetic but incomprehensible, as they had neither teeth nor tongues. Neither did they have fingernails or toenails, because they had no fingers or toes. But all of them had healthy eyes so they could watch the process and feel the humiliation of being naked in front of those who had once seen them as almighty. The degradation was unimaginable, punishment enough to make the prisoners regret ever having betrayed Dracula. Unfortunately, it was too late to repent.

Knowing how Dracula had respected his father, one mercenary screamed at him, "Cursed is the man who brought you into this world!" In response, one of the vovoid's boyars approached him and beat him in the pit of the stomach with the handle of his mallet, and another boyar armed with a huge stone delivered a powerful blow to his mouth and nose.

The aggressive traitor had paved his own horrible path to hell. *I'm going to die!* He thought desperately . . . but his punishment was just starting.

The process was the same as before: the same pain, the same anguish, the same vultures, the same fear of eternal damnation.

For the people, the scene was unforgettable. Those almighty men they had respected, feared, and hated were now naked and could not even complain of their unbearable pain. And that is how they ended. That day was recorded in the memories of the inhabitants as one of the most horrible days of their lives. At night they had terrifying dreams that continued to haunt them after they woke up. If they had ever intended to steal, kill, or rape, or overthrow their vovoid, now they wouldn't even think of it.

That day Dracula impaled sixty-eight traitors. The other fugitives were identified in a blacklist; they had to be apprehended in order to fulfill the law of the vovoid.

Then Dracula summoned the group of Saxons who had requested the liberation of the traitors, and addressing Moses, he asked, "Would you like to be impaled alongside these traitors?"

The Saxon was shaken. "What for?"

"For being a traitor! Do you think I am a stupid boy who doesn't know you conspired against me? You are damned traitors . . . and traitors have only one place." He summoned his boyars, shouting, "Impale them!"

"We are the members of the town council," Moses protested. "We are untouchable!"

Dracula looked back at him coldly. "Explain that to the vultures who are going to eat you," he said. "Impale them!"

The threat of horrible punishment was enriched by the fate of those traitors. All the Saxons were more cautious now; they knew they could no longer toy with this ferocious ruler.

To further his governmental agenda and give him more resources to defend himself from his enemies, Dracula promulgated another law: all the commercial activities of all the inhabitants of Wallachia, including the Saxons, were to pay taxes according to the official tax table. However, in each community the Saxons gathered and decided not to pay the tax charged to them, which they considered insulting.

———◆———

So Dracula made a shrewd plan to force them to pay. Knowing it was practically impossible to fight with all the Saxons at once, he decided to create a precedent so they would begin obeying the new law. In the Saxon town of Brasov, where coins were made, Dracula approached a man named Levi, who oversaw the mint. "I want you to mint a coin," Dracula said. "On one side it must show the Wallachian eagle and on the other a dragon."

Levi hesitated and then said, "And if instead of the dragon we put a cross, how do you think it would look?"

"I prefer the dragon, so my people will remember that the coin was minted when Dracula was vovoid. I want them to know that I am a descendant of Dracul, and that our dynasty will always be remembered as the defender of the faith in our God." The men negotiated and agreed upon a price and delivery date, and Dracula departed.

Then, in order to improve his relationship with the powerful men of Wallachia, Dracula wrote a letter to the craftsmen of Brasov, where the coin was being minted:

Saxons of Brasov,

You are honest men, worthy of doing such a delicate job for the State. I consider you sincere friends, and I hope our commercial relationship will be long-lasting.

Signed,
Your friend in everything,
Wladislaus III, Dragwlya

The day of the delivery arrived, and the treasurer paid what had been agreed upon but deducted the taxes. Levi counted the payment twice and then said, "There is money missing!"

"What you consider to be missing," Luga said, "are the taxes you have to pay for your commercial activity."

Levi was furious. "We have never paid taxes!"

Luga shrugged. "From now on you will," he said. "That is my job, and I am going to charge taxes to everybody."

"This is a robbery! We had never paid . . . I refuse!"

"I do not care what you think. Say what you want! Good-bye!"

When they heard Levi's story, the Saxons hurried their plot against Dracula. That ruler had already caused them damage enough.

51

Dracula missed Zalesha terribly, and as he had now recovered his power, he wanted to be with his family. So he sent Ivan to bring them to Tirgoviste.

Following Dracula's directions, Ivan went to the home, where he found Kestywz. "My vovoid ordered you to appear with all your family in Tirgoviste," Ivan said.

Kestywz smiled broadly. "Then, Dracula is fine?"

"He is very well!" answered Ivan, and he repeated Dracula's order: "You shall join me with all your family in Tirgoviste!"

Kestywz was euphoric. "If Dracula invited me to hell itself I would go there gladly!" he exclaimed. Then he looked around at his house, his land, and his animals, and asked wistfully, "What am I going to do with my things?"

The boyar answered with a slight smile. "Are you joking? This is nothing! With Dracula you will have what you have never imagined! Don't you know who he is?"

Kestywz remembered him as an industrious, intelligent, young man . . . but powerful? That was hard to believe. However, he issued an order to his older sons: "Harvest the crops and sell them. We will be waiting for you in Tirgoviste."

The grandmother decided to stay with her grandchildren so she could cook and take care of them. Her good will compensated for her advanced age and slowness; there was no doubt that the old lady felt, and was, very useful.

When they arrived in Tirgoviste, Kestywz and his family were accommodated in the palace. They were not used to this way of living and felt strange amidst all the luxury.

While Ringalya stayed behind with the younger children, Kestywz and Zalesha were taken to where the vovoid was attending to important matters of state. They felt intimidated by all the guards, luxury, and formality. They passed through several huge rooms decorated with great care and good taste before they finally arrived at their destination.

Zalesha could not believe what her eyes were showing her. There was her lover . . . but was he really the same man? This one seemed extremely important and powerful, and his Turkish-style clothes made him somehow mysterious. Kestywz had the same thoughts. The two stood petrified, waiting their turn to be seen.

Dracula was focused on the negotiation of an important deal with some emissaries of Matthias. Then he happened to glance at the door, and when he saw Zalesha, he forgot all about formalities. He jumped from his chair, leaving the emissaries bewildered, and shouted, "Zalesha!"

Zalesha felt her heart would leave her chest. If before she had not cared that her lover was a poor man, now she did not care that he was a rich and powerful one. Letting her feelings guide her, she started running toward him with tears in her eyes. Then they were hugging, and she was crying too hard to say a single word.

Dracula kept saying her name over and over again, as if it were the only name in the world. He still hadn't fathomed that he was not going to be apart from her ever again. Glowing from happiness, he spoke to Kestywz and with his arms wide open exclaimed, "Give me a hug, Father!"

Kestywz was speechless. He could not believe that Dragomyr, the young man who had obeyed his orders without questioning them, was now Dracula, the most powerful man in Wallachia. He knew that the man who had arrived at his house poor, hungry, and humbly dressed was the same as this man—but how different he was!

"Did the cat eat your tongue?" asked Dracula.

Kestywz answered with difficulty. "Forgive me, my lord . . . I do not understand any of this."

"Again! Please don't call me lord. I am Dracula, your relative . . . your son! Did you forget the past?"

"How could I?" Kestywz said. "You asked us to come . . . and here we are"

"Your life is going to change from now on. You and your sons will be my boyars, and your family will be part of my court. I hope you still will grant me Zalesha's hand in matrimony!"

Kestywz turned to his daughter. "Do you want to marry Dracula?"

Zalesha smiled. "He is already my husband; our Lord was our witness. I just want to reconfirm it in front of the altar wearing my white dress. That has been my greatest desire!" She gazed happily at Dracula, saying. "I have prayed for this day to come. I don't want to be apart from you again!"

Without letting go of Zalesha's hand, Dracula said to Kestywz, "We are going to marry in a church, and it will be the most elegant and beautiful wedding Wallachia has ever seen."

Zalesha's cheeks were bathed in tears of excitement.

Dracula looked back at her solemnly. "I am a defender of Jesus Christ," he said, "and my highest ambition is to die defending him." Addressing Kestywz, he asked, "Do you and your sons accept my offer to be boyars, defending the Christian faith and our beloved Wallachia?"

That was more than Kestywz had ever dreamed of. Him, a powerful boyar? And his sons, too? He did not even have to think about it. "We accept!" he said. "And we are eager to die at this moment for our faith!" That is how Kestywz and his sons became part of Dracula's new militia, and how his family became part of the rising court of the powerful vovoid.

Dracula had new boyars who would be faithful to him until death. Now his life was complete. On December 20, 1456, Dracula and Zalesha were married in the most elegant, beautiful wedding Wallachia had ever seen. And from the first day of their union, their married life was like a paradise on earth.

52

Then Dracula sent for Kardotas to be brought with all his family.

Ivan arrived at the home of the peasant and told him, "It is an order of Dracula that you join him with your family in Tirgoviste."

Kardotas, who was an intelligent man, did not think twice. He took his family and his most precious belongings and left his humble home. When they arrived at the palace, he saw that the humble young man who had shown up at his house one day had turned into an elegant man dressed in an expensive, Turkish-style suit. He approached Dracula respectfully, bending one knee and taking his hand as if to kiss it.

Dracula laughed. "Stand up, Kardotas, and treat me like you did the night I met you! Where are your curses? I summoned you to offer you a job of high risk but high rewards: do you and your sons want to be my boyars?"

Kardotas wondered if Dracula was joking; that offer was like the entrance to heaven. He was speechless.

Dracula knew the man and knew he was definitely the most intelligent of all his subjects. "To be a boyar is to join me as a defender of our faith in God," he explained. "Our greatest desire is to die on the battlefield with the name of our God on our lips."

Kardotas' excitement betrayed him, and his eyes filled with tears. He wanted to speak but couldn't, so he nodded his head in affirmation. He couldn't believe his luck, and he said a silent prayer thanking God for the opportunity. He was very happy!

"The horse you gave me when I met you—you cannot imagine how helpful it was," Dracula said. "Now it is my turn to return your courtesy. Please join me." They went to the stables together, where Dracula showed him the most beautiful of his horses and told him, "This animal is all yours!"

Kardotas was astonished; he had never imagined he could have the most beautiful horse in Wallachia. He said humbly, "It is too much, my lord. I cannot take it!"

When Dracula saw his humility, he said, "You are my boyar and you have to obey me. The first order I will give you is this: take this horse. And do not call me lord!"

Kardotas looked at the beautiful horse again, and then he looked back at Dracula. "Thank you!" he said, and then he asked in a whisper, "Can I ride it?"

"It is all yours!" answered Dracula.

Quickly, with a huge smile, Kardotas mounted the fine horse. When he gave it free rein, it was so fast and light he felt like he was riding on thin air.

———◆◇◆———

Dracula summoned many of the men he'd met when he was a fugitive—humble men who had shown him fidelity and courage in adversity. Knowing he could trust them, he appointed them boyars. He had come to value that period of distress; thanks to it he had found reliable people and the kindest, most beautiful, woman in all Wallachia. Now, surrounded by true friends, he saw that all his bitterness, pain, and suffering during those difficult times was worth it. His new boyars were simple but faithful men, and he could rely on them.

When he had gathered an adequate number of boyars, he said, "You do not know how difficult it was for my father, who was forced by the sultan to charge the tribute and punish the peasants who couldn't pay." With a faltering voice, he told them how he had found his father crying alone after the sultan's band of tormenters had gone, how it hurt him when people called him "son of the devil" when his only intention was to protect them. Then Dracula asked for forgiveness for the irreparable damage his father had caused to their families and loved ones. "I know my pain will not repair your sorrow," he said, "but I want you to understand that my father was not evil; he was just trying to avoid war and cause as little damage to Wallachia as possible." He wanted to repeat the same anguished plea over and over again until they understood.

The new boyars could see that he was being sincere. "There is nothing to forgive!" some exclaimed, while others apologized for having thought wrongly of his father. Now that they knew the truth, they felt ashamed by their attitude.

Dracula was heartened by their trust in him. "I am sure that Wallachia is going to change," he said.

53

Since Stanyzkwl encounter with the thief Gjon, his life had changed completely. He had lost his land, his dignity, his honor—everything. Now he had a single obsession: to kill the bastard. He hated Gjon with every fiber of his being. When he found out that Dracula had released Gjon from a prison in Tirgoviste, he traveled there, extremely upset.

Stanyzkwl knew the new law, but like almost all the subjects of Wallachia, he did not trust his ruler. He had heard that the town council had been abolished, but he didn't believe it, and he assumed that by releasing the criminal, Dracula was behaving like yet another puppet of the Saxons. Stanyzkwl's festering hatred now extended to that Turk ruler—he wanted to kill the miserable bastard! However, he could not risk acting on that impulse . . . his family needed him.

It didn't take Stanyzkwl long to locate Gjon on the streets of Tirgoviste. He decided to set a trap for the thief. Making sure he had some witnesses, he approached Gjon to see if the wretch recognized him, but Gjon had stolen from so many people that he did not even know who was who. "Do you have change for this coin?" Stanyzkwl asked him.

The thief immediately smiled and held out his hand, saying, "Yes, of course . . . allow me!" As soon as the coin was in his palm he turned to run, but since Stanyzkwl and his accomplices were expecting that reaction, they grabbed him and took him to Dracula.

Dracula stared at Gjon in silence; he never forgot a face.

"I gave you one last chance to be a good man," he said. "I freed you because you did not know the law, hoping you would reform yourself and not steal again. But now you know the law, so do not call me executioner. I am simply your judge. Due to your own action, you will be impaled on Sunday, after Mass."

Although that was the law imposed on all the inhabitants of Wallachia, Stanyzkwl still could not believe it. He had wanted justice, but with that sentence he was also getting revenge: he was going to watch the man who had ruined his life die slowly and painfully.

Gjon, meanwhile, was screaming and cursing the new governor, but the thief's protests had no more effect than a pig's squeals before it is sacrificed.

Sunday arrived, and the execution was what everyone was talking about. They discussed Gjon's liking for other people's belongings, and how finally, with the help of one of his victims, he had been found and caught in a simple trap. When Mass ended, the drumbeat began at the outskirts of town, and the public square began to fill with busybodies. Up front, near the place of the impalement, there were seats reserved for Stanyzkwl and his family and other victims of the busy criminal.

The routine was the same as always. The traitor was brought in chained in a wooden cage, and the people could see him on his knees, shaking and crying and begging with all his strength, "The blood of Christ was shed for the forgiveness of our sins! I am much repented! Forgive me, Dracula!"

The people he hadn't been affected by his way of living did not care if a pardon was given, but Stanyzkwl was waiting anxiously for Dracula's justice.

Finally everything was ready. When the vovoid appeared, the drum fell silent and he said, "By his actions, this criminal has condemned himself to the punishment all thieves deserve." He briefly paused and then gave the order, loud and clear: "Impale him!"

A scream tore from the criminal's throat, "I swear by my God that I will never steal again!"

Dracula looked at him in silence, and although the square was filled with people, they all fell silent, too; everyone was waiting for the vovoid's pardon. Instead, without changing his imperious tone, he said, "I'll make a better promise. I swear by my God that you will never steal again. And I always keep my promises." Turning to the boyar in charge, he reconfirmed the sentence. "Impale him!"

This time, the order took a little while to be carried out. The boyar in charge seemed baffled and was clumsy at his job. But finally Gjon was pierced and displayed up high. Dracula had applied the law. As he turned to leave, Stanyzkwl knelt down before him, and with tears in his eyes and a faltering voice said, "Forgive me, my lord . . . a thousand times forgive me!"

Dracula frowned in confusion. "Why should I forgive you if you haven't offended me?"

The man was now sobbing openly. "Forgive me for hating you! For not trusting you! Forgive me for having wished you dead with all my heart! You are the fairest and wisest man I know—God bless you! I would give you anything you asked me for . . . but I have only my life."

"Raise your head," Dracula said.

Stanyzkwl obliged, his face bathed in tears, and Dracula saw in his eyes one of the most honest and sincere looks he had ever seen. Acting on instinct, he declared, "I am going to ask for your life!"

Stanyzkwl was stunned. Yes, he had offered his life to Dracula, but now that meant the ruler could impale him! He wanted to flee, but it was impossible.

"You will give your life for the defense of our Christian faith and Wallachia's freedom," Dracula said. "From now on, you will be my boyar."

Stanyzkwl nearly fainted. He, a powerful boyar? He was speechless from excitement. "But I do not know anything about militia!" he finally stammered.

"But you have the attitude and the heart!" Dracula said. "You will learn everything else quickly. The first order I will give you is this: enjoy the impalement of this miserable thief, and I will be waiting for you at the palace." As he walked away, he called over his shoulder, "I repeat—that's an order!"

Stanyzkwl's world had changed in an instant. He never could have imagined that so much pain would bring him that huge reward; he had recovered a lot more than what he had lost. He looked up at Gjon and said, "Thank you! You made me a defender of the faith! I do not hate you anymore, nor do I feel wrath toward you. Now I pity you, and I forgive you for what you did to me. But you earned your punishment . . . you knew you should not steal again. Have a good death!" And with that Stanyzkwl he headed off to the palace.

Dracula summoned the soldier in charge of the impalement and asked him, "Why did it take you so long to carry out my order?"

The boyar looked down at his feet. "My lord, Gjon was the son of my sister Erzherzogin. Although he behaved terribly, my sister loved him very much—after all, she is his mother. But I fulfilled your order."

Dracula thought about the exchange and then summoned Ivan. "Hire a group of mercenaries who are not from Wallachia," he said. "We will call them Vitesji, and we will use them to do the jobs that are difficult for our boyars."

"I do not understand," answered the faithful commander. "All our men are reliable."

Dracula frowned worriedly. "What if we have a revolt one day? I trust in all of you, but it is better to be prepared for anything. Besides, these mercenaries could help us fight the Ottomans."

54

Dracula rode through Tirgoviste and was upset to see Kazymiers, a lame Gypsy, asking for alms. He approached Kazymiers and said, "I told you I wanted to see you working. No one shall beg in Wallachia; begging is a variation of theft!"

"But I am lame!" the beggar complained pitifully.

"You have two strong arms, and I offered you an honorable job helping build my castle of Poenari. You have no dignity!" Turning to one of his boyars, he said, "The law must be applied to him!"

Realizing he was going to be decapitated, Kazymiers began to scream. "I swear I am going to work!" he said. "Please, don't kill me!" But his pleas did not touch the ruler's heart.

The next day at sunrise, the people awoke to the sharp noise of the drum. That could mean just one thing: someone was going to be favored with Dracula's justice. So the people gathered, and the lazy man was brought in a carriage, bound at the hands and feet. When Dracula arrived, the drum and the crowd fell silent. "Kazymiers did not want to work because he is missing a leg," Dracula said. "But in my kingdom, we all work. If someone does not have a job, I will provide one in my castle of Poenari, where there is plenty of work to do, and all the workers receive a fair wage." Looking at the convict he said, "Your actions were your executioner! You wanted to rest? Well, now you will do it for all eternity. You will never work again. That is my promise!" He looked at the boyar in charge. "Apply the law!"

The miserable man started to scream with all his strength. "I swear—I will work without rest! I promise I will never beg again!" Looking at Dracula with tears in his eyes, he began pleading. "For the love of God, forgive me just this one time and I will be the hardest-working man in Wallachia!"

Dracula watched him in silence; all the pleas and promises did not seem to move him.

When Kazymiers saw the soldiers heading for him, he became enraged and began shouting at Dracula. "Damn you, son of the devil!"

One of the soldiers, making a great display of initiative, did not wait for the order: using an ax handle he hit the beggar in the mouth hard enough to knock out most of his teeth. Then some soldiers grabbed the lazy man, who was bleeding profusely, and pushed him down roughly until his head lay on a log. Another soldier swung his ax, and within seconds the head was detached from the body and had rolled away, leaving a trail of blood.

Dracula murmured, "Now, lazy man, rest as long as you want." Then, looking out at his subjects, he declared, "Today is a beautiful day to exalt our beloved Wallachia with our work! Let us exalt it with joy!"

And everyone went about their jobs.

55

As usual, the Saxons of the town of Bristritza were conspiring against Dracula. One, Canain, addressed the others. "We have to weaken the bond between Dracula and Matthias Hunyadi," he said. "We will say Mikhail Szilagyi has robbed us, and we will demand his impalement." They appeared before the vovoid, and Canain said, "Mikhail Szilagyi is a thief! He stole from us, and we demand that your law be applied."

Dracula frowned. He had deep respect and admiration for his brother Dragon. "Can you prove your serious accusation?"

"Of course!" Canain said.

Dracula summoned Mikhail. "Someone has made a serious accusation that you are a thief."

Mikhail was dumbfounded, and his denial was categorical. "I have never stolen anything in my life! Who dares to say such a lie?"

Dracula summoned the Saxons who had accused him, and they repeated their claim in Mikhail's presence. "You are a thief!" Canain shouted at him. "You stole 120 silver coins last month!"

Mikhail was stunned by the attack. "I gave that money to Luga!" he said. Then he took from his papers a receipt for that amount and showed it to Dracula, saying, "I did not steal anything; that money was the taxes these miserable men had to pay for their commercial activity."

When Dracula heard Mikhail's version of the events, he became angry. "Do you dare to sustain this is a theft?" he demanded of Canain.

"Yes!" the Saxon answered boldly. "Taxes are a theft. We have never paid them!"

Dracula raised his eyebrows. "Are you calling me a thief?" he asked. "Where do you want us to get the money to administer our government? And where will we get the resources to defend us from our enemies?"

The Saxon, shaking with anger, shouted, "The product of our work is being stolen from us! *Taxes*? What an elegant way to disguise theft! Besides we do not agree with the way you spend it, building those Orthodox churches and monasteries. We were enraged to learn you are helping pay down the debt of Mount Athos. They are Orthodox!"

Dracula did not need to hear more. "Guards!" he shouted, and the place filled with soldiers. "Arrest these traitors . . . and impale them!" Turning back to the Saxons, he said, "Orthodox or Catholics, we all worship Christ, our God."

Knowing they were all going to die, Abraham answered furiously, "What God? The only true God is Yahweh. You are crazy!"

"You are a Jew?" Dracula asked.

"And I will die as a Jew!" the Saxon answered bravely.

At that moment the Saxon's hypocrisy was revealed. *They said they were Catholics just for convenience,* Dracula thought. *Actually they are Jews.* His hatred was rising toward the descendants of Abraham. Now whenever a Saxon claimed to be Catholic, Dracula wouldn't know if he was telling the truth. "Impale them!" he ordered again.

Amidst tears and complaints, the offenders met their destiny. They knew they were going to die, and they knew if they resisted they would be savagely beaten first. They were taken to the town's entrance and impaled naked, with all the pain, shame, and fear that came with that punishment.

Alive on the stakes, the impaled men wanted to curse the demon who sentenced them. They wanted to kill him. They wanted . . . there were no words for their emotions, and the pain did not allow them to scream. They simply moaned, trying not to move and increase their suffering.

From that day forward, Dracula suspected that most of the Saxons were hypocritical Jews disguised as Catholics. His fear of Jews was growing.

The Saxons who had not spoken out were mute witnesses to Dracula's actions. His boyars burned down the homes of the impaled Saxon leaders, and then they went to the town of Szekler, where, as in the rest of Wallachia, the Saxons were displeased at having to pay taxes. The town was defended by Oswald Zuzgany, who wanted to show King Ladislaus V that he could be useful in his army.

Dracul took Szekler, Oswald fled, and the Saxons who stayed to face Dracula earned the destiny of the traitor: impalement.

56

In 1457, Dracula received a surprise visit from a relative. "Cousin!" Dracula gave a shout of joy and felt his heart begin to pound when he saw the familiar face of Stephen. The men hugged each other hard. "I can't believe it!" Dracula exclaimed. "I am so happy to see you!"

"It is a pleasure to me, too!" answered Stephen, and then he added, "I heard you recovered the throne. I am really glad!"

Dracula smiled. "You cannot imagine all the enemies I have," he said.

The cousins talked for hours, reminiscing, and then Stephen said, "Do you remember our oath?" He held up his palm with the cross-shaped scar.

"How could I forget?" Dracula replied. "The first one of us to get his power back will help the other one recover his, we will always help each other, and there will never be rivalry between us. We swore it with our God as witness."

Stephen said, "I have come to get your help recovering Moldavia."

"I have a lot of enemies around me at the moment," Dracula said again. Then he told Stephen in great detail about each of the contenders to the throne of Wallachia who were trying to overthrow him. "If I am helping you before I appease them," he said, "it is because my God was witness to that oath."

They kept talking until sunset, remembering the hard times, and at the end of the day, before going to sleep, they prayed as they had always done: together, on their knees before their Christ. That old custom was still part of their lives.

Dracula prepared to carry out his promise and organized a battle plan. A few days later, just before sunrise, the soldiers celebrated a brief Mass, and after they all had had Holy Communion, the vovoid stood up in front of his army and shouted, "For Jesus Christ of the Blessed Sacrament!" And the battle began.

When Petru Aron saw the aggressiveness and determination of his enemy, he fled, nearly reaching Poland before he was captured.

Stephen was effusive in his praise of Dracula. "I cannot believe it!" he exclaimed. "You recovered my throne! You are a brave and honorable man, cousin. No one else, having won it, would have handed it over. Thank you!"

"I just kept the oath that I made before God," Dracula said. "Now I must leave immediately. I have many traitors to attend to. Good-bye, Cousin!"

57

Vlad Calugarul the Monk, half-brother of Dracula, was recalling what his mother had told him when he asked her what it meant that he was an illegitimate son of the ruler of Wallachia. "You are a recognized son of Vlad II, the great Dracul," she had reminded him. "Through your veins runs royal blood. One day you are going to inherit your father's power—as long as you respect the Saxons' interests."

Augustine, a Saxon who lived in Amlas, came to the Monk with a proposal: "We have decided to give you our complete support—we will place you in power. But you must immediately reinstate the town council and give us our previous privileges, the same ones your grandfather, your uncle, and your father gave us."

"I promise by my Christ that once I have assumed power, all your petitions shall be granted," Vlad Calugarul replied.

"There is something else you have to do," Augustine said. "Our king, Ladislaus V, is a Catholic, and so you, too, must profess this faith. You have to become a Catholic!"

Vlad Calugarul did not care much about the Orthodox religion; he was simply thirsty for power. So he answered without hesitation. "That's not a problem," he said. "I will be baptized right now."

Augustine nodded his approval. "You will be established in Amlas," he said. "You will receive all our military and economic support, as well as the support of our allies, Dan III and Basarab Laiota."

❖

In the Saxon town of Sibiu, Dan III made a similar pact with the Saxons there, while Basarab Laiota also conspired against Dracula with the support of another group of Saxons.

Therefore in that year Dracula had two foreign enemies. One was the powerful Ottoman Empire, which threatened to destroy the divinity of Christ; and the other was the Holy Roman Emperor Frederick III, who supported Ladislaus V. As professed Catholics, neither Frederick nor Ladislaus allowed the Orthodox Church in their lands, nor did they recognize Wallachia as an independent nation.

In addition, Dracula had three internal enemies: Dan III, Basarab Laiota, and his half-brother, Vlad Calugarul.

After these five enemies was his most dangerous one: the sinister, anonymous, cowardly, and evil men who acted as a treacherous group, always looking for new ways to overthrow Dracula. These were the Saxons, and of all his current enemies, they were the most formidable, because they had the most economic power and because Dracula needed them to help make Wallachia an independent nation. Without their capital, achieving that objective would be almost impossible.

Dracula was a ferocious anti–Semite, and he knew that some of the Saxons were Jews who only claimed to be Catholics. But he remembered his father's advice: he would have to be the chameleon again to defeat this powerful and dangerous enemy. Little by little, with the law in his hands, he would destroy the Saxons and expropriate their wealth for the benefit of his people. He wished that, instead, he could eradicate with a single blow those heretics who considered his God just a prophet.

Fortunately he had already ended his battle with his worst enemies, the ones who were near him, the ones who knew his movements and could kill him at any moment: the treacherous mercenaries and unfaithful boyars. They were dead, still hanging from their stakes as an example for would-be traitors.

58

On September 12, 1457, Dracula happily held his newborn boy in his arms. His son's eyes were as green as his. Showing the baby to his beloved wife, he said proudly, "Tell me, isn't he a little doll?"

Zalesha smiled. "He looks a lot like you. He is beautiful!"

"We will call him Minhea, like his great grandfather," Dracula said. "He will also be Minhea the Great. What do you think?"

"Whatever you do is fine with me," she said. "You know my greatest joy is to see you happy."

Time passed pleasantly for Dracula. He spent all his free time playing with his son. At night he told the boy the same stories his own father had told him. The boy would listen until he fell asleep, a placid smile on his face.

Dracula's sexual nature was in keeping with his character, and his wife was always willing to enjoy the highest pleasure God had given them in this life. Their relationship could not have been better. He was always thinking about Zalesha and she was always waiting for him, and they considered their stable marriage another precious gift from God.

59

In an Orthodox Church in Tirgoviste, the most important people of the region gathered. The powerful Dracula, highest pontiff of the Orthodox Church in Wallachia, was dressed in a ceremonial suit, prepared to appoint the metropolitan. This honorable and noble charge would be received by a humble monk whose highest ambition had been to lead his small monastery.

In a ceremony enlivened by beautiful Gregorian chants, Brother Barbat was appointed metropolitan. Barbat vividly recalled his first impression of that strange Ottoman. He had never imagined at first that Dracula would turn out to be the most pious Christian he had ever known. He remembered how he had defended Dracula, hiding him and rejecting the bribe to turn him in, and he thanked God for having crossed paths with him.

Dracula was happily remembering the same. *Of all the monks I have known,* he thought, *Barbat is the holiest, and the one who most deserves this great privilege.*

Then he appointed the most important ecclesiastical authorities. In this way the Orthodox clergy of Wallachia felt kinship and responsibility to the pious Dracula, while the Catholic monks became jealous, resenting the obvious preference of their ruler.

60

On November 23, 1457, King Ladislaus V shamelessly unveiled a portrait of himself showing off his beautiful golden locks and effeminate good looks. The next day he did not wake up. He had been poisoned.

Shortly afterwards, there was a meeting of the three bishops and four archdukes who were part of the clique previously called the town council of Hungary. Their objective was to defend the interests of the powerful men they represented through the appointment of a new king. They carefully considered the possible successors to Hungary's crown, analyzing the candidates one by one.

"We must be careful and take our time," Swerige warned. "Remember that when we placed Sigismund on the throne, once he became king he ignored us. We had to wait a long time for him to die."

Iactu sighed. "I wish everyone were like Ladislaus. He was docile and very compliant."

"But a sodomite," Brantowky reminded him.

They kept analyzing the candidates, and when they got to Matthias Hunyadi, everyone agreed that the timid character of the adolescent—he was barely sixteen—made him the perfect choice. Surely they would control him as they pleased! Until Matthias arrived at the ruling age, they appointed an Italian regent named Benfini, whose obedience to their interest had been tested beforehand. They did not need to keep looking; it was the perfect combination.

They planned a strategy to justify to the people their appointments of these puppets. They began to advertise the incredible Matthias, who was wise, fair, and honest. They said that at night he went out dressed as a beggar and gave gold coins to the poor. He would punish the bad governors, they said, and was highly educated: he spoke Latin, Croatian,

Hungarian, German, and Czechoslovakian. What an amazing teenager, to have all those virtues!

On January 20, 1458, Matthias was declared king of Hungary and a regency of Italian counselors was appointed, led by Antonio Benfini. This regency had a decisive role in the history of Hungary, as it was influenced by the most talented artists and creative men of that time, the Italians. Benfini established a library surpassed only by the one at the Vatican; it was known as the Corvian Library, and of course all the effort and work of Benfini was ascribed to the teenager, Matthias Hunyadi.

One day King Matthias Hunyadi went out hunting and his royal ring fell off his hand. A crow saw it and quickly swooped down and snatched it. Matthias chased the bird, and after many vicissitudes he recovered the ring. As he thought about what that crow had made him go through, some questions came to his mind: *How could a small animal like that be so smart? How could a simple crow demand all the attention of a powerful king? How could an insignificant bird make a king think and sharpen his mind?* He kept asking himself questions and thinking so much about the answers that he ended up attributing exceptional qualities to the crow and adopting it as a symbol on his heraldic coat of arms. Before long he identified himself with the smart animal, and since in Latin the word *crow* is "corvus," he decided to change his last name of Hunyadi to Corvinus. It did not bother him to disown the last name of his heroic father just to pay tribute to that talented little animal; and perhaps on that time, something inside the Corvinus head think as an animal

61

Dracula had both internal and external enemies, and it was impossible to fight them all at once. Therefore while he attended to some with the sharp edge of his sword, others he treated with diplomacy to see if they would reform their behavior and abandon their intentions to overthrow him, but they only responded with mockery and rejection. He kept sending emissaries with goodwill offers, inviting them to join forces with the army of Wallachia to fight the real enemy, the Ottoman Turks; he offered to forget any old quarrels and issues between them, promising before God that if they joined his army there would be no retaliation.

The answers were always the same: rude rejections and cowardly derision.

The priests and monks of the Catholic Church, as good medieval politicians, had their favored party: Holy Roman Emperor Frederick III, the recently elected Matthias Corvinus, and the opportunistic and hypocritical Saxons, who now supported King Matthias after having attacked him with all the strength of their miserable beings

The Catholic and Orthodox Churches had not reconciled their dogmatic differences, having as an excuse their quarrel about the origin of the Holy Spirit. But their differing interests went beyond the ecclesiastical orthodoxy. Both churches sought, through different actions, enough money to provide their ministers and leaders a carefree life. This fact was noted by many ferocious critics of the time, who were of course considered heretics for making such observations.

The Catholic Church was accepted and respected by Dracula in Wallachia. He was a knight of the Order of the Dragon and a subject of King Matthias Corvinus, who promoted, supported, and professed the Catholic faith. So if the Orthodox Church flourished, it was by the decision of Wallachia's strong vovoid.

However, the Catholic clergy supported the sinister Saxons, the hidden enemies of Dracula, who had a habit of giving huge tithes and profitable alms. The clergy were also jealous of the vovoid's open and brave preference for their Orthodox rivals.

The treacherous Saxons did not want to pay the vovoid's taxes, but they paid the tithe without regretting it and were generous with their alms to avoid problems with the Holy Father and his feared tribunal defender of the faith, the Holy Inquisition.

While the Orthodox Church—90 percent of the population—survived by the good will of the humble peasants and the support of Dracula as their guide and shepherd, the Catholic Church flourished, having enough money to satisfy its needs and squander what was left on luxuries, after sending the corresponding amount to the Vicar of Christ on Earth.

It was not difficult to see that, even though the Catholics accepted Dracula due to his great power, they quietly considered him a heretic whom they had no other choice but to tolerate.

A select group of Catholic bishops met with King Matthias Corvinus and demanded action. "You must force Dracula to turn into a Catholic!" the leader of the group said. "The Holy Scriptures state it clearly: no one can serve two masters. Force him to change. He and his people must be Catholics!"

Matthias, who was docile and easy to manage, immediately called his subject. "I am getting a lot of pressure by the Holy Roman Emperor Frederick II and the Holy Father in the Vatican. I can accept no excuses: you and all your people must become Catholics and renounce your Orthodox faith immediately. And that," he said imperiously, "is an order!"

That order made Dracula feel like he'd been struck by lightning. He wanted to take out his dragon dagger and pierce that little king, who was made of the same material he was and just stared at him in silence.

Matthias was expecting an affirmative answer but instead received a great silence that stretched out so long he felt like he was in an abandoned crypt. Finally, after another long space of time, Dracula took a deep breath and answered, "I love, worship, and respect my God." He drew his sword, took it in both hands, and pointed it to the sky, saying, "The Orthodox Church worships the same God as the Catholic Church, and no one is going to take away from me the beliefs that my father instilled in me! I grew up among Ottomans, with everyone around me professing faith to a savage god, but in my heart there was only room for the real one. And now you ask me to turn to Catholicism? I will tell you this: one day, back when only your mother, your uncle, and your brother supported you, I had the chance to consolidate my power by making an alliance with the emperor. I didn't do it because I knew that if I supported you, someday you would be my king, and I could ask you to give me the freedom to profess the doctrine my father instilled in me. If my Orthodox faith and actions are not defending the same God as yours, not only will I renounce my religion, but I also will renounce my life! I was born Orthodox . . . and I will die Orthodox!" Saying this he turned his sword on its side and handed it to the young king. Then he knelt down before him, exposing his neck. "I prefer to be dead than to be a Catholic!"

Matthias was speechless; the faith of that Christian was great! There was no doubt that what his father had told him was true: Dracula was an exceptional man. Matthias was starting to understand why his father had admired him so much. Without further arguments he said, "Dracula, continue with your beliefs and the defense of your faith in our Christ." Then they dined together, and the next day Dracula went back to Wallachia; there were still many traitors to attend to.

62

Life in Wallachia with the new vovoid was different. For the first time, the townspeople felt they were respected by the boyars, who in the past had always abused their power. They also were free from harassment by the Saxons, who as members of the now-defunct town council were always stepping on their rights and stealing the fruit of their work.

It wasn't long before the boyar in charge of the prison paid a visit to the vovoid. "Lord, the jail is empty," he reported. "I am bored without work. It has been a long time since a crime was reported in Wallachia."

One day Dracula summoned Kestywz to discuss a new plan. "Father," he said, "I cannot move you from your commander position, because I have great confidence in you and your work, and I need you. But I want you to organize the farmers and advise them on how to improve their crops so that the crops grown in Wallachia satisfy the demands of the entire region. Do not let all of them plant cotton; make sure there is a variety of crops grown. And don't stop there: travel around and organize Wallachia's agriculture system based on your own experience until it is working as it should. Then, when you are done, come back to me."

Kestywz was pleased. "Do not worry, Son. I'll take care of this, I promise you. Wallachia will never have problems feeding its people again." He traveled among the peasants, giving each farmer advice about what seeds to sow according to a master plan. As a result, Wallachia and its farmers were protected by a new agricultural prosperity.

As life began to flourish in Wallachia, Dracula decided it was a good time to face his half-brother, Vlad Calugarul the Monk. The treacherous Saxons of Sibiu, including Jared the gunsmith and his wealthy partners, supported the Monk with money, weapons, and anything else he needed.

Dracula sent a spy to follow the Monk. A few weeks later the spy returned with troubling news: "Your half-brother, Vlad Calugarul, has hired mercenaries, among which is Albu Cel Mare, (Albu the Kingmaker). He has the support of the Saxons, mainly the ones from Amlas."

———◆≈◆———

In April 1458, with a keen wit, good intelligence, and the right military strategy, Dracula attacked the Saxon town of Brasov. When the rebels saw that he was going to capture them, they ran off, terrified. In the process, Vlad Calugarul, Albu Cel Mare, and a considerable number of boyars and mercenaries escaped.

Dracula and his men pursued them to Sibiu, where he sought out his trusted friend and main ally on the side of the Saxons, the talented Master Jared, who when he saw Dracula, stuttered, "really nice to see you!" The gunsmith then hugged him with extreme effusiveness but also a certain nervousness. There was definitely something strange in his attitude, voice, and look.

"I am chasing my half-brother, Vlad the Monk. Have you seen him around here?"

"With so much work it is impossible to me to know who comes and who goes," Jared said anxiously, and then his face brightened. "Let me show you the improvements we have made in our armaments! These muskets have much more reach and precision. You can take some!" he added.

The faithful Dracul was now grown. Wagging its tail energetically, it did not leave Master Jared's side. The gunsmith, meanwhile, did not miss an opportunity to call the dog by its name, hoping to strengthen his relationship with the powerful son of the late governor.

It was their custom when Dracula visited to enjoy a fine meal, and then, after they finished, Dracula would go to the kitchen and compliment the cooks for their excellent seasoning. The cooks were always smiling, polite, and kind, and they greatly appreciated it when important clients took the time to recognize their good work.

This time, however, when Dracula noticed Jared's odd behavior, he got a strange hunch. He went to the kitchen as the meal was being prepared, and there he found that the cooks were quiet and a little nervous. Speaking to the main cook, he asked, "Does the stew taste good?"

The Saxon blushed slightly, and without answering the question, he took some of the stew with a spoon and offered it to Dracula, who waved it away with a smile and said, "You taste it. See if it has enough salt!"

The cook put the bite in his mouth but did not swallow it; he just nodded vigorously, eyebrows raised, and turned around and left the room. Once out of Dracula's line of sight, he discreetly spit the soup out into his apron.

To Dracula, the cook's attitude spoke for itself. He took the spoon again and put it back into the pot, saying, "This looks delicious!" As he brought the spoon to his mouth, he spilled it on the floor near Dracul. The dog rushed toward the spot to enjoy the unexpected treat, but Jared gave it a strong kick, saying, "Get out, filthy dog! Don't be so voracious, Dracul!" But the dog ran right back and managed to devour the spilled food despite the maneuverings of its master, who looked worried.

Dracula did not need to see more. He took another spoonful of stew from other pot and offered it to the little animal, saying, "Poor thing! Take this, Dracul. Eat this stew and tell me if it is delicious."

Jared laughed nervously. "Dogs can't talk . . . you are joking, right? How is it going to tell you if it liked it or not?" This time, Dracula noticed, Jared did not kick the dog away but watched as it lapped up the stew. When it finished it wagged its tail and looked up at Dracula, waiting for the next bite.

Then Dracula put the spoon back into the first pot, and the gunsmith said, "Do not give any more food to that filthy dog! It is never satisfied!"

Dracula obliged, having reconfirmed his suspicions. At the first opportunity he pulled Ivan aside. "No one should start eating until I do it, and everyone will do exactly as I do." Staring into Ivan's eyes, he said, "This, Ivan, is an order. The one who does not obey will be impaled!"

The commander could not understand that strange order. Why would Dracula impale his beloved boyars if he loved them like brothers? But Ivan was used to obeying without questioning, so he communicated the strict order to the boyars, who were furious; they wanted to eat already.

The guests sat down to eat. At the center of the table were the host and Dracula, to the left of the vovoid sat his hungry boyars, and to the right of the gunsmith were his sinister Saxon partners.

The smell was irresistible, and the boyars' appetite was ferocious. They could not understand why the vovoid had issued such a strange and ridiculous order, and some of them were tempted to eat a few bites on the sly, but they knew not to mess with Dracula. They imagined themselves paying the price for their disobedience; when they remembered the unbearable pain of impalement, they decided to bear the unbearable hunger instead. But deep inside they wanted to attack their leader for being such a tyrant. Some of them were so hungry they felt faint.

Dracula was watching everything carefully. The atmosphere felt tense. Dracul, the dynamic dog which did not leave his master's side, began to seem calmer than usual. The cooks served dinner, and as Dracula had assumed they would, they placed the poisoned stew near the hungry and desperate visitors, and the other pot near the plates of the Saxons.

Dracula took up his spoon with his right hand and held it near his plate. He then looked at his boyars. Every one of them did the same. (Costea wanted to kill him, and he was the only man brave enough to eat on the sly—but in that position, how could he?) Dracula waited patiently for the Saxons to start eating, and when they did, he looked at his boyars as if he were giving them an order. Then he took the plate of Master Jared and exchanged it for his own, to the amazement of the host. The boyars did the same, exchanging their plates for the Saxons', and prepared to eat.

The Saxons were terrified. Who had discovered their plot, which they had planned with a lot of care and secrecy with Vlad Calugarul? There was no doubt . . . Dracula was a demon!

The boyars served themselves more untainted stew and ate until they were full. Now there was no doubt in anyone's mind that one pot was poisoned. Since the Saxons had not even tasted their food, Dracula took it upon himself to summon the servants, instructing them to pick up the untouched plates and offer them to Jared's children and other children who were there. "Have some," Dracula said warmly. "This food is delicious!"

When the hungry children were about to start eating, Jared could no longer take it: from his throat came the desperate scream, "No! The food is poisoned!"

Now the Saxons were wishing they had eaten the poisoned food, as their death would have been less painful than the one that they could expect as traitors. But it was too late.

"Make these miserable men confess," Dracula said to Costea. "I want them to remember everything, even the day they were born!"

Costea did that very well. The traitors were chained and taken to the dungeons for interrogation. The faithful Dracul could not get up and died from the poison it had eaten.

Without asking any questions, Costea pulled two nails from Jared's fingers, and that was enough. The traitor screamed in pain. "Stop! We planned this plot with the Monk! That is it!"

Costea pulled another nail and made him a solemn promise: "Every time you stop talking, I will pull out another one. And when they are all gone, I will take your fingers one by one. Then I will cut out your tongue, and when I take out your teeth one by one you are going to beg me to kill you, I wonder how you would look without ears and a nose?" Then he shouted, "If you do not talk soon and tell me everything, I am even going to take out your eyes!"

The Saxon, crying and trembling, said in a faltering voice, "I am not going to stop! Please don't torture me! Here in Brasov, Amlas and Fagaras built some hideouts behind the chimneys in the building of the town council. There is enough food and water for someone to remain there for several days. They have a secret door, and it opens by moving a lever hidden on a high shelf, just like that one. We also sold the Ottoman sultan the secret alloy to make the great cannon, the one they used to take Constantinople. We sent part of that money to Germany, and what we have here is hidden in the vault of the town council building. And that's it! I swear to you I do not know anything else! Please do not cut me into pieces!"

When Costea told Dracula everything that Jared had told him, Dracula stormed into the room where Jared was being held. "Why in hell did you sell the secret of the great cannon to the sultan?" he screamed. "That belonged to the people of Wallachia! They gave you the money to develop that weapon! Do you know what you did? Damned traitors—because of you, our Lord Jesus Christ was divested of his divinity in Constantinople!"

Jared began trying to justify his actions. "My partners and I saw the opportunity to become immensely rich—the sultan paid us thirty thousand gold coins. You would have done the same!"

"I wouldn't have stolen! That secret was not yours!" Dracula shouted furiously.

The Saxon added, "At that time your family was not in power, and we saw the opportunity to sell it."

"You're not just thieves, you are traitors! And you chose your destiny." He nodded to Costea, "Impale them!"

"For the love of God, do not do it, Dracula! We promise to support you and always to be faithful, but please, do not impale us!"

Dracula then addressed Luga. "Expropriate the wealth of these miserable men," he said, and looking back at Costea he said, "Start the impalement tomorrow at sunrise!"

The pleas, the crying, and the manifestations of extreme pain did not move the vovoid.

The next day at sunrise, the church bells in the town of Sibiu pealed, joined by the sharp noise of the drum. The town's inhabitants were curious to witness the justice Dracula was going to apply there. When everyone had gathered, he spoke. "These Saxons did not just betray me. They also betrayed you, because they used your taxes to pay for the development of the secret technology of the great cannon, and then they sold that secret to our enemy, the Ottoman sultan, without caring that because of their treasonous action Constantinople fell at the hands of the infidel. These damned Jews sold Christ again—this time for thirty thousand gold coins! This time they also betrayed our God! Thanks to them, our Christ is not God in that place—this is unthinkable!" Looking at the offenders, he said, "You are going to die as you chose by your actions. The punishment you will receive will be the most painful I know; if there was another, greater, punishment, I would definitely use it. I know that taking your miserable lives through your well-deserved punishment is not going to restore the damage you have done, but at least we will enjoy watching you die slowly." Looking at Costea, he said, "Impale them!"

The vice-governor, Nicholas of Ocna, could not believe it: he was going to be impaled along with his wife, who also had been an accomplice of the traitor. They were supposed to be untouchable! And yet the process started. They began with five traitors, each attended by a group of soldiers who carried out their job efficiently and carefully. Blows to the traitors' bodies were very helpful in convincing the main guests to cooperate. Undressing the traitors to humiliate them was another part of the routine.

The inhabitants were watching, both horrified and satisfied to see those traitors on their stakes. The Saxon traitors who had not been identified were frightened and wanted to ask for help overthrowing Dracula. They would support Dan III, Basarab Laiota, or Vlad Calugarul, offering all their resources to rid themselves of that damned demon. In the meantime, they had to content themselves with hating that son of Lucifer and telling themselves, *Things cannot stay like this!*

63

Dracula's spies informed him that Vlad Calugarul was heading to Brasov, so the vovoid followed the Monk like a wolf stalking its prey. He had to end that enemy who, despite being his half-brother, wanted to overthrow him. Dracula and his boyars passed through Fagaras, but that was not their objective. They finally arrived at their destination and the same story repeated itself, with the exact same results. In the building of the abolished town council they found the secret room that was the Monk's hideout, but it was already empty. Vlad Calugarul and Albu Cel Mare had escaped again, with a handful of mercenaries and boyars. The apprehension, trial, and impalement of the Saxons who had supported the fugitives was similar to the scene in Sibiu.

In Amlas, the vovoid summoned the local Saxons and their wives. Many of them had managed to hide in time. Dracula asked the others, "Where is the Monk?"

They looked at each other in silence, and the Saxon Naggai answered with a trembling voice, "We don't know."

Dracula looked at Naggai. "Why are you shaking?" he asked. Then, addressing them all, he said, "You are traitors! But if you tell me where he is, I am going to reward you with decapitation . . . I am feeling especially magnanimous today."

Absolute silence was the resounding answer.

"Fine," he said. "You chose your destiny." He activated the secret lever and the door opened; there were the Monk and his henchmen. Seeing the numeric superiority of their enemies, they handed in their weapons and were immediately apprehended and chained.

Again Dracula addressed the traitors. "You chose your destiny," he said, and then shouted to his men, "Impale them! And let me speak with the Monk." The order was carried out, and when he was alone with his half-brother, he remembered the little blonde boy he'd seen running after a chick, and how his father had lifted the boy in his arms and given him a tender kiss. At the time, witnessing that scene had hurt Dracula and Mircea. Now, however, it occurred to him that the human being in front of him had the same blood and worshiped the same God as he did. Looking him in the eye, he asked, "Why did you turn to Catholicism if our father instilled in us the Orthodox faith?"

The Monk knew that he was a traitor and his destiny was impalement; as he was going to die anyway, he did not answer.

"It is difficult for me to order your impalement," Dracula said. "You are my half-brother—I cannot kill you. Just answer me. Why did you never respond to the letters I sent you to join to my fight?"

Again, absolute silence was the answer to his question. Dracula stared at him for a few moments and finally stood up. "Do you like to be in silence? I am going to please you!" He turned around and left.

The next day the inhabitants of Amlas witnessed a show similar to those in the other towns, the miserable bodies of the traitors serving as macabre decorations at the entrance to the town square.

Dracula arrived at the monastery of Tismana and said to the abbot, "Father, this is my half-brother. Please give him lodging, feed him only what's necessary, and do not let him be a victim of idleness. Do not speak a word to him; just give him orders that he must obey blindly. He is going to remain here in complete silence until his death."

Feeling powerless and very frightened, the Monk began to protest. "That is not fair!"

"Look, you do talk! And I was starting to believe you were mute. Too late, Vlad. Now, do not say a word!" Dracula turned away from his half-brother and addressed the abbot. "For every word he speaks or every order he disobeys, you will put him in the dungeon for one day. Leave him there and do not feed him. He has already spoken four words, which is four days locked up and without food."

The Monk wanted to complain, but he knew his half-brother had had the last word. His martyrdom was starting, and he would spend it in a silence that was going to torment him beyond his imagination.

Dracula looked for Caltuna, the mother of the Monk, and said to one of his boyars, "Take her to the monastery of Tismana and tell the abbot that she is the mother of my half-brother, that she also will be taking a vow of silence, with the same punishment when she speaks. Tell the abbot that we do not want her to be a victim of idleness either, and that by no means should there be any speech between them."

The abbot received Dracula's envoy, who said, "My lord orders that the mother of his half-brother receive the same treatment, and that there be no speech between them for any reason."

The abbot, addressing Caltuna, said, "From now on we will call you Mother Eupraxia. You, like your son, will do cleaning work at the monastery. Every time you say a word or disobey an order, we will put you in the dungeon for one day without food. Your first order is to clean the excrement out of the latrines."

Caltuna wanted to defend herself. Why had that damned monk changed her name without asking her? Who had authorized him to give her that stupid, horrible name? She knew that it would cost her to defend herself, but already her liver was involuntarily sending poison to the rest of her body. Over time, her profound dissatisfaction every time she heard that damned name turned her life into a real hell. And those miserable monks managed to say that name all day, giving her orders that forced her to hold her fury inside her, gritting her teeth and praying for obedience, while endlessly cursing in silence her new and fatuous jailers.

I have already defeated three of my enemies: Vladislav II, my traitor boyars and mercenaries, and my half-brother, the Monk, Dracula thought. *Now I have to focus my attention on Basarab Laiota.*

64

In May 1458, King Matthias Corvinus was visited by a group of Saxons. One of them, Matatias, addressed the king, saying, "We are the productive strength of Wallachia and hold its economic capital, and do you know how Dracula treats us? He impales us without mercy and charges us taxes—surely because we are Catholics! And since he appointed himself highest pontiff of the Orthodox Church in Wallachia, he mocks us by building monasteries and Orthodox churches with the taxes he forces us to pay. Besides, he is sending money to pay the debt of Mount Athos to the Ottomans, and that place is Orthodox. It's not fair! You are the king, you are Catholic, and only you can stop this damned heretic, who is killing us and robbing us without mercy. If he keeps acting that way, we are going to return to Germany!"

Another Saxon, Joseph, added, "You must intervene; we are frightened! Dracula is a demon who is determined to end us. He has even dared to impale our wives!"

Matthias listened while the Saxons continued to complain. Finally, when they stopped, he said, "I promise you that I will speak with him immediately."

The king of Hungary received Dracula in his palace, where the two allies talked. Finally Matthias asked Dracula, "I have had many complaints that you are brutally impaling innocent Saxons throughout all Wallachia, and that you are charging them taxes. Why are you doing this?"

"I abolished the town council and expropriated their immense wealth for the benefit of Wallachia, because those bastards had oppressed the population, charging them arbitrarily—whatever they wanted for any reason that pleased them. They took the peasants' property whenever they wanted to without giving them any explanation. And besides, they sold justice. They charged fines to rapists, thieves, and murderers, and then freed them without caring about the victims who were crying out for justice. Now they are furious because I am making them pay taxes for their commercial activity . . . and, yes, I have impaled many of them for being traitors. But I am making my law effective. They tried to poison me in Sibiu and so I impaled them, just as I impaled the Saxons who supported my enemies. All my actions toward them are based on the same law I have established for all the inhabitants of Wallachia."

Matthias asked with morbid interest, "Don't you think it is an extreme punishment to impale murderers, rapists, thieves, and traitors, and decapitate lazy men?"

Dracula replied, "If a thief is not stopped decisively, whenever he feels hungry, cold, or thirsty he will take what doesn't belong to him over and over again. To him, 'other people's belongings' means 'mine,' and the word *work* is an insult, something he wasn't born to do, I assure you, we all work in Wallachia, and we all have food, a roof over our head, and a good salary. I can assure you that there are no thieves or lazy men in Wallachia; you can walk around peacefully there and no one will try to kill you. Everyone is going to respect you. The concepts of robbery, murder, and rape do not fit into the minds of the Wallachians; they know that satisfying their greed, rage, or lust is not worth the punishment. As a result, our jails are empty. And as far as traitors go . . . do you know how many enemies we are facing, Matthias, inside and out of Wallachia? They are a swarm, and we have to kill them one by one. Let me ask you something: do you think that because we order them not to betray us, because that is against the law, they are going to obey us like gentle lambs just because we ask them kindly? No! Like the thieves, the rapists, and the murderers, they only understand terror and shame. I have eliminated most of my internal enemies; the only ones missing are Dan III and Basarab Laiota. Then we will continue with the Ottoman Turks, who are our greatest external enemies. I cannot act freely knowing that those miserable men want to kill me and can. If I face the Ottomans now, they can make a coup d'état

"I invited our internal enemies to join us to fight against the Turks, and they laughed at me and answered me with ridicule and insults. So do not ask me to treat them like friends; they are enemies and must be eliminated! Tell me how you treat your enemies. Do you give them advice? No, you treat them like what they are! Remember how Ladislaus V treated your brother, Laszlo? Did he think twice before cutting off his head? And you were next! Thanks to God our allies rescued you in time! Do not let those traitor Saxons influence you. They are behind all this because they do not want to pay taxes. Besides, most of them are hypocritical Jews who just pretend to be Catholics. We cannot treat them as if they were good citizens. Unfortunately they have money and hold the productive power in Wallachia, so we cannot kill them all. But I recommend that you not listen to them; those who came to you are definitely traitors who are afraid because they know that sooner or later they will end up with a stake piercing their bodies."

Matthias was not like his father; to him the Jews were not criminals. He proposed a compromise. "Let us have a negotiation in which each of you gives in to something. That way we will arrive at an agreement."

Dracula frowned. "Negotiate with the Saxons? Give in and recognize their authority? This, Matthias, cannot be negotiated! However, with the intention of coming to an agreement, I accept your decision, as long as Dan III and Basarab Laiota are not protected for any reason."

Matthias was silent for a moment and then said, "I am going to think about a negotiation to reconcile these interests. In the meantime, I exonerate you from any responsibility."

65

In June 1458, King Matthias Corvinus said to Mikhail Szilagyi, "There are big problems between Dracula and the Saxons of Wallachia. You have an excellent relationship with the vovoid, and I know that with your intervention we can make a negotiation that he will accept."

Mikhail shook his head worriedly. "Conciliation on either side is practically impossible," he said. "The Saxons do not to pay taxes for any reason, and Dracula needs to charge them taxes to keep the government running well."

But the king just shrugged and passed the problem to his uncle. "I do not know how you are going to do it, but your mission is to come to an agreement with the Saxons. Make them yield in some way; just don't accept any deal that protects Dan III or Basarab Laiota. Then we'll figure out how to make Dracula accept it."

In Brasov the atmosphere was tenser than anyone could have imagined. The Saxons remembered with hatred and resentment how because of that damned negotiator, Dracula had impaled their brother Saxons of Bristritza. However, they had no other choice but to negotiate.

Mikhail Szilagyi appealed to their reason, saying, "I have to return to Hungary with a signed treaty regarding your conflict of interest with Dracula."

But the Saxon David began arguing immediately. "We need to be released from paying the unfair taxes, and we want to remove Dracula and put Dan III, Basarab Laiota, or Vlad Calugarul in his place. We will accept any of them as vovoid of Wallachia . . . they are all Catholics."

Szilagyi had already been informed by Dracula about the hypocritical stance of those pseudo-Catholics. He was silent for a while, and then, obviously upset, he took a deep breath and replied, "Where do you want to get the money to pay the army and the activities of the government of Wallachia? Do you want in power traitors like Dan III, Basarab Laiota, or Vlad Calugarul, who although they call themselves Catholics, make voluntary pacts with the Ottomans? No! What you ask for is definitively impossible!"

The Saxon Enoch said, "We have already explained this to the point of exhaustion: the ones who pay taxes are the peasants! Is that so difficult to understand? Our income is tax exempt! Besides, part of that tax money helps Dracula build Orthodox monasteries and churches and pay the debt of Mount Athos. We are Catholics, so that is heresy!"

Knowing that it was useless to argue with hypocrites who would never accept reason, Szilagyi looked them in the eye and said in a determined voice, "I did not come here to argue about religion. I came to make a pact. I want to know why you refuse to pay taxes if you live in Wallachia and your wealth has come from here."

The Saxons were furious. They could see that Dracula and Mikhail were strangely similar; they seemed to be cut from the same cloth. The Saxons felt that they were swimming against the current. "This negotiation is over," Enoch said drily.

"Is that what you want?" Mikhail shouted. "Then when Dracula comes and you have more issues with him, do not go crying to King Matthias, because he is not going to help you. You're not behaving like adults! If you want me to leave, I'll leave, but let me be clear: the king was willing to fix this conflict. If you don't wish to arrive at an agreement, that is your responsibility!"

After hearing Mikhail's impassioned argument, the Saxons changed their attitude and agreed to the following provisions: First, they would pay taxes on the products they sold in Brasov. Second, they would have the freedom to trade their products, and by paying taxes they wouldn't have to pay duties. Third, they would not support another candidate to unseat Dracula as vovoid in Wallachia. The agreement was signed by Mikhail Szilagyi and, reluctantly, by the Saxons.

Mikhail delivered the treaty to his king, who in turn delivered it to the messenger Benedict of Bothar. "You must take this to Dracula and convince him to accept it," the king said. "Tell him Mikhail Szilagyi made the negotiation."

Dracula read the agreement in silence. Finally he said, "These Saxons always get their way . . . but they'll see where that gets them!" He wrote a brief letter and then called to his envoy. "Give this to my king," he said.

Some time latter, the governor of Hungary read Dracula's response:

> My King Matthias,
>
> I accept the decision and support the negotiation made by my lord Mikhail Szilagyi. I do not agree with the attitude of the Saxons. As long as they do not betray us I am going to respect the agreement . . . but their attitude will have serious consequences.
>
> 1458 Year of our Lord Jesus Christ
>
> Signed,
> Wladislaus III, Dragwlya

Meanwhile Dracula said to Luga, "I want you to develop a system of trade between the peasants. They are the ones who know how to make the products; they just need us to support them with some capital. So we are going to lend them economic resources." And that is how vigorous commercial activity started to develop in Wallachia, creating strong competition against the Saxons by offering much lower prices for similar products—and, of course, bringing in the corresponding taxes.

66

When a group of Saxons from Germany arrived to sell their products in Wallachia, Luga contacted Shem, their Saxon representative. "You must pay the corresponding tax of two gold coins for your economic activity," he said.

The Saxon was livid. "We have never paid taxes before, and we are not going to pay them now."

Luga told Dracula about the encounter. "The Saxons who came from Germany refuse to pay the tax," he said. "They're threatening to complain to the king."

So Dracula visited Shem himself. "You were charged two gold coins for your commercial activity and you refused to pay," he said. "As a result, I had to get involved, so now the tax is double. You must pay four gold coins immediately."

"This is robbery!" the enraged merchant protested.

"Are you calling me a thief?" the vovoid asked quietly, staring steadily at him.

Shem stood frozen. He knew that insulting the powerful ruler was more dangerous than playing with death. In a quavering voice he said, "Forgive me, my lord . . . I would never say you are a thief." As he spoke he produced four gold coins and offered them to the vovoid.

Without breaking his stare, Dracula shouted, "If you want to sell in Wallachia, you have to pay the tax that I charge you! If you do not like it, go away! We do not need you!"

On his way back to Germany, Shem stopped to see King Matthias and make his complaint. "We went peacefully to sell our products to Wallachia, and Dracula stole four gold coins from us with the excuse of charging us taxes. He almost impaled us! For a second I thought it was the end of us!"

"My subject is violent but very fair," Matthias explained. "As long as you do not steal, kill, rape, or betray us, you have nothing to fear. If I were you, I would seek a new market for your products. If you want to sell in Wallachia, you must pay the tax Dracula charges you."

The Saxon left, disappointed. He had expected the king to support him, but now he saw that between Matthias and Dracula there was a powerful alliance.

———◆———

Not long afterwards, Matthias received another visit from a group of Saxons—this one led by a foul-tempered man named Kennan. In a voice shaking with rage, the Saxon said, "In Wallachia, Dracula allows any peasant to fabricate products that before, only we made! That is retaliation against the treaty we negotiated with Mikhail Szilagyi. He also keeps charging his unfair taxes. We need your help!"

The king summoned Dracula again. "I am tired of all the Saxons' complaints," he said. "They are unhappy about their new competition, and they keep asking me to tell you to repeal the taxes. What is happening?"

Dracula answered impatiently, "Ever since the treaty with Mikhail, I have watched those opportunists closely. They are always seeking a way to elude taxes. We've given special terms of credit to the peasants who make the products. Not only do they sell them more cheaply, but they pay the taxes happily. So I would ask you the same question: what is happening?"

As usual, his ally and good friend Matthias trusted the judgment of his wise subject.

Over time, the foreign Saxons who arrived in Wallachia to sell their products were surprised to find that the local merchandise was both of better quality and less expensive than their own. The town's inhabitants began to buy locally made products so the money would stay in Wallachia; as a result, a new prosperity was established there.

"This is a catastrophe!" the Saxons said to one another. "Just how far is Dracula capable of going?" The vovoid had turned from a monster into their biggest nightmare. They started devising a plan to defend their interests with more energy—with treason, of course, at the core of their plan.

67

Even before he became pope, the life and career of Pio II were interesting. As a young man he had had a shady existence. He liked to visit prostitutes, and as evidence of these relationships he had two illegitimate children, one in Scotland and the other in Strasburg. He and his young friends boasted about their misdeeds, but otherwise his life was mundane. Even after Emperor Frederick III crowned him imperial poet, he continued with his licentiousness, as the oratory was easy for him—more than easy, in fact, as he was quite gifted.

In March 1446, Christ touched his heart and at that moment he experienced a divine transformation, a change that can only be explained by those people who receive the strength and power of the Holy Spirit. He was ordained a deacon and then, in 1447, bishop of Trieste, and bishop of Vienna in 1450. He continued to receive more prestigious appointments until he was appointed pope on August 19, 1458. A skillful politician, he cultivated the support of and mutual cooperation among Emperor Frederick III and the kings of Poland and Hungary. Pio was the perfect leader. Unfortunately, the Catholic Church was experiencing a schism, which was very convenient for the infidels.

Mehemed II continued his plan of expansion, and Dracula had experienced firsthand the fall of Constantinople. Although he was not Catholic, he was worried that Rome would fall—and if that happened, he could not guess the dark future that awaited the Christian faith. So he decided to seek a military alliance with Pope Pio II, who had the history of a real crusader—a martyr who, in his youth, made a penitential vow to walk ten miles barefoot in the snow. It almost cost him his life to fulfill that penance; he suffered from gout as a result. To Dracula, this man was the personification of the defense of the faith. He had worn a knight's armor, brandished a sword, and attacked heretics without concern for his own life. If his brother Dragon Janos Hunyadi was the greatest Christian warrior, then Pope Pio II was in second place, although both of them were Catholics. Dracula sent the following letter to the pope:

Holy Father Pio II,

In the year of our God 1459

I write to you to request your help to organize a crusade against the Ottoman Mehemed II and his infidel religion, Islam. I have lived with him. I know his army, his techniques, and his ambitions, and I know that only you have the moral and religious strength to summon princes and powerful kings to stop this infidel monster. He has already conquered Constantinople; my people and I are practically in his hands. I am terrified to think he may take Wallachia and keep expanding to Rome. My Orthodox heart burns with the fire of our God. My greatest dream is to die in battle defending my faith and with the name of our God Jesus Christ on my lips. If we crush this filthy infidel, I am sure that the faith in our God will prevail.

Holy Father, I am a knight of the Order of the Dragon, established for the defense of the faith of Christ by the late Holy Roman Emperor, may he rest in peace, Sigismund of Luxemburg. I am sure that his passion for our God will encourage you to take actions suitable to your greatness.

I am a subject of King Matthias Corvinus for the glory of my God. Nothing would make me happier than fighting our enemies under your blessed direction. May God protect you and bless you, and I would appreciate it if you sent me your Holy blessing.

Signed,
Wladislaus III, Dragwlya

The Holy Father was alarmed and excited when he received Dracula's letter. Here was someone who followed his actions, someone who, though

Orthodox, believed in him, and that was very motivating. He immediately summoned all the Christian kings and princes to attend the Council of Mantua on June 1, 1459. Representatives of Venice, France, Germany, Bohemia, Hungary, Russia, Spain, Poland, Moldavia, and Wallachia were among those invited.

The objective of the Council of Mantua was to recovering Constantinople, establish a great crusade against the most powerful enemy on earth, the Ottoman Turks. All the Catholic and Orthodox kings were invited, but only the representatives of Wallachia attended; they intended to support the pope with everything they had.

The Holy Father almost cried when he saw that only the most interested party attended. He postponed the council until September 26, 1459. Again he sent letters to the Christian kings and princes, but this time he explained that the faith was in extreme danger, and he demanded that those who could not go send representatives with enough power to make decisions in support of the crusade.

Now the monarchs recognized the great mistake they had made; they all apologized and promised that they would attend the council without fail.

On September 26, 1459, the Council of Mantua opened, hosted by Pope Pio II and attended by representatives of all the main kingdoms Catholic principalities, all of whom shared a similar objective. "The Ottoman Turks have already taken Constantinople, and in that place our Lord is treated as a prophet," Pio said. He made a great display of his oratorical skill, and the participants enjoyed listening to such an interesting speaker. When he proposed a vote to decide if they would go on a crusade to defend the faith, the decision was a unanimous yes.

He then proposed that the crusade last three years, and that proposal, too, was accepted unanimously. Then the council got to the most important matter: what would each kingdom or principality offer in terms of men, equipment, and money?

The representative of Venice said, "We are not saying no . . . but we will decide later how we will contribute to the crusade."

Pio was a politician. He understood clearly that their answer was no.

The representatives of France, in deference to their French pope, reiterated their agreement with the proposed action. "But we need to discuss it with His Holiness," they said. "We will notify you later regarding our contribution."

Again, Pio understood clearly: no!

Gregorio of Hamburg did not bother to look up as he gave the pope his answer. "We will contribute thirty-two thousand infantrymen and ten thousand cavalry," he said arrogantly, his cynical smile a sign that his offer was a poor joke. Pio looked at that Christian and saw a wealthy and shameless man. It would have been easier just to say no—and of course, he never kept his word.

The representatives of Frederick III from Germany said, "The emperor appreciates and esteems with great affection your Holiness, but at this moment we have serious internal and external issues." He continued with his explanation, trying to justify Frederick's cowardice and lack of commitment to such an important crusade.

The representatives of the king of Bohemia, George of Podiebrad, said, "We support this holy crusade, but right now we have serious issues with the heretic Hussites. It is impossible for us to go." Pio was not surprised by the refusal; that king had problems with his religious convictions, and the pope was seriously considering excommunicating him.

The representatives of King Matthias Corvinus said, "Our king has ordered us to support the crusade, but it is impossible for us to do so right now because we have serious internal issues and an economic crisis. As soon as these resolve we will be available to support you." The Holy Father remained silent: Matthias was another coward.

The Russians, too, voiced their support . . . and the reasons they couldn't contribute. ("Right now we have problems with nomadic tribes that are attacking our towns.") The other representatives had the same response. Everyone, it seemed, supported the crusade, buts . . .

All those "buts" and refusals! *Is anybody going to help the crusade?* Pio asked himself desperately.

Only the representatives of Wallachia had not yet spoken. When their turn came, the metropolitan, Barbat, said, "Our vovoid, Dracula, has instructed us to give you all our support for the crusade—not just our military men, but all our people, who are willing to defend our faith in our God. We are ready to start fighting right now."

Pio could not overcome his amazement. How was it possible that of all the Catholic and Orthodox kings and princes, only Dracula had agreed to defend the faith? Pio was furious. Looking out at the council, he made them an offer that would force them to participate. "I will give one hundred thousand gold coins to any participant in the crusade," he said.

That offer would have tempted any saint; it was a stratospheric amount. But it also came at a great risk. The crusaders would face the best army of that time—the best-trained, best-fed, best-armored, best-paid, and largest, motivated by a heretical but well-structured religion. All the representatives attending the council had specific orders from their governors not to support Pope Pio II; they preferred to hide their heads in the ground like ostriches. The council was a disaster.

However, the Holy Father was a man of word and action, too. Undeterred, he organized the collection of money for his crusade, establishing the Order of Saint Mary of Bethlehem to accomplish that specific objective.

The men in charge of the collection requested that the kings and princes voluntarily contribute to the holy crusade against the Turks, but all of them claimed to have greater economic priorities. So this order was another failure of a pope who was one of the greatest defenders of the faith. Fortunately there was another Catholic institution that was always willing to defend the faith of God : the Holy Inquisition.

The pope gathered his subalterns and ordered them to make an initial collection of one hundred thousand gold ducats for the crusade against the infidel Ottomans. He also instructed the holy grand inquisitor that he and the holy inquisitors must seek out heretics more zealously, as the faith of their God was in more danger than ever.

Barbat, the metropolitan, returned from the council bitterly disappointed. "I cannot believe it!" he said to Dracula. "Of all the representatives who attended the council, only I had orders to participate in the crusade with our full resources."

"And the representatives of Matthias?" asked the vovoid.

"They said no, albeit diplomatically. The pope was desperate; he offered one hundred thousand ducats in gold to any king who participated in the crusade, and still nobody else joined. The Holy Father will send you that resource through King Matthias."

But Dracula was pleased for Wallachia. "At least we have a real ally!" he exclaimed. "There is no doubt the Holy Father is a real saint."

68

In a small town in Spain, Monica cured her neighbors with herbs, ointments, eggs, and prayers. The poorest inhabitants of the town considered her their doctor, and she accepted their merchandise—or sometimes just a thank you—as payment for her services. But she also attended to people who did well with their crops or the sale of their animals, and they showed their gratitude with money.

The woman saved her coins when she could, and as sick people continued to come and go, her little savings increased, bit by bit, without her even realizing it.

———◈———

One day an important-seeming fellow dressed like a monk arrived in town, joined by other pious priests. They introduced themselves to the local priest. "I am Friar Hector Blass de Torres y Barraza, holy inquisitor and defender of the faith of Christ, and these are my helpers. We have come because the faith is in danger. The mission of His Holiness is to seek heresy with more zeal."

The town priest, feeling intimidated by all those important people, said, "Holy Father, tell me: what do I have to do?"

"The first thing we have to do is look for 'familiares' among the population."

"Pardon my ignorance: what is a 'familiar'?"

"He is a civilian who helps us look for heresy among relatives and friends. He must dress in black and has permission to carry weapons."

The priest brightened. "I know some people who would be happy to contribute with such a delicate and pious labor," he said.

Soon three new 'familiares'—Hugo, Francisco, and Luis—were seen around town, dressed elegantly in black, their steps now purposeful, their voices authoritarian. Without a doubt, they were considered solid supporters of that blessed institution, the Holy Inquisition.

⬦

"My head hurts—I cannot stand it!" Petra, Monica's goddaughter, had come to her mother with this plaintive cry.

"I am going to take you to your godmother," Josepha said soothingly. "She will cure you like she always does."

Before long the little girl was describing her pain to Monica. "Godmother, I cannot stand the pain," Petra said. "My head hurts horribly—right here!"

"Do not worry honey. I will make you as good as new in a second— you'll see!" Monica started praying as she vigorously rubbed an egg on the child's head. There was a smell like burning herbs, and then Monica broke the egg, which smelled quite bad. She tipped the egg into a cup of water, which took on a strange, dark color. Then, addressing her goddaughter, who was studying the cup and its contents, she said, "See how easily I got the ill out of you?" Quickly Monica went outside, dug a small hole in the ground, poured the egg into the hole, and covered it. "You are cured!" she said, brushing the dirt off her hands. "Now just sleep. Tomorrow you will be fine."

But in the morning Petra was no better. "I cannot stand it!" she said. "Please take me to a doctor . . . I feel like I am dying!"

The doctor who attended her did everything he could, but the pain did not disappear. Now desperate, Josepha went to the priest and, in the course of her confession, told him about her daughter's problem.

The priest began to scold her. "Are you a heretic?" he said. "How could you take your daughter to a witch? That is why the doctor could not cure her. The only real doctor is our Christ. You must report the witch to the holy inquisitor. That is your penance."

Josepha was scared stiff—doing that, she knew, would condemn her good friend to a very strict ecclesiastical process. "Monica has always cured us, and she has never charged us anything," she explained.

"It is not the payment—it is the action," the priest said. "Your penance is to report her, and I am not going to give you absolution for your sins until you do it. Meanwhile, you committed a mortal sin!"

235

Josepha was torn. If she reported Monica, she could be burned at the stake. If she didn't, she could not receive Holy Communion—Christ wouldn't be in her heart, and her soul might end up in hell. In her mind there was a fight to the death between the two choices.

After several days passed, Josepha returned to confession, anguished. "My daughter still hasn't healed—she is screaming from the pain! I am desperate . . . help me, Father!"

"If your daughter is sick, it is because you allowed the demon to possess her with your attitude. When are you going to report that witch? You are a traitor to Christ, and traitors deserve excommunication. Your soul will surely go to hell if you do not report that witch. Do not come to this house of God—get out!"

Back on the street, Josepha waited sadly for a 'familiar' to pass, and when she saw him she said, "Monica is a witch . . . I will take you to her house." Then, walking in silence and with tears in her eyes, she guided the steps of that good Christian.

The 'familiar' arrived at the house of the infernal heretic and grabbed her abruptly by the hair, "Come with me!" he shouted.

Monica's greatest fear had materialized; the presence of that Christian character, who looked sinister to her eyes, confirmed it. Unceremoniously, the witch was taken from her home. On the way out she exchanged glances with her friend Josepha, who looked down at the floor, ashamed.

"Why, friend?" Monica asked simply. Without receiving an answer she was taken to the dark, cold, and humid dungeons of the Holy Inquisition, where she was chained to the wall in a locked cell. She would be there indeterminately.

The 'familiar' said to the holy inquisitor, "Holy Father, I locked a witch in the dungeon. I know her address—shall we go there to look for evidence of her activity?"

The inquisitor did not say a word; he was a man of action. Immediately he headed to the woman's small home, where they found plenty of evidence of her heretical activity: eggs that when they were cracked open stank horribly, strange ointments, herbs of all kinds, and an endless number of diabolical-looking amulets. There was not the least doubt—that woman was a satanic witch.

The inquisition process began with the holy inquisitor in the middle of the room, flanked by some secretaries acting as the jury. They sat on an elevated platform so the accused would feel the power of the Holy Office. Then the defenders of the faith sat behind a huge table with a red tablecloth; on the wall behind was the coat of arms of the Holy Inquisition, and above this was the main witness, a crucifix. Two strong armed guards served to discourage the accused from trying to run from divine justice.

The accused, meanwhile, sat far away from the saints, on a small, shabby stool with three weak legs.

A secretary rose and said, "We give thanks to God the Father Almighty, his only son Jesus Christ, and the Holy Spirit, because today, March 8, 1460, the year of our God, before the presence of the holy inquisitor, we gather to carry out a trial against a person who calls herself Monica . . ." He kept talking for a while and then finally ceded the floor to the holy inquisitor.

That great man simply stared at the woman without saying a word. Finally, he broke the silence with a harsh command: "Tell me the truth!"

Monica felt her body aching. She had heard about these trials, but now that she was in the middle of one, with the holy inquisitor before her, demanding information, she was speechless. She felt like a mouse about to be gobbled up by a snake. She could not move a muscle; she could not articulate a single word.

The silence was broken again with the same shouted command.

This time Monica answered quietly. "I am innocent. I am Catholic."

The holy inquisitor had witnessed firsthand the evidence of that witch's devilish activity. He felt like a red-hot coal was burning inside him. "Tell me the truth!" he screamed.

Monica was now very worried. She had told the truth and he did not believe her. So she repeated with difficulty, "I am innocent, and I am Catholic."

The holy inquisitor's patience was reaching its limits before the heretic's obstinate attitude. Once again he commanded, more upset, "For the last time, tell me the truth!"

Monica answered in a louder voice: "I am innocent, and I am Catholic!"

Enraged because she did not acknowledge her heresy, he issued his order: "Take her to the dungeon!"

Monica was terrified, but her fear did not match the pain that awaited her.

She was taken to a huge hall underground. She could not believe what she saw—the place had no windows; the gloom was illuminated by weak torchlight. She saw different instruments of torture, just the sight of which would have chilled the blood of even the bravest man. From the ceiling hung several very small metal cages, and inside each one of them there was a naked, immobile, and very much alive human being who stared out at the new guest without saying a word. A heretic was being tortured naked on the rack; he looked unnaturally long and very thin. Monica couldn't help herself: she burst out crying. "Where am I? My God! Help me!" She began screaming, terrified.

Like any other heretic she was undressed completely and placed on the rack, tied by her feet and hands. Then the holy inquisitor arrived, and he saw the face of the accused up close—she was certainly very beautiful. Obviously, her figure had been sculpted by the lust devil, and the holy man was being made his victim through the tempting body of that satanic witch. Summoning all his patience, he said, "For the last time . . . tell me the truth!"

Monica answered again, "I am Catholic, and I believe in Christ!"

The holy inquisitor looked at one of the torturers and nodded. The man immediately walked to a crucifix that was in the room and covered it with a black cloth to prevent their Lord from witnessing the defense that was going to be made in his name. When the holy Christ was shrouded, the inquisitor called, "Give it a spin!"

The torturer's face was covered with a black mask so that only his eyes were visible. But his mask was hiding a sadistic smile; he was going to do what he liked most, and so he happily carried out the sacred order.

When Monica felt the rack pulling, she gave a shrill scream that tore her throat.

The objective of the holy inquisitor was clear: defend at all costs the faith of their God. No matter how hard the devil tried to divert him from his holy mission, he was not going to listen. Now he was starting to fight against a powerful demon that had put temptation in front of him and was using lust to beat down his resistance and his virtue. Staring steadily at the beautiful body of the heretic, he shouted, "Tell me the truth!"

Monica did not know what crime she was being accused of committing. "I am Catholic! I am innocent!"

The holy inquisitor was starting to worry that the devil was winning the battle—he wanted to take that helper of Satan from the rack and possess her. But first he had to make her confess, so he shouted his order again. "Tell me the truth!"

"I am Catholic, and I am innocent!"

The inquisitor looked at the torturer and nodded. "Give it another spin!"

Monica began screaming before the pull. "For the love of God! Don't torture me!" But the torturer gladly carried out the order.

The inquisitor was defending himself with all his might, but he was only human. He could feel the strength of the devil, who through lust was overwhelming his virtue, leaving part of his vulnerable body enflamed and rock-hard. His reason blinded, he knew the demon was winning the battle, and in a confused and faltering voice he said, "Take the accused off the rack!"

The torturer already knew that tone of voice and what that order meant. He took the heretic off the rack, carried her to a room with a bed, and threw her down as if she were a sack of grain.

Left alone, barely able to move from the pain, Monica sought the refuge of her God. At that moment the inquisitor arrived, closed the door behind him, and without saying a word took the aching body of that diabolical heretic. The holy man was dragged down into a turmoil of lust and passion, and he possessed her against her will over and over again until he was exhausted.

Realizing that the devil again had blinded him, he humbly sought the forgiveness of his God. The priest who heard his confession understood that the holy inquisitor was a human being who, in the course of his delicate mission, was regularly exposed to the dangers and traps of the devil. He reminded the inquisitor that Christ shed his precious blood for the forgiveness of mankind sins, and that through this sacrifice the inquisitor received not only forgiveness, but absolution and Christ's divine grace. The penance the priest imposed on him was to reinforce his faith in their God. The inquisitor immediately had Holy Communion and then bravely continued with the difficult interrogation, but the accomplice of Satan did not admit her fault because the devil had possessed her. The holy man understood this. According to the writings of Saint Augustine of Hippo, there was just one way to break this devilish alliance: to raise the severity of the torture.

Following the procedures of the *Directorium Inquisitorum* (written by Saint Nicholas Aymerch and authorized by the pope in his fight against the devil), the inquisitor placed the heretic on the rack again and, with the formality and seriousness the case deserved, had the torturer apply the highest level of violence possible. When he saw with desperation that even this could not break the bond between the devil and the heretical woman, he knew without a doubt that the witch was being protected by Satan. And still he kept fighting bravely, giving no quarter, until the guilty woman finally confessed, screaming, "I am a witch! I made a pact with the devil! I make spells . . . I'll tell you everything you want! But please . . . no more!"

The holy inquisitor was pleased with this confession; it was pretty clear that the suspect was a heretic. Saint Augustine was right: pain had broken the devilish bond. Now only the sentence was missing. The holy inquisitor remembered that they would soon have an 'auto de fe', in which a large group of heretics was going to be sentenced and punished. "Your sentence and punishment will be administered on April seventeenth," he said, and Monica was taken to a dungeon to wait.

The holy inquisitor confiscated the witch's house and possessions, taking the money that was a product of her wickedness and selling everything else. Part of the money was used to pay for her trial and execution, and the rest was sent to the Holy Father in the Vatican. That dirty money, generated by the evilness of Satan, when it fell into holy hands was purified by God.

———◈———

At the church of the Sacred Heart, the priest spoke from the pulpit. "I remind you that in thirty days the 'auto de fe' will be celebrated in Seville, and we all must go to receive indulgences. Those who do not assist may be considered heretics, so do not miss this for any reason. We will be reminding you every day."

The day before the trial, the holy inquisitors made 'the procession of the Green Cross', and the most important Christian authorities were there. "Father, what does this procession mean?" a 'familiar' asked the holy inquisitor.

Fray Hector Blass de Torres y Barraza made a great display of enlightening that ignorant man. "It symbolizes the hope of the prosecuted," he said, picking up two banners and handing him one. "I will carry the banner of the Holy Office, and you the banner of Jesus of the Holy Sacrament." The men then headed to the place where the 'auto de fe' was going to be celebrated. The procession was received by other ecclesiastical authorities amidst beautiful, sacred chants, and then Mass was celebrated.

The next day a 'familiar' announced, "Get up, heretics—it's three o'clock in the morning. You don't want to arrive late to your party . . . you are the main guests!"

Monica had been unable to sleep. Knowing that within hours she could lose her life in the middle of unspeakable pain kept her in the worst kind of suspense, and she wanted to end it once and for all. *What kind of punishment will I receive from these hypocrites, who dress like saints but behave like demons?* There was no doubt: desperation was making her think like a heretic.

She was instructed to put on a 'San Benito' with the Cross of Saint Ignatius and a long hood. "This is black, with demons and flames, and the long hood you gave me says I am a witch! This is a lie . . . I am not wearing it!"

"Are you calling the holy inquisitor a liar? Do you want to be interrogated again?"

"No . . . please, no more!" she answered, quickly putting on the garment. Then a rope was tied around her neck and she was given a yellow candle.

"Damned demons! Sons of Satan!" shrieked one of the accused, throwing punches at the pious 'familiares'. The heretic was subdued by means of a savage beating; then he was muzzled, chained, and dressed in a long hood. "Just give us a reason and we'll drag you around to get a beating from everyone!" one of the 'familiares' growled.

Understanding that he could not disobey those virtuous ecclesiastical authorities, the heretic cooperated against his will.

"Five o'clock in the morning!" a 'familiar' yelled. "Let us give thanks to our Lord for our blessed 'auto de fe' and pray that it will be celebrated without setbacks." And the prayers began. The great holy inquisitor was at the front, carrying the banner of the Holy Office, and behind him were the holy inquisitors, among them Friar Hector Blas de Torres y Barraza, carrying a banner of Mary. Behind them were the heretics surrounded by pious familiares.

The atmosphere was enlivened by the beat of several drums, the sharp noise punctuating the deepest fears of the accused.

"There goes Monica!" said one of her former clients, pointing at her. She wanted to take off that hood and that 'San Benito', but how could she if she was being closely watched by a 'familiar' for being a satanic witch? She decided she was dreaming; she had had this very nightmare many times, and so she was expecting to wake up in a sweat at any moment.

The procession was made more ghoulish by the cartoonish, life-size dolls the 'familiares' were carrying on their shoulders. They symbolized the cowardly heretics who had escaped rather than bravely facing trial for their actions; it made sense that the souls of these cowards had a place reserved in hell, and according to the holy saints, these souls would be attended in person by Satan and his devilish minions. Other 'familiares' carried boxes of the bones of those who had died during interrogation or in the dungeons of the Holy Office. These boxes were decorated with flames symbolizing the flames of hell, which is where their souls were by order of the ecclesiastical authorities.

In the midst of sacred chants, they arrived at the main square. At the front of the square was a huge platform; on one side of it was the king, and on the other were the distinguished and holy ecclesiastical authorities. When the grand inquisitor took his position on the platform, Mass began. One of the inquisitors stood to describe the dangers facing the faith. He explained at length and in great detail about Christ's sacrifice and the nature of his wounds, and how he shed his blood for the forgiveness of our sins. He concluded by recalling Christ's glorious resurrection in body and soul on the third day.

Then they started to judge the heretics. Some were condemned to wear the 'San Benito' for life; they were assigned to the atrium of the church, where they had to arrive before the bells tolled at noon Angelus and had to remain on their knees, praying and asking forgiveness, until sunset. (If it rained or was cold or snowed, this would serve as a lesson for those growing apart from the faith.) These penitents would live from alms and could not work or do any kind of job. Other heretics were sentenced to life in prison; others were forced to labor in the galleys until the day of their death; and finally, some were sentenced to die in a cleansing fire due to their satanic activity. Among this last group was Monica.

Although she fought with all her strength, she could not overpower the pious 'familiares', who quickly tied her to a pole surrounded by firewood. Friar Hector Blass de Torres y Barraza was carrying a long white walking stick, on the end of which was an iron crucifix. He put the cross into the fire until it was red-hot, and then he brought it near the mouth of a heretic tied up next to Monica. In a gentle voice he said, "Kiss our Christ and ask forgiveness for your sins!" The woman next to Monica respectfully kissed the crucifix, burning her lips.

As a reward for her humility, the inquisitor issued an order to the executioner: "Death by garrote! And burn the corpse!"

The obedient executioner raised a club and gave her a potent blow to the head. The heretical woman lost consciousness and her neck was broken by the rope around it, so that she was sent to hell without pain.

Next Friar Hector Blass de Torres y Barraza held the red-hot crucifix before Monica, who still did not understand the holy mission of that saint of God. When he suggested she kiss it, she spit in his face. "Damned hypocrite demon!" she screamed.

The holy inquisitor had developed tolerance, and on this occasion he decided to apply it. Like every exemplary Christian, he turned the other cheek.

The heretic screamed again, "Cynic . . . damned devil!" And the sainted man received another wad of spit.

Making a big display of humility and composure, the inquisitor did not abandon his delicate mission; he went on to another heretic, while Monica did not stop offending him.

Unnoticed under his black cloak was the huge smile on the face of the sadistic executioner. He knew that the devilish heretic would soon know what real hell was.

The 'auto de fe' was an expensive but important process. Religious criminals received public humiliation, and helpers of Satan were burned to death for moving away from the faith of their God.

Immediately after sentencing, the drums resounded again, a choir of parishioners started to sing, and the executioner lit the firewood. As flames started to devour her flesh, Monica tried hard to wake up, realizing too late that she was not dreaming. She had never felt such excruciating pain. And amidst desperate screams, her life was taken from her.

The holy inquisitor watched how the cleansing fire destroyed that work of Satan who had made him sin, dragging him to the swamps of lust and concupiscence. As a defender of the faith, he thanked God that the heretical witch could no longer hurt him with her spells and her lustful body; now that diabolical being was going to hell, where she belonged.

With blessed actions like this, the holy inquisitors began gathering money to serve the noble cause of the Pope Pio II: the war against the infidel Ottomans.

69

The agreement made in Brasov was extended to all the Saxons of Wallachia, where a strange and false calm had taken hold, as if the region's problems had disappeared. That apparent calm made King Matthias Corvinus make another bizarre decision typical of his juvenile nature: he summoned Mikhail Szilagyi and relieved him of his duty. "Uncle, from now on you won't be military commander of Transylvania," he said. "You are old and tired, and we are at peace; there are no issues of any kind. I want you to rest and spend time doing what you want."

Mikhail was stunned. "The most important thing to me is my military career," he protested. "If you take it away, you are taking my life away! I want to die in a battle defending my faith with the name of my God Jesus Christ on my lips."

"But you are an old man. You are already sixty years old, Uncle," answered the monarch.

"But I feel like I am twenty-five!" Mikhail said. "Strenuous exercise and the healthy life I've led have allowed me to feel young! Nephew, for the love of God, do not make me retire!"

"I have made my decision, and nothing is going to change my mind," the king said categorically.

Mikhail lapsed into deep depression. He did not want to eat or talk or do anything at all. When his daughter Ilona saw him on the verge of tears, she was terribly concerned. "What is wrong, Daddy?" she asked.

In a choked voice he answered, "Your cousin fired me from the army. He says I am an old man and that I have to rest."

Ilona tried to cheer him up. "It is a good thing that you are going to be here at home," she said. "I am going to enjoy your company just for myself!!" And she hugged him lovingly, giving him many tender kisses on his white head.

As the days went by, however, Ilona started to worry more. She regularly found her father crying, and that made her cry, too. One day she plucked up her courage and asked him, "Why do you cry so often, Daddy? I have never been happier! Having you close fills me with joy."

Mikhail could no longer take it. He wept like a child as he said, "My girl, I always dreamed of dying in a battle defending my faith. But look at my destiny. I am going to die of old age, sitting in this chair."

The beautiful Ilona was starting to understand her father's sorry. "I wish I could make things different, but I cannot send you to fight, and my cousin is stubborn; if I suggest that he send you to the army, he will refuse. I know him well."

"There is a way for me to meet my destiny, Daughter!" Mikhail replied.

"What, Father?"

"I can go to Dracula. He is a brave and active warrior." He continued to talk about Dracula, about his determination, his character, his strength, his kindness, his toughness, and, most of all, his great love for his Lord. Ilona also respected the man. Her father had told her so much about him that she felt she knew him well. However, when she met him she had been a little girl, and he had treated her as such. *What is it about Dracula that makes my father admire him so much?* she wondered.

One day Mikhail called Ilona to his side. "Do you want to see me happy?" he asked her.

"More than anything in the world!"

"Then I want my last will to be done."

Ilona was alarmed. "But you are not dying!"

"I am sixty," he said. "Soon I will be in heaven at the side of my God. My last will is to die in a battle defending him, and with his holy name on my lips. I will achieve that only if I go to fight at Dracula's side."

Having seen him so depressed—and so cheered by just talking of his plans—Ilona said, "Father, whatever you decide will be done."

Two days later, Mikhail bid his daughter good-bye. "Remember me always as a strong man and a passionate worshiper of our God," he said. "I will write to you from time to time. Pray for me to die in battle—and now kneel down to receive my blessing. May it be God's will that this is my last."

Ilona knelt down, and her heroic father gave her a solemn blessing as she cried and prayed in silence, *My God, your will be done!* Then the brave knight of the Order of the Dragon, Mikhail Szilagyi, went to Wallachia to meet his destiny.

Ilona stayed there, still wondering, *What is it about Dracula that so attracts my father?*

Dracula was visited by one of the men he admired most. Effusively hugging his brother Dragon, Dracula asked him, "To what do I owe the great honor of your visit?"

Mikhail answered him simply. "Matthias dismissed me from the position of military commanding officer of Transylvania."

"I already knew," Dracula admitted. "I was enraged when I found out!"

"Look at me: I am no longer a soldier. I can scarcely believe it!"

Dracula was silent awhile. "Matthias might look like a nineteen-year-old man," he said, "but he acts like a child pretending to be king. What was he thinking when he did such a stupid thing?"

"And yet he is our king, and he has the power," Mikhail added. "We must obey him without questioning or criticizing him."

Dracula knew his ally was right, but that did not stop him from expressing his opinion. Taking advantage of the great trust between them, he said, "Janos is dead, but he will always be the best Christian warrior I have ever known. After him, I can honestly tell you, is Pope Pio II. You follow them in braveness and courage—it is an honor to consider you my brother!" And he hugged Mikhail again, saying, "Even though he is your nephew, our king is a perfect idiot!"

Mikhail agreed; however, he preferred to obey the king without criticizing him. Taking a deep breath he made a request of his brother

Dragon: "I want to join your army and fight against our enemies. I am sure that by your side I will find the path I have sought all my life—"

Dracula interrupted him. "To die in battle defending the faith of our God, . . . and with his holy name on your lips."

Mikhail nodded solemnly. "Who doesn't wish that?"

"That is also my greatest ambition," Dracula said. "I hope God will grant it. Welcome, brother! Consider yourself my man of trust—and from now on you are my commander general."

Dracula later introduced his commanders to their new superior. "This is my brother Dragon, Mikhail Szilagyi. From now on he is our general commander. When he orders something, respond as if I were ordering it." Mikhail was then introduced to the army, and the men gave him a sincere welcome. Their first battles were noticeable successes thanks to the braveness and courage of the seasoned warrior.

When the Saxons found out that Mikhail Szilagyi was no longer military commander of Transylvania, they started organizing to overthrow Dracula. The Saxon Boaz contacted Dan III to say they wanted him to take power in Wallachia. "What we are going to ask you is obvious," he said, "but we want to be really clear: when you take over, you must reinstate the town council. Then we will appoint you vovoid, and you will give us our former privileges."

"As it always should have been!" Dan III responded heartily.

The Saxons supplied him with new, more powerful muskets, and he ordered his commanding officers to have their men familiarize themselves with the weapons.

Meanwhile, Dracula's spies reported strange movements in Tampa Hill. Dracula summoned Mikhail and explained the situation. "Are you ready to offer your life in this battle?" he asked.

Mikhail answered bravely, "May it be God's will that this is my last!"

"Let us fight for Jesus Christ of the Holy Sacrament!" The great Mikhail gave the rallying cry, and then, joined by Dracula, he led the attack against the traitor Dan III. The army's spirited horses did not startle at the noise of the muskets that were decimating their ranks. Ultimately, the Dragons' bravery and intelligence gave them the victory. In the end, the Saxon traitors were identified and, together with their soldiers, received the punishment reserved for them: impalement!

The vovoid's spy ring informed him that Dan III had sought refuge in Brasov, and so, with the courage that characterized them, Dracula and Mihail led their army in a repeat of the strategy. The traitors were more slippery than soap: they could not be caught! But again, the Saxons who protected and helped them, along with the soldiers who were taken prisoner, tasted the destiny of the traitor.

Soon afterward, Dan III wrote the following letter to his Saxon followers:

> To all Saxons of Wallachia,
>
> I represent the scream for freedom of the Saxons. "The Son of the Devil" has committed the worst atrocities against our innocent and brave people. I am the one and only vovoid of Wallachia, thanks to your support. The fight against the demon is hard, but we must not withdraw.
>
> March 2, 1460
>
> Signed,
> Dan III

The gunsmiths of Sibiu delivered to Dan III new and effective arms, the range of whose ammunition surpassed anything else imaginable at that time.

70

On April 4, 1460, A new battle begins the two Dragons led from the front, so when the enemies threw out the lethal discharge, Dracula was wounded in one leg and the Saxons' new ammunition pierced Mikhail's reinforced armor, wounding him in one shoulder. These setbacks only filled the soldiers with more courage, and their attacks became bolder. The battle was bloody. Mikhail was attacked by two soldiers; while he fought one, the other fired into the back of the sacred crusader, who felt the deadly wound and looked at his murderer as if to thank him for what he had done. Then, lifting his eyes to the sky, he said, "Bless you, my God Jesus Chr—" And with that he gave his life to the creator, dying just the way he had always wanted.

This time Dan III was taken prisoner, along with the boyars, soldiers, and Saxons who supported him.

It was not difficult to guess the destiny of those miserable traitors. In the main square of Fagaras, a routine trial took place. This time Dracula addressed Dan III: "I invited you to forget our differences and join the army of Wallachia to face our greatest enemy, and together defend the faith of our God and fight for Wallachia's independence. It is a shame that because of your ambition you have become the executioner of these traitors. For your actions you are condemned to die impaled. That is the law." Dracula had a lump in his throat; he was grieving the loss of his brother Dragon. But he did not want to show his sadness, which would only please his enemies, so with a strange and enigmatic smile, he added, "And thank you! You gave my brother Mikhail the death he always sought. At this moment he must be at the right side of my God."

"You are lying!" Dan III shouted. "Mikhail is in hell! You are the sons of the devil! Die, damned traitor!" His screams were the manifestation of sheer helplessness.

That traitor, along with his boyars and soldiers and the Saxons who supported him, died impaled, with all the horror and unbearable pain that punishment wrought.

Dracula continued to follow the enemy he was missing, hoping to eliminate him and then wage his larger battle against the Ottoman Turks, but it seemed that the elusive man had fallen off the face of the earth. Dracula realized too late that Basarab Laiota was the smartest and most intelligent of all his internal foes—that he should have started by eliminating him first. Every time Dracula looked for Laiota, the man disappeared like a ghost and Dracula ended up following another enemy instead. In fact, his spy ring informed him that Laiota did not appear to be anywhere in Wallachia. Dracula asked King Matthias Corvinus for help, and his spies could not find the man in Hungary, Moldavia, or Poland. *Is he disguised as a peasant?* Dracula thought. *Has he hidden in some monastery, as I did? This is not possible—no one can find him!* Then Dracula had a realization: he was with the Ottomans.

Still, as he traveled around Wallachia, he kept looking. The peasants he encountered greeted him respectfully. He answered their effusive displays of affection by raising his right hand, Roman-style, and looking at them in silence. Their vovoid was like their protective father.

71

On May 6, 1460, determined to defend the faith, Dracula planned his next move: to seek allies to help him attack the Ottoman Turks. Then he headed to Moldavia, the land ruled by his beloved cousin, Stephen.

When Dracula arrived, he was received with honor. He was given the finest food and the best treatment, as appropriate for the most important guest in Moldavia. But at bedtime, Dracula and Stephen continued their humble tradition, kneeling before a crucifix and praying with devotion.

Dracula's first full day in Moldavia began with a solemn Orthodox Mass and Holy Communion officiated by the metropolitan. After a succulent breakfast he and Stephen went riding together, remembering the old times—their religious education with the monk Urbano; Stephen's escape from his uncle Petru Aron; their flight from the boyar who died by the dragon dagger; and their sacred pact to help each other in times of trouble and never to be rivals.

After a while, Dracula spoke: "Cousin, I have killed almost all the aspirants to the throne of Wallachia. Just Basarab Laiota is missing. He knows I am looking for him and so I know he would never dare to come here. I suspect he's with the Ottomans, and I think it's time for us to face those enemies. I have come to ask for your support to attack them."

"Who else is going to the crusade?" Stephen asked.

"I am going to invite my king, Matthias Corvinus, because—"

Stephen interrupted him sharply. "Not Matthias, please! I have bad relations with him. In fact, I hate him with all my soul, and I do not want to know anything about him as long as I live. He is Catholic!"

"Cousin, I have to invite him," Dracula said. "Remember, I am his subject. Someday Wallachia will be independent, but in the meantime we must face reality. What's more important than being Catholic or Orthodox is defending our God, who is a beloved and respected God in both faiths. I would welcome any help I can get!"

Stephen and Dracula continued talking for hours, but Dracula's arguments did not seem to move Stephen, who finally said, "Besides, you have already solved your problems with your internal enemies, but I still have my problem. I will give you my support . . . but it needs to be later."

Frustrated, Dracula stopped his horse and asked, "And what about the oath we sealed with our blood—with Christ as our witness—promising always to help each other?" He looked at the scar on his right hand and sighed. "I was dealing with plenty of my own enemies when I helped you recover your power."

It was clear that Stephen understood the hint, but he was not going to make an alliance with Matthias Corvinus.

That night, for the first time, they said their prayers separately. The next day Dracula headed back to Wallachia. It was unbelievable to him that his beloved cousin would not fulfill the pact they had made before the presence of their God.

When he arrived home he resumed the search for Basarab Laiota, but he seemed to be nowhere in Wallachia. Dracula's boyars had inquired at the Catholic monasteries, but when the monks denied he was there, the boyars took it no further; they had specific orders from Dracula not to disturb those houses of prayer. Dracula recalled how the monk Barbat had defended him from his perceived enemies; Barbat had not treated Dracula like a traitor. So Dracula could forgive the monks' present attitude, justifying it as appropriate for bearers of the secrets of confession, who must be allowed to continue their ministry in peace.

Dracula arrived at the palace of King Matthias Corvinus, who received him with unusual warmth. "I eliminated my enemies," Dracula told him. "Just Basarab Laiota is missing, but I am sure he is hiding with the Ottomans. It is time to start a crusade against the enemies of the Cross."

Matthias was not half as brave as his father was. Janos Hunyadi was a sacred warrior who fought the infidels all his life, a hardened defender of the faith. But Matthias? Matthias was Janos's biological son, but he might as well have been the son of a cowardly peasant. He professed to be Catholic, but he did not want to rise in arms to defend the faith with the fervor and braveness of his father. "How are we going to organize this crusade?" he asked fretfully.

Dracula felt the blood boiling inside his veins. How could the king to whom he was subject ask him that question? He looked at Matthias with his green eyes and answered slowly, "We are going to fight the Ottomans with all the strength of our hearts. Our God will show us the way to defeat them. But we have to act now!"

Matthias could not believe it: until that moment he had not considered going to war against such a powerful enemy. "Let me talk about it with the town council," he said. "I will tell you my answer later."

Dracula felt alone. He could not argue with his king; all that was left for him was to accept the refusal. *When Matthias changed his name, he chose the wrong animal to honor,* he thought furiously. *He should have changed it to chicken. Matthias Chicken better reflects the way he acts.* Then Dracula began to pray, seeking comfort in the only ally who would never abandon him.

He traveled to Poland to seek the support of King George of Podiebrad, with the same outcome. Unable to find a solution to his problem, he went back to Wallachia. He was facing a great dilemma. He knew he could always join the Ottoman Empire, and he would have it all. Mehemed II was like a brother, and with his army he could surpass the war deeds of Alexander the Great! But what about Christ? Was Dracula going to step on him? And what about his Orthodox faith? Was he going to step on that and betray it? Never! He made his decision: he would fight with his people! He would enliven their hearts with the strength of his faith in God—and he would face the Ottoman Empire, even if he were alone, himself against the world.

72

A large retinue sent by the sultan arrived in Wallachia and delivered to Dracula an invitation to negotiate peace on October 2 at the Fortress of Giurgiu. Dracula already knew the intentions of the powerful man, he had a big dilemma. If he made peace with the sultan, he would be betraying his God and his people. If he didn't, the sultan would take Wallachia; Dracula would not be able to defend it alone. He remembered his father's advice: "Son, be like the chameleon and deceive your enemies." *It is time,* he said to himself, *to wear the skin of that animal.* And he went to the Fortress of Giurgiu with some of his boyars to meet the infidels.

When Dracula arrived at the fortress, his reception had been planned just as he'd anticipated it would be: gifts, good food, many women—three days of pleasure—and after that, the negotiation. Dracula was prepared for this, and so he spoke to the commander in charge, saying, "I have a lot of work to do back in Wallachia. I would like to attend to the important matters right away."

"You are not giving us the opportunity to treat you like a great governor deserves," the man said, "but it will be done as you wish." Handing Dracula a document, he said, "We are proposing that you sign this treaty, which will be extremely beneficial to your people."

Dracula saw that the treaty had nine provisions, many of which would benefit his people. But the core and most important provision was unacceptable: he had to deliver to the sultan one thousand children of conscription and ten thousand gold coins per year. He wanted to tear up the treaty and impale the Ottomans, but of course he couldn't. Enraged by the helplessness of being unable to do what he wanted, he signed the treaty against his will.

When Dracula faced the world, his will was as strong as an oak. But when he was with his beloved Zalesha, he showed his vulnerable side. He arrived home and told her all his worries. "I am depressed, discouraged . . . humiliated," he said. "I don't want to do anything. I cannot believe that the most powerful Christian kings are not defending their faith with passion, that they've let fear get into their hearts. I am going to face the sultan—and if I have to do it alone, I will! It is hard for me to believe that I have signed that damned treaty with those miserable Ottomans, that I've promised to give them our children . . . but they forced me! Now I feel what my father felt!" As he said this he began sobbing, and his wife put her arms around him lovingly, saying, "How I wish I were rich and powerful enough to hire an army of soldiers to kill your enemies. It is a shame I am just the daughter of a poor peasant."

When he had unburdened himself of his repressed anguish, Zalesha said, "Come, honey, let us seek refuge in prayer." Together they knelt down before their Christ and indubitably their God listened to the voices of those pious hearts.

Mehemed's treaty with Dracula was part of a greater strategy; he made the same treaty with Skanderbeg in Albany. That way he could use his allies as shields in case of a war against Asia.

From 1460 to 1461, while the Inquisition made its blessed defense of the faith to gather the resources Pope Pio II had promised in the fight against the Ottomans, Dracula continued ruling Wallachia. He made the peasants happy and enraged the Saxons; one group considered him a kind and fair ruler, while the others thought of him as a bully, a thief, and a murderer. The Saxons pointed for proof to the fact that their income had diminished due to unfair taxes and duties. They also complained that their economic activity had diminished due to unfair competition that Dracula had promoted among the peasants, who now made the same products as the Saxons but actually sold them at a lower price! Worst of all, they said, innocent Saxons had died impaled, suffering unthinkable pain for having dared to defend their rights.

Dracula assimilated the truth: he was alone. He had only one ally, and that was Pope Pio II; no one else wanted to join him on the crusade. Expecting the resources offered by the holy man, Dracula prepared to face the most powerful army in the world. With his inexhaustible energy, he made a plan to visit the 225 villages of Wallachia, sending his boyars before him to each village square or meeting point to gather the townspeople.

When the peasants knew that their beloved ruler was going to visit them because he needed them, they were overcome by excitement. He addressed each village with the same speech:

"I am the highest pontiff of the Orthodox Church in Wallachia, and I tell you that the faith of our God, Jesus Christ, is in danger. The infidel Ottoman sultan took Constantinople and divested our Lord of his divinity, declaring him a simple prophet on the same level of Mohammad. The Christians who lived there were beaten, humiliated, raped, and then sold as slaves—and the sultan wants to do the same with us. He has forced me to sign a treaty in which I promise to deliver to him one thousand children of conscription for his army every year. In the two years since, I have not carried it out—I have only delivered him promises. I swear by the souls of my parents and my brother that I would rather change my name and you can call me 'Dog'; than allow a single Wallachian child to be delivered to the damned sultan. But I need help from all of you: the elderly, the children, the pregnant women, the lame—we all are soldiers of Christ in this fight! Some of you may be wondering, *What about my crop? What will happen to my animals?* I am asking you to ask yourselves some better questions: *What will happen to my God? To my children? To my women? And what will happen to my life? To my freedom?* I was a prisoner of the Ottoman Turks for five years. They took my family away from me, and I never saw them again. We are going to serve our God and the freedom of Wallachia! We are going to fight as disciplined soldiers—and if my soldiers and boyars give you orders, obey them blindly! Carry them out as real soldiers do, with no discussion, even if you don't understand them! I was born to serve our Lord and our beloved Wallachia, and I promise you that I will do everything possible, even die on the battlefield, to defend my God and you. I pray to my God that I will die with his holy name on my lips. When the time comes and you are called to war, do not think of yourselves. Think of our God, Of your children and your nation! And finally, let us honor our God by participating in a holy Mass."

By the end of his speech, the people were screaming from joy and excitement. The faith of their monarch had gladdened their hearts. Where did they have to go? What did they have to do? They would go to hell itself to fight the devil! They were just waiting on Dracula's orders, and they would follow him blindly.

———◆◆◆———

When the vovoid left each village, some boyars would stay behind to instruct the women and elderly:

"You, too, will participate actively in the war. You will seek refuge in the forest, preferably in caves. You will take water, food, and grain to those places and hide there, quiet as rabbits. A war is not won just by soldiers. You will help, too, by digging wells, covering them with wood, and building something on top of them. When we give you the order, you must burn your crops and kill your animals, and throw them, along with human excrement, into any water sources that are not hidden. Then you will go to your shelters and hide, praying with all the fervor of your heart that our God will guide us to victory. When the danger passes, you will come back, uncover the hidden wells, and with the seeds you have stored away you will replant the fields. When the war is over, other animals will be sent to you."

Dracula visited every village and town, encouraging his people, so that everyone in Wallachia was not just willing but impatient to die defending his faith and seeking freedom through war with the enemy—everyone, that is, except the Saxons.

73

"Dracula is organizing his people in Wallachia to declare war on the Ottoman Empire!" a spy breathlessly reported to the powerful Mehemed II.

The sultan burst out laughing. "That is a good joke! And what is he going to attack us with—clubs and stones?"

One of his advisors furrowed his brow. "You should investigate him," he said. "He can be a dangerous adversary."

"I know Dracula well," Mehemed said. "He said he was a worshiper of Allah, and now he appoints himself highest pontiff of a savage church. He has no ideology! And his army? What army! A bunch of peasants and beggars playing at war! It would be ridiculous for me to worry about a rebellious, resurrected louse." By now the sultan was holding his stomach because it hurt from laughing. This was the funniest joke he had heard in his life! It had been a while since he had laughed so hard.

His wisest advisor spoke up: "Kill him now, when he has no strength, lord."

"You are right," the sultan said, still catching his breath. "Bring me Hamza Bey and Thomas Catavolinos."

After a while the summoned men arrived and asked respectfully, "How can we serve you, my lord?"

Mehemed stared at them blankly, making an effort to remember why he had summoned them, while the thugs waited patiently. "Oh . . . now I remember!" With a huge smile on his face he said, "I want you to kill Dracula!" And without bothering to offer more details, he resumed his more important business.

Catavolinos was the mastermind. He made the plan, taking advantage of some privileged information his spy had received from one of Dracula's commanding officers about the potential border dispute at frontier at the Danube River. Catavolinos then explained the strategy in great detail to Hamza Bey.

———◆———

Dracula was visited by an emissary from the Ottoman Empire; he had an invitation to solve the future problem of determining the border at the Danube. It was asked that Dracula not send representatives; the powerful sultan wished to resolve the problem face-to-face to arrive at a friendly agreement. Dracula was also informed that Wallachia's tribute of money and children of conscription, which had been pending for two years, could be paid the next year.

Dracula said to the envoy, "In two more months, without a doubt, I will be in the Fortress of Giurgiu, and I will bring the pending tribute." The envoy departed with the message for his sultan, leaving Dracula deep in thought. After considering the situation carefully, he called Ivan.

"How can I serve you?" the boyar asked.

Dracula looked at him with distrust and asked himself in silence, *Is this the one who betrayed me?* But no . . . he was not that kind of man. He, along with f Kestywz, represented Dracula's real family. After a long silence, he said, "One of our commanding officers is a traitor."

Ivan was speechless. That accusation was reason enough to draw the sword and challenge the one who uttered it. But in this case, how could he? The one who had said it was the most intelligent and shrewd man he had ever known. Ivan took a deep breath and asked, "Who is he, my lord?"

"I would like to know that, too. The commanders and I were the only ones who knew about the border problem at the Danube, and now the sultan has summoned me to resolve it! We have a traitor among us, and we are going to make a plan to identify him."

Ivan set his limited brain to work and quickly realized that he was meant to obey, not to think. "What shall we do, my lord?" he asked.

Dracula kept thinking and finally answered, "We will send an emissary to the sultan confirming that we will take advantage of our meeting to give him the tribute we owe. We will also offer him some Dutch horses and, to make their delivery more entertaining and interesting, we will reveal our plans to present him with the most exotic and beautiful gift in the world. But he must guess what it is before we deliver anything. I bet he will never know what it is until delivery And that is a challenge!"

Ivan did not understand the strategy, but as usual, he had blind faith in his vovoid. "Consider it done," he said.

The next day an emissary left town for the Ottoman Empire to deliver the challenge. The sultan received it and said to Hamza Bey, "No one stops paying us tribute. This miserable louse is going to pay with his life for having tried to attack the empire. And to think that at one time I considered him my brother! His destiny is set, and only Allah can change it."

The sultan thought for a while and then gave Catavolinos an order. "Investigate the mysterious gift and find out what it is. I have to know before the delivery. No one defeats me in a challenge!"

By means of a spy, Catavolinos sent Senesval an order to investigate the mysterious gift. "It is not a problem," Senesval told the spy. "I am going to investigate, and I will tell you what I learn later."

Dracula summoned his boyars and said, "We must gather two thousand children of conscription from throughout all Wallachia. On this occasion I want them all to be older than fourteen, but they must look young."

"Isn't fourteen the highest age for the conscription?" Kardotas asked.

Dracula glared at him and shouted, "I do not need to give you explanations! Fulfill my order!"

"Dracula is a liar—a damned Ottoman 'Dog'!" "Demon 'Dog'—may the souls of your parents burn in hell!" These and many other curses came out of the mouths of the Wallachians as their young men were chained to pay the conscription of the hateful sultan. Meanwhile, the young men were confused and truly scared. From that moment on, their destiny was uncertain. But there was one feeling shared by all the people affected: they wanted to impale the traitor!

———◆———

Meanwhile Dracula had a meeting with his six commanding officers. "We are going to the Fortress of Giurgiu to pay the sultan the pending tribute," he said. "We are going to give him some pretty gifts—and a mysterious one."

Kardotas, Kestywz, Swerige, and Luga were curious, "What is it?" they asked.

Senesval kept quiet so as not to look suspicious; the others had already asked, anyway.

Ivan smiled knowingly. "It is beautiful, it is unique, and it is a gift worthy of a great sultan."

Dracula was watching and paying attention to every detail—every reaction, every involuntary movement of his commanders. When he saw a slight flush but no expression on Senesval's face when they spoke of the gift, it did not take Dracula long to identify him. However, he needed to be sure; there was a lot at stake.

When the session was over and the boyars had gone, Dracula went to Ivan. "The traitor is Senesval," he said. "Watch him closely. We must wait for the plan to work to confirm he is guilty."

It wasn't long before the traitor invited Ivan to drink together. After a few glasses of wine, Senesval asked, "Do you know what the mysterious gift is?"

"Of course!" answered Ivan.

Senesval smiled and slapped Ivan on the back. "And what is it?"

Ivan held up a hand. "I promise I will tell you the day we deliver the tribute. How would you like to go hunting tomorrow?"

"Sure," Senesval replied amiably. But as they kept on drinking, Senesval continued to ask about the gift—his insistence confirming his guilt.

They killed the animal

The next day they set out to hunt, again Senesval's actions confirmed his guilt: during the entire hunting expedition he did not stop asking about the gift. "I am dying to know!" he said. "Please tell me. What is it?"

Following Dracula's instructions, Ivan finally gave in and said, "It is the most beautiful and exotic ruby I've ever seen, with a truly unique color. But please don't tell anyone! Just you, Dracula, and I know the secret."

"Can I see it?" Senesval asked.

"I have it well hidden," Ivan replied. "I'll show it to you later—and when you see it, you are not going to believe it!

With that, Senesval had the information he needed; he did not care about anything else. He told the spy what he had learned, describing the gift. Meanwhile, the traitor was already being watched, and in that way part of the sultan's spy ring started to be identified.

Dracula and Ivan met to discuss the situation. "It is so sad that Senesval has betrayed us," the vovoid said. "Two days have passed since you told him what the gift was. If he really was simply curious about it, he would have asked you again to show it to him. This reconfirms his treason! However, we must pretend we do not know anything. Three days before our departure, take the spy, without anyone noticing, and make him tell you the sultan's intentions. The next day arrest Senesval, interrogate him, and get the truth out of him, too."

After a while, an envoy of the sultan arrived with a brief letter addressed to Dracula. "Your gift is a ruby with a unique and strange color," the letter said. "Don't ever underestimate or challenge your sultan! I expect you in Giurgiu. Signed, Mehemed II." As Dracula read it, a strange smile spread over his face.

At the right time, Abraham was taken to the mousetrap for interrogation. When he entered he began shaking. "Why did you bring me here?" he asked, fearfully.

The boyars' silence and the energetic activity around him told him that he was going to be submitted to torture. He was tied by his feet and hands, leaving him defenseless. Then, without saying a word, one boyar stretched the ropes taught while another pulled out his toenails. The traitor was terrified; those demons had not asked anything yet, and already they were torturing him to the limits of his resistance. He started to scream. "I am a spy! I will give away the others! But please, do not hurt me more!" And he started to name his co-conspirators, all of whom were Saxons with the exception of Senesval.

One of the boyars left to report to the vovoid. "You were right. One of his accomplices is Senesval."

Two days before the planned delivery, many sacks full of metal arrived in Tirgoviste, simulating the gold coins owed for the tribute. The two thousand children who had been chosen from throughout Wallachia also were gathered in Tirgoviste to be delivered to the sultan.

"Come in, please," Senesval's wife said kindly.

When Senesval saw his fellow commanding officers step into his home, he gave a warm smile. "I want to invite you to take—" Before he could finish welcoming them, he was surrounded by swords pointed threateningly at his body. "What is happening?" he asked, as his astonished wife and children looked on.

"Come with us, traitor!" Ivan ordered.

Senesval felt the weight of the world upon his shoulders; Dracula was smarter than he had imagined. He knew his future: he was his own executioner. Now he had to pay with his life the consequence of his actions. He joined the boyars in silence and was taken to the mousetrap. Ivan stopped and turned to him. "Save us the torture—you know your destiny. Tell me what is going to happen at the Fortress of Giurgiu."

Senesval had no hope; he knew that one way or another, he was going to die impaled. He kept his silence.

Ivan frowned. "You don't want to talk? That is your decision. Remember that you are going to die the way you chose, and your family will stay in Wallachia. Dracula is our hope. We trust in him; he is going to free us from the Ottomans. If you don't tell us what you know, your family will pay the consequences: your wife and daughters will end up in the Ottoman brothels, and your sons will be Janissaries."

Speaking slowly, Senesval confessed. "You are going to a trap," he said. "When you arrive at the fortress they are going to kill Dracula and all the rest of you, too." And then, without hurrying, the traitor described in meticulous detail the strategy the sultan had planned for eliminating them.

"Who are your accomplices?" Ivan demanded.

"Accomplices?" Senesval replied. "My contact is the Saxon Abraham— and to convince me to work with him, he had to give me a lot of gold. What use do I have for it now? I want to speak to Dracula!"

Ivan turned and left to find the vovoid. "The traitor wants to talk to you," he said.

Dracula went to see what additional information he could get from Senesval. Standing in front of the traitor, he asked him, "You wanted to see me? What useful information are you going to give me?"

Senesval began pleading, "My lord, I am very ashamed and sorry for having betrayed you. Our God forgives any sin if there is repentance. You are the highest leader of the Orthodox Church, and I ask for your forgiveness in the name of the blood of our Lord!"

Dracula had a noble heart, a pure soul, and an obsessive sense of justice. Looking Senesval in the eye, he answered, "If you had shown your repentance before you were discovered, I would have saved you from impalement and shown mercy by beheading you. However, you were discovered committing treason. To show you that I am fair and there is no rancor inside me, I will forgive you your offenses against me. But concerning the punishment, you earned it with your actions. After the death of your body comes the final judgment of your soul, and only God knows what awaits you. Hell, glory—how should I know?" He turned around and left as the cowardly traitor screamed, begging to be decapitated, imploring Dracula to consider the blood of Christ as mediator. The vovoid left without bothering to give the traitor the least explanation. *No one wastes time speaking to corpses,* he thought.

Meanwhile the young men who had been called for conscription were confused, asking each other a million questions: Why did the 'Dog' deceive us? Doesn't the 'Dog' care that he is sending his parents' souls to hell? Are we going to see our own parents again? Many of them were crying.

Just as the young men had plunged into the depths of sadness, a familiar figure appeared before them. They felt they now were seeing who he really was without a mask: a monster who used the holy name of God to lie, a heretic who carelessly damned his loved ones to hell. Some of those gathered started to bark, reminding him that he had promised to take the name of 'Dog' if he allowed even one young person to be delivered for conscription to the infidel sultan.

When Dracula heard the barking, he understood the pain and confusion of those innocent children. He raised his hands for silence, and when the noise subsided he began talking:

"As I am sure you can understand, we could not explain to you or your parents the strategy of this battle. I know we have caused you deep pain and incredible sadness, and I hope you will accept my apologies. It never was my intention to cause you so much damage. I know you look at me as a liar and call me 'the Dog' because you think I am going to deliver you to our enemy. But those who know the nature of the war understand that you cannot always tell the truth lest you reveal the tactics you are going to use against the enemy.

"The war against the Ottoman Turks has begun! Each one of you can be a soldier in this battle—no more pretending to fight. And your participation is critical if we hope to win the battle. You are going to help us deceive our enemies. Yes, you will be chained—but all the chains will be open. We will deliver you to the sultan, and while you are being delivered you must cry and show fear and sadness. Then, when the order to attack is given, the battle will start. At that moment you must throw aside your chains, run to the nearby carts, take up weapons, and attack the enemy. You are soldiers of Christ! We are going to fight for our faith. We are going to free Wallachia. Do not allow our families to be slaves! If any one of you does not want to go, you are free to return home. I will not consider you traitors, as you are practically children."

The young people felt as if they had been struck by lightning. What was happening? They were not prisoners—they were free to leave the chains that would take them to war. Now they felt their bodies fill with a strange kind of energy, and not one boy abandoned his leader. Everyone wanted to die defending his faith and the freedom of Wallachia. Now they felt ashamed for having insulted their vovoid with that nickname. They cried tears of joy, smiling all the while.

When Dracula saw the brave attitude of those new soldiers, he said respectfully, "We are going to dedicate this battle to our God—and we are going to win it! Those of you who have the honor of offering your lives as martyrs, defending the faith and the freedom of Wallachia, will be honored and forever remembered by all Wallachia. You will give prestige to your lineage and go the kingdom of God. Imagine when you arrive home bathed in glory . . . you will be beside yourselves with joy, and your parents will be very proud of you. We must seek to be at the side of our God. So let us seek death with joy! Let us serve our Lord!"

The anguish, fear, and desperation those young people were feeling changed to joy and a fierce desire to serve their vovoid. Now they trusted him more than ever, and they felt like powerful soldiers, smiling in the face of battle. To celebrate the initiation of his new soldiers, Dracula invited them to participate in a solemn Mass, sharing Holy Communion and praying with them. In that place they all could feel the presence of the Holy Spirit.

Then Dracula summoned his boyars and outlined the details of his military strategy.

The next day all those who would be participating in the delivery to the sultan gathered. They began with a Mass to entrust their actions to God. With the help some monks, Holy Communion was distributed, and then, after praying in silence, the group prepared to head into the trap laid by their enemy.

Their departure was enlivened by the townspeople, who did not stop barking at the hypocritical ruler as he led away the children of conscription reminding him from this point on, he is the 'Dog'. Those unchained captives were smiling disconcertingly, as if they were going to a party; their parents shouted at them, encouraging them to run, and were exasperated when the children did not obey.

One parent took his child by the arm and tried to force him out of line, but the son pulled away, upset. "Father, behave!" he said. "I am going to serve the sultan!" And so, among barking and curses, the beloved children walked away, breaking the hearts of their parents, who were crying profusely and blessing them, sure that this was the last time they would see their boys.

Meanwhile Kardotas went ahead with part of the retinue, and they took their positions.

Dracula was at the front of the boyars, who in turn led the two thousand children of conscription. When the group got close to the front, they passed back chains for the children to carry so they looked like prisoners.

The soldiers in the fortress watchtower saw them on the horizon. "Enemies in sight!" they called. Immediately the soldiers who were going to ambush the group took their positions deep in the forest, moving stealthily and in silence. When Kardotas' soldiers, dressed like Ottomans, approached the sultan's men in the forest, they never imagined they were actually the enemy . . . until it was too late.

From the fort, the Ottomans saw Dracula approaching with children of conscription, and then they watched Ottoman soldiers emerge from the forest, surrounding and disarming the group. They never imagined their treason had been discovered.

Dracula's retinue was led to the fortress as planned. With the enemies captured and unarmed, the sultan's men opened the door of the fortress to chain the missing prisoners.

"For our God Jesus Christ!" At Dracula's battle cry, the children of conscription experienced for the first time the exotic taste of adrenaline. They threw aside their chains, exchanged them for swords, and showed their fierceness. Within moments the fortress was captured

After defeating the enemy, Dracula shouted, "Impale them all!" He looked at Hamza Bey and Catavolinos and addressed those Byzantine renegades. "Traitors!"

The boyars and the new soldiers impaled the infidel enemies

Hamza Bey watched, horrified, how he was going to end. What scared him most was the fact that his soul would not rest, because he was going to die impaled and then go straight to hell. He heard the heart-rending screams of his companions when they were pierced by a stake and placed naked up high, while in the sky above them, a flock of birds prepared for the great banquet.

The infidels killed in battle were cut into pieces and their parts impaled. Dracula had the fort burned, and he left in its place a flag of the Order of the Dragon, to give himself credit for the victory. But he also knew that the war had just started; it was only a matter of time before the sultan threw himself at Dracula's forces with a great part of his huge and powerful army.

The vovoid then addressed the children of conscription, saying, "Today you showed your faith and love to Christ by defending him from our enemies. You showed you have a soldier's heart by fighting for Wallachia. But I still need your help! You will now return to the places you came from, and you must talk about how you participated in this battle. You must also glorify the martyrs who at this moment must be rejoicing in the eternal glory of God. We must uplift the hearts of our people—do not let their spirits fall! Let our greatest desire to be to die for our Christ! The war has just begun. Now we must be prepared to fight for the freedom of Wallachia!"

The boys were excited. They wanted to be like Dracula. They wanted to die for their faith and with the name of God on their lips, defending the freedom of their homeland. They envied the destiny of the martyrs.

While this was happening, Dracula was becoming known as 'the Dog' throughout Wallachia. He had promised that he would never deliver a child to the sultan, and he had lied. The rage against him was so great that all the dogs in Wallachia were renamed 'Dracula' to the dishonor the evil liar.

Dracula arrived in Wallachia with a huge smile of satisfaction on his face. He was riding at the front of his retinue, and everywhere could be heard the anonymous barking of the people, a concert embellished by screamed insults like "Die, liar 'Dog'! You sent the soul of your father to hell!" and other offenses. But no matter how the crowd insulted him, Dracula appeared unfazed. In fact, he seemed to enjoy the confrontation. How cynical! The townspeople started to whisper among themselves,

"Has this damn 'Dog' gone crazy?" Then a shout rang out: "The 'Dog' has gone crazy!" And the crowd took up the shout: "The 'Dog' has gone crazy!" But even if that were true, no one could take away the immense hatred the people felt toward the lying vovoid. "He is a traitor!" someone shouted. "We have to impale him!" As more shouts rang out, the crowd was watching the traitor, infuriated by his cynical smile. His arrogant attitude made the blood boil in their veins.

Dracula was hearing the screamed insults. The more upset his people became, the happier he felt, and he smiled even more broadly.

Seeing him up close, one furious parent shrieked, "Die, damned 'Dog' of the dev—" but then stopped himself. "Son!" The father ran to his boy and hugged him with all his strength, his face bathed in tears. Those who were watching the scene were confused. *What is happening?*

Zygmund, the boy, explained, "I am a soldier of Dracula! He never had any intention of delivering us to the Ottomans, but he kept the secret because it was part of his strategy to win the battle . . . and we did it!" Then he added with obvious pride, "I am a defender of the faith in our God! I fight for Wallachia's freedom, and my leader is Dracula! The war has started, and we all are soldiers of Dracula!"

The townspeople began sobbing when they heard the truth; they were ashamed for having insulted their good leader. Kneeling down with tears in their eyes, they cried, "Forgive us, lord! Show us the way and we will follow you, even to hell! If you ask us to fight against the devil, we will do it . . . gladly!"

Dracula understood their emotions, and he was excited and happy as he greeted his subjects. Raising his right hand, Roman-style, he said, "The war has begun with this attack . . . it is unavoidable!"

All the dogs in Wallachia continued to be called 'Dracula', but now the name was meant to honor the people's greatest hero and defender.

74

Soon afterwards, Dracula went back to visit the most powerful man in Moldavia.

"Cousin!" Stephen said. "It is great to see you! You look strong as an oak—look at you!"

Dracula gave him the great news. "We took the Fortress of Giurgiu! You should have seen it . . . it was incredible. With the help of our children, we defeated the enemy!"

"You used an army of children?" Stephen asked, astonished.

"Surprise was an important factor," Dracula said. And then he told Stephen in great detail about the battle and how he was received by his people when he returned home. At the end he said, "As you can see, Cousin, the war against the Ottomans has started. I need your support now more than ever!"

Stephen frowned. "Uncle Petru is still conspiring against me—I have spent a lot of money to defend myself from him. Right now I have serious internal and economic problems."

"When you asked for my help to recover your crown, I had Basarab Laiota, Dan III, Vlad the Monk, and many other Saxons of Wallachia wanting to overthrow me—and what did I do?" Dracula raised his hand to show Stephen his scar.

"You helped me recover my kingdom," Stephen replied somberly.

Dracula put a hand on his cousin's arm. "Let us fight the sultan together," he said encouragingly. "The Holy Father offered me one hundred thousand gold coins as support for the crusade, but you are my only ally. Do not leave me alone!"

Stephen looked skeptical. "When do you think the pope is going to give you what he promised? Because it is easy to make a promise, but to deliver one hundred thousand gold coins is another thing altogether. I agree with Saint Thomas: seeing is believing."

"He will send me the money through King Matthias."

"And you think Matthias is going to give it to you?" Stephen gave a short laugh. "If it was one thousand coins, I would not doubt that. But we are talking about a lot of money! You are too gullible, Cousin! Do you still believe that Zeus is divine? I am sorry, but I am not going to your crusade."

Dracula's pleas, his arguments for the defense of the faith and the freedom of their nations—nothing made Stephen change his mind. Dracula looked his cousin in the eye and asked him, right palm outstretched, "What about our oath? And our blood? And our witness, Jesus Christ?"

Stephen kept silent, preferring not to answer and look like a coward.

The next day Dracula said good-bye to his not-so-beloved cousin, leaving with this reproach: "I hope that our God enlightens your heart and takes away your cowardice! The only thing I will take from you is disappointment."

Stephen received this farewell like a slap in the face, but his shame prevented him from answering. Like every good coward, he kept silent. He watched his cousin leave the room and he felt really bad. Was he a coward? A liar? A traitor? Was he even a man? Why hadn't he fulfilled the promise he had sworn before God? Over time, those questions and a thousand more would make his conscience seek and find the light; but in the meantime, he was what he was, and no one could change that. He was a perfect coward . . . and a traitor to Dracula and Christ.

75

Matthias was pleasantly surprised by Dracula's visit. "To what do I owe the pleasure of your company?"

Dracula smiled. "I have come to inform you of the occupation of the Fort of Giurgiu."

"I have been informed," Matthias said. "I still can't believe it! Only you would think to take a fortress like that one supported only by a group of children without military training."

"Ah, but with the hearts of dragons . . . you should have seen them in battle! They were more ferocious than many soldiers I know, and they are ready for the upcoming war. There's no doubt that the sultan is planning an attack. That is why I have come to ask for your help and military support."

"It would only occur to you to go into the lion's den! How are you going to face the sultan? His army is too powerful!"

"I am sure we will defeat him with your help," Dracula replied.

Matthias shook his head. "I don't know how to face that army! At moments like this I wish my father were alive. You do not know how much I miss him . . . sometimes I would like to dig him out of his grave. It is difficult for me to openly support your fight, but I'll see what I can do."

It would have been easier and more honest simply to have said no. Dracula was shocked by the cowardice and insecurity of this man, who was wrapped in elegant and sophisticated military attire. Staring at the king, he thought, *You would think Matthias was the son of a peasant. I cannot believe that I am the subject of this miserable coward. But with or without his help, one day I will free Wallachia.* Then he said aloud, "I am really worried! How are we going to finance the crusade? Did you receive the money promised by the Holy Father?"

"I haven't received anything yet," the king said. "I sent some emissaries to His Holiness, and he asked us to be patient; the resources are still being gathered. As soon as he has the money he will send it immediately."

Dracula felt desperate. "We are running out of time, and it is impossible to make any crusade without money," he said. "Please keep insisting—I need those resources urgently! I am leaving because I have to prepare for the inevitable war. I hope that God enlightens you and you send me reinforcements . . . I will be waiting for them! And please, as soon as you get the money from the Holy Father, send it to me immediately."

When Dracula arrived back in Wallachia, he talked to Barbat, the metropolitan, saying, "I am going to entrust to you one of the greatest responsibilities of our fight."

Barbat answered, "I know that whatever you request is for the defense of the faith of our God. I will not rest until I achieve what you ask of me."

Dracula nodded and took a deep breath. "All the religious ministers in Wallachia must exalt the spirits of the congregants so they will come to the defense of the faith—which is in danger now more than ever. We have to enliven the hearts of all the inhabitants of Wallachia, making them feel like soldiers of Christ and preparing them for war by instilling within them a fierce desire to shed their blood to defend him, and to blindly obey my soldiers and boyars.

So on Sunday, throughout all Wallachia, the Orthodox churches radiated an energy that made the hearts of their parishioners swell. The priests encouraged them to defend the faith and consider death in battle their highest ambition.

76

"Damn Dracula!" The sultan's scream echoed through the palace. He had just learned the news that had already spread throughout his empire, about the smart strategy his enemy had used in the occupation of Giurgiu. What upset Mehemed most was that people had exaggerated and distorted the facts; his subjects were talking about it as if it were a great epic adventure led by a giant demon—an invincible power who had sent the souls of the Ottoman soldiers to hell, and neither the sultan nor Allah been able to prevent it.

Muhamat, one of his counselors, rushed into the room, his eyes bulging with fear. "He dared to impale our people!" he exclaimed. "Their souls will suffer in hell for all eternity!"

"They deserve it for being fools—naïve and overconfident," muttered the sultan, "I hope this serves as a lesson for all my army that they should be more careful when they go fighting against cockroaches. That resurrected louse did me a favor: now my army knows fear. And I know exactly how to pay him back—when he steps on my territory, I am going to crush him like an insect!"

77

Dracula had a meeting with his commanding officers and told them, "I know that what I am going to propose will seem like a crazy military tactic, but if we think it through, we can have great success. We will attack the Ottoman Empire by crossing the Danube River when it is frozen. I assure you, we will kill a lot of infidels and therefore provoke the rage of the sultan. He will without a doubt attack our territory."

"What if we wait for the cold to pass?" Kestywz asked.

"No, Kestywz—it's the intense cold that is going to be our best ally in this case. You'll see . . . trust me!"

Oblucita was the first place to receive a visit from the blessed crusaders. There was no a battle cry; everything transpired in complete silence.

Abdullah was in his small, comfortable home, surrounded by his large family; his little children were happily playing hide-and-seek. Suddenly someone slammed the door and the crusaders entered and headed toward him. They beat Abdullah and tied him up while his terrified family watched, none of them understanding why the men had to inflict so much harm.

When the men arrived, little Shereza was hiding, waiting for one of her brothers to find her. She saw everything from her hiding place without being discovered. She watched the mean men brutalize her beloved family; she saw the men tie them up and then savagely beat them. Trembling and unable to help them, she started praying, begging Allah to protect and look after them.

The same scene was repeated throughout the town, and by mid-morning the crusaders had absolute control. "Impale them!" Dracula cried, and his orders started to be carried out immediately. Then he turned to a boyar named Costea and said, "Cut the ears and noses off these infidels and put them in a sack to keep count of the enemy's casualties."

The process of impalement was so painful and humiliating that the inhabitants refused point-blank to cooperate; convincing them required a savage beating. In this case the intense cold became part of the torture. While on the one hand it raised the intensity of the pain, on the other, it diminished the time of death, freeing the victims from that suffering, since the impaled ones died frozen the next day. The ones who died defending themselves in the occupation were cut into pieces and the pieces impaled, so that the Ottomans who witnessed the punishment would have no doubt that the souls went to hell.

Night fell, and Costea was carefully counting noses. Finally he turned to Dracula with a satisfied smile. "One thousand three hundred twenty-five infidels died in this place! It was an excellent day . . . we must give thanks to God!" So that is what they did. Then the men prepared to go to sleep, pleased at having fulfilled their duty.

Little Shereza was mute from fear. The scenes she had witnessed would be with her for the rest of her life, and they would be her greatest torment. The intense cold made time go by more slowly than ever; she could not sleep a moment due to that infernal cold. Her mind was on the verge of madness.

The next day Dracula gave a new order: "Let us go to Novoselo!" When everyone was about to leave, he yelled, "Burn all the houses!"

Nooo! The scream resounded in Shereza's mind, but her energetic mental refusal did not prevent the solders from carrying out the terrible order. Anguished and desperate, she spoke to her God: "Help me, Allah! Why are you punishing me in this way?" She heard her home starting to burn, but she was waiting for the bad men to go away so she could run; she knew that if she was captured she would end up impaled and her soul would go straight to hell. But those men, who to her were the sons of Satan, were like wolves lying in wait. The fire was consuming all the corners of her house, and she waited and waited until the fire surrounded her . . . it was hell on earth! But if she fell at the hands of those demons, they would surely send her to real hell. The flames began to devour her little body, and still she endured the torment until she could take it no longer. Then she couldn't help herself: she went running out into the snow, engulfed in flames. There in the snow, in the grip of unbearable pain, she went to the heaven her religion had assigned her—without a doubt to the side of her God, Allah.

The military men watched, amused, as human torches came running out from God knows where; they smiled watching the destiny of those infidels, who had almost evaded justice. "Should I cut the ears off those flaming demons?" Costea asked Dracula.

Dracula gave a dismissive wave. "Forget about those miserable infidels!" he said.

When they withdrew from the place, they placed a flag of the Order of the Dragon among the impaled to award themselves the victory.

Then it was the turn of Novoselo to receive a visit from the blessed crusader army, whose military tactic was similar to the one they used at Oblucita. At Novoselo they counted 6,868 noses and twice as many ears. Then they moved on to another place, and another and another. The scene when the crusaders left was similar in every town, as if made by an artist who always painted the same picture. The only thing that changed was the number of impaled people.

In January 1462, Dracula's men completed their holy crusade. The vultures followed the army home, as it had been such a dependable provider of succulent eyes and fresh meat.

78

On January 25, a visibly shaken Ottoman arrived before the sultan and said, "Dracula surprised and murdered in cold blood more than twenty thousand of our subjects who lived along the Danube River—and he impaled them all! He did not even spare the women and children."

At that moment Mehemed understood that Dracula was not an insignificant little foe, but his most bitter and wicked enemy—a demon who was sending children's souls to hell. Mehemed had to crush him as soon as possible. Summoning his chief falconers, he said, "I want to attack Dracula immediately. Prepare the invasion of Wallachia!"

Mehemed II was extremely discreet in his relationship with Radu; anyone who saw them together would have assumed Radu was just his reliable counselor. The sultan had a wife, lovers, and children, but none of them filled the void occupied by his real love. That night Mehemed II told Radu his plans: "We are going to kill your brother and invade Wallachia."

Radu looked at him steadily with his beautiful blue eyes, and then, in sweet, hoarse voice, he said, "Kiss me first—love me. I do not care about anything else!" Their mouths merged in a long, passionate kiss, and then their bodies also became one. As their hearts beat one next to the other, they shared a strange, intoxicating energy, and their love took them to the edge of madness. When they had ended their passionate encounter, Radu spoke in the same whisper, "I love you above all, and I do not want to lose you for any reason. Do you know Wallachia? There are forests, swamps, bogs, rivers . . . it is easy to get lost. Do not attack my brother there—you have no idea how shrewd he is. Wait for him to attack you here in the empire, and then crush him like an insect. Why do you think he attacked the Danube and then went back to Wallachia? To force you to attack him when you were blind with rage—that way, he would have an advantage. Do not let that happen. You are more intelligent than he is. Take your time, think with a cool head—don't think with your gut."

The sultan smiled. "What is it about your voice and your words that hypnotizes me and convinces me?" the sultan asked softly.

"Love—all the love in the world!" Radu replied.

The next day the chief falconers appeared before the sultan. "My lord, everything is ready for the occupation of Wallachia," one of the men said.

"Cancel the invasion," Mehemed said.

The falconers looked at each other. Why was he ordering that? What was wrong with him? They could destroy Dracula in just a matter of weeks. Nevertheless, the men obeyed him in silence, not daring to comment on the absurd order, even among themselves.

Feeling superior because of his great army and his prestigious reputation for having conquered the most important city in the world, the sultan summoned his most aggressive, intelligent, and brave tribute collector and issued the following order: "Take a group of emissaries and a large retinue of Janissaries, go to Dracula, and force him to show respect to his master by paying the pending tribute. If he does not have it, then collect it as we did in the times of his grandfather, his uncle, and his father—and do not come back without it!"

With the confidence that came from long experience, the collector said with firm voice, "I have always fulfilled my duties by collecting all the tributes you have entrusted to me. When I come back I promise you, by Allah, that I will bring you twenty thousand gold coins and two thousand new soldiers . . . and the respect of that rebellious and irreverent governor!"

Some time after, an impressive retinue left the empire, headed toward Wallachia.

79

In Hungary, a different retinue was received by Matthias. The man leading the retinue bowed his head respectfully and said, "My king, we are envoys of our lord Dracula. He sent you this letter and these two sacks."

He opened the sacks and felt faint. *What wicked joke is this?* The sacks held thousands of noses and ears! Terrified, the king opened the letter and read:

My King Matthias Corvinus,

I have started the actions to provoke the war against the enemies of the faith in Christ. I haven't paid tribute for two years; I attacked and took the Fortress of Giurgiu and impaled all the Ottomans defending it; I undertook a crusade through the Danube, impaling 23,884 infidels. This number is not the product of exaggeration or false confidence: this letter is accompanied by two full sacks of noses and ears from the people impaled. Not included there are the ones who died burned, as we did not take their noses and ears. With this you will realize that the war against the infidels has started and there is no time for excuses. I am counting on your military support, as I expect to face hostility at any moment.

February 11, 1462, year of our God

Signed,
Wladislaus III, Dragwlya

Matthias was shaken. What was his crazy subject doing? Why would he walk right into that lion's den? How could Matthias face such a powerful enemy? Where was his father when he needed him? The truth was, Matthias was not prepared to face such problems; he was a young, immature, and cowardly king. The town council of Hungary had placed him in power seeking only their personal welfare and knowing that the young man could be played like a puppet, and they were not wrong. He was docile and perfectly malleable. Who cared about the real interests of Hungary or the defense of Christ?

Pope Pio II, knowing the bravery, determination, and fierceness of the great defender of Christianity, asked for solemn Te Deums, holy masses, rosaries, and prayers to be offered on his behalf. So throughout all of Europe, people prayed with devotion for Dracula's fight; it was all anyone talked about. Leading his brave army, Dracula massacred thousands of infidels, quickly establishing himself as the most holy defender of Christianity.

But Dracula needed something more than Te Deums and acknowledgment, so he wrote the following letter to the pope in the Vatican:

> Holy Father Pio II,
>
> The crusade against the Ottomans has started! I haven't paid tribute to my enemy for two years; I attacked the Fortress of Giurgiu and impaled all the Ottomans who defended it; and I made a crusade along the Danube, sending my king two sacks with the ears and noses of the 23,884 infidels that I impaled there. At this moment they must be in hell. Because of these actions, I expect an attack by the sultan's army any minute now, and I urgently need the resources you offered to send through my King Matthias Corvinus. I appeal to you for your help because I am desperate—you are my only ally. I need the resources now! If it arrives later, it might be too late. I need to buy weapons and support the expenses of the crusade. Do not allow those infidels to destroy the faith in our God.
>
> You are Catholic; I am Orthodox. But we love, worship, and revere the same God.

I need your help desperately! Please send us your holy blessing, also. At this moment we need it more than ever.

Signed,

Wladislaus III, Dragwlya

The Holy Father was deeply touched when he received the letter; he immediately sent part of the promised money to King Matthias for the crusade to be a success.

———◆———

An envoy of the pope, heavily escorted, delivered sixty thousand gold coins to King Matthias. "This money must be delivered immediately to Dracula," the envoy said. "Sign this receipt."

Matthias received the money and put it in his treasury. A wicked idea had entered his mind and now would not let him rest. *What if I used the money to buy the crown of Saint Stephen? That would give legitimacy to my crown as king of Hungary—and I would become the holy Roman emperor.* But no . . . that would be treason to his God—and theft from his subject Dracula, who had never failed him.

80

Meanwhile, Dracula was asking himself desperately, *What is happening with my cousin? Why won't he help me?* Then an idea occurred to him that at first upset him, but then became fixed in his mind: *Why didn't I take Moldavia for myself? I delivered it to my cousin, and for what? He is a perfect coward! For the sake of my God I am willing to make war against him, because he broke our oath—but now I have to concentrate on my attack against the Ottomans.*

Dracula and his commanders planned carefully the deadly route by which they were going to guide the Ottoman army once it arrived in Wallachia. With the help of the peasants—including children, elders, and even pregnant women—they planted hidden traps along the route, digging huge holes with sharp stakes at the bottom and then covering them with branches and dirt. They also made other clever traps and diversions, and even built dams to flood some areas and turn them into swamps.

Still, Dracula was desperate for resources. "The help from the Holy Father still has not arrived," he told his commanders. "Every day we've sent an emissary to King Matthias, and every day he reports that he has not received the promised payment. We need to buy weapons and move the troops! What are we going to do?"

The intelligent Kardotas thought for a while before speaking. "What if we go to the monasteries and churches and ask for help?"

Dracula liked the idea and implemented it right away. He and a retinue arrived at a nearby Orthodox monastery and told the monks, "We are in a campaign for the defense of the faith in our God, but we do not have any money. We are begging for your help!"

The abbot broke into a broad smile. "This is the greatest honor we have received in all our lives. That our lord would ask us to contribute to the crusade against the infidels . . . it is more than we ever dreamed of! Allow us, lord!" He entered a little room and came out with a small chest full of gold and silver coins. Then he gave it to Dracula, saying, "These were our savings." Then more monks emerged from the room with another small chest containing sacred relics of gold. "Melt them and sell them," the abbot told Dracula. "And come back next week—we are going to ask our parishioners to get their savings and bring them to us."

Dracula was speechless. Taking a deep breath, he said in a voice shaking with emotion, "I accept your offering, and I promise you that as soon as the war is over, I will pay you back with interest for the sacrifice you are making for the defense of our faith." He then ordered his retinue to kneel down before the abbot. "Father," he said, "please give us your blessing."

On March 16, 1462, Dracula arrived at the monastery of the Catholic monks of Bucharest. "We need and beg for your help," he said. "We are defending the faith in our Lord. The Holy Father in Rome has offered to send us one hundred thousand gold ducats for our crusade, and in the meantime we have come to ask for your help."

For the Catholic monks, their moment of revenge had arrived. Standing before them was their bitter enemy—the one who called himself the highest pontiff of the Orthodox Church; the one who was depleting the wealth of their most important and faithful clients, the good Saxons—and now here he was, humiliated in front of them, almost begging on his knees. It was time to teach him a severe lesson.

The monk in charge said, "My good lord, this is a house of prayer. We are poor. You would do good to contribute to us some of the resources the Holy Father is going to give you. If you want to take something, I can give you my blessing."

Knowing about the great tithes and profitable alms these liars received, Dracula considered that hypocritical statement a cynical mockery. Feeling like a hot coal was burning his chest, he looked directly into the monk's eyes and said, "I do not need your damn blessing! Do you not understand? The war against the Ottomans is going to start, and there is no future for any of us if our enemies win. The churches will disappear. There will be no monks. Our God is going to be divested of his divinity—he will be a simple prophet, just as he is in Istanbul. Give me your money!"

That monks was really happy. That was how they wanted to see Dracula: begging, humiliated, at their feet. The abbot answered him cynically, "We do not have any money. Do you want my blessing, or not?"

Dracula turned to the shrewd and attentive Kardotas and said, "Find the money!" Then, looking back at the abbot, he said, "If it is true that you do not have money, I will beg your forgiveness and ask for your blessing on my knees. But if you have deceived me, you will be a traitor . . . and your actions will be your executioner!"

The monk remembered the law; he knew what happened to traitors. He became nervous and started to shake as Dracula's men carefully searched the monastery. Finally Kardotas returned to Dracula. "There is nothing here," he said. "These monks are really poor."

But Dracula noticed every detail about people. When he saw the monk's demeanor, he knew that he was lying. Addressing the suspect he said firmly, "You have hidden the money! You speak not with your mouth, but with your attitude. I am going to give you one last chance: give me the money, or you will die impaled!"

The monk was confuse. If he lied successfully he would keep his wealth, but if he was discovered he would end up impaled. If he told the truth he would save his life, but the monastery would be poor. The treasure, however, was well-hidden; the demon would never find it! With a silent prayer asking God's protection, he answered in a trembling voice, "We do not have any money."

Knowing he would never get the truth from that liar, Dracula issued the order: "Impale him!"

The abbot cried and prayed for divine help as the soldiers undressed him in the courtyard of the monastery. He did not understand what was happening, and his horrified companions watched the shameful process. When the soldiers prepared to put the stake in his anus, the abbot screamed with all his strength, "I will give you our wealth! But do not impale me!"

The soldiers looked at their leader, waiting for his instructions, but when he remained completely quiet, they continued with their job and the stake started to pierce the body. The impalement was punctuated by the terrifying screams of the traitor and the prayers of his companions. At the end he was naked and stuck on a stake in the middle of the courtyard, where he would remain alive for a few days before his body would serve as carrion for the birds and as an example for the other monks.

Dracula knew that it was impossible to interrogate the abbot in that position, since the pain would not allow him to talk, so he set his gaze on another monk and said, "If you do not tell me where the money is, you will accompany that traitor!"

The monk to whom he addressed the question was on the verge of hysteria. "Follow me, lord," he answered in a faltering voice, and then he led the soldiers to the corner of a secret basement. "It is buried there!" he said, pointing.

On Dracula's orders, the monks dug a hole and took out a chest filled with gold and silver coins and relics.

Dracula and his men returned to the courtyard, where he looked at the monks and said, "You have proven that you care more about money than defending the faith in our God. However, you will live." Then he pointed a finger at the impaled abbot. "But if you take that traitor down, I will impale you all!"

The monks were horrified at having lost their spiritual leader and their life savings, but what they did not realize was that they had lost something even more valuable: Dracula's trust.

As they rode away from the monastery, Dracula made an observation to his commanders: "We must identify monks by their actions and give them the treatment they deserve. I hope you understand now that Orthodox monks are our friends . . . and Catholics are our foes."

News of the impaled monk spread like wildfire throughout all Wallachia. And the peasants admired their vovoid all the more.

"Dracula is doing more than giving us justice," Olagu said to Jerzy. "He is forcing the Catholic monks to contribute their huge wealth to our crusade."

"I am glad he is impaling those traitors," Ianco added. "They have always despised us. They just care about the Saxons and the enemy boyars because of the large alms and tithes they give them."

Dracula visited several monasteries, with the same outcome. The Orthodox monks were willing to give all they had to the warrior, even if it was just their habits. He thanked them their willingness to help and asked them respectfully to give him their blessing. The Catholics hid their wealth; he had to take it through threats, and if they still did not accede he turned to impalement. When he left, they uttered their curses.

81

"Some Catholic monks are sending their wealth to Hungary and Europe," an informant from Dracula's spy ring reported.

"Kardotas!" Dracula shouted. His commander arrived before him immediately. "I want you to organize our soldiers to check the loads of all the peasants and merchants who travel through Wallachia."

"And what shall we look for?" Kardotas asked.

"Gold, silver, and money. The Catholic monks are exporting their wealth, and we have to stop it. Bring to Tirgoviste anyone who does that. He will be treated like a traitor."

"I will attend to this issue right away," Kardotas said. He left and summoned all the commanding officers, giving them the instructions from their leader. The officers then organized their boyars and soldiers, who immediately began the detailed search.

On a road from Wallachia, a boyar stepped in front of a departing cart. "Stop! In the name of Dracula, we are going to check the load!"

The driver of the cart dropped his gaze. "We are just some poor peasants on an errand for good monks," he said.

"And what are you taking?" asked the boyar, while his solders checked the load.

"Grain," another of the travelers replied, looking down at his feet.

"And why don't you look me in the eye?" the boyar asked in an authoritarian tone. He waited a moment to see if the travelers would lift their heads. When they didn't, he asked, "What are you hiding?"

"Nothing!" the driver said nervously. At the same time the soldiers reported, "Nothing but grain!"

The boyar raised his voice. "Did you know that taking wealth out of Wallachia is now considered treason . . . and that traitors will be impaled?"

"Yes," the driver muttered, without looking up.

The boyar moved to the back of the cart and looked closely at one of the driver's helpers. "Why are you trembling?" he asked.

"I am sick!" the man offered.

"Maybe you are sick," the boyar said. "But you are also lying. Now . . . look at me in the eye and tell me where the money is! If you do not tell me, I will find what you are hiding anyway, and you will also die impaled!"

The peasant knew it was useless to hide the treasure. "The cart has a false bottom," he said with a quavering voice. "Please do not impale me!"

"I promise you privileged treatment, but these miserable men will die as the law has established."

With that the driver said, "Fine—we are carrying gold and money! Take it, but please let us go! I am sure that with this treasure you won't have to work again in all your life."

The boyar was furious at the insinuation that he would deceive his friend Dracula. "How dare you propose to betray our father! To Tirgoviste!"

"Dracula, these traitors say they are peasants. They were trying to take this treasure out of Wallachia."

Dracula stared at the men. "What do you do?" he asked.

The men answered at the same time. "We are peasants."

Remembering his time as a peasant, Dracula asked, "Which moon cycle is best for harvesting wheat?"

They looked at each, scared, and that was enough for Dracula; there was nothing more to ask. "Stretch out your arms with your palms up!" he demanded. They obeyed, and the shrewd vovoid took their hands in his, looking for the calluses that every peasant earned through hard work. These hands were clean and callous-free. Dracula dropped their hands and looked at their faces. They were not sunburned.

"You are Catholic monks!" he shouted, and some of the men blushed, confirming his suspicion. "Liars! Traitors! Who are you running from? Is this how you defend the faith? Is this how you seek Wallachia's freedom? You do not even deserve the stake with which I am going to impale you!" He looked at Kestywz and said, "Prepare the impalement for tomorrow!"

One of his soldiers took the vovoid aside and pointed to the monk who had revealed the treasure. "My lord, I promised this monk that he would not be impaled if he told the truth, and he did. I would like to fulfill my promise."

"And you will," Dracula answered calmly. Then, addressing the monk in question, he said, "The punishment for committing treason is impalement. But since the word of my soldiers is as good as mine, I am going to show you mercy. You will be decapitated!"

The next day the sentences were carried out. The impalements took place with the usual routine—the same shame and the same message for all would-be traitors. One head rolled away from its decapitated body as the impaled ones watched from high on their stakes, amidst unthinkable, unbearable pain, envying the favored one's destiny.

82

In Europe the Holy Inquisition had done an excellent job, gathering enough money to give the pope what he had requested and keep its holy and blessed mission. It had punished the heretics according to the stipulations of the Catholic orthodoxy. If someone died writhing from excruciating pain or screaming from being burned alive, that was the way heresy was cleansed: the real torture was being drawn apart from one's Catholic faith. The Inquisition, that blessed institution, was a living example of the real defense of the faith in Christ.

In support of the cause, the Vatican sent some envoys to King Matthias to announce further allocation of resources. "The Holy Father Pio II sends you forty thousand gold coins," one of the envoys declared. "Added to the sixty thousand that were delivered previously, that makes a total of one hundred thousand, as promised. Please sign the receipt."

Matthias signed it, sealed it, and returned it to the envoys.

The main envoy then handed Matthias a sealed letter, saying, "Give this to Dracula and tell him the Holy Father considers him a sacred warrior due to his courage and devotion to the defense of the faith. Tell him that all of Europe is praying fervently that he will prevail in his fight."

Now that Matthias had the money, an idea that once seemed remote had become a real possibility. He was experiencing a very big dilemma: a battle between his moral and material values. After a great deal of thought, he finally made his decision. The one hundred thousand coins—money that the Holy Father had gathered as a sacrifice for the crusade against the Ottomans—Matthias would save in his treasury.

83

On March 18, 1462, a large Ottoman retinue arrived in Tirgoviste, guarded by an even larger group of Janissaries. "We have come to speak to the sultan's subject called Dracula," the tribute collector announced

The gatekeeper, seeing what little regard those strangers seemed to have for Dracula, replied, "By disposition of my lord, everyone who comes to see him must uncover his head as a sign of respect."

The collector frowned. "Don't you know who sent us? We are representatives of your real lord—the Ottoman sultan! He has ordered us not to uncover before anyone . . . that is our tradition!"

"I do not have any other lord but Dracula," the gatekeeper said. "And if you want to speak with him, it is necessary that you uncover your heads as a sign of respect. Do it, and then you may come in."

"Insolent louse!" the collector screamed. "Who do you think you are?" He turned to his main guard. "Go ahead!"

The gatekeeper tried to oppose them but the arrogant Ottomans pushed past. Speaking in his Turkish language, the tribute collector stormed into the room where Dracula sat. "We have come to speak with you, and your people treat us like strangers!" he shouted. "What is happening?"

Dracula listened to his insolence in silence. How dare they appear before him wearing turbans? What a lack of respect! His green eyes flashed with rage, although he patiently listened without saying a word.

The Ottoman assumed that since Dracula had not answered, he did not speak Turkish. The Ottoman barked an order to one of his subordinates in that man's Turkish dialect. "Bring the soldiers in and take this idiot prisoner!" he said.

Dracula, of course, had mastered Turkish and most of its dialects, including this one. He leaned close to Kardotas and murmured, "They are going to attack us . . . do what is necessary!" Dracula knew he could trust his intelligent commander. Kardotas quietly walked away.

The Ottoman subordinate also left to carry out his superior's order, but he was stopped in the halls without his companions noticing.

Kardotas returned a few minutes later and made an announcement to the huge Ottoman retinue: "When my lord and our men have gone to make treaties with your magnanimous sultan, the sultan has always received us with an elaborate party. Now you are our lord's guest! Please form three groups and follow us into the building next door."

The Ottomans happily divided themselves into three large groups, and when they entered the building they were told, "In a moment the women and food will arrive. In the meantime, please enjoy some music and help yourself to wine until you are satisfied." With that, the wine was served and the music started.

The Ottomans felt really happy that they were going to eat, drink, and enjoy the beautiful women of that place. Disguised as servants, Dracula's boyars took the first group of Ottomans and led them into a room, where they disarmed and chained them while the other two groups still waited for the women and food. Then, with the first group subdued, the boyars led away the second group, and then the third. In that way they took the huge retinue.

While this was happening, convinced that within a few time the situation was going to be completely under his control, the tribute collector said in an authoritarian tone, "We are messengers of the sultan. We have come to complain in his name for your incursion in our territory and impaling innocent Ottomans. We also have come to charge you the pending tribute. We are going to take two thousand children for the conscription and twenty thousand gold coins—and these must be paid immediately! If you do not have the money, we will collect the tribute the way we did with your father, your uncle, and your grandfather. This is an order from our sultan!"

By the time he finished speaking, his entire retinue had been apprehended. Kardotas signaled to Dracula, indicating that everything had gone according to plan.

Meanwhile, Dracula's patience had reached its limits. When the infidel finished with his demands, Dracula continued staring at him in silence—a silence that foretold a storm. Suddenly, with a voice like thunder, Dracula began speaking in the Turkish dialect the collector had just used to order his capture. "How dare you infidel Ottomans appear before a great lord with your heads covered, insisting that your stupid sultan is our master?"

The emissaries were petrified: they had never imagined that the man could speak their language so well, and with a perfect Ottoman accent.

There was a long silence, and then the tribute collector, thinking of his master's strong support and the large retinue of Janissaries who had accompanied him to Tirgoviste, said in a commanding voice, "Our lord—the sultan!—has marked the customs we have to follow. We just obey! We all are his subjects . . . including you and your people!"

Dracula looked at the intruders in silence. Then, taking a deep breath, he answered in a booming voice, "First of all, the Wallachians are not subjects of your damned sultan! And tell that coward that I remember how his father kidnapped my father, my brother, and me and forced us to obey him, and that I have not forgotten that my brother Radu is an obedient servant and changed his faith for a savage religion whose god is falser than the sultan's manliness. Tell him that he is a bastard, a demon, and a complete coward! Tell him that if he is so brave, he should come here himself with his army of chickens to charge the tribute to Wallachia! Tell him to forget about taking one child! The worst mistake he made was kidnapping us! And to you . . . I am going to reinforce the customs ordered by your damned sultan."

He asked a servant to bring him some small nails. Addressing the tribute collector, he said, "Tell your little sultan that he can protect the customs of his kingdom in his kingdom, but in Wallachia he has no authority—and I am waiting to fight him to the death! Mehemed is a coward, a chicken who is afraid of us. What do we have to do to try the strength of his army? We did not pay tribute! We killed all the infidels in Giurgiu! We killed more than twenty-three thousand infidels along the Danube! And now you will be punished! After that, if he still does not dare to attack us it is because he is a complete coward—a woman in a man's body!"

The emissaries could not believe that someone could talk like that about their powerful master; nevertheless, they heard with their own ears the rude remarks of that irreverent Wallachian.

Still dissatisfied, Dracula handed the nails to Kestywz. "Nail the turbans to the skulls of these emissaries . . . and impale the others. And let these miserable men witness their punishment."

Within moments, all the Ottomans were disarmed, and Dracula's men began preparing for the next day's impalement.

"For the love of Allah! Stop!" screamed a terrified Ottoman as the nails entered his skull.

"Don't be a crybaby," his punisher said. "They are just a couple of little nails! You are as cowardly as your little sultan. Besides, I have finished— and you'd better not take off the turban! Because if you do, my lord will get mad and you will receive a real punishment." When he saw the Ottoman's face bathed in blood, the soldier added in a mocking tone, "There is no doubt about the great personality that horrible piece of cloth gives you . . . you are the bloody nail!" And he burst out laughing.

As night fell upon the imprisoned, one of them said, "I am going to take out these damn nails . . . this pain is unbearable!"

"Do not even try it!" another whispered. "Who knows what else that crazy man may do? Tomorrow we will leave, and then we will take them off."

"I cannot take it any longer!" the first man said, prying the nails out with his fingers. "The pain is killing me!" The last nail fell to the floor. "What a relief!"

The next day everything was ready: the stakes, the grease, the horses, the anxious victims, and the vultures. (Those last did not need an invitation, and they never missed the party.)

"The party is going to start!" That was the invitation received by the emissaries with the nailed turbans. They filed out of their cells in silence and were led to the spot where the mass impalement was going to be held.

Dracula appeared with a stake in his hand—a long, specially made one painted gold—and addressed the emissaries. "I swear by my God that I will do my best to impale your chicken sultan. I have had this stake reserved just for him!" Then he issued the standard order: "Let the impalements begin!"

There was a symphony of screams from the guests as they realized that a catalog of horror was going to be inflicted upon them. The sound was terrifying; it would have given goose bumps to the devil himself.

As the emissaries watched, one exclaimed in a soft, choked voice, "Poor men . . . their souls won't have rest!"

After a few hours the macabre show still had not stopped. There were a lot of Ottomans to impale. Then the one who had taken out the nails sneezed with such strength that his turban fell to the floor.

When Dracula saw him, he said to his soldiers, "Bring that disobedient man here!" He frowned at the Ottoman. "Why did you take off the turban?" he asked, curious.

"Because my head hurt really badly!" the Ottoman replied, clearly terrified.

Dracula smiled slightly. "I would really like to relieve that pain in your head—in fact, it would be easy to do; we just have to cut it off and your problem will be solved. But instead I am going to show you that you were wrong, that the pain you say you felt was just a fantasy. You are now going to know real pain, whether you want it or not. And you are not going to disobey one of my orders ever again." Then, addressing a nearby soldier, he shouted, "Impale him!"

The Ottoman knelt down and began begging, "No! For the love of God! Nail it to me again—I swear I won't take it off and I won't complain! For the love of Allah . . . nail it again!"

Dracula waved his hand. "Fine, fine . . . you win. Today I'm feeling especially magnanimous. Nail it again!" he shouted. "And impale him!"

The Ottoman's screams and refusals were useless. When he again felt the turban fixed to his head and he knew that he was not going to escape his punishment, he started to curse Dracula.

The vovoid feigned bewilderment. "I do not understand you! I satisfy your whims, and you get upset and offend me? Didn't you ask me to nail the turban back on your head, and didn't I just do so? You are ungrateful!"

"Yes," the Ottoman replied, near tears. "But after nailing my turban, you should have freed me with the others!"

Dracula shook his head, disappointed. "You are as ungrateful as a sucker calf. Do you know those? They suck and then they charge against the cow! You want to have it all. Do not be so greedy." He paused and then addressed the same soldier. "Impale him!"

84

On the way back, the emissaries took out the nails and covered their heads with their bloodstained turbans. Of the huge retinue that had been sent to Tirgoviste, only seven men arrived back, and they were in an appalling state. When they reported to Mehemed II they were still shaking. "Dracula is not human . . . he is an impaler demon!"

The sultan was shocked at their appearance. "Where are the others?" he asked.

"That demon pierced them all on stakes, and he swore he would do the same with you. He showed us a huge golden stake he has reserved especially for that purpose. Then he said things about you that are so horrible . . . we do not dare repeat them."

"Maybe you understood wrong," the sultan said. "There is always some misinterpretation when translating a language."

"That impaler demon speaks Turkish to perfection," the emissary said. "His accent is similar to ours. You never told us that, and he overheard our plan."

The sultan, frightened by the thought of dying impaled, asked, "You are going to tell me word for word what that damned demon told you!"

The emissary shook his head, answering categorically, "Forgive us, lord! Even if you punish us, we are not going to pronounce a word he said!"

The sultan needed to know now more than ever what that demon had said. "Either you tell me what he said," he growled, "or I will cut your heads off!"

"Fine," answered the emissary. "But remember that you forced us to tell you. Prepare yourself, lord, for what you are going to hear. I never would have repeated it, and if I'm doing so now, it is because my life is at stake. I nev—"

"Stop that nonsense and start talking!" the sultan shouted.

And so the Ottoman started to repeat all that Dracula had said, with the others confirming his story by nodding their heads.

The sultan stood frozen, shocked by the incredible lack of respect that damned impaler demon had shown by professing it aloud. It was hard for him to remember the exact words of his emissaries, but still the idea of them resounded in his head as if they were the greatest offenses imaginable. Dracula had said the sultan's religion was savage. He had cursed his father—even after hypocritically treating him like a father. He had damned his name and called him a bastard, a demon, a coward, a chicken! But what hurt the most was when he said that Allah was as false as Mehemed's manliness, and that Mehemed was a woman in a man's body. Had he not sworn by Allah that he would never reveal Mehemed's secret? There was no doubt, Dracula was a hypocritical liar . . . and he had never believed in Allah!

At that moment, the head of the impaler was Mehemed's most coveted trophy. But at the same time, he was consumed by dread from the threat made by that crazy murderer. Dracula had sworn to impale him; he even had a huge golden stake especially designed for him. That had become fixed in his subconscious and was now his greatest fear. He gathered his falconers and told them, "We will attack Wallachia immediately! Prepare most of our army!"

Then he met privately with Radu in one of the chambers. "Prepare yourself," he said. "We are going to take Wallachia—and I am going to impale your damned brother."

When Radu saw Mehemed so inflamed he approached him with graceful, feline movements, and looking at him with beautiful, enigmatic blue eyes, whispered, "I love you." A long, passionate kiss kindled a fiery encounter: their hearts beat together again, their bodies became one flesh, they were in their paradise! At the end, calmness brought them back to reality. Radu, running his delicate fingers through the sultan's hair, told him in honeyed tones, "I do not want to lose you—not for anything in this world!"

"And that is never going to happen!" answered the powerful sultan.

"We are going straight into the lion's den," Radu said. "Have you not noticed that my brother is provoking you so you will attack him in his territory? I know, you are going to tell me that you will win the battle—and of that I do not have the least doubt! But ask yourself: at what cost? A lot of our men are going to die there! And if by some misfortune he captures you, he will impale you—there is no doubt about it—and your soul will be lost in hell! Please think this through. I love you! Please, do it for me; I do not want this life without you. Dracula might be my brother, but he is not human. He is an impaler demon!"

The sultan became still as stone. He had heard that last phrase before and wondered if it had been a premonition. "Repeat the last thing you said!"

"I said that although Dracula is my brother, he is not human . . . he is an impaler demon."

The sultan felt a wave of fear. "Fine," he said. "You are right—again. I will wait until he attacks us on our territory, and then we will crush him like an insect!"

———◈———

Again Mehemed gathered his chief falconers. "Suspend the attack on Wallachia!" he said.

They wanted to ask the reason for that absurd decision—To take Wallachia and kill that rebellious man would be child's play—but they kept silent and obeyed the strange order. *Is our sultan really afraid of that little vovoid, Dracula?* they thought. *Is Radu his ally against the sultan, or is Dracula really a powerful demon that can send our souls to hell?* These and other questions were spinning through the heads of those military men, but none dared ask them aloud.

85

Brother Hans, abbot of the monastery of Bristritza, gathered all his monks and told them, "We must be prepared for when the demon Dracula appears. He is going to want to steal the product of our selfless Christian mission, and we must deceive him with shrewdness. When he asks you something, do not answer: I'll explain that you have taken a vow of silence, and I'll take care of the rest."

On April 15, 1462, Dracula and his boyars appeared at the monastery. Brother Hans opened the door, joined by Brothers La Porter and Jacob. Quickly stepping in front of the others, Hans greeted Dracula, saying, "Praised is our Lord!"

"In every place and at all times," Dracula answered respectfully.

Hans looked into the vovoid's eyes, saying, "Lord, we were waiting for you. We want to contribute to your holy crusade against the Ottomans. Here you have our savings . . . and we are giving them to you with glad hearts."

Dracula was dumbfounded. Were they Orthodox monks? No, they were Catholics! Then why were they behaving in that strange way? *This monk's valuable contribution to the defense of the faith in our God has disarmed me,* he thought. Impressed by their generosity, he issued an order to his men: "Everyone kneel down to receive the blessing of these saints!" Then, turning to Brother Jacob, he asked, "Have you been in this house of God a long time?"

Brother Hans answered for him. "Forgive us, lord, but all the monks have taken a vow of silence. They cannot talk."

Dracula did not address them, respecting the vow taken by the good monks, while his soldiers accepted the chest that was being delivered to them. He smiled at Hans. "Father, I will always remember your generosity and your help to our fair cause. Bless you." With that he and his men bid the monks farewell and prepared to leave.

"Carry the tribute!" Kardotas called to some of his soldiers. The men stooped to lift the chest, used to the difficult task of carrying heavy chests from monasteries. But this one was extremely light. "This is not heavy at all," one of the soldiers remarked in surprise.

"Open it!" Kardotas ordered. When they checked inside they saw that the box held only a few copper coins. Kardotas glanced at Dracula. "It is almost empty," he said.

Dracula had visited many monasteries and had gathered a considerable amount of money from each of them. This, however, was a joke, an offense to his sharp intelligence. Visibly upset, the vovoid looked at the monk for an explanation. "Why are you doing this to me?" he asked.

Brother Hans was expecting that reaction. "Lord, we are giving you what we have—we have nothing to hide. The defense of our God is at stake, and if there is little in the chest it is because, just as we are generous with your holy cause, we are also generous with the poor who request our help. We share our alms with them."

Dracula doubted the words of that monk. He didn't know if he was lying or telling the truth. The vovoid's keen intelligence challenged the monk, and his penetrating green eyes searched for any signal that would give the man away as a liar. But the monk did not tremble or blush or look away; he did not even bat an eyelash. *Either I am standing in front of a perfect chameleon, or he is speaking the truth*, Dracula concluded. He glanced over at Kardotas—that was one of the few times he'd sought another opinion before possibly committing an injustice. His intuition had never failed him before, and this was not going to be the exception.

The monk gazed back at Dracula with a slight smile on his face, as if he knew that he had managed to deceive his foe.

Dracula had no easy options. If he left and the monk deceived him, his reputation as an intelligent man would be stained and he would be the butt of jokes among all the Catholic clergy. If he impaled an innocent man, his reputation as a fair man would end up in the garbage. So he appealed for help to the only one who could give it, his God. Then his intuition spoke: *Impale him*. He came back from his little trance; everyone was awaiting his decision. "I am going to give you one last chance," he said to Hans. "Give me all the money . . . and I promise to respect your life."

Brother Hans felt a certain superiority over the demon who was only going to steal from him, and with chameleonic naturalness he replied, "Lord, we have given you all we possess."

For the first time Dracula was indecisive. What if the kind monk really was innocent? Turning to Kardotas, he issued the difficult command: "Impale him!" The monks were terrified. They had never imagined a reaction like that. They had given the man money—this was not fair!

Kardotas ordered some soldiers to carry out the command. The soldiers were well experienced at this activity; they began undressing the monk in front of his companions. When he felt the shame of being seen the way he had come into the world, the monk began crying. Meanwhile the soldiers placed shackles around his wrists and ankles, brought out the stake, and began greasing it.

Dracula had done all this to scare the monk. Clearly, he thought, he had gone too far—he was now convinced that the monk was not hiding anything. He was just about to order the soldiers to stop when the monk screamed, "Do not impale me! I will tell you where we have the money . . . but for the love of God, do not impale me!"

With a cold voice Dracula said, "I was about to stop the execution because, for the first time, I doubted my own judgment. You are a very skillful liar. But now no one can save you from your punishment on earth, and it is not within my power to judge your soul. I do not need you to tell me where you hid the money. I'm sure that your brothers—despite their vow of silence—are going to tell me. And if they don't, they will end up joining you in hell."

The impalement of Brother Hans was astonishing to his companions. They could not believe that their smart leader was meeting this cruel destiny. They dropped to their knees and begged God to help him, their prayers accompanied by the traitor's horrible screams of pain as the stake was entering his anus. Finally the stake came out through his back, where a soldier expertly fixed it with a huge nail, making sure it would grab the bone. Then, as usual, the stake was raised until the impaled was up high: naked, alive, and ready to start the second part of his punishment. In the air above him, the birds circled patiently, waiting their turn. They were not willing to respect the high ecclesiastical status of that important representative of God.

With Brother Hans hanging high, his open eyes showing a terror that cannot be described with words, Dracula turned his attention to Brother Jacob. "This traitor cannot speak because the pain he feels does not allow him to! Where is the money?"

Brother Jacob felt the penetrating and inquisitive look of the monster, whom he considered the devil incarnate. Without wasting a minute, he said, "Follow me." He led Dracula down into a basement, where he pointed to a carpet, saying, "It is buried here!"

As Brother Hans was dying from his painful impalement, across Europe people were commenting upon and praising the deeds of the holy Christian crusader. The energy of their blessings went up into the quantum space, combining in a strange symphony of Te Deums, masses, rosaries, and other prayers supporting Dracula's fight, along with the curses of those monks who defended their money over their God. While some blessed the saint, others cursed the demon.

The soldiers dug in the place where the monk had pointed and took out a chest of the same size as the previous one, but full of gold, silver, and valuable relics. They smiled broadly at their good fortune while the monks watched in silence and with tears in their eyes, bidding good-bye to their real god . . . money!

Thanks to the Catholic monks' thrift and obligatory generosity, all the necessary arms were bought for Dracula's army and his valuable allies (the slaves) in Wallachia. Most weapons were bought from the Saxons, who kept producing them without rest, but arms were bought from other places, too. New, quiet, and precise crossbows were bought in Venice.

86

Stephen of Moldavia was a guest of the Ottoman Empire, enjoying a party that had lasted three days. The food and the beautiful women surpassed his wildest imagination. At the end the festivities, he paid the obligatory visit to the trophy room. "These are the heads of the enemies of the empire," the sultan said, smiling. "This is my most important trophy—it belonged to Constantine XI. And *this* space is reserved for your cousin Dracula: here he will join all those who do not want to be our allies and friends."

Stephen understood perfectly well the implicit meaning: either he joined the empire or he would die, and his people would have an uncertain destiny. The powerful Mehemed II looked him in the eye. "Do you want to make a pact of alliance with the empire?" he asked. "Or would you prefer to be our enemy?"

Putting aside his religious convictions, Stephen knew that with this alliance he would end up being his cousin's enemy, breaking the blood pact made before his God. But he accepted the forced decision. "I will make a pact with you," he said.

"You must deliver ten thousand gold coins and one thousand children of conscription every year," the sultan said. "In return, we will assure you peace. From now on I am your only master; you are not subject to any king of Europe or any Catholic pope."

Stephen returned to Moldavia heartbroken, feeling guilty and repentant. He was both sad and worried about having rejected the alliance that Dracula had offered him against the Turks. *Why was I such a coward?* he asked himself over and over again. At night he could not sleep for worry. *My God, how did this happen? What about my oath? I have broken it twice.* He then began begging desperately. *Forgive me, my God. What am I going to do now that I am a subject of the Turks? I have turned into Dracula's enemy . . . and I did not have the courage to defend you!*

87

Dracula met with his commanding officers. "I am really worried," he admitted. "I do not understand the sultan. We killed everyone at the Fort of Giurgiu, we did not pay the tribute, we made a crusade at the Danube, we punished his emissaries . . . and still he has not attacked us! I keep asking myself what his strategy is. I am really worried!"

"What if we attack him?" Luga suggested. "I think he is afraid because we impale."

Dracula shook his head. "That is what he wants us to do. But if we did, we would last only three days in that foreign place. We must find a way to get him to attack us in Wallachia." The room fell silent, the men watching their leader as he thought. After a while his face brightened. "I've got it!" he said, and he summoned a scribe and made the following proclamation:

To all the slaves, wherever you are,

The time has come to take revenge on those who took your God away, killed your loved ones, sullied your women, stole your families, and sold you as slaves. The damned Ottomans must pay with their blood for their monstrous crimes. On June 1 on the banks of the Danube, in the place indicated below, we will gather to attack the chicken who answers to the name Mehemed II and calls himself "the Lord of Both Seas" and "the Conqueror of Constantinople" but is missing the title of "Dracula's Subject." Do not be afraid of him—he is the greatest coward who ever existed. He hides his cowardice by saying that he conquered Constantinople; let us see if he can take Wallachia! We must not be afraid. The hand of our God leads us, and he is without a doubt more powerful than Allah. We are going to die for our faith! Remember what you have lost, and come to the Danube to die fighting our enemy!

Signed,
Wladislaus III, Dragwlya

Dracula gave the paper to Kestywz. "Make sure this proclamation is made immediately in Serbia, Greece, Bulgaria, and Istanbul—and then, later, in the Ottoman Empire."

The Black read the proclamation and rushed to his fellow slaves, arriving excited and with a tearstained face. "A man called Dracula, the vovoid of Wallachia, is summoning us to join his army to fight against the Ottomans. I lost everything I had to those demons—I know that part of my family was sold as slave in the southern part of the empire. I do not care if I throw my soul to hell—if I can recover them I will, or I'll die trying. At least I'll know that my life was worth something! I am going to escape and join that army!"

"I am going with you! They killed my loved ones, and my highest ambition is to meet with them in heaven!" The Mute left the other slaves flabbergasted; they had never heard him speak a word.

"I am also going with you," the Crow said. "We all lost everything— even our names."

Those slaves invited others, and those others invited others, and night after night these new crusaders escaped, seeking their unknown leader.

"Damned son of the devil!" The sultan's rage-filled scream echoed throughout the palace when a copy of the proclamation fell into his hands. "How does that imbecile dare to do this?" Summoning the chief falconers, he said, "Prepare to invade Wallachia! I want the strength of our full army! On June first we are going to crush that insect!"

When Radu found out that his lover planned to attack Dracula in Wallachia, he made the same strategic argument to try to protect him, but this time it did not work. "No one treats me with disrespect! If I do nothing about this, I will be the laughingstock of my people. I will not change my mind even if you beg me on your knees. This time I am determined: the time of your brother's death has arrived!" Mehemed looked at his lover and his expression softened. "Stay in the empire . . . while I kill him."

"I won't let you go alone!" Radu said, taking Mehemed by the shoulders. "Do you even *know* my brother? He wants to impale you! If he captures you, I will be the only one who can rescue you from death! He would never kill his brother—remember how he forgave the Monk because he was his half-brother? You are not going to leave without me!"

Mehemed II thought of his own impalement and got chills. The pain, the humiliation, the damnation of his soul . . . it made him tremble just imagining it. He considered the personal benefits of having his lover along to defend him. "Fine," he said. "You will go with us."

88

·

"I want you to gather from throughout Wallachia all the people who are ill with the plague, leprosy, and other strange and fatal illnesses, and have them isolated and ready for war," Dracula told Stanyzkwl. "Put them a comfortable place, and try to give them everything they need."

After the sick people were gathered, Dracula addressed the large crowd. "We Wallachians are at war against the sultan. He wants to take our land and destroy the faith in our God. His soldiers will sully our women and sell our children as slaves, and you will be put down. I am asking for your help to save the faith, our Wallachia, and your children. You are our secret weapon to win this war! In fact, whether we win it or lose it will depend upon your valuable participation. Because all of you have an incurable illness, I am going to ask you at the right time to join our enemy's army to make it sick. You will die, without a doubt—but you will die fighting against them, and you will be remembered as martyrs and heroes by all those you leave behind. I give you my word as crusader knight that your families will be given an honest job and will live in peace to remember you with respect and love. Who wants to be a soldier for Christ?"

A unified shout was heard from those excited and brave Wallachians: "I do!"

"You will live in this special place," Dracula said. "You won't lack for anything. Your families will be able to visit you here from a security distance as the time of your participation approaches. And to consolidate this alliance, the metropolitan, Barbat, is here with us. Together we will celebrate Mass." They had shared Holy Communion, Dracula addressed the gathering again. "Your first order is to study the Turkish language until you can speak it with our enemy's accent. I will provide teachers who will help you." Then he bid farewell, satisfied with his special new soldiers.

After Dracula left, Staico remarked to his companions, "I was thinking I would die like a mangy dog, reviled by everyone. What tormented me most was not knowing where I would get my food. Now it turns out that we all are going to have what we need, and at the end we will become martyrs and heroes, having helped free Wallachia and defend the divinity of our God. I am ready to face our enemy!"

The others felt the same way—they were anxious to get into the action.

89

The moment of truth had arrived. Without excuses or pretext, Matthias had to deliver immediately the one hundred thousand gold coins Pope Pio II had sent him for Dracula's crusade. But how could he? And what would happen with his crown of Saint Stephen and his appointment as holy Roman emperor? If he hoped to keep on with his plan, he had to do everything just right, and that meant just one thing: Dracula had to die. Without caring that Dracula had been his ally in his fight to King Ladislaus V, without caring that he had been his father's best friend and, above all, a ferocious defender of the Christian faith, Matthias designed a treacherous plan. He summoned his commander, Bathory. "You will go to Dracula and order him to take his army and help you win the Fort of Chilia, once you have the control of the fort, you stay there with our men and protect it, and send Dracula back with his army to face the Ottomans."

Bathory, confused, repeated the bizarre order back to his superior: "I must go to Dracula, and with all his army he will help me take the Fort of Chilia, and then when we take it, I will send Dracula and his army to face the army of the sultan alone, and I will stay to protect the fort."

"You understood clearly," Matthias said. "Now carry out my orders immediately! And I am going to give it to you again in writing. I don't want any misunderstandings'"

Actually, Bathory still did not understand anything. To his way of thinking, that order would send Dracula to the slaughter. "My king, Dracula has summoned his army, his people, and all the slaves to defend themselves from the Ottoman attack," he said skeptically. "If we do what you say, the Ottomans will surely consolidate in Wallachia, and it is very likely that Dracula will die there with his army . . . and we will lose the battle."

Matthias turned red in the face. *Who cares about the battle! I just care about the crown of Saint Stephen!* He wanted to scream that to his wise military commander, but instead he simply glared at him and asked, "Do you want me to explain my orders again?" Then, not waiting for a response, he yelled, "Fulfill them!"

Bathory arrived in Tirgoviste just as Dracula was heading out toward the Danube River. "Good thing I found you!" the commander called. "Our king sends you this order!"

Dracula read it and exclaimed, "Matthias has no brain! Tell me, Bathory, do you find sense in this foolishness? If we obey this madness, we are going to die and the sultan will go straight to Rome!"

Ever the good military man, Bathory replied, "I am just obeying orders. Are you going to disobey our king?"

Dracula was silent. He had to obey his king; he, too, was a military man, and he always carried out the orders of his superiors. But this time it was not about a king or some orders; it was about the defense of the faith in his God. "I will obey partially," he said. "Part of my army will go with you, but I am going to face the Ottomans. I have a war to win, and I am not going to lose it for any reason. We are defending our faith!" Speaking to Costea, he said, "I appoint you one of my commanding officers. You will be leading six thousand of my men, who will join Bathory and, under his direction, fulfill the orders of our king. The rest of my army will join me on our date with our enemies."

The disapproval from Dracula's army was unanimous. All the commanders and soldiers openly criticized the bizarre order of the stupid king. What kind of donkey was that monarch? They never imagined that the objective of that order was the death of Dracula, because only Matthias knew that he had never given Dracula the one hundred thousand gold coins the pope had sent.

90

When the sultan began receiving reports that many of the slaves in his empire had escaped to join the rebellious Dracula, the powerful man did not give the news much thought. But when similar reports kept coming, he screamed until his throat was raw: "Damn that impaler demon!" But his scream was not enough to stop even more reports about fugitive slaves.

"It is an order from our sultan that you must give access to the ships that are going to attack Dracula;" said the commander of the Fort of Chilia, and Stephen obeyed. But when he saw the ships moving upstream, his heart screamed, *Traitor! By allowing these ships to pass, you will destroy the man who helped you recover the throne when you had no one!* He knew that when Dracula died there would be no one left to remind him of his treason, but there was another witness who would remind him for the rest of his life: his God Jesus Christ, who even now was working through his miserable conscience. *Traitor, traitor, traitor . . .*

Dracula said good-bye to his family, hugging his son and kissing him on the head. "My beautiful child, take care of your mother and obey her," he said. "I am going to defend the faith in our God, and I am sure I won't see you again. Follow my example, and when you grow up, fight to the death for his defense!"

Zalesha had a great pain in her heart, but she was also beside herself with pride. Her eyes brimmed with tears, although she did not know whether it was from excitement or sadness. Her men was the most ferocious defender of the faith.

Dracula was both happy and sad. Taking Zalesha by the hands, he said, "My love, we came to this world to serve our God. My greatest desire is to die on the battlefield with his name on my lips. Pray for that to happen! I love you more than my own life, but my God comes first. Instruct Minhea to follow my steps." Then, giving his wife and child a long, close hug, he said, "I am sure that the next time I see you it will be in celestial glory. I love you both!" He gave his wife one final kiss, drew away from her, and then slowly walked up the road, turned back just once to see, for the last time, the loved ones who were his reason for living.

A group of soldiers went through all Wallachia to notify the citizens that the war had started. The brave Wallachians were willing to make the highest sacrifice before surrendering to their enemy. With Dracula leading them, they could fight even the wicked sultan and his infernal allies!

The pope summoned Matthias to the Vatican and asked him, "Did you give the one hundred thousand gold coins to Dracula?"

Regretting that he could not go back in time and do things differently, Matthias looked steadily at the pope and said, "I did, your holiness!"

"And what kind of support did you give your subject?"

"I sent a great part of my army, led by the commanding officer Bathory, your holiness."

"Well done, Matthias! Kneel to receive my blessing."

Matthias was terrified, although he knew he had nothing to be afraid of. He had no doubt that, thanks to his clever plan, Dracula would meet his death.

The Holy Father Pio II, supportive of Dracula's cause, ordered solemn Te Deums, holy masses, rosaries, and prayers to be said throughout all Europe so that the brave crusader and his army would succeed in the defense of the faith. All these positive thoughts arrived at the cosmic center and returned as a strange energy that would shape the events that were about to unfold.

Dozens of ships loaded with Janissaries, soldiers, horses, cannons, and all kinds of weapons sailed in a line through the Danube to the point where Dracula had summoned the slaves to rebel against the sultan.

The sultan had witnessed with his own eyes the way the wicked impaler demon punished his enemies. Along the shores of the Danube were the corpses of those who were once the sultan's subjects. A shiver ran through his body as he imagined the unbearable pain those unfortunate people had suffered before dying, but what he lamented most was that the souls of those innocents had been thrown mercilessly to hell for having died impaled. It was hard for him to understand that the beautiful man he had once tried to seduce was the same man who ordered that massacre. Those scenes were more than even a crazy man could take! There the bodies would remain, waiting to be buried by slaves. His fear of dying impaled was rising. The impaler had promised to stick into his body a huge golden stake. He could not believe he was going into the lion's den—but then again, with the army he had with him, who would be able to touch even one hair on his head? As he fought down his fear, the vomit came unannounced, and then the headache had him in its clutches. He was a desperate man, unable to find peace despite being protected by the best army in the world.

The river was wide, deep, and therefore very navigable. The sultan's troops arrived at the meeting point and disembarked on one bank of the river to prepare for the next day's occupation of the other side. For this they had to gather the bulk of the army. Ships, ships, and more ships kept arriving, along with narrators and historians. Then a huge ship arrived transporting the central figure of the operation,—Mehemed II, joined by his inseparable advisor, Radu the Beautiful.

Mehemed said to Radu, "I am worried because your brother knows all our military strategies. He once became chief falconer."

"What worries me most," Radu replied, "is that no one knows these lands—not even I who was born in them. May Allah protect us and guide us with his holy hand so that we return safely!"

When Dracula arrived at the meeting point along the Danube, he was greatly impressed. Where had all those people come from? There were many men of different races, all of them unknown to him. They were, without a doubt, the fugitive slaves that had answered the call of his proclamation. There were also children, elderly people, and women—even pregnant women—all his subjects, and all armed with whatever weapon they could get. His voice trembling from excitement, Dracula addressed those weaker subjects. "You cannot go to the front of the war because the fight there is bloody and aggressive; you will be easy victims for our skilled and clever enemies. But I accept you as soldiers in my army behind the front lines. You, too, will make war! And the first thing you must do as good soldiers is obey orders. The first order I will give is to go back to your places of origin and wait and fulfill blindly the orders we convey to you through our boyars and soldiers. I assure you, with our God as witness, that the actions you will carry out as soldiers behind the front lines will help us win this war."

All of them obeyed their leader happily, like good soldiers.

Then Dracula addressed the slaves. "You have lost everything—your families, your land, and even your names—but today you recovered your freedom when you decided to join my army. My fight is for the defense of the faith of our God Jesus Christ, and for the freedom of Wallachia. You are here because you are thirsty for justice or want to meet your loved ones, either here on earth or in the celestial glory. Together we are going to make this dream come true. We are going to fight against the best-paid, best-trained army in the world. Well, you are not mercenaries! You do not fight for money; you fight for your families—either to avenge or recover them. You do not have the best military training, but your hearts are full of hate and anger against that damned sultan, and that is worth more than any pay or the best military training in the world. Wallachia is your new homeland! Even though you are not her children, by fighting for her liberty and offering the most valuable thing you have—your life and your blood—you have become her adoptive children. Whenever you wish you will be welcomed here along with your honorable families, if you can recover them. For those who cannot, we have good and honest Wallachian women with whom you can rebuild your lives. You are our new brothers—you are part of our family. You are Wallachians, and Wallachia is your new native land. Tomorrow will be the big day! Welcome, brothers!"

Some of the newly free men were really excited. Who was that holy man who was leading them? At that moment they felt they belonged to an incipient nation and that they had a new family. They were sure of one thing: they would follow that leader to hell and obey him blindly until they either achieved victory or found the death that would take them to heaven with their loved ones. Equipped with weapons that had been bought mainly with the obligatory contributions of the generous Catholic monks, the fugitive slaves waited impatiently for the order to start the fight.

91

On May 31, 1462, while the battle was being organized, the sultan's warriors talked among themselves. "We are the most powerful army in the world!" one Janissary said proudly. "I was in the battle of Constantinople, and that battle was hard—those soldiers were real professionals who were used to making war. These scruffs are not even going to last the warm-up."

Another Janissary laughed and said, "Can you believe it? I've heard Dracula is using slaves for soldiers, and children, elderly people, and even pregnant women."

"I'll take care of those," added another, lustful Janissary, making an obscene gesture.

"Would you like a little help?" asked another one, smirking. The troops were all happy; they seemed confident and calm and their spirits high. None of them doubted that the next day the disembarkation was going to be an easiest thing . . . just a routine matter.

Dracula planned his war strategy with his commanding officers. "I lived with the Ottomans for five years," he said. "I came to be chief falconer there, and I know the military tactics of these miserable men better than they do. A supplier army will follow the sultan's men at one day's distance. Their objective is to provide the front lines with water, food, clean clothes, and sharpened weapons. All the soldiers on the front lines need to do is not stop until they achieve victory. The suppliers also receive the injured soldiers and transport them to a safe place where they will be given medical attention." Dracula then addressed Kardotas. "You must eliminate the supplier army . . . but before that, let the first load of supplies depart. Then the next day before sunrise, start by killing the guards and then the soldiers who protect them. Capture all the others and force them to dig up the dead bodies and bring them to Tirgoviste in carts. There you must impale the dead ones and lock up the prisoners. Send the carts with the Ottomans' clothes to the sick people to wear and sleep in. Recover the supplies you can, throw into the river what you cannot take, and burn all the ships you can. When you have fulfilled this order, meet me."

"Consider it done," Kardotas answered.

92

On June 1, 1462, at sunrise, Dracula ordered a brief Mass attended by the soldiers, peasants, and allied slaves. At the end he held up a banner with the image of Jesus of the Sacred Sacrament and said, "The day has arrived! We should give thanks to God for this opportunity to defend his faith! Today we will seek death defending our God! Those of you who are lucky enough to die today will be remembered tomorrow with respect; you will give prestige to your lineage and live forever at the right hand of God. I welcome the new free men who answered my proclamation! When you are fighting, remember your loved ones; remember what the Ottomans took from you. The time for revenge has come! Either our blood or the blood of our enemies will be shed on this field of honor."

As he was speaking, the Janissaries were approaching, crossing the river in barges protected against arrows. The vovoid took his sword and lifted it up high with one hand, and with the banner in the other he shouted, "Praised is our Lord Jesus Christ!" Then, with his characteristic fierceness, he threw himself upon the enemy, with his soldiers close behind him. The peasants and allied slaves followed, too, astonished: their new leader had not just given the order to attack, but he had attacked first and was up front! The fight was bloody; the banner was covered with the enemy's blood. That disembarkation would be the last and a nightmare for those Janissaries!

On the other side of the river, the sultan watched, pleased that his Janissaries would do whatever it took for the rest of the army to cross without problems. Then his elite group approached the shore and he watched in surprise as riff-raff soldiers—inexpert peasants and undisciplined slaves—did not run away terrified, like other soldiers he had fought against. They were supposed to be running away, but no, they were putting up a hard and violent fight. There before his very eyes, making a great display of unusual fierceness, they defeated his two thousand experienced and fierce Janissaries.

Mehemed's horror grew. Had they taken liquor or some strange elixir to be so brave? He would never realize that their bravery came from the rage those slaves held inside their broken hearts and the strength their God had given them through the cosmic energy generated by the many prayers, thoughts, and petitions in favor of Dracula.

Then the defenders of the Christian faith took stakes and quickly pierced the enemies' bellies or any other place. Having done this, they cut their throats and fixed them in the ground, leaving the victims hanging in the air. The remaining Ottomans were trembling, terrified; they imagined that if they fell at the hands of those wicked demons, the enemy would not settle with just killing them; instead they would steal their souls and send them to hell.

Mehemed II watched from a distance what those savages were doing; he could hear the screams of pain of his impaled soldiers. He issued an order to one of his chief falconers: "Attack with the bulk of the army!"

The chief falconer obeyed immediately. "For the glory of Allah! Everyone against the enemy!" But when the soldiers saw what those savages did with the souls of the ones who disembarked, they were terrified and refused to fight against that diabolic and wicked enemy. If those demons captured them, they would throw their souls to hell, and no sultan could rescue them from that place.

Meanwhile Radu was begging desperately, "Wait—please! Don't you see that is what my brother wants? The most vulnerable moment for any army is disembarkation. And you saw it yourself: if we attack in that way, we will make it to the other shore, certainly, but we will to lose a lot of men! Do not let anger guide you; think militarily and strategically!" Then he took Mehemed by the shoulders, shook him hard, and, looking him in the eye, said, "Calm down!" Some of the sultan's falconers discreetly watched this severe scolding and silently thanked God for Radu's bravery and positive attitude.

Mehemed understood that his lover was always right and had consistently given him good advice. He was silent, trying to think of a way to convince his men to fight against the impaler demon. Finally he had a strategy. Addressing his army he said, "I promise by Allah that at the end of the disembarkation I will distribute thirty thousand gold coins among you! And I will award ten thousand gold coins to the one who brings me the head of the impaler."

The Janissaries were the best-paid army in the world, earning the stratospheric amount of one gold coin per year, free of expenses. When they heard that generous offer, they were greatly motivated to keep fighting and earn that fortune.

93

The next day Mehemed II issued a new order: "Fire the cannons!" And 130 cannons fulfilled the order perfectly while the soldiers were disembarking downstream.

Dracula knew that their disembarkation was unavoidable: the Ottomans were too many and had the best weapons in the world. At the right moment, he called to his bugler. "Play retreat!" he said.

The Ottoman sultan stepped on the shore of that enemy land and considered it one of his multiple conquests. Cognizant of having his historians as witnesses, in an arrogant tone he issued a ceremonious order: "Today, June second, 1462, this land belongs to the Ottoman Empire. Its new name is Cehennem because it is infested by demons. From today on, the real God who will be worshiped in this place is Allah; Jesus Christ will be a respected prophet, just like Mohammad. All the inhabitants of this place are from now on our slaves." He turned to his chief falconers, "Take the impaled men down immediately!"

The chief falconers heard the strange order and looked at each other skeptically. Finally one of them plucked up the courage to say, "With all due respect, my lord, I do not think any of our men would like to lose his own soul by taking down from the stake a body whose soul will never get out of hell."

"Do I have to repeat my orders?" Mehemed screamed. "I said, get the impaled men down!"

The chief falconer relayed the sultan's order to the soldiers, and they were really afraid of carrying it out. They were trying to think of a way to get their companions down, but when they even tried to start the action, their fear stopped them. This was an order, however, and they had to obey it—even if their souls ended up in hell.

Radu began speaking to Mehemed in a low, urgent tone. "You are a father to all your soldiers—so protect them like a father! Why do you risk their souls if the ones who went to hell cannot be saved from it?

Do you want them to say their father was their executioner? Give them confidence—lift their spirits!"

The sultan thought for a moment about that wise proposition, and then he summoned the chief falconers and told them, "I think my advisor Radu is right: the souls of our men are too valuable. The dead ones can stay there until we send slaves later to bury them."

After he left, one chief falconer asked another one in a low voice, "What could the advisor have said to convince him?"

"I don't know!" answered his comrade. "But there is no doubt that Radu is our best ally." When Radu was congratulated by the chief falconers for his valuable advice, he was so happy he wanted to kiss his lover in front of everyone . . . but he just smiled slightly.

Meanwhile, ladders were in place, and Ottoman soldiers shaking from fear prepared to take down the corpses of their fellow soldiers. Just then the chief falconer appeared. "Stop!" he called. "By order of our sultan, you must leave the impaled men in their place . . . he won't risk your souls unnecessarily!"

When the relieved soldiers investigated the origin of the change of decision, the news spread like wildfire among the Ottoman soldiers. "Radu is our sultan's best advisor!" they said. "What would we do without him?" If at one time the chief falconers and soldiers had distrusted the brother of the impaler demon, they now began to trust Radu's wise judgment.

In the distance the enemy was practically inviting the Ottoman army to chase them. They had lifted the huge golden stake and were waving it slowly to provoke the sultan. When he saw it he got a chill, and in uncertain tones he issued an order to his chief falconers: "Let's go get the enemy!" The order was carried out immediately, and the soldiers headed into Wallachia, where Dracula had drawn his route of death.

Radu's voice was trembling when he spoke to Mehemed. "I do not like this at all! Nobody knows this place, and I feel like we are going straight into a mousetrap. This is even more dangerous than I had imagined! We should go back!" Trying a final tactic to convince his lover, he said, "That huge golden stake those demons have is the one with which they want to impale you. I do not want to lose you . . . let's go back!"

"Quiet, Radu," the sultan snarled. "You are making me more nervous. I already know that if your damned brother gets me, he is going to impale me!"

"That is what I am talking about!" Radu said pleadingly. "Let's get back! We still have time! We are going from bravery to stupidity!"

"My prestige is at stake, Radu! Can you imagine what the people would say about me? That the Conqueror of Constantinople ran away from the impaler demon? In your dreams!" Mehemed's voice dropped to a whisper. "I *am* really afraid—I can say that to you—but can you imagine if my army knew?" He cleared his throat and called to a chief falconer. "We will set the camp here!" he said firmly.

The order was carried out immediately, and the servants set to work. Some imams faced Mecca, intoning chants to Allah, while the rest of the faithful knelt down with their arms outstretched and their faces to the floor. They were making their sacred prayers, the most important of which was the desire for a long life for their powerful sultan. As was the custom among them, a cannon salute punctuated their prayers.

At the end of preparations, a comfortable camp had been installed with all the commodities the great Ottoman sultan was used to. The main tent was maroon, the ones around him belonging to his commanding officers were blue, and those along the edges of camp, where the Janissaries slept, were green. There was also food, water, and pasture for the animals. They did not lack anything. At night some soldiers who had slept during day took their turn at guard zealously.

Dracula said to his commanding officers, "The strategy is going perfectly. We have to go where the traps are! They won't take long to receive provisions, and then they will go on without suspecting anything. Let us rest, because tomorrow will be a long day." As always, before going to sleep the pious Dracula said his prayers.

94

"How are we going to do to defeat them?" Luga asked Dracula. "They have more than twenty men to our one."

"By surprise attack," Dracula answered. "We are going to attack from a distance and catch them off-guard. As soon as they are ready to attack us, we will run away."

"Isn't it cowardice to attack and run?" asked Kestywz.

"In war anything goes, and we must take the necessary actions to win. We are not defending a whim—the divinity of our God and the freedom of Wallachia are at stake! Our way of making war is completely valid. No one should be ashamed of fighting to win."

When the supplier army arrived at the place of disembarkation, everyone was speechless and terrified by the scenes they had witnessed. But the commanding officer, seeing that his troops were losing their courage, said with nervous determination, "We are going to do our job as usual. There are always casualties in war!"

The soldiers did not respond. They seemed like automatons without a will of their own. But they had work to do, and a swarm of Ottomans installed the campsite and prepared the food, water, and supplies.

Sweating from the intense heat, one of the employees dared to say, "I am really afraid!" And then everyone was saying the same thing. Despite the general fear, the first load of supplies departed that same afternoon, carts and mules packed with the all the necessary things. Smart, well-trained trackers followed behind them, assuming that, as always, the journey would be problem-free.

Just before dawn, Kardotas gave the order with a quiet signal: "Attack!" And by the dim light of the sweet sunrise, some faint shadows moved stealthy along the shores of the Danube. The guards there saw that they were going to be attacked, but before they could open their mouths their throats filled with blood and they began their agonizing deaths. Then the rest of the employees there were taken by surprise; before they realized what was happening, they were chained at the wrist and taken prisoner. The few who fought were subdued easily. With that, the first part of the mission was complete. By full daylight, the sultan's servants were some in chains and the other dead.

"Go tell Dracula that the supplier army has been taken and the rest of his orders will be carried out without problem." Tepelus received Kardotas' order and immediately prepared to fulfill it; meanwhile Kardotas was carrying out the rest of the plan.

By the time Tepelus arrived before Dracula, he was overwhelmed by the intense heat. He gave the vovoid a detailed report of how the events had unfolded.

Meanwhile a boyar took carts loaded with Ottoman clothes to the sick people and said, "Here is your order: you must wear and sleep in these clothes!"

The sick people knew that they were soldiers of Christ and that that important order had been given by their kind and brave leader through his soldier. They obeyed with military zeal, without arguing or even commenting. They kept studying industriously the language of their enemy, and some of them had already mastered the language and an excellent Ottoman accent.

95

Bathory the Elder arrived at the Fortress of Chilia and issued the following order to his emissaries: "You will make negotiations for our enemy to turn in the fort. Explain to them that we are superior in number and that if they offer resistance, the front will be taken at all costs and a lot of blood will be shed unnecessarily. With these white and dragon flags, they won't attack you."

The unarmed emissaries took the flags and bravely headed to the door of the fort.

Stephen remembered the oath he and Dracula had made: there would never be rivalry between them. When he saw the dragon banner he shouted to his guards, "Open the door!"

But the Ottoman in charge, gave a different order: "Shoot to kill!" The sky filled with arrows. The brave emissaries died in that instant, and the battle had started.

Stephen headed to complain to the Ottoman and ask him why he did not respect the white flag. He was infuriated by the attitude of his ally. But at that instant an arrow flew through the air and stuck in his ankle. Seeing the ferocity of the enemy and the great number of attackers, he decided to flee to Moldavia, and the fort was taken by Bathory and the Dracula's men. Now Stephen could not deny he was Dracula's enemy. The thought tormented him and made him feel like the most ungrateful of traitors. In theory he never would have broken his promise, but reality was different, and his actions spoke for themselves: Stephen of Moldavia was a miserable traitor to the Christian faith.

The commander Bathory said to the commander Costea, "The fort is taken! You can go back to Dracula. Thank you for the support!"

96

When the sultan received his first shipment from his supplier army, the commanding officer said, "My lord, the supplier army consolidated, and so you will receive supplies without problem or delay."

But the sultan was worried. "Be prepared!" he said. "This land is full of demons—that is why I named it Cehennem." Then made his farewell salute, leaving the Ottoman horrified . . . what kind of name was that? He wanted to run away from that devilish place!

Dracula caught the men in charge of the supplies on their way back and took them to Tirgoviste. Then he said to his commanding officer, "Now that the line of provisions from the enemy's army has been eliminated, we are going to attack the sultan. Lead him to the traps!" And his order was immediately carried out. His troops took their new positions, and suddenly a huge group of unarmed peasants were making obscene gestures a short distance from the Ottoman soldiers, while other peasants were screaming in unison, "The sultan is a woman! The sultan is a woman!" Still others were waving the huge golden stake, which had pierced a female cloth doll dressed as the sultan.

When he saw how close the peasants were and how little respect they had for his magnanimous self, the sultan felt his anger turn to blinding wrath. What kind of cynical mockery and provocation was this? He felt his blood boiling in his veins, and for a moment he lost his mind, forgetting all military strategy. A loud, visceral scream tore from his throat: "Damn demons! Go after them! Do not leave one alive!" And with that, the disorganized attack started. The cavalry fulfilled the energetic order immediately, and behind them was the infantry. The speed of the horses made a thick dust cloud that blotted out the sunlight, so that the soldiers behind the horses could not see anything. Then the cavalry suddenly disappeared as though they had been swallowed by hell, and behind them, into the same hell, marched the infantry.

The dust did not let them see what was happening; they could only hear screams of pain, shrieks that sounded that sounded like they had come from the crypt. The attack stopped, but by then it was too late: the traps had taken many victims. Some brave soldiers went to the rescue of their comrades, and many of them became martyrs, falling into other traps in the process.

"I do not want to go to hell!" Forty-three Ottomans were screaming at the bottom of a trap with stakes piercing their bodies. The horses, on the other hand, were resigned to their deaths, accepting their unfair destiny. From all the traps came Ottoman screams for help.

"What do I do?" the desperate sultan asked Radu.

"You are their father! Act like one! What would your soldiers say if they saw their father allowing a demon to take the souls of his children to hell? We have to take the soldiers out carefully. Cure the injured ones and give an Ottoman burial to the dead ones. You should not allow the demon to take their souls to hell . . . do not let him impale them!"

Addressing the chief falconers, the sultan said, "Rescue the injured and dead soldiers carefully, and give an Ottoman burial to the dead ones. Take the injured ones back to be cured."

"The souls of all these lucky men are basking in the glory of Allah for having died in battle," said one Ottoman after having buried the last body.

"I'm jealous," said another, who was sweating profusely from the intense heat, "And here we are in this hot, ugly place. No wonder they called it Cehennem. I can even feel the presence of the impaler demon near us! I am terrified!"

"You'd better shut up!" his fellow soldier said as they nervously tracked their enemy. "And don't say that name—it gives me goose bumps!"

Dracula summoned Swerige. "Exhume all the dead and take them to Tirgoviste. There you will impale them!"

From a distant hiding spot in the forest, Wallachians watched the actions of the Ottoman invaders and prepared to attack them at the first opportunity. Finally the intense heat of June forced many Ottoman soldiers to make a fatal decision: they took off their armor, trusting in the great number of their army.

When Dracula ordered his soldiers to leave several people impaled near the forest, the sultan's army approached to witness the event and await orders from his leader. Suddenly the sky was filled with so many arrows that they partly blocked the sun. The Wallachians hunted the unprotected Ottomans as if they were rabbits, killing many of them.

Meanwhile the sultan's chief falconers retreated to make a plan of attack, while Dracula's soldiers spread out and hid in the forest. The Ottomans' military strategy was exactly as Dracula had anticipated, and Dracula's own soldiers carried out their mission perfectly. When the Ottomans passed near the impaled bodies, they could not avoid the arrows that rained down upon them. Some were fortunate enough to find death quickly; they were spared days of agony. Those who survived walked ahead, searching among the trees for their cowardly enemies, but they seemed to have fallen from the face of the earth. Upset at having no one to fight against, they went back to join the bulk of the army. When they passed near the impaled ones, a chief falconer said, "I need some volunteers to take these soldiers down!" No one wanted to lose his soul; not a single man offered to take on the risky mission. They knew that those souls were already in hell and there was no one in heaven or on earth who could rescue them from that place.

Meanwhile, Dracula's soldiers were fulfilling his order to unearth the corpses of the soldiers who fell into the traps. They would take them to Tirgoviste to impale them.

The sultan was worried because he had received only one delivery of supplies, and so he summoned one of his chief falconers. "Send a large retinue to retrieve the wounded and investigate why we haven't received more provisions," he said. His order was fulfilled immediately, and a group of soldiers left to investigate.

When Dracula saw part of the sultan's army leaving, he called to Kestywz. "Capture them and take them to Tirgoviste," he said. "Lock up the live ones and impale the dead ones."

———◄≫———

The sultan set his campsite and again summoned a chief falconer. "Send some explorers to find out where we are," he said. And again, Dracula watched the group of soldiers separating from the rest, and he captured them immediately to take them to Tirgoviste—dead or alive.

By now Radu was worried. "You see? I told you we were going to get lost!" he complained to Mehemed. "And I am losing sleep over that damned golden stake!"

"If you feel that way, imagine how I feel—I am the one that could end up impaled," the sultan replied. "Fortunately I feel safer with my army nearby, but every night I dream your damned brother is impaling me."

Radu tried to be reassuring. "They are just dreams, my love. It is very likely that we will lose more men, but at the end we will defeat our enemy." He approached Mehemed with feline movements and with sweet, rasping voice whispered, "Give me a kiss!"

"Are you insane?" the sultan said, pulling back. "Don't even think about that! If anyone suspects the truth about us, I will lose my army's respect. We must be really careful."

"You don't want to kiss me because you already have someone else!" Radu snapped jealously.

"Quiet, my love! It's only that if they discover us, we will be in trouble." Mehemed took Radu's hand and gave it a discreet squeeze. "I love you," he whispered. "Now go to sleep. May Allah watch our dreams!"

While they were sleeping, Dracula's soldiers, under cover of the shadows, were killing the army's horses and mules to make their march slower. The next day the chief falconers arrived breathless before the sultan. "The explorers did not come back," their leader said, "and many of our beasts are dead."

What kind of enemy am I facing? the sultan asked himself. "That damned impaler demon is a coward!" he screamed furiously. "He will not face us and will not fight like an honorable soldier! Double the night watch and make sure the animals are well-protected. Now, let's go straight to Tirgoviste!"

When they heard the absurd order, Radu said, "We are lost!" and the chief falconers just looked at each other. Their general silence confirmed the fact.

The sultan broke the quiet. "Another group of explorers must leave—but this time it has to be a bigger group to help us map the area. Let's not lose sleep over a few rebellious soldiers. Meanwhile we will wait until tomorrow for new supplies."

And so a larger group of brave Ottoman soldiers departed to explore the area. They shared the same destiny as their companions. New captives filled Dracula's already packed prisons, and new corpses decorated Tirgoviste.

The female cloth doll dressed like the sultan and impaled on a golden stake moved slowly and incessantly in the distance, but it still could not provoke the mobilization of the enemy. The Ottoman sultan silently stared at it with his black eyes, trembling with fear. Just the thought of ending up impaled on that stake gave him goose bumps. *What will happen to my soul?* he wondered. *The impaler demon will surely send it to hell.*

"Not even the ones who went to investigate the delay in the delivery of supplies have come back," he said aloud. "Nor have the ones who went to explore the territory. What would you do if you were me, Radu?"

"Follow Dracula and eliminate him without separating your army," Radu replied. "Those ragged soldiers of his are not better than we are. We have better weapons and discipline, and there are a lot more of us."

So the sultan issued a new order to his chief falconers. "Follow the enemy and destroy him! The army must remain together!"

"I am suffocating in this heat! I cannot take the thirst!" said one Ottoman soldier. "Pass me some water."

"We must save our water," another soldier scolded. "The new supplies have not arrived yet. I wonder if the impaler cut them off."

"We've never had to fight like this," the first soldier complained. "The heat is unbearable—I feel like I am going to die inside this armor. It's like a hot iron. I've got to take it off!"

"Don't even think about it!" his comrade said. "It is better to be burned alive than pierced by the arrows of the impaler demon."

"You're right—I won't take it off. But I don't know how long I will be able to take this hell. It is very strange to fight against an enemy that does not exist."

"He does exist—but he is a coward. He won't face us, but just hits and runs. He fights like a woman!"

In Tirgoviste Kestywz had a big problem. "The jails are packed," one of his soldiers reported. "The prisoners are standing—not one more can fit in the cells!"

When he received that report from Kestywz, Dracula came up with a new solution. "Use the mousetrap," he said. "And when they no longer fit in there, chain them up in the courtyard with their heads covered."

"I am really thirsty—I would kill for a sip of water! And the supplies still have not arrived. I am dying of fear!" When one soldier dared express his misery, another picked up the theme, and then another one and another. Soon all the soldiers were complaining of thirst; it was distressing. The intense heat seemed to get worse by the minute. "We are in hell!" a soldier moaned.

"And the impaler demon is stalking us," another replied, scared.

"He is playing with us . . . we have already come this way."

The sultan said worriedly. "We are following a coward ghost that does not face us and has us walking in circles." Addressing to a chief falconer he said, "Let's take a shortcut—keep going northwest!" And the order was carried out straightaway.

"They are changing the course!" Swerige informed Dracula.

"Where are they heading?"

"They're headed toward the village where I live," said one of his soldiers.

"Swerige, go ahead and prepare the population for the arrival of our enemy!" Dracula said. Then, turning to the soldier who lived there, he said, "It would be really helpful if you would join them—go with them!" The soldier left at once.

Dracula summoned the rest of his soldiers. "Impale three enemy soldiers and plant them in the sultan's path. We must delay his march." The unlucky three were among the Ottomans who had fulfilled the sultan's latest order for a search party. By the time the rest of the Ottoman army caught up with them, they no longer had eyes; the vultures had devoured them quickly.

A chief falconer asked, "Is there a volunteer who would like to take down those impaled men?" A deep silence was the answer.

Then one of the impaled men moved slightly. "They are alive!" one of the soldiers screamed.

The sultan knew they were not going to survive. "Behead them," he said. "And give them an Ottoman burial!" With that order, those three souls had been saved from going to hell.

Meanwhile the soldier Tihomir was leading Dracula's well-nourished soldiers. When the villagers saw him arrive, Tihomir was received as a great hero. Without dismounting his horse, he said, "The time of truth has come! We all are soldiers of Christ, of Wallachia, and of Dracula!" With that, the townspeople knew that they were going to participate in the war as military men and women.

Swerige then spoke. "You know what you have to do—it is time to do it!"

Each one of the villagers did a job that had been planned well beforehand. Some of them burned the crops; others killed the animals and threw the dead bodies and human feces into the wells, to poison them; and others unearthed already decaying animals and threw them into the water deposits, as well.

Little Lionel and Santa Lucia saw all the adults doing strange things and they wanted to help, too. They asked if they could help burn the crops but their mother wouldn't let them. Since many adults were capturing animals, they decided to grab one too, and began insistently chasing a chick, but the little bird was not willing to be captured. Finally their mother, Alexandra, with a strong Spanish accent shouted, "Let's go to the refuge, children!" And they headed to the hiding place while others erased their tracks with branches.

When Santa Lucia saw so much movement, so many armed men, and her mother so worried, she asked, "mommy, why are there so many soldiers?"

"Because we are at war against the Ottomans, Daughter," Alexandra said.

Lionel was watching the action all around him with curiosity. "What is a war, mommy?"

"It is a fight," she replied. "And if the bad people defeat us, they will take us away and treat us like animals."

Opening her eyes wide, Santa Lucia said, "But we are going to be like chicks, mommy! We are going to run very fast so nobody can catch us!"

Little Lionel looked frightened. "If the mean men grab us and take us away . . . will we see each other again?"

Alexandra didn't answer; she just kept walking in silence, looking very worried. The children began crying. "We are so afraid, mommy!" Santa Lucia said, why don't we get back to Seville?

"Now see? We are at the refuge! Don't be afraid, children. Dracula will protect us. He is our commander, and we are all his soldiers. He is fighting hard against our enemies, and we, as good soldiers, must obey him to win this war. Our orders are to pray with devotion to our God!"

Santa Lucia asked, "Dracula is our commander?"

"Yes, Daughter . . . he is our commander."

"Am I a soldier in this war?" Lionel was beaming.

"A very important soldier!" Alexandra said, smiling. Knowing they were safe in the refuge, she added, "Go and play around, little ones!"

Santa Lucia, who was older, took little Lionel by the hand and said, "We are soldiers of our commander, Dracula, and we must obey him!" And they headed to one of the crucifixes in the refuge, knelt down, and began to pray.

Half an hour later, Alexandra looked around, shaken—she did not see her children among all the ones playing. She immediately began searching for them, anguished. When she found them praying, she held a hand to her pounding chest and went to hug them. Then she knelt down alongside them, and with her cheeks wet with tears, she joined in their prayer: "Our Father who are in Heaven, hallowed be your name . . ."

To the collective strength of the prayers being said all over Europe were added the prayers of these clean and pure hearts. The cosmic center received them, and these prayers were, without a doubt, the most potent kind, strong enough to become a physical force, shaping history before it happened.

Smoke guided the sultan's army straight to the village. "A town!" an Ottoman soldier shouted euphorically. "There must be water and food there. Thank you, Allah! Finally you heard our prayers!"

The army broke ranks and desperately searched for food and water, but they found only ashes. The water was red and brown from the animals' blood and stank horribly from the feces the villagers had thrown into it, but the soldiers' thirst was greater than their disgust at the putrid water, and some of the soldiers drank it only to vomit later. Again they were in hell!

Livid, the sultan shouted to his chief falconers, "Catch and kill that damned impaler! That is an order! Fulfill it!"

His men retraced the tracks of their enemy but could not find him: he was a cowardly ghost who hit and run. After hours of searching, one of the chief falconers reported back to the sultan. "Some of the men are exhausted, and the supplies have run out!" he said.

"Then sacrifice some horses!"

Once the army was fed the men had renewed spirits; however, the march was slower. Finally the lack of water and the intense heat forced some of the Ottomans to take off their armor—and when they least expected it, arrows came from the sky, piercing many of the men. But when they tried to face the enemy he had disappeared again, as if he had fallen from the face of the earth. They buried their dead with a quick Ottoman ritual and then proceeded with the tortuous march, now carrying their wounded as well.

Dracula and his soldiers arrived behind them. "You know what you have to do," he said, and his energetic men dug up the corpses and took them in carts to Tirgoviste, where they were impaled.

Kardotas asked Dracula, "I know there must be a good reason for exhuming the Ottomans. What is it?"

"When a Turk dies defending his faith in Allah and receives an Ottoman burial, his soul goes to heaven," Dracula explained. "But when we exhume his body and impale him, we are taking his soul out of paradise and throwing it down to hell, where no one can remove it! This follows the religious beliefs of our enemies, so with this action we fill them with terror. They now know that even if their soldiers receive an Ottoman burial, we will attend to their souls personally and with special eagerness. I assure you they consider us wicked demons."

97

The sultan now was speaking frankly to Radu. "I am terrified of dying impaled!" he said. "We have a lot of men, but we don't have food or water, and we are lost and have no idea when are we going to get out of this damned mousetrap. I am sleepless from worry. Please, help me get to sleep."

Mehemed lay with his head in Radu's lap, and Radu touched his lover's hair and started stroking it gently. Slowly, the sultan felt sleep overwhelm him—a deep and refreshing sleep.

Suddenly there was the noise of a thousand cannons. Mehemed looked toward the entrance of the tent, and there was Dracula, Radu's head in his hands, looking at him with his deep-green eyes. "Your time has come!" he said. "Impale him!" Then Dracula's soldiers were dragging him out of the tent, and he saw in horror that his entire army had been impaled: all of them were moaning, but none of them could talk. The soldiers undressed him and tied his feet and hands, and he was ashamed at being seen humiliated and in that state He had never imagined that he would end at the hands of the feared impaler demon. The golden stake that had enticed him to war now was entering his anus, and the pain as it pierced his body was unbearable. "Noooo!" he screamed. "For the love of Allah, don't do this to me! I am going to lose my soul!" He had never known such fear or felt such pain. He would have preferred to die in any other way than that! He screamed again and again, until he felt himself being shaken violently.

"Wake up, Mehemed! You are having a nightmare!" It was Radu.

Mehemed lay bathed in sweat, staring fixedly into space. Then he hugged Radu and told him, shaking, "Your damned brother was impaling me! Help me! I am really afraid!" After a moment, when he began to recover from that nightmare, he looked around him and saw that he was surrounded by his chief falconers. They had heard the screams coming from the main tent and had run there to help fight the enemy. Instead they had been unwitting witnesses to the great fear of their master.

Mehemed now felt deep shame coupled with great hatred for the impaler demon, who had made him look like a fearful coward before his men. Collecting himself, he joined his men to walk the entire campsite and make sure it was secure. But inside, he still wanted to die. He had been ashamed and humiliated. Now he hated that miserable man more than ever. Lifting his eyes to the sky, he made a solemn vow: "I swear by my God Allah that I will not rest until I have the head of the impaler!"

Abdulla, a soldier in the sultan's army, felt like he was suffocating. "I cannot take this heat any longer," he said desperately. "It is killing me!" Even as he spoke he was taking off his armor.

His companion put a hand out to stop him. "Put it on," he said. "You are going to make yourself a target for the enemy cowards."

Abdulla shrugged and looked around. "The forest is far away," he said. "I am safe here. You should rest, too . . . take it off for a while!"

His comrade shook his head vigorously. "I am not crazy!" he said, and continued on his way.

"I am ashamed," the sultan admitted. "The entire army knows about my nightmares and my fear of your damned brother. I am also worried, because I think my nightmares are a clear premonition that I am going to die impaled."

Radu put two fingers to Mehemed's lips. "Don't even mention it! Now I am scared, too! What would you think if we slept in the tents with the Janissaries?"

Mehemed smiled. "You always give me the best advice! I think that's a wonderful idea. I don't want to die pierced by that golden stake that does not let me sleep."

At the camp where the terminally ill people were in quarantine, Ianco was on the verge of tears. "I feel like I am dying," he said. "Everything is getting cloudy. I want to go to war!"

Udriste put an encouraging hand on his shoulder. "Cheer up, Ianco. You are not dying yet!"

But Ianco knew his fate was near. "Please take my disease to our enemies," he said. "My God is calling me!" His eyes were fixed in anguish at not being able to go to war. With a shallow breath, he gave his soul to his creator.

His companions were sad that yet another one had departed before he could fight the enemy. They desperately wanted to go to action! In their prayers they asked their God to give them strength to bear their sicknesses long enough to join the war and defend him. Then everyone in quarantine approached the new corpse, with the most fortunate ones sleeping beside it. They knew it carried a deadly disease, and they wanted to take that disease to their infidel enemies.

In the meantime, the sultan's army continued its silent walk. Finally an Ottoman soldier turned to the fearless Abdulla, who was walking beside him. "Did you know that our sultan is so afraid of the impaler demon that he has started to sleep in our tents?"

"Incredible!" Abdulla replied. "The most powerful man in the world feels fear? I've also dreamt that the impaler is killing m—"

Abdullah gasped and dropped, and then everyone hit the ground as a rain of arrows fell on them. Abdullah's companion watched helplessly as his imprudent friend lay dying in agony.

When the attack finally ended, the surviving Ottomans scrambled to fight the enemy—but where was he? "Damned cowardly ghosts!" screamed a chief falconer, angry at not having anyone to confront.

At night the camp filled with a negative energy that invited fear, and the sultan's powerful anxiety spread among all his subordinates, who, strangely, at the end of their dreams ended up impaled. At night screams of fear and nightmares became widespread, so the scene was less like a military camp than a mental asylum full of paranoid patients.

98

On the night of June 17, 1462, Mehemed said to Radu, "The spirits of my men are low. If I had known what was going to happen to us I never would have come to this place, this Cehennem. My men are terrified, and I am desperate!"

Radu chided him, "It was stupid of you to name it that—'hell'! Only you would have thought of that!" Then he added, "The accumulated insomnia has made us crazy; our soldiers are like the living dead. I hope we get out of this mousetrap soon." When they arrived at the tent of the Janissaries, where they would sleep, Radu said good-bye to his lover. "May Allah give you a satisfactory rest, my love," he whispered. "I will see you tomorrow."

Screaming was now part of the process of rest for those poor military men; everyone dreamed the same dream, and everyone feared the same impaler demon. The nightmare-fueled cries rang out, with all kinds of variations. "I do not want to lose my soul!" "Do not impale me, demon!" "Ahhh!" Those were just some of the anguished, desperate screams heard in the Ottoman camp at night—and even in the daytime, sleep was elusive. One night watchman complained to another, "No matter how hard I try to sleep during the day, I haven't been able to do it, and now I am exhausted."

"Do not fall asleep!" his companion warned. "If you do, you'll be punished!"

"What bigger punishment is there than coming on this stupid adventure? No one has even seen the enemy in battle."

The second watchman shrugged his agreement. "It is difficult to keep watch in this mental asylum, but I am going to my post."

<hr />

A Janissary who was trying in vain to sleep looked toward the door of his tent and saw the shadowy image of a soldier of Dracula. He knew he was in the middle of another nightmare, but then he saw the soldier attack his tent mates, piercing them with his sword. The Janissary tried to wake himself up, but before he managed to do it he felt the tip of a sword pierce his body. Putting his hands to the wound, he saw blood and realized that he was dying—he was not dreaming. It was a reality as true as his death! He screamed in horror and then groaned in pain; the sounds became part of the strange symphony of screams that punctuated the macabre attack.

Dracula and Ivan, joined by a group of soldiers, went to the sultan's tent. Dracula entered first to identify the occupants. When he saw that none of them was Mehemed, he had his soldiers kill them all. Then they began searching the other tents.

In one of the Janissaries' tents, Radu grabbed Mehemed's hand. "Do not let go of me for anything!" he said, and amidst the chaos they escaped toward the forest.

By then a chief falconer had commanded his bugler to signal the beginning of organized battle. Despite the confusion, the Ottomans were a strong and experienced army, and soon they had organized to fight the longed-for battle against the enemy, who finally faced them.

"That bastard is nowhere!" exclaimed Dracula when he heard the signal from the enemy's bugler. "It is a gamma formation! We are not going to be able to contain their attack—there are too many!" He turned to Ivan. "Order retreat!"

"Play retreat!" Ivan called to his bugler. The order was carried out at once, and the soldiers of Dracula withdrew and went deep into the dark and sinister forest.

The world's most modern war machine, the best-armored and best-trained fighting force, was willing to kill any enemy—but where was that damned enemy? Dracula had run away again like a cowardly hare! Helpless and disappointed, the chief falconer said quietly, "The enemy attacked us and then escaped."

When the sultan went back to the camp, he saw it was a real disaster. There were dead men everywhere, and the men who were left were more scared than ever. "He called me chicken!" he screamed at Radu. "Chicken is your damned brother! He hits and runs like a coward! Why doesn't he face us and fight like a military man—with honor?"

A chief falconer issued his report. "The casualties are more than seven thousand, sir."

Mehemed II put his hands on his head. "There are so many!"

"And sir, we did not count the missing ones. We will not know the precise number until tomorrow."

The following day the corpses were given an Ottoman burial. At the end of the ceremony, the sultan, filled with hate, told his chief falconers, "I am going to give twenty thousand gold coins to the one who brings me the head of the miserable impaler demon."

The news spread like wildfire throughout the army, motivating the solders and raising their spirits, which were very low.

Dracula summoned Stanyzkwl. "It is time to make use of the very ill people," he said. Then he gave his specific instructions, and the commander prepared to obey them.

"The time to defend our God, our Wallachia, and our children has come!" Stanyzkwl announced to the ones in quarantine. That news was received with great joy. Finally, these humble peasants were going to participate actively in the war! Everyone was willing to die fighting; they were anxious to be in battle.

"We are going to put these contaminated clothes in the sultan's way," Stanyzkwl told them. "Meanwhile, you will quietly join his army to spread your disease to the enemy. Try to sleep near them. You are the most lethal weapons we have: our victory is in your hands."

The sick people wanted to contaminate those hateful enemies. They were desperate to be among the infidels and give them what they deserved.

"And those?" asked a chief falconer, pointing at some carriages along the road before them. His soldiers obediently checked their contents.

"They are Ottoman clothes!" a soldier shouted back. "And they are clean!"

Delighted, they began exchanging the clean clothes for their own dirty ones. While the soldiers were changing clothes, the sick people discreetly came out of the forest dressed as Ottoman soldiers and silently joined the ranks of the sultan's army.

With water in short supply, the army rationed it zealously. Each soldier got three gulps. They did not pour it out into cups for fear of wasting even a drop of the vital liquid. The sick people took full advantage of their turn, and on the third gulp they spit in the common vessel in order to spread their disease to the others.

"Unearth the enemies from the last battle and impale them in Tirgoviste!" Dracula commanded. "From now on, however, we are not going to exhume the dead because we may get contaminated. We are going to pass these infidels through our hidden traps and make them go in circles while the sick people contaminate them."

Night covered the Ottomans with its cloak, and as the sultan prepared to sleep, his hardened face showed his anxiety. The bags under his eyes were as big as his fear.

After several days, one of the chief falconers came to the sultan, visibly alarmed. "We have an outbreak of plague!"

"Plague?" the sultan repeated anxiously. "What are we going to do now?" He began praying desperately, as only Allah could give him comfort in his terrible misfortune. The army's march had become much slower, and the sense of alarm was general.

"Radu, I am watching my men die and I cannot do anything," Mehemed confessed. "I am really scared—I feel Allah has abandoned me. This plague is the ruin of my army! Look how it has decimated us already. And I have passed my fear to my soldiers. We all want to go back, but we can't!"

The days went by slowly, and each brought its own misfortune. The number of dead due to disease surpassed the dead from battle by a considerable amount, and the powerful sultan was watching, powerless, as his army grew smaller and smaller.

The vovoid guided the enemy army where he needed them to go, and he attacked them at the least expected moment, decimating them slowly but effectively. Meanwhile the diseased keep falling.

When Dracula had used all the traps and the time was right, he gathered his commanding officers. "We are going to direct them to Tirgoviste!" he said, and then he explained his carefully planned order. "The sultan must arrive in Tirgoviste exactly in seven days," he said to Kardotas. "Stay at the front of this part of the army and take whatever actions you consider adequate so they arrive at the right moment. I trust in your intelligence and wit. I will see you in Tirgoviste!"

Kardotas stood at attention like the soldier he was and answered, "In exactly seven days we will see each other there! Not a day more . . . not a day less."

99

When Dracula arrived in Tirgoviste, the stench was unbearable. Thousands of Ottomans were hanging impaled, partially eaten by the vultures. "We must impale all the Ottomans we have in prison," he said to his commanding officers. "We have to hurry, because they are too many!"

The commanders organized squads to carry out the delicate activity, and the men immediately prepared to fulfill their leader's command.

Kestywz had a group of impalers in his charge, and they worked with ruthless efficiency: they quickly took an Ottoman, beat him, undressed him, and tied him to the saddles of four horses amidst a concert of horrifying screams. Everything was ready to introduce the stake through his anus.

With the expeditiousness of his leader, Kestywz had requested that they introduce it quickly—and then he saw the two birthmarks on the Ottoman's back. He stood petrified and breathless, and everything became cloudy around him; his legs suddenly could not hold him and he felt like he was about to faint—but there was no time for that. Pulling himself together, he looked at the enemy's face and let out a muffled scream. "My beloved son!"

Terrified and bewildered, the boy exclaimed, "Dad! What are you doing?"

The soldiers were left speechless by the strange encounter and let the boy go. Kestywz hugged him as if he wanted their souls to melt together. But he knew that he was a defender of the faith in Christ, and his son was an infidel. He had to do his duty. He had to make a choice between Christ and Dracula or his son and that savage god. Looking the boy in the eyes, Kestywz dropped to his knees and begged: "Forgive me, Son! I love you more than my own life . . . but my God comes first!" Turning to his soldiers he said with a dispirited voice, "Impale him." And the execution continued on its course.

The boy began screaming desperately, "Dad, don't do this to me! I love you and I need you! It was not my fault! You know I was forced to! If you do not help me, who is going to do it?"

Kestywz would have liked to be deaf so as not to hear the voice that was speaking directly to his heart and shaking him like a volcanic eruption. Plucking up courage, he took the stake and placed the tip at the boy's anus, but when he started to impale his son he stopped and sank back down on the ground, crying. "Forgive me, my God! I cannot do it!" He threw down the stake and hugged his son, and his words were muffled from crying. "God forgive me! But I can't!"

Dracula had been watching the strange scene from a distance. Was Kestywz hugging a naked Ottoman? He approached to find out, asking, "What is happening, Kestywz?"

Kestywz, still on his knees, said through his sobs, "Forgive him, Dracula! He is the son the sultan stole from me and turned into our enemy! I cannot kill him—impale me, but forgive this innocent!"

Dracula stood frozen. What was he going to do now? He had to choose between Christ and his foe. But his agile mind worked quickly. "Stop the impalement!" he shouted. His strange order was obeyed immediately, and then he gave another one: "Free this child of conscription!" He approached the released boy and asked him, "Can you identify other children of conscription from Wallachia, Moldavia, or Transylvania?"

The boy nodded and pointed with a shaking finger. "Those are Wallachians, and those are from Moldavia. And I see some impaled from Transylvania, too!"

"Gather them," Dracula told Kestywz. "I am going to speak with them. Behead the impaled ones who are still alive, and give all the dead a Christian burial."

Kestywz was a strong man, but now he could not stop crying. He could not find the words to thank God for having put that angel on his path. He wanted to thank Dracula, as well, but he couldn't manage to speak; instead he approached him, knelt down, and took his hand with the intention of kissing it. But Dracula gently took his hand away, saying, "Get up, Father. We have a lot of work to do." He could not help but notice that a single tear from his grateful and faithful father-in-law had fallen onto his hand. That little drop was more eloquent and expressive than all the words in the world.

Then he spoke to the children of conscription, who now were young men. "You were victims of the sultan," he said. "From now on you will be my soldiers, and you will defend the faith of our Christ!"

Karyotins, Kestywz's son, was impressed. This saint who was forgiving him and saving his life was the same man the sultan called 'impaler demon'? He had been told that Dracula was the bloodiest murderer in history—so why had this murderer forgiven him? Why did he call his father "Father"? A thousand questions came into his head, and only time would answer them. But he was sure of one thing: from that day on and until his death, he would be faithful to that saint who had saved his life, given him freedom, and allowed him to recover his God and his family.

"Continue with the executions!" Dracula said.

One of the freed Janissaries said to another, "I felt like a new person when they told me I was a child of conscription. I cannot believe it! We will recover our families, our religion, and our lives—and now we are soldiers of Christ!"

"And all thanks to Dracula!" the other young man replied. "I am going to fight by his side until I'm dead!"

"As will I," said the first one.

Kardotas used his tactics to guide the Ottomans until one of the soldiers shouted, "I can see a few houses in the distance!"

The sultan was relieved and happy. "We got out of the mousetrap!"

But when they entered the village, the fetid smell of death permeated the atmosphere. It was so strong they felt compelled to investigate, so they followed the birds overhead until they found before them the most terrifying scene they had ever imagined: more than twenty thousand impaled Ottomans. *How is this possible?* the sultan asked himself in horror. All the soldiers who had disappeared, as well as the ones they had buried, were hanging there, pierced on stakes—some were still alive. The air was full of vultures; others had landed and were feeding energetically.

The Ottoman soldiers were horrified by what they saw. Those souls had earned their place in paradise, having died in battle defending Allah, but by exhuming their bodies and impaling them, Dracula had taken them from their eternal rest and mercilessly thrown them into hell, and they would never get out. The soldiers' fear was so great that they were silent for a long time.

Finally Mehemed II turned to Radu and asked desperately, "What do I do? Some of them are still alive!"

"Behave like a father," Radu said. "Take care of the soul of the soldiers who are alive, and save them their pain. All your army will thank you."

So the sultan issued an order in a loud voice: "Search for the ones who are still alive and take them off the stake! Behead them and give them an Ottoman burial!"

"Identify the live ones—take them off and behead them!" shouted the chief falconers to their soldiers.

One Janissary had been impaled for two days and was waiting impatiently for the arrival of his death—his only hope for ending the hell he had endured against his will, the painful and slow torture of his punishment. The vultures had been delighted by the taste of his succulent eyes, and he could feel that parts of his skin were missing. The pain was unbearable, and then there were the cold, heat, hunger, thirst, and other pains he couldn't identify. But they all were overshadowed by his main anguish: he was going to lose his soul. Strangely, however, his hearing had sharpened, and he heard the order of one chief falconer. His hope to die quickly and receive an Ottoman burial was a fact! His body filled with happiness, and he felt that in spite of his misfortune, he was very happy. He wanted to move to show them that there was still life in his body; he was making superhuman efforts to show his existence . . . but his body did not obey him.

He was deep in concentration, trying to achieve his objective, when he heard a couple of voices directly below him.

"Is this one alive?"

"Look at him!"

The impaled man concentrated all his attention on moving one hand—it was the right time! But no matter how hard he tried, not one muscle of his body obeyed the order.

"He is dead—he's not moving."

There was a pause and then a doubtful voice, a little closer. "He does not smell like a corpse."

"Then get him down!"

This challenge was answered with a fearful voice. "What if he is dead?" There was another short pause, and at that instant the impaled man felt his hand moving—and he was filled with joy. He did not know that the soldiers had briefly looked away and had not seen his movement. They left him, sad at not having been able to save the soul of that unfortunate man.

The impaled man was calling them desperately with his mind: *Help me! For the love of Allah! I am alive! Allah, do not abandon me—I trust you!* He was sending all kinds of mental messages, imploring his God to save him. He knew that his friends had good intentions and wished to help him, and he felt that Allah had abandoned him. Now he was left with his sole companion, the dread of being lost forever in the hell to which his religion had assigned him, and he had to keep bearing his indescribable pain as the process of death stayed on its slow and seemingly endless course.

The Ottomans were terrified. They had given an Ottoman burial, with all the spiritual assistance of their religion, to the ones they had taken down alive. As for the rest, Allah would take care of their souls; the soldiers were not going to risk their eternal lives to gain the same for others. Their fear had by now surpassed the limits of reason. They were haunted by a single question: What if they had been the impaled ones? Imagining that destiny, they were more horrified than ever and wanted nothing but to leave that hell, to be far away from the wicked impaler who was stalking them.

The sultan could no longer take it. Radu's beautiful eyes, his masculine beauty, their immense love, all that torrid romance was being overshadowed by the dark actions of the impaler demon. Mehemed had to choose between his love and his ambition to expand the empire, and his ambition was easily more powerful. Looking for a solution to the problem he told Radu, "You are going to stay here. You will keep Tirgoviste, and later you will take all Cehennem." Then in a reassuring tone he added, "This separation is temporary. When Cehennem is at peace, I will put in your place another ruler and we will be together again. Trust me!"

Radu's blue eyes filled with tears. He did not want power or wealth. The only thing he wanted was to be near his lover. In desperation, he turned to threats. "I love you more than my own life, and if you leave me alone . . . I am afraid I will end in the arms of another man!"

Mehemed was silent a moment, and then, furious, he exclaimed, "If you do it I will kill you!"

When Radu heard this threat he was happy: Mehemed loved him! And he decided to keep putting pressure on Mehemed not to leave him in that wretched place. "Can you imagine another man kissing me?" he asked, smiling slightly.

With that Mehemed lost his temper. He hit Radu again and again.

Radu considered each blow that hit his body a clear manifestation of Mehemed's love: the more he hit and hurt Radu, the more Radu knew he loved him.

Mehemed, in turn, kept imagining his lover in the arms of another until he was blind with fury. Radu ended up badly beaten and crying pitifully. When Mehemed saw him so weak and defenseless, he knelt down before him and asked him sorrowfully, "Can you forgive me? It is just that I love you so much!"

Radu did not answer; instead he just hugged Mehemed by the neck. They kissed passionately and then consummated their love until they were satisfied. It had been so long, so long since they touched. The impaler demon had stolen their intimacy!

Mehemed pulled Radu close and whispered, "I trust in you more than I do anyone else. I am sure you will send me the head of your brother. Remember that he broke his oath of silence made before Allah, and therefore betrayed him. He deserves death!"

Radu knew he would obey his lover because Radu knew Dracula, and Dracula would never accept Islam.

"I will leave you this money and part of my army to stay in power and fulfill my orders," Mehemed said. "You must kill your brother immediately, before he gets stronger—I trust you! I must go back to the empire now. I promise that I'll see you later!"

Radu stood up, looking anxious. "But what will happen with Cehennem? And the faith in Allah? And your proclamation that says Jesus

Christ is a prophet, just like Mohammad? These savages are going to declare that Jesus Christ is God, almighty and real, as soon as you leave!"

The sultan sneered. "What do I care about the salvation of the souls of these savages?" he said. "As far as I'm concerned, they can continue believing what they want, and go to hell when they die. I just want to leave this place immediately. And you . . . you had better send me the head of your brother!"

"What about me?" Radu said in a quavering voice. "You don't care about me, do you?" He clasped his hands against his chest dramatically. "Do not leave me," he whispered.

But Mehemed took advantage of a distraction outside the tent and left quickly. Radu wanted to stop him, but he got to a place where there were witnesses; he knew he could not behave as he did privately in front of the other soldiers. So he watched his loved one leave, and the pain he felt was so intense he was sure he would not survive.

When Mehemed returned to the empire, he was no longer commanding the victorious army whose spirits were sky-high from having conquered Constantinople. Yes, it was still an army, but it was decimated and sickly. The men seemed less soldiers than frightened children, terrified that the impaler demon, without warning and without mercy, would take their souls and throw them into hell.

The way back home was not as difficult as the journey to Tirgoviste had been. With experienced and trustworthy Saxons as guides, the Ottomans continued their march without fear of getting lost; since they knew about the lack of food and water, they had brought many mules loaded with enough provisions. But the nights were terrifying, and at dawn the soldiers were always thankful for another day of life. There were still plenty of frightening incidents—like mules and horses that died by arrows from God knows where—to make their way more tortuous.

Every step along the way, the sultan was in fear; he knew the enemy was surrounding him and wanted to impale him. His fear increased every day as his army continued to diminish, and he began praying constantly to be delivered from that hell. Each minute was precious, and because of the men's hurry and their fear of being contaminated, the dead were abandoned and later attended with special attention by the voracious vultures—no Ottoman burial for them!

When they arrived at the Danube, the sultan was sad to see that a lot of his ships had been sunk. With some difficulty they recovered some of the ones that had been left on the other bank of the river, and with a lot of work they organized their shameful escape, always in anguish for fear of an attack. Finally, when the sultan felt he was safe, he exclaimed, "As long as that damned impaler demon lives, I will not step again on Cehennem!" He turned back to see that place and got his final, parting image: his two thousand Janissaries, impaled.

With the defeated sultan was a "soldier" named Udriste, who felt terribly sick. War had not ended for him, and as he struggled along he was praying in silence, *My God Jesus Christ, please give me the strength to contaminate all our enemies. Do not take my life—let me live just a little longer . . .*

100

Not long afterwards, an emissary arrived at the palace of King Matthias. "Good news, my lord! Dracula has the Ottomans terrified, and he survived the war! Mehemed has fled to his empire!"

Matthias felt everything spinning. Certain he was about to faint, he leaned against a table to keep from falling down.

Seeing the king's ashen face and shocked reaction, the worried emissary asked, "Do you feel all right, my lord?"

"I am fine!" answered the king. Pulling himself together, he added hypocritically, "It is a good thing that my subject succeeded."

"He still has not won," warned the emissary, "but the most difficult part of his fight has passed."

Matthias Corvinus stood before the powerful holy Roman emperor, Frederick III, and said, "It is very likely that Dracula will ask for your help fighting his crusade against the Ottomans. I definitely refused—the man is insane! How could he attack the most powerful army of the world by himself? That would occur only to him!"

Frederick III hated Dracula and still considered him an enemy. "It angers me that the pope has ordered Te Deums in his support. He forgets that Dracula is a heretic Orthodox, and he treats him like a saint. Pio has already forgotten he once was my subject, and now he feels superior to all of us. I feel he looks down on me by treating me like an allied subject. You can count on me! I promise you I won't help Dracula."

Neither monarch told the truth: that they hated and envied Dracula because somehow, with a small group of soldiers, some humble peasants, and some slaves with no military training, he had fought against, decimated, and chased away the most powerful army in the world. Both men were consumed by jealousy.

After dinner the host said to his guest, "Let us have fun for a while!" and he summoned his jesters. Among them was a man named Michael Beheim. He wore a tight harlequin decorated with yellow and blue squares; cloth shoes with huge, rolled pointed toes; and a funny cloth hat with four points and bells. In one hand he held a maraca, and in the other a little puppet. He started to sing and play a ridiculous little guitar he had hanging from a ribbon, and then he began dancing, too, spicing up the show with spectacular rehearsed falls and jerky movements. At the end, to top it all, he started reciting a poem about the violent, crazy Prince Dracula of Wallachia, who nailed the turbans onto the heads of some of the sultan's emissaries and impaled the others. He also recited a joke in which a donkey and a monk ended up impaled on the same stake. When he had finished his ridiculous performance, the two monarchs laughed and clapped with special enthusiasm.

The jester thanked them excitedly and bid them farewell, delighted by his unusual, even incomprehensible success.

Matthias, pleased, turned to the emperor. "Your jester is ridiculous! Where did you get it?"

"He arrived here by himself," Frederick responded. "He was wandering around. Apparently he was thrown out of everywhere else for being a nuisance, but he always makes a big effort to entertain me."

"Poor little thing!" Matthias exclaimed. "When you do not want it anymore, send it to my court—I would be happy to have it with me. Tomorrow at dawn I will leave for Hungary."

101

The Ottoman army led by Radu was very large; confronting it directly would be suicide. But Dracula had gone through the most difficult stage of his fight. It was only a matter of time before he would meet his brother in battle. So far, everything was going well.

When Zalesha saw Dracula she was so excited that she cried. She hugged him and then knelt down before her crucifix and prayed fervently, "Thank you, God, for having lent him to me for more time!"

Dracula smiled. "I have a surprise that is worth more than all the gold and silver in the world. If you can guess what it is, I will give it to you."

Zalesha tried to guess. "The war is over!"

"No, it's not that," he said. "Now close your eyes . . ." Suddenly she felt someone strong lift her from behind, so high she felt like she was flying. Then she heard the voice of a young man she could not identify, saying, "I've got you, Zalesha!"

Startled by the strange welcome, she opened her eyes and saw that her husband had a huge grin on his face. Finally the strong arms stopped spinning her and set her down on the ground. She turned around and was so stunned she might have been struck by lightning. She put her hand over her mouth and gave a muffled scream and then hugged the young man for all she was worth. "Karyotins . . . Brother! I cannot believe it!"

When Dracula saw his wife so happy, he looked at the sky and, speaking from his heart, said, "Thank you, God. Bless you!"

Minhea, Dracula's son, was also happy; he had never expected to see his father again. Now he was looking at his new uncle in amazement.

"I am alive because my God wanted it that way," Dracula said. "My brother Radu is after me with a large part of the Ottoman army, but that does not worry me anymore. The most difficult stage of my fight has passed. I am going to take you to King Matthias, but you must follow my orders and fulfill them without questioning them or arguing. My main objective is to save your lives."

Mother and son began praying, still thanking God that the family was still together.

Along with some faithful boyars, Dracula made a plan to move his family where King Matthias was. There they would be safe while he planned a strategy to go back and finish the enemies of the cross.

A peasant, who like every other peasant loved his vovoid but was a servant of the Turks, heard that as soon as the sun began to rise, the Ottomans were going to capture Dracula—they had located him on one of his properties. Plucking up the courage to risk her life, the peasant stood in front of Dracula's propriety and shot into the tower window an arrow with a note that said, "You are going to be captured in the morning. Run away!" When the woman saw the arrow enter the tower and Dracula's wife pick it up, she felt she'd accomplished her mission.

Zalesha read the note and said, "They have located us!" Then she gave the note to Dracula. "What will happen if they capture us?"

He answered honestly. "My commanders are carrying out my orders in other places, and right now I do not have a way to confront them. If they capture us they are going to rape you, and then they will kill the three of us . . . and I won't be able to stop them."

When Zalesha imagined herself falling into the clutches of those lustful Ottomans, she was wild with fear. "I love you more than my own life," she said to Dracula, "and I will always wait for you with our God!" Then she kissed him, her eyes filled with tears, and she began backing away from him, repeating as if she'd confirmed her decision, "I will always wait for you with Christ!" And before he could stop her, she threw herself out the window and into the Argens River.

Dracula was shocked by the loss of his faithful wife; his emotions were in turmoil. Still, he knew he had to act, if for no other reason than for the sake of his son, who had always followed him like a shadow. He called to a boyar. "Put the horseshoes back to front on some of the horses," he said, and his order was immediately carried out. Then he bade farewell to his men, saying, "I will contact you when the time is right. Thank you for everything you have done for me."

"We should thank you," several of them responded.

He hugged each one of them and then said, "Fire your cannons to confuse my brother's army while we escape."

Dracula and his son left on horseback and rode until they reached some dangerous cliffs, which they descended with instructions from some local guides. Their destination was a fortress in Fagaras. At one point Dracula reined in his horse and spoke to Minhea, who was riding behind him. "Son, we have been through many adventures together, and today we are going to go through the most dangerous adventure of all. If something happens to me, defend Christ and be his bravest warrior, and seek the freedom of our people." With that he kissed the boy on the forehead and set off again. But in the confusion he lost Minhea in the dark night. He could not light a torch or shout at him because the enemy would capture them. The best thing, he knew, would be to leave his son there, as Dracula was the one being pursued. So, heartbroken, he continued on his way. He knew where to go—he would find his way to his trustworthy ally, King Matthias Corvinus. Matthias would help him . . . he was sure of that.

The King of Hungary, Matthias Corvinus, was more scared than ever. If Dracula decided to go directly to the Vatican, everything would be lost—. He wanted to give back the money for the crusade, but he had already assured the Holy Father that he had delivered it to Dracula. If he told the truth now, the whole world would know that he was a liar and a thief too. He had to find his vassal before it was too late. With the help of insomnia he desperately sought a solution to his problem. He was willing to do anything just to get out of that hellish situation—he would sell his soul to the devil, with no negotiation, if he had to! Suddenly the cruelest of ideas came to his mind. If he followed it, he would not only eliminate his dishonor at being a thief, but he would also be appointed holy Roman emperor. The first thing he had to do was find an accomplice who hated Dracula—and that was the easiest thing in the world.

While Matthias was discreetly looking for the right candidate among the Catholic monks to carry out his wicked plan, he gave an order to one of his commanders: "I need you to locate Dracula and immediately bring him to me live or death.

The commander nodded. "We will start looking near the border with Wallachia."

Then Matthias traveled to Sibiu. He stayed there until October while his informants looked for the fugitive, and then he went to Brasov.

Matthias found out that Brother Jacob hated Dracula, so he paid him a visit. "Do you know where Dracula is?" he asked.

The brother just stared at him with a murderous look, and without saying a word he got up to leave.

Matthias stood in front of him and asked again, "Do you know where Dracula is?"

"In hell!" answered the monk, trembling with rage. "I will not tell you what I am thinking because you would punish me!"

"Do you hate Dracula?" asked the monarch.

"And all his allies!" the monk said sharply. Then, nervously, he said, "And please do not ask me anything else. You are a powerful king, and I am just a humble monk." He again tried to leave the room, pushing Matthias aside. "Let me go!" he begged.

"Why do you hate him so much?"

"Because he impaled the man I loved and respected more than anyone—Brother Hans—just to steal from him."

"I am not an ally of Dracula," the king said. "In fact, I am looking for him to put him in prison." Matthias fixed the monk with a serious look. "What would you do to destroy Dracula?"

Brother Jacob was silent awhile, and then he took a deep breath and answered, "Anything. If I weren't a religious man I would probably even sell my soul to the devil to see that monster impaled!"

"Do you know how to write in Latin?" Matthias asked.

"Not very well," the monk admitted. "I am clumsy writing in that language, and I make a lot of mistakes. But I can generally convey what I want to say."

"Would you like me to take your foe prisoner and lock him in a cell forever?"

The monk's answer was immediate: "What do I have to do?"

Matthias instructed him to write three letters in Dracula's name: one to Sultan Mehemed II, another to the Great Vizier Mohmoud, and another to Stephen of Moldavia. The monk had to call them by titles that denoted Dracula's absolute submission to them: Mehemed would be "Emperor of Emperors," Mohmoud would be "Lord and Master," and Stephen would be "Great Lord and Master." (At that time Stephen was an ally of the Turks, an enemy of the Catholic Church, and a traitor to the Orthodox one). In the letters, the vovoid would offer his military service and propose to kidnap Matthias and to defend and protect Islam.

Brother Jacob made the three letters and gave them to the king. "How much do I owe you?" Matthias asked.

The brother stared at him and said, "You will pay me by getting that demon into a cell—and not giving him food or water!"

"It is necessary to ruin Dracula's reputation," Matthias said. "Right now he is considered a living saint. We need him to be seen as a real demon."

"It angers me when I receive orders from the Holy Father to pray and participate in the Te Deums in his support," the monk agreed. "I who know what he has done, and it enrages me!"

"Make up stories using real facts and then distort them," the king suggested. "I am sure that with the help of other monks you can do it."

"I know that Brother Johan is furious because the demon arrived at his monastery, stole everything they had, and impaled Brother Hoover. He almost got killed, too."

Matthias thought for a moment and then said, "In the court of Emperor Frederick III there is a jester named Michael Beheim. He sings very funny and bloody stories about Dracula. Look for Brother Johan and then go to the jester and write stories together. Write real ones or make them up, but either way, exaggerate! Do not stop to consider if the stories are true or false: write a bloody book, and with the help of the new printer, publish it."

"We need a lot of money to do that, and I am just a humble monk. Where am I going to get the money?"

"Here—take twenty-five gold coins," the king said. "Spare no effort or expense. If we don't act quickly, the pope may canonize him alive."

Sensing a motivation beyond deep hatred, the monk asked him skeptically, "Why are you giving me so much money?"

"Because I do not want you to have any excuse not to make that book—and I want it as quickly as possible."

"Consider it done," the monk said.

Brother Jacob immediately found Brother Johan and told him the good news. "Believe it or not, we are going to get our revenge on Dracula!"

"How?" Johan asked quizzically. "We are not military men."

"The king of Hungary has entrusted me to write a book about the demon's atrocities and to embellish it with other stories, too. Then we will publish it and take it to the king."

Johan frowned. "But we are monks, not writers!"

"There is a jester at the court of Emperor Frederick named Michael Beheim," Jacob said. "He sings fantastic stories about Dracula. The king ordered me to get in contact with him—and believe it or not, he gave me twenty-five gold coins to work with! We have no excuses not to do this job immediately."

"That's a fortune!" exclaimed the astonished monk. "Well, let's get to work."

The monks arrived before the Emperor Frederick III. "We have come on behalf of King Matth—"

"I was expecting you!" the emperor interrupted. "What took you so long?"

"We were making plans for the book," Johan responded.

"Jesters!" Frederick shouted.

And suddenly there appeared a group of clowns who amused the emperor when he had company. "Stay, Michael," he said to one. "You others, get out!"

The monks were surprised. There in front of them was a man in the tight clothes of a harlequin, down to the funny cap and shoes. He was obviously prepared to do his usual, ridiculous routine. But the emperor held up a hand. "You are going to do what these monks say."

Jacob explained. "There is something we all have in common: hate and rage against Dracula that will not stop until that demon is destroyed."

Beheim was looking at them, astonished, while everyone, including the emperor, nodded vigorously.

"Our objective," said Brother Jacob, "is to ruin Dracula's reputation. At this moment he is considered a saint, and all of Europe is praying for him. If he died right now he would indubitably be canonized. But we know what he has done, and we want him to pay for his crimes."

"That is why," said Johan, "we wish to write a book to tell the world of his crimes and end his prestige."

"Let's get down to work," the emperor said. He turned to the jester. "From now on you will dress as a man of letters and start writing. You will stop being a jester and become Imperial Poet Michael Beheim—because I say so." Then he turned back to the monks and handed them a small sack. "And here: you now have another twenty-five gold coins. So work quickly and make no excuses."

The intelligent monks looked at each other, thinking, *Why are they giving us so much money? What powerful interests are behind all this?*

Beheim, with less gray matter, suspected nothing; he thought only about himself, and tears of joy fell from his eyes. He had been born to make a fool of himself and be humiliated, and so this was the first time he had ever been treated with respect.! He left with the monks, carrying his new, pompous title of imperial poet. With all the excitement of the day's strange events he remembered too late that he barely knew how to read and could not even write his own name—but surely the monks would help him. The three started working immediately.

Jacob said, "I have the perfect title for our book. Let's call it, *The Story of a Bloodthirsty Madman Called Dracula of Wallachia.*"

"That's very long," Johan said, "but it sounds good. All right, that will be its title."

102

One of Dracula's spies came to the vovoid in his hideout. "King Matthias received copies of the letters you sent to the sultan, the vizier, and Stephen," the spy reported. "He is furious with you."

"What letters?" asked Dracula. "I do not know what you are talking about!"

"Matthias received copies of three letters in which you offer to betray him and the cross of Christ."

"What? That is ridiculous—I would never do that! I am going to write a letter to Matthias. I want you to take it to him immediately."

A few days later, Matthias received the following letter:

My king,

I found out that you received three letters in which I offer to betray you, kidnap you, and renounce my Christian faith. Those letters are a lie! I would prefer to die before committing an atrocity like that. I am faithful to my God and to you, and my greatest desire is to be in your trusted custody.

Signed,
Wladislaus III, Dragwlya

When Matthias finished reading, he issued an order to Litovoi, the faithful commander who had always accompanied his uncle. "Prepare some troops: we are going to capture Dracula."

"But Dracula is your subject and your faithful ally!" answered the surprised commander.

"He promised to kidnap me and fight for Islam," Matthias said.

"Do you believe that lie?" Litovoi asked. "Dracula might betray you, but our God? That is just impossible. There is something strange going on, and you should investigate it."

Matthias was visibly anxious. "Are you going to argue against my orders?" he shouted.

Litovoi stood at attention like the good military man he was. "No sir!" he answered firmly. And he went to fulfill the strange order.

———◆———

For years, Litovoi had fought under the direction of Mikhail Szilagyi, and he remembered how his superior always talked about the great passion with which Dracula defended the Christian faith and the great respect he had for the son of his best friend, Janos Hunyadi. So Litovoi wrote a letter to the vovoid:

Dracula,

I am well aware of the great respect and admiration Mikhail Szilagyi felt toward you and your defense of the faith. Therefore I am compelled to warn you not to entrust yourself to the custody of King Matthias. Do not trust him!

Signed,
A friend who admires your fight

Litovoi then gave the letter to a trustworthy soldier, saying, "Deliver this into Dracula's hands . . . and be discreet."

When Dracula received the letter, he could not believe it. How could he not trust in his king? He always be Matthias's ally! Still, his keen wit told him to be cautious; he prepared himself for a possible attack by the king.

Soon afterward, emissaries of Matthias arrived at the fortified suburb where the fugitive was hiding. Led by Litovoi, they were unarmed and carrying a white flag. They requested an interview with Dracula.

"We have come on behalf of King Matthias," Litovoi said, arms crossed. "Now you are under the protection of the king. Do you wish to join us?"

Why is he asking me instead of ordering me? Dracula thought. *Why does he have that corporal posture? What is he trying to say to me?* Looking Litovoi in the eye he asked, "Is Matthias with you?"

Litovoi did not answer immediately. For several long moments he stared back at Dracula. "Yes," he finally said. "He is . . . outside."

Sensing that there was something the military man wanted to tell him, but couldn't, Dracula asked, "If he is out there, why did he send some emissaries with a white flag instead of coming himself? Am I not his subject? Tell me the truth!"

The soldier did not answer.

"Leave us alone," Dracula said to the others in the room.

When they were alone, Litovoi told him quietly, "I sent you the letter! Mikhail always told me that you were Christ's bravest soldier, and I do not believe that you have offered to defend the crescent moon. I am a friend who admires your fight."

Dracula looked steadily at Litovoi and replied, "I swear to you by my soul, and by the souls of my ancestors and my children, that I would never be a traitor to my king, much less to Christ! Thank you for warning me. What is your name?"

"Litovoi," answered the commander, adding, "I believe you."

"I sense the hand of a very powerful man is behind all this," Dracula said, frowning. "Do you think Frederick III has something to do with Matthias's attitude?"

Litovoi shook his head. "I really do not know," answered the honest commander. "If I told you I did, it would be a lie."

After Litovoi and his retinue had departed, Dracula issued a strange order that left his soldiers dumbfounded, "The emissaries have left. Prepare to fortify against Matthias."

The weeks passed, and the king did not attack Dracula; there were only negotiations between them through mediators. After a while the vovoid said to his men, "I am going to turn myself in on the condition that you are not taken prisoner."

The protests were immediate: "You must not!" "Over our dead bodies!"

"You will do what I say! Tell the vovoid that I am going to turn myself in on that condition . . . and that is an order!"

The military men accepted reluctantly, fulfilling the order against their will. A message left immediately with the following note:

My King Matthias,

I offer to turn my weapons and myself directly to you in exchange for the absolute and unconditional freedom of my men.

Signed,
Wladislaus III, Dragwlya

With that Dracula's weapons were handed in, and Matthias, like any honorable king, fulfilled his part in the process by going in person to arrest him. When the king was in front of Dracula, the vovoid simply looked at him sadly. "Why, Matthias?"

Matthias handed him the three letters and replied, "Why, Dracula?"

Dracula read them quickly. "This is an infamy! How can you believe these lies?"

"Still, they exist! These letters were not written by themselves. I am going to have to hold you while we investigate."

"What are you going to investigate?" Dracula asked. "Are you going to investigate whether the man who always was your ally is now a traitor? Are you going to investigate the man who gave you his complete support when you and Laszlo were in jail and only your mother and your uncle were on your side? What is really happening, Matthias? You know I would gladly give my life for you. What does Frederick III has to do with all this? Tell me the truth!"

Matthias did not know how to answer, and without daring to give the order to apprehend him, he turned and left, saying quietly, "I am sorry, Dracula—we have to investigate." As soon as the king was out the door, his soldiers chained Dracula and took him prisoner.

368

In his cell, Dracula was thinking about the biggest liar, hypocrite, and fraud of all mortals—Pope Pio II, who had offered to help him but never did. *Where is that demon's conscience?* he wondered. *I hope his soul rots in hell!*

With Dracula safely behind bars, Matthias went to the Vatican. "Holy Father, I am worried," he said. "I intercepted these three letters—here, look at what they say."

Pio read them and answered, "Do you believe these lies? It looks like a donkey wrote these, they are so poorly written and have so many misspellings. Has not Dracula shown fidelity to the Catholic Church by courageously defending Christ despite being Orthodox?" Then the pope said something that shook Matthias to the core. "The hundred thousand gold coins we gave Dracula to fight the enemy were the best investment ever made by Christendom. He almost destroyed the powerful army of Mehemed! And now the Ottoman soldiers refuse to fight against him. I've heard that the sultan has nightmares and can't sleep for fear of Dracula; he trembles just to hear his name—and now he is afraid to attack Rome, too. The Ottomans are terrified by him! Dracula would be a fool to approach him! He has everything with me! The sultan declared our God a prophet in Wallachia and changed the name of that place to Cehennem, and Dracula made him swallow that stupid and heretical declaration. Then he made the sultan run away like a great coward. If it weren't for him, Rome be in real danger right now—not to mention the divinity of our God." By now the pope had worked himself into a frenzy, and he stood up and fairly screamed in the astonished king's face. "Because of what Dracula has done, he is the favorite son of our church! If it were up to me and he became Catholic, I would canonize Dracula here and now—even though he's still alive!"

Matthias was in trouble. He had never imagined that Dracula—the highest pontiff of the Orthodox Church in Wallachia—had earned an important place in the heart of the Catholic Church. He wanted to confess, to beg for forgiveness through the precious blood of his God, and return the one hundred thousand gold coins he had in his treasury; however, he knew the Holy Father, and he knew that the Catholic Church would forgive any sin, no matter how monstrous, as long as it was not affected. If he confessed, he was going to be treated like a heretic and traitor to the Church and to the blood of Christ, and the only thing he would get in return would be excommunication. Surely he would be turned in to the holy inquisitor—and if he fell into those hands, he would never be found innocent, even if he were a saint! He would be judged according to the strictest ecclesiastical standards. He preferred to keep silent rather than be judged a heretic.

"Free him immediately," Pio said. "These letters are the most absurd libel I have ever seen in my life. Besides, I want to meet Dracula in person; I am very curious to know a living saint. Bring him to me immediately!"

Matthias felt the ground open under his feet—this would be his ruin! After a moment's thought he said, "Holy Father, I promise you that I will free him and bring him to you later. Just let me investigate the content of these letters."

The pope frowned. "All right, investigate it . . . but do it soon. And in the meantime, do not even consider keeping him in prison. Treat him like what he is: the greatest defender of Christ on earth. And if something happens to him, you will be responsible for it! Kneel down to receive my blessing."

Matthias was desperate. What would happen when Pio discovered the truth? He sent an emissary to the court of King Frederick III, where three men were working hard to finish their book as soon as possible.

103

The resentful monks had some pictures painted in which Dracula was shown sacrificing saints. One showed the crucifixion of Saint Andrew, patron of none other than the sinister Saxons. The picture showed the holy apostle who joined |Christ being crucified by the boyars; behind them was the mastermind of this wickedness, the demon Dracula. They had other pictures made, too, and in all of them the main character was the wicked Dracula, always hurting the saints most favored by the Saxons.

Meanwhile, Dracula was taken to a prison in Alba Lulia, where he had all the necessary accommodations. From there he was taken to the palace of Visegrád on the Danube. King Matthias Corvinus often went there to dine with him. His conscience was so dark that he lived in fear of his treachery being discovered, and he always ordered his soldiers to be present and watch the guest closely in case he planned a surprise attack against the king.

One evening, Dracula asked him bluntly, "Why am I prisoner, my king?"

Matthias smiled. "You are not a prisoner," he said. "You are a guest of honor! You live in a palace, you have servants . . . you are being treated like the great vovoid you are."

"And why can't I go out of the palace?"

Matthias gestured toward the window, where they could see the river and the beautiful scenery illuminated by moonlight. "Here you have everything you need," he said. "Wait a while, and I promise you that in time I will help you recover your throne in Wallachia."

Dracula knew there was some reason behind this farce. He never imagined that there were one hundred thousand reasons, in gold.

They finished dining, and Matthias bid him farewell.

104

In Wallachia, Radu was grief-stricken. He missed his lover terribly; the pain he felt in his chest every time he thought of him wasn't disappearing. Desperate, he sought a solution to his pain. His fiery nature was screaming to be satisfied. Radu knew that if he allowed himself, he would be unfaithful to Mehemed—and hadn't he begged him not to go? He began thinking of ways to justify his possible infidelity . . . and he kept on thinking.

In the army of Wallachia there was a soldier who stared at Radu with strange intensity, a look that invited him to sin. Every time Radu saw the soldier, sparks seemed to fly from his beautiful blue eyes, and Radu felt his body tremble when the soldier was near. After a while, Radu could not get the man out of his mind. He tried by every means possible to avoid an encounter with him, but finally nature won the battle, and Radu summoned him alone.

When the soldier arrived, Radu watched him closely, noticing that he was even more beautiful than he had thought. "What is your name?" he asked.

"Vajk," the soldier replied.

"Why do you look at me in that way?" Radu asked.

With startling honesty, Vajk said, "Lord, I know that after I tell you what I think, you are going to have me killed—and I'll deserve it. But I cannot stop admiring you. You are the most beautiful man I have ever seen, and I am very attracted to you." He looked down. "Now you can kill me," he said simply.

Radu was dumbfounded by the young man's brave declaration. A strange silence surrounded them, and Radu gazed at him, again contemplating his enigmatic and masculine beauty. Then passion took care of the rest. They forgot their respective ranks and even their names and let themselves follow their nature. When at the end of their encounter they lay next to each other, their hearts beating together, Radu remembered Mehemed—and for the first time, he no longer felt the pain in his chest that went along with the sultan's memory.

Vajk looked stricken. "My lord, please—nobody should know about this. I am married and have a family. I need to be discreet."

That was what Radu needed, too, and Vajk was begging him for it, putting his family first. Radu agreed, saying, "This will be our secret; no one will know. And from now on, you are my personal guard."

Vajk smiled shyly. "I have never been with someone as beautiful as you are," he said, sighing. "I think I am falling in love."

Radu felt the same way; the beauty of that man had awakened something inside him, and he knew that it would turn into a great love.

<hr/>

Vajk was a vigorous man; he always was in the mood for sex. He did it with women, men, and even animals, and he excused himself by saying, "God made me this way . . . it's not my fault!" One day he arrived with a present. "Look, my love, and see what I brought you so you'll remember me."

"What a beautiful little dog!" Radu exclaimed. "And it is of a good breed. I am going to call it Matthias, to dishonor that bastard."

Radu was living in a dream beside his new love. ten months after they started their romance, he saw strange, round wounds on intimate parts of his body, but since they did not hurt he didn't pay attention to them. Unbeknownst to him, his body was fighting a new and mortal enemy, syphilis; the wounds were the aftermath of that battle.

105

In the meantime, the pope was becoming impatient to free Dracula. Worried, he sent an emissary to demand the prisoner's immediate liberation.

After lengthy discussion of the book, Jacob finally said, "Enough talking. Let's start writing. The first thing we need to do is defame Dracula and his family before the world, portraying them as infidels and heretics so the Holy Father will reject them." Then he read aloud a few lines he'd written.

> One time an old governor murdered the old Dracul. His son Dracula and his brother renounced and rejected their Christian faith, which they had sworn to protect and defend, turning into heretics.

"What do you think of that?" he asked.

"It is excellent!" the others said.

So that became story number one.

Beheim looked crestfallen. "I need you to teach me to write! Since the emperor gave the appointment, I have been studying really hard—remember, I am the imperial poet! If I don't learn soon, the emperor can take my title away. This appointment was given to me by the Holy Father. Please, you are my teachers and my only friends . . . I am alone."

"You must practice calligraphy exercises—a lot!" Jacob advised.

Johan was still thinking of story ideas. "Let us write about the death of Vladislav II, the one known as Dan II, brother of Dan III," he suggested. "We can describe in great detail the cruel way the monster impaled him."

But Jacob energetically opposed the idea. "That won't work. Vladislav II was Catholic and an ally of the Saxons. We cannot stain his memory by narrating the details of his impalement. It is a shameful and painful process. Besides, we will be publishing the fact that his soul was lost in hell for not having been properly buried. We'd better say he was decapitated and given a Christian burial."

"Poor man, to think he died impaled." Johan shook his head sadly. "I agree with you."

Beheim, who was practicing his calligraphy, watched the monks in silence, not understanding why eyewitnesses to such murders couldn't just state the facts. And so the monks dictated story number two to Beheim. The teachers, with the patience of Job, waited for their pupil to write his first sentences:

> During that same time, Dracula usurped power in Wallachia and crowned himself "vovoid." The first thing he did was send Ladislaus of Waboda (Vladislaus II), who was the genuine ruler of that region, to prison. There he killed him.

The Catholic monks thus protected the memory of their ally by not explaining the manner of death of this traitor to Dracula.

The jester enthusiastically displayed his penmanship. "How did it come out?"

The monks looked at each other, neither wanting to tell the new poet that his handwriting was completely illegible. Johan patted him on the shoulder. "For a first writing, it is not bad," he said. "But keep practicing . . . you need to do many calligraphy exercises!"

"The pope considers Dracula a living saint," Jacob continued. "We have to end with a shocking image. We are going to say that Dracula was cruel to all Catholics—that he burnt their villages, castles, and monasteries."

Beheim listened attentively while Brother Jacob explained the scene in detail, conjuring from his creative mind the burning of the Catholic buildings. Then the new poet started writing with difficulty—but great enthusiasm—story number three:

> After that, Dracula appeared in Transylvania near Hermannstadt (Sibiu) and burned down villages and castles. Then he headed to

the monasteries of Holtznowdorft and Holtznetya (Hosmanul)
and, without qualms, burned them to ashes.

"I am sure that with this story we will assure the enmity of the
Catholic Church toward Dracula," Jacob said, satisfied,

Jacob and Johan had many ideas in their heads. One by one they told
Beheim of the many crimes the monster had committed, impaling and
burning people. The jester began to understand their thinking. "We should
write that he impaled children and women," he proposed.

Johan scratched his head. "The only children he impaled were the
ones from the crusade in the Danube, but those were infidels. He never
impaled children in Wallachia, and he only impaled the wives of the Saxon
traitors."

"If we write the facts as they were, the stories are not going to have an
impact," Beheim reminded him. "It is essential to include children." And
he started to write the infamous fable he called story number four:

> He went to Berkendorf (Benesti) in Wistzerland (Tarabirsei)
> and set fire to everything until it all turned into ashes. All
> the inhabitants—men, women, elderly, and children—were
> chained and burned, and then he impaled them all.

"That is a terrible handwriting, poet—it is barely readable!" Johan
said, examining his work. "But you are making progress."

The simpleton took this as a compliment. "You do not know how
happy I am that you can understand it!" he said eagerly.

The monks looked at each other in silence, exchanging a discreet and
mocking smile.

Johan read the last story again and shook his head. "I don't know," he
said. "I think it is a little risky, Dracula always took care of the children,
especially the children of the peasants. He said they were going to be his
future soldiers."

"True," replied Beheim, "but imagine the indignation and rage this
fable is going to provoke."

Then Jacob said to Johan with a sly wink, "Do you remember that in
Wuetzeerland Dracula killed the Saxons and robbed them?"

Johan at first did not know what was he talking about, but then he understood the plan. "Yes," he said, "um, it is true . . . I remember perfectly well that he stole their merchandise . . . and impaled many of them."

Beheim was listening attentively; his clumsy pen started to create another lie. This one was story number five:

> He took as prisoners the innocent merchant Saxons of Wistzerland (Tarabirsei) and had them impaled the first day of festivities.

So far Dracula had burned and impaled plenty of people, but now the writers' inspiration had run out. They sat in silence, trying to think of new atrocities. Johan brightened. "We shall write that he killed one hundred innocent young men who were just there to learn the language."

"Let it be two hundred," Jacob proposed. "Twice as horrible."

"If we are exaggerating," Beheim said, "it had better be four hundred. So that's it: story number six. Let us shape it."

> He gathered the young people who had come to Wallachia from many places to learn the language and some trades, and he treacherously forced them into a room; there were four hundred. Then, in cold blood, he ordered them burned alive.

"It is kind of exaggerated, but I think it is fine," Beheim remarked.

Brother Jacob said, "We have to remember the most pious boyar that has ever existed—he was appointed by the town council of Wallachia—Albu Cel Mare, the Kingmaker. He was Catholic and always fought on the side of the good ones: Vladislav II, Dan III, Vlad the Monk, and Basarab Laiota. Unfortunately he fell at the hands of the monster, who impaled him. But when we tell the story we must not say his name so as not to stain his memory."

Brother Johan proposed a more general version of the story:

> And he impaled the most faithful boyar that existed, the Kingmaker. Even the tears of the boyar's sons did not touch the demon Dracula.

He finished reading and waited for the approval of his accomplices, but all he received was absolute and reproachful silence. Finally Beheim said, "How about if we wrote story number seven like this?"

> With the cruelty that was typical of him, he ordered the impalement of an entire family as well as their friends who had joined them, from the youngest to the eldest. With this action he destroyed a complete family without leaving a single survivor.

Brother Johan looked skeptical. "But will they believe he impaled children?"

"Who is going to refute it?" Jacob said as Beheim nodded. "Do not be afraid!"

Then Brother Johan made a valuable observation. "We just keep writing about people being burned and impaled," he said. "We must give life and action to these stories; otherwise they will become monotonous and people are going to get bored."

"What do you propose?" asked Beheim.

"What do you think about this story?" Jacob said. "It will be number eight."

> He enjoyed cruelty. He buried men up to their bellies to be targets for his weapons. He took others and roasted them, and skinned alive some others.

"Very nice!" Beheim exclaimed. "Imagine the face of our masters and the people when they read it! This is definitely going to be number eight."

The monks then remembered their protector, Dan III. His death high on a stake was particularly horrible, as he was eaten by the vultures.

Immediately the jester's slow pen started to describe that real and horrifying event. When he had finished, the brothers told him, "You are improving your handwriting—this is very good. But if we leave this as you wrote it, it will stain the memory of this great Catholic. Where did his soul go? To hell! The least this martyr deserves is for us to say that he died tortured with spiritual assistance and that his body received a Christian burial. Write, Beheim."

> When he captured young Darin (Dan), without understanding the reason he allowed a representative of God to give the victim spiritual assistance, and then he allowed him to make a grave according to the Christian tradition. Afterwards, the holy man's body was massacred in the grave.

The brothers were pleased with this lie. They knew Dan III did not receive a Christian burial; he died naked with a stake through his anus, as befitted a traitor. And Dracula never allowed spiritual assistance, arguing that no traitor deserved it.

Beheim did not like that story—the one he'd written was more shocking—but he was trying to stay on good terms with his teachers, and so he allowed the monks to narrate story number nine as they pleased.

Time kept its fast course, and the days passed quickly with all their discussions and projects. Then one night, Brother Jacob said to Brother Johan, "King Matthias asked us to stain Dracula's image. All we've done is write little stories that won't make anyone angry. Impale, burn, and behead? Others have done far worse things! I feel we are writing a story in which the villain isn't bad enough. We must make a larger effort."

The liars fell asleep with that problem in their heads. The next day Jacob awoke with an idea. "I've got it," he said. "Last night I dreamed about many impaled people in a churchyard—there was a hill covered with martyrs and Dracula was sitting among them, eating."

So they visited the jester and told him how Dracula had committed more bloody acts, and the clumsy pen started writing story number ten:

> The king of Hungary sent fifty-five Saxon ambassadors from Transylvania to Wallachia. To terrorize them, Dracula had some stakes placed there, and he took them prisoner. The ambassadors thought they were going to be impaled, too, and so they were intimidated. Oh what a great problem they had! They thought Dracula had detained them because he suspected they had betrayed him. When five weeks passed they concluded that they were going to die impaled, as some of them

had the intention of betraying him. Indeed, he impaled them without mercy. The next day he took his army and headed to Wuetzeerland. Early in the morning he visited castles, towns, and villages. He destroyed all the grain and burned what he could not take out of the city of Kranstatt (Brasov). He impaled men, women, and children around Saint Jacob's chapel; those hills were filled with blood, horror, and death. Then, when he was hungry, the demon demanded that his soldiers set a table there and serve him food and drink. And so, amidst so much pain, Dracula enjoyed his food like a wild animal, watching the impaled around him inexpressively.

Johan read what Beheim had written and was astonished. "They are not going to believe us," he whispered to Jacob. "This is completely unrealistic. We should modify it!"

"How are you going to modify it?" Jacob scolded. "Are you going to say he impaled the ones that did not want to pay taxes and the ones who betrayed him, murdered, raped, or stole? Then he would be canonized! No, Johan, we must write more scandalous stories."

Brother Johan was becoming worried about the tone the stories were taking. Still, since he was good at drawing, he made some detailed sketches and showed them to Jacob. In one, Dracula could be seen eating among impaled people, while in front of him, a boyar was cutting another Christian into pieces. When Jacob saw them he exclaimed, "These drawings are perfect. It seems like they are alive! You are good at drawing, Jacob. Congratulations!"

Jacob then turned to Beheim. "Write this down. We are going to make the pope really angry. Let's see what you think; if you like it, it will be number eleven."

Dracula headed to Saint Bartholomew's Church in Brasov and burned it down to its foundation. He stole the monks' clothes and sacred chalices to desecrate them, and then he sent some of his soldiers to do the same in the church of a great village called Zeyding (Codlea). But when the inhabitants realized this sacred place was being desecrated, they confronted him and made the soldiers withdraw. When Dracula's captain told him that he could not take the place because its inhabitants had defended it with spectacular braveness, the demon looked directly into his eyes and screamed, "Impale him!" That captain ended up at the top of a huge stake.

At that, Johan took Jacob aside. "Dracula was very kind," Johan said. "He never attacked a church or monastery until he started his campaign, and he even then he did it only to the ones who did not collaborate with him."

Brother Jacob was furious. "Shut up! I witnessed with my own eyes how he impaled Brother Hans. I assure you that when he hears this story the pope will be enraged and despise Dracula. If the story is exaggerated, even better. This is what the king asked us for! Besides, no one is going to refute it, and the peasants are like crickets: they make a lot of noise, but no one pays attention to them."

The buffoon Beheim was happy, and he was anxious to put his clumsy but poisonous pen back into action.

The brothers went to sleep that night feeling desperate. Their inspiration wasn't keeping up with their stories; they needed more variety. As of now, there were just people impaled, burned, and cut into pieces. They had to find something new. Finally Jacob said to Johan, "Tomorrow we will tell Beheim that Dracula stole merchandise from the Saxons and then impaled them."

Johan shook his head, surprised. "Dracula never stole," he protested. "He demanded money to make his crusade!"

"Do not refute it!" Jacob told him, and the next day he went to the jester and gave him an exaggerated story: "Dracula captured a caravan of forty Saxon merchants; he stole their merchandise and then impaled them." Beheim immediately started writing story number twelve:

In Wuetzeerland near Thunow and Pregel, he impaled two hundred Saxons and stole their merchandise.

When he read that, Jacob exclaimed, "Two hundred is too many! There are no merchant caravans of this number."

Beheim looked at him and asked, "Do you want me to put forty?"

"Put one hundred!" advised Johan.

"We'd better put it this way," Beheim said:

> In Wuetzeerland near Thunow and Pregel, he impaled six
> hundred Saxons and stole their merchandise.

The brothers were astonished but pleased; they had accused Dracula of being a thief—so now, according to his own law, and he must die impaled.

"I think we should invent a variety of deaths," Jacob said, "because reading only about impaled people is boring." They looked at the various tortures that were used in the Holy Inquisition to defend the faith in their Christ, and using them for inspiration, the three writers made up story number thirteen:

> He had a great saucepan made with two handles on it and put
> his victims inside, and then he put planks with holes above
> them. The men stuck their heads out, trying to get out of that
> hell. Then he set the saucepan over a fire and poured water
> inside it so the men would cook. The men began screaming,
> desperately begging for celestial help. The demon was watching
> them, expressionless; their screams for mercy could not soften
> his heart of stone. He also had many men, women, old men,
> and young men impaled.

The writers were satisfied with their story and made a drawing to reinforce the fable.

Beheim then wrote another story about impaled people, number fourteen:

> One day Dracula appeared in Steenburgen and in Talmetz
> (near Sibiu), where he took some men and cut them up like
> pumpkins. Then he impaled their remains on small stakes.

One night the brothers in Christ started talking about their project and Jacob said, "We have to think of some truly bloody and cruel punishment, something deviant."

Johan thought for a while. "What about some newborn babies and their mothers suffering and dying in a lot of pain?"

Jacob smiled. "That sounds fabulous! You are improving!" The next day they told the jester they had seen mutilated mothers, murdered children, and anything else their sick minds could imagine. Beheim listened carefully and then slowly wrote out legend number fifteen:

> This demon without a soul used many unspeakable methods to cause pain to innocent people. He took mothers and cut off their breasts, and through the holes in their chests he stuck the heads of their infants. Then he impaled the mother, so that both mother and child died amidst indescribable horror. He took one—and two-year-old children and impaled them without mercy. His cruelty was unsurpassed even by the most ruthless hunters of Christians, like Nero, Herod, Diocletian, or other heartless pagans. Without a doubt the most wicked and bloody man of all time was Dracula.

The liars were impressed with their latest story: it was shocking and ingenious. They congratulated each other effusively.

I think we should add something new to the impalement, said Brother Jacob, and the three started to come up with ideas. When they had finished, they had story number sixteen:

> If his victims tried to defend themselves against impalement by kicking or punching, after he impaled them he would have his soldiers twist them on the stake as if they were frogs. Then Dracula would cynically mock them, saying, "Oh, how funny they look twisted!" And that was the fate of many of his victims, whether pagans, Christians, heretics, Jews, or Wallachians. He impaled everyone: men, women, young men, and old men alike.

The men got more creative as they went on, staining Dracula with their fantastic stories, until Brother Jacob got a new idea. "We must say he was a cannibal," he said to his companions.

Johan shook his head. "They won't believe us—it's too much! But we can say he forced others to eat human meat."

So Beheim again went back to work and haltingly wrote what would become an infamous story, number seventeen:

> A gypsy was arrested for stealing, and Dracula condemned him to die by hanging. When the gypsy's friends begged Dracula to forgive him, offering to restore the damage, the monster looked them in the eyes, and in his icy voice he said, "Hang him!" They refused to hang their friend, saying that was not their custom, and Dracula became enraged because they disobeyed him. So he ordered the thief boiled alive, and then he made the gypsy's friends eat him.

"This came out pretty well," said Jacob. "Plus your handwriting is improving. I would like to see the pope's face when he reads this." The jester grinned happily.

Johan proposed yet another plot twist. "What if Dracula impaled one of his boyars for being lazy?"

"Better than that," said Beheim, "what if he impaled an important man for complaining too much?" And they started to shape story number eighteen:

> One day a nobleman visited the demon as he was amusing himself among a forest of impaled people. They had been dead for some days and stank horribly, and the man covered his nose and complained about the smell. "Does the smell of death upset you?" Dracula asked. "Yes!" was the good man's answer. At that, the monster ordered his soldiers to bring the longest stake they could find and impale the man. When he was about to be lifted in the air, Dracula said, "Up where you are going, the smell of corpses will not reach you."

Brother Johan frowned. "Will they believe that he took a man's life for something so meaningless?"

"This is about destroying the reputation of saint, not sanctifying a murderer," Beheim answered cynically. "We will write one in which a man of God has issues with him." And story number nineteen began to take shape.

> A priest stated in his sermon that a sin could not be forgiven unless the act of injustice was made in the sight of God, and so Dracula put a piece of bread in his meal. When the priest took the bread with his fork and prepared to eat it, Dracula reminded him what he had said in his sermons. "What I told you is true!" the priest said. The monster answered, "Why do you take my bread, which I have unjustly placed in your meal?" Having said that, he ordered the priest's immediate impalement.

The brothers resented Dracula, and with this story they felt they had been avenged. This man had killed their companions in order to steal from them, and he was going to get what he deserved: they would destroy his reputation as a saint.

The brothers now recalled the boyars who had been their faithful parishioners and always fulfilled their promises of alms and tithes, those sixty-eight Catholic martyrs that Dracula murdered the first Easter of his second rule. In memory of those good Christians, the monks told Beheim about the event, and he began writing more quickly and a little more fluently the story that would become number twenty:

> One time Dracula invited nobles and landowners to his house, and when they had eaten and drunk he asked them, "How many lords have you served?" One of them replied, "I don't remember, there have been so many!" Therefore they all started to answer, trying to recall the exact amount. One answered fifteen; another thirty, and still another, twenty. The youngest said seven. Dracula was furious. "Impale them all!" he cried. And that is how five hundred innocent men ended up pierced by a stake.

Johan looked dubious. "We should adjust that number. Five hundred is too many. Put one hundred."

But Beheim held firm. "No!" he said. "People have no idea how many there were. Remember, this is all about exaggerating."

"I disagree," Jacob said. "I think it's too much, too. But if you think that's a good number, I won't oppose you. Let it be five hundred!"

A huge smile broke out on the jester's face.

At this point they remembered that Dracula had the reputation of being a good father and an affectionate and faithful husband. He was not like his predecessors; he did not have bastard children. They started wondering how to defame him, how to stain his personal reputation. After a while Beheim said to the brothers, "What do you think of this idea? If you like it, it will be number twenty-one."

> One of Dracula's many lovers informed him that she was pregnant, and the monster knew that having children would mean problems with his legitimate descendants. So, without mercy, he had that innocent woman's womb opened while he said cynically, "Let the world see where I have been and know where the result of my sin goes." Then he had her cut into pieces.

"Are they really going to believe that story?" asked Brother Johan-.

"Sure! Can't you see that Dracula is a crazy man? They are going to believe it and love it!" answered the jester with his typical smile.

More time passed, and one night as the monks were trying to sleep, Jacob said to Johan, "This needs more blood. We are describing a murderer and a violent, crazy man—and there are many such men. We need to make a monster look like an innocent child compared to Dracula."

Jacob was listening attentively, but his brain could not think of anything else beyond impalements, burning people, and cutting people into pieces. *Always the same tortures,* he sighed. They went to sleep and when they got up the next day, Jacob was inspired. "I dreamed of thousands of impaled people!" he said excitedly. "It was the most macabre dream I have ever had in my life!"

When he saw the jester, he told him about the dream, and Beheim immediately got a picture in his mind. "Great!" he said, and he started writing story number twenty-two.

> One morning in the year 1460, on the day of Saint Bartholomew, the demon appeared with his servants outside the village of

Humilasch (Amlas), where he started a macabre activity: he began cutting people like pumpkins and throwing the remains into huge piles. He allowed some people to go back to their houses to describe the horror they had witnessed, and then he went to the village and stole the people's belongings. Between the cut-up corpses and the impaled, there were thirty thousand.

Johan threw up his hands. "This is an exaggeration! Thirty thousand trees! he said. "Where would he have found thirty thousand people to kill? Besides, they would have had to cut up all those trees for the impalements. That's an entire forest . . . no one is going to believe it!"

Beheim was silent awhile. Then he said, "If we say there were just forty-three Saxons, he won't look like much of a monster, and we will also have to explain why he killed them. What are we going to say—that he killed them because they refused to pay taxes or betrayed him? No, Johan. This is about creating a monster."

That night after the monks went to sleep, Beheim presented the stories to Emperor Frederick III, who was astonished by the bravery of that ignorant man, contender for the title of poet. He couldn't believe it! The whole thing was absurd and illogical. It was one thing to tell lies . . . but this! Still, the one who was going to be making a fool of himself was the annoying jester himself—and had he not been born to do just that? With a huge smile of admiration on his face he said, "You are doing great!" Meanwhile he was thinking, *I am going to have a lot of fun watching the rage and the ridicule that is going to be directed at this jester, who considers himself a man of letters!*

Beheim returned to the monks looking delighted. "The emperor is pleased with the project, and I am even happier. For the first time in my life, I feel like I am good at something! I feel respected."

The monks looked at each other, amazed, and then looked back at Beheim. "Why do you say that?" Johan asked finally.

"Because you do not know how hard and sad it is to go from court to court looking for a job as a jester. Once the masters know our jokes and tricks, we no longer amuse them, and they throw us into the street without consideration. Then we have to look for another master. Not having an education, as you have, is horrible! I have barely learned how to write."

Then, inspired by the amount of violence in the last fable, he said brightly, "Since we've begun to create a monster, we should continue our new stories with the same numbers. What do you think if we made this story number twenty-three?"

> In the year of our Lord 1462, the monster came to a heavily populated city where there lived Christians, pagans, Jews, and other kinds of people. The women from that place were very beautiful, and many of them were maidens. When the members of the court saw these women, they begged the monster to let them marry the women and turn them into honorable wives. Instead the monster formed groups of men and forced them to rape the women—first some, then others—and in the end he impaled them all. There was a forest of impaled people: twenty-five thousand found their death. From there he went to a neighboring region and burned it completely; many of its inhabitants burned to death, too, and he impaled the rest. There were another twenty-five thousand innocent victims.

Brother Johan was silent; he did not like that tale at all. Finally he said, "Fine—let it stay like that . . . but I am not going to say that I wrote this book."

Knowing that Johan was wise to remove his name from this absurd and fantastic project, Jacob said, "I will not say I wrote part of this book either."

The jester, however, had been encouraged by the book's unconditional support from the emperor. "You are cowards!" he said. "What are you afraid of? The monster is in prison! Maybe they are not going to believe these stories in Wallachia, but Radu is reigning there now, and he is also Dracula's enemy. I assure you they are not going to be forbid the book in that place, and we are releasing these stories to the world. Besides, I have nothing to lose. I am used to being humiliated and despised and having problems. I am not going to give up my title of poet for anything in the world!" Then, in a wheedling tone, he said, "We should let our readers use their imagination. Since we already gave them a few details, now they can imagine the other details as they wish. See what you think of story twenty-four."

Wallachia took the appearance of a gloomy, horrible hell, where people were wounded, roasted, and skinned, and there were thousands and thousands of innocent impaled people.

"I like it!" Jacob said.

Johan smiled, nervous but pleased.

The brothers could not believe the jester's bravery when it was clear that he would back these fantastic stories with his signature. They were silent awhile, and then Jacob said, "Well, let's see what you think about the twenty-fifth."

He surrounded Fugrash (Fagaras), chained the inhabitants of that place, and took them away. Men, women, and children followed his path of suffering until they arrived in Wallachia, where they were impaled. He mercilessly beheaded the men who had helped him bury his treasure so they would not steal it.

The brothers were impressed by their own creativity, and knowing that they did not have to answer for the truthfulness of the story, they were silent, thinking, *What is going to happen to that ignorant jester? As soon as the book is published, he is going to have all the problems in the world and he is never going to get a job again.* Still, they knew those scandalous stories about Dracula were going to be talked about.

Beheim started writing the next story he proposed:

He liked to behead and roast his enemies and then invite their relatives to eat at his house. When the food was served and they had consumed that macabre food, he informed them what they had eaten. When they refused to continue eating, he impaled them.

"You are a genius!" Jacob exclaimed hypocritically. "In my opinion, that should be story number twenty-six."

Johan, on the other hand, complained. "We are repeating the same stories over and over, and the days are going by," he said. "We have to hurry and think of something new."

After long thought, Jacob said, "I think I have an original idea. What do you think of this?"

> On one occasion when he was patrolling his dominions, he saw a peasant with a short shirt. He approached him and asked him, "Do you have a wife at home?" The peasant answered, "Yes, my lord!" "Bring her. I want to ask her some questions," the monster said. "When she was brought in front of him, he asked her, "What do you do, woman?" She answered, "I do the laundry, I cook, and I do errands," she said. But since the innocent woman did not say she made the peasant's shirts, he ordered her impaled. The monster gave the peasant another woman and ordered her to make him a long shirt or he would impale her, too.

"I think it is too simple," Beheim said. "There is very little pain and just one person impaled."

"Nevertheless, it is different," Jacob insisted.

"Well, that can be story number twenty-seven. Keep thinking."

The days were passing quickly. They had never written a book before but they knew there were not enough stories in this one yet, so they kept trying to come up with new ideas to complete it.

Trying to find inspiration, the poet Beheim put on his ridiculous jester costume, took his guitar, and started singing the fables he had invented about Dracula. Then he danced and sang the song in which a donkey was impaled on the same stake as a monk. It was so funny that the monks burst out laughing. At the end of the song, Beheim asked, "What would you think if we made that song come true?" And he proposed the following story:

> He impaled a donkey and, with the same stake, a Franciscan monk. Then he planted it in the ground.

Jacob rolled his eyes. "Now your fantasy has reached its limit, Beheim. What do you mean he impaled a donkey? That is practically impossible!"

"It is as possible as impaling thousands and thousands of people," the jester answered.

"Yes, but think of this: how are they going to get a donkey on a stake? And how are they going to raise it up high? Moreover, how are they going to fix it there? No stake would hold it—it would break. And if it did hold it, it would fall. Please admit that that is impossible!"

"No, it is not," the jester insisted. "The donkey is first on the stake, and above him is the monk! The point is to annoy the pope with our stories, so leave it like that. You'll see, people will be both angry and amused."

The jester needed variety in his stories, and so he said, "That will be story number twenty-eight." The monks looked at each other skeptically. They could not believe the boldness of that slanderer, but they kept silent. Neither of them would be signing as the book's author anyway.

After more days went by and the hoped-for inspiration still did not arrive, the monks received a messenger from King Matthias. "It is necessary that you hurry," he said. "The king needs the book immediately."

"Tell Matthias to wait a little longer," Jacob said. "We are working on it day and night."

It was a race against time. They searched and searched their imaginations until the well-lubricated mind of Brother Johan finally produced more lies. He dictated them to his companions, and the jester started to write slowly.

Three hundred gypsies went to his land. He took three of them and boiled and roasted them, and then he made the others eat them. "You will be eating each other until there is no one left," he said, "or I will send you to fight against the Turks." Because of their fear, they decided to do as Dracula ordered them to do. He dressed them and their horses in cowhide skin. Then the Turks ran away because of the cowhide clothes and they all drowned.

"Yes, Johan, that should be story number twenty-nine," Jacob said.

The men of letters kept thinking and thinking, the days went by, and Matthias became desperate. Every night the brothers sought inspiration to make new stories. One night Johan reminded Jacob about Dracula's animosity toward lazy people, "Remember how he cut their heads off if they did not work?" Johan asked. They concentrated on that action and the next day mentioned it to Beheim. He immediately started writing.

He invited poor people to eat at his house and then he put them in a little room and burned them. One time he burned two hundred.

The monks smiled, satisfied with the jester's imagination, and told him, "Excellent! This should be story number thirty."

But the men's pool of inspiration was becoming increasingly shallow. No matter how hard they thought, they could not find something really shocking, something worthy of the book. They could say he impaled or burned thousands of people, but it would be just more of the same: impalements, impalements, and burning. But the book had to be completed, and so they kept thinking. Meanwhile, time ticked away.

Finally Brother Jacob proposed to the jester, "What do you think about this?"

He roasted children and forced their mothers to eat them. Then he cut the women's breasts and forced their husbands to eat them. Through the holes in the mothers' chests he stuck the heads of the infants, and with the wickedness of an evil demon, he impaled the survivors.

"Without discussion that should be story number thirty-one," said Beheim. "I like it. It is gruesome and those actions are unthinkable. You were inspired, Jacob—congratulations. But we have to hurry. Almost four months have passed since King Matthias gave us the assignment." And they kept thinking.

A messenger from the Holy Father arrived at the palace of King Matthias and delivered the following letter:

Matthias,

This has been a long time to be investigating a saint! Free Dracula immediately and bring him to my presence. Receive my blessing.

Signed,
Pope Pio II

Matthias got really nervous and wrote the following letter:

> Holy Father,
>
> Everything is becoming clear. I promise you that in a few days you will receive news. Thank you for your blessing.
>
> Signed,
Matthias Corvinus

He handed it to the same envoy to give to the pope, but the messenger held his ground. "No Matthias. I will not leave without Dracula. We must leave immediately."

Matthias felt the weight of the world upon his shoulders when he saw the intransigence of the envoy. He began begging. "Give me enough time to find the proof I need," he said. "I am going to send an emissary to Emperor Frederick III, and we will take it to him as soon as I receive it, I promise!"

"Fine, I will wait," the envoy said. "But just the necessary time—not a day more!"

The jester and the monks received the visiting envoy from King Matthias, who said to them, "You must leave with me now to see the king. I will not leave without fulfilling my command!"

The literary men felt pressured. "We still have not finished!" Jacob said. "Tell the king to wait just a little longer."

"Not even a minute longer! We must go immediately!"

"Fine," Jacob said. "We will go to the printer's—we're just missing the last story. Tomorrow at sunrise, we will go to the king." To complete the book they included a story they had rejected:

> Some ambassadors from the west visited Dracula, and when they were in front of the demon they uncovered their heads but were still wearing red skullcaps. Dracula was enraged and asked them, "Why didn't you take your skullcaps off before

appearing before a great lord?" And they answered, "Lord, that is not our custom." So Dracula sent for some nails and had the caps nailed to their heads.

"This is going to be the last story," Beheim said. "Number thirty-two."

They went immediately to the printer's, where they worked all day and into the night without stopping, filling in the stories that were missing. At sunset, they left for Hungary.

"You have waited too long!" the papal envoy said to Matthias. "Bring Dracula to me, and let us go to the Vatican."

"Give me one more day," the king said beseechingly. "Just one. Please!"

The envoy sighed. "This will be the last, because tomorrow we depart. I don't want any excuses."

"Fine," said King Matthias. He sounded confident, but inside he felt such anguish that he wanted run out of the castle and throw himself off a cliff. Dishonor, shame, and surely excommunication awaited him. He had no other choice: he had to kill Dracula. He realized that he should have done it before—doing it now would only arouse suspicions.

106

Shortly afterward, one of his servants approached. "The messenger you sent with Frederick III has returned, accompanied by two monks and an ambassador of the emperor," the servant told him. "They wanted to give you this." The king nodded his assent. The servant handed Matthias a pamphlet and ushered the monks and the jester into the room as the king began browsing through the work of his accomplices. *This is appalling!* Matthias thought. *It's horrifying! It will scare off anyone!* He felt a surge of happiness that made him quiver, but he kept a straight face. "Who thought of this?" he asked.

When the monks heard the king's tone of voice and saw his stern expression, they grew frightened. "This work is Beheim's," Jacob said quickly. "We just told him stories, but he wrote the book alone—we swear by Christ." The monks stood in silence, awaiting the harsh sentence.

Beheim, in particular, was tortured by the suspense; he never imagined that the king would react that way. Feeling desperate and anguished, he also waited impatiently and in silence for the harsh reprimand that would surely be followed by a terrible punishment.

King Matthias looked at the jester and broke into a broad smile. "This is a work of genius!" he declared. "Congratulations, poet!" With that he gave the jester a warm hug.

The monks then realized that they had been wrong all along—they never thought that the book would make such a positive impression on the king. Now they were looking for a way to reverse what they had said. They wanted to say that they, too, had participated actively in that great literary work, but they had sworn in front of a king, with the holy name of their God as their witness, that they had just told the jester some stories. If they cleared up the situation, they could even lose their status in the Church.

The jester, on the other hand, was elated: the credit was all his, and nobody could dispute it. Privately he could share his triumph with his sidekicks, but nobody else would ever know.

"Poet," King Matthias said, "we will go immediately to Rome, where you will explain your book to the Holy Father. After that you will go to Vienna to print more and will distribute them immediately everywhere." At the king's words, tears of happiness rolled down Beheim's face.

The monks were about to cry, too. What a huge mistake they'd made—and they could not do anything to fix it.

Johan made a petition to the king: "My lord, could we go with you? We can tell the Holy Father that we were witnesses to the gruesome and unholy actions of that damned demon, and we can help Beheim with his titanic mission."

Matthias, swayed by the monks' self-serving argument, answered, "Wherever Beheim goes, you will go! I want you to be his special secretaries and help him with the printing and distribution of this book all over Europe. You must take up this enterprise as if it were your own."

Now the brothers wanted to cry from happiness. Soon they would know the Holy Father in person! Thrilled, both monks kissed the hand of their king as a sign of gratefulness.

Beheim was astonished. He, an insignificant, clumsy, uncultured court jester, now had two learned secretaries. It all felt like a dream, and he did not want to wake up.

Matthias reminded them. "If you take economic advantage of it, it will be even better for you." So that they would have no pretext to fail, the king generously gave them another twenty gold coins.

"My lord, we already have thousands of books ready," Jacob said. "They are on the carriage."

"Then we are off to the Vatican immediately," Matthias said. He summoned his servants and told them to prepare for an urgent departure, and he instructed some of his special commissioners to distribute the books in Hungary, Wallachia, Transylvania, and Moldavia. Then he took some of the books himself and got ready to travel to Rome with his precious proof.

King Matthias and his literary accomplice and his secretaries stood in a hall in the Vatican, waiting the vicar of Christ on Earth. The place shone, reflecting the presence of the sacred warrior and ferocious defender of Christianity, Pope Pio II.

The monks were unable to speak or move when the Holy Father appeared. Beheim also was speechless, but when he saw that the king make a show of reverence, he promptly imitated it. The pope offered Matthias his ring, which the king kissed with respect; then he offered it to the king's companions, who followed their leader's example, giving silent thanks to God for their great happiness.

When those formalities were over, the pope looked at Matthias and threw open his arms with the clear intention of giving a warm hug to one of them. "Which of the three of you is Dracula?" he said in a booming voice.

"Holy Father," Matthias began, "Brother Jacob and Brother Johan have witnessed the atrocious acts of Dracula against the Catholic Church, and based on their accounts, the emissary of Emperor Frederick III, the man of letters and poet Michael Beheim, wrote this book. I hope that all this will become clear when you read it." And then the king gave Pio a copy of the book.

The pope looked through the pages and read a few lines. Then he looked at Beheim, incredulous. "Is this true?" he demanded. "Dracula is the greatest defender of Christianity! Why did you write such evil things?"

Matthias quickly turned to Jacob. "Tell the Holy Father about Dracula's actions against the Holy Catholic Church in Wallachia," he said.

So Jacob began to explain. "Dracula named himself maximum pontiff of the Orthodox Church in Wallachia," he said. "He plundered the Catholic Church, mistreated the bishops, murdered the priests, and burned the churches." Then Jacob described how the monster had impaled the Catholic monks after brazenly stealing from them the resources that were to be sent to his Holiness. Jacob also recounted how Dracula came to his monastery and demanded that the people's alms and tithes be given to him, and how, when he had them, he impaled the naked Brother Hans. In vivid detail he described the horrible and painful process of impalement, to which he was a witness. (Jacob made some slight changes to the story so that the Holy Father would not realize that he had kept a hidden treasure that he had no intention of sending to the Vatican.)

When Jacob finished, the Holy Father turned to Johan. "And you? What problem did you have with Dracula?"

Brother Johan gave his version, also taking care not to mention the hidden treasure that was kept from the Vatican.

After they had told their tales, the two Catholic monks explained to the Holy Father that Dracula stole from and burned churches and monasteries and impaled the innocent Catholic monks who lived there.

The Holy Father then began to read the jester's book more carefully, and he didn't stop until he had finished it. By the time he reached the end he had tears in his eyes. "And all the while I thought he was a saint . . . I even wanted to canonize him!" Turning to Matthias, he asked, "How is it possible that a man who received one hundred thousand gold coins would steal even more money and attack the hand that feeds him? Did you let him loose, Matthias?"

"No, your holiness!" answered the monarch respectfully.

"Well, don't do it!" said the pope. "Dracula must remain incarcerated for being such a violent person—he's a madman and a murderer! I should go now. So much crime and so much blood is making my head ache."

King Matthias said "Yes! I have no problems! Let the world know of Dracula's evil ways!" Inside, the king's conscience was accusing him: *You are destroying the reputation of a good man. You are defaming a Christian knight, a true warrior who has defended with passion the Christian faith.* His conscience was right, but it was him or Dracula, and for Matthias, the balance always tipped in his own favor. As for Dracula . . . he might as well go to hell.

The king's return trip to Hungary was relaxing and very quiet. He slept long hours trying to recover from so many sleepless nights. At last, there was nothing to fear!

107

Beheim's book sold very quickly: everyone wanted to buy it and collect it as a great treasure. The book turned into a huge source of popular entertainment; in fact, people talked about nothing else. Time and time again they read it—or, more likely, had it read to them, because most of the population couldn't read. It was the first published book to become a commercial best-seller in several languages—after the Holy Bible, of course.

Holy Roman Emperor Frederick III was proud to have a celebrity among his court jesters. King Matthias visited one day, and after the standard post-dinner entertainment featuring jesters and clowns, an announcer said, 'As a main attraction, the author of the noted and famous book, *History of a Bloodthirsty and Mad Man Called Dracula of Wallachia* . . . the great man of letters, Imperial Poet Michael Beheim!"

Amidst enthusiastic applause appeared the famous court jester, now with a new identity. Dressed in an elegant black suit with gold buttons and decorations, he recited the stories by heart, and at the end the audience gave him a warm ovation.

108

On June 16, 1463, there was a great ceremony in the cathedral of Esztergom. Accompanied by the chant of a solemn Te Deum, the crown of Saint Stephen was placed on King Matthias's head, giving him the magnificent title of holy Roman emperor. He was twenty-three years old.

Inside the young monarch's head there waged a confusing battle of values, a fight between his ambition and his conscience, which screamed *This crown cost you eighty thousand gold coins—the result of your treason against your most faithful subject, the one who always be your ally and support you. You are the holy Roman emperor, the most powerful man in this part of the world—but that money is like the silver coins that Judas received for betraying Jesus.* The strong headache he had developed almost forced him to take off the crown and go rest in a dark room in silence.

"You are going to make sure that Dracula never knows about the existence of the book of Beheim," Matthias ordered his commanding officer, Olagu. "Train your people to inform all his visitors that they cannot talk about that subject—and if they do, they will die."

Olagu nodded. "I will instruct my men never to leave Dracula alone," he said. "He will be watched always."

"Excellent," said the new emperor.

To shut out the voice of his conscience, Matthias periodically dined with his guest. "Dracula, become a Catholic," he said one night. "It has been a long time since you had Holy Communion, and you have committed a mortal sin."

Matthias had made the proposal before, but as always, Dracula was resolute. "I will confess and have Holy Communion when an Orthodox priest assists me," he said. "I was born an Orthodox, and I will die an Orthodox!"

"But you know there isn't one Orthodox priest in Hungary."

"Summon Barbat," Dracula said. "He will come immediately."

"I cannot," Matthias said. "Remember that I am Catholic—if I do that, I will be in trouble with the Holy Father in the Vatican."

His face distorted by sudden rage, Dracula shouted, "Do not mention that rat in a habit! He is the most despicable enemy of God, the greatest liar, fake, and hypocrite of all mortals! He dared offer me money for the defense of our God and then did not keep his word . . . I wish I had him here so I could impale him with my own hands!"

Matthias was pale from the shock. If he had spoken such words to another person it would have been his end. He dropped the subject, and when he left he said to Olagu, "It is forbidden to mention the pope to Dracula. The one who does it will die."

In 1464, Pope Pio II, who was a practiced crusader, decided to defend the cross of Christ once again with the strength of his sharp sword. Dressed in expensive armor and accompanied by his brave army, the pope started toward his homeland, where a great fleet of brave crusaders was waiting to join him in his fight against the infidel Ottomans. Pio's fight was twice as hard now, as his gout caused him excruciating pain. When he reached his destination, however, his bravery was fully tested. In the distance were the ships of war that would take him to his epic battles, and when he saw them up close, he cried from frustration: there were three little boats and a handful of brave men whose weapons, instead of provoking fear, made people laugh. Pio's sadness was so great that he delivered his soul to his God then and there.

For days afterward there was the steady tolling of bells from churches across Europe. Soon everyone knew the news: the pope had died.

Matthias could not believe it; he could now set Dracula free. As he traveled to the Vatican to present himself to the new pope, he decided that as soon as he arrived back from Rome, he would release Dracula and return him to power in Wallachia. But when he met Pope Paul II, the new pontiff said, "Matthias, you are a saint for having imprisoned Dracula. It disturbs me that even after the demon received one hundred thousand gold coins, he still stole from the Catholic Church and impaled our monks. I recommend that you put him in the hands of the inquisitors."

Matthias's blood ran cold. This pope, too, knew about the coins! If he set Dracula free, Matthias's own act of theft would surely be revealed, and he would end up shamed and excommunicated. If he turned Dracula over to the holy inquisitors, the truth would be known, too! And so he answered very carefully. "Holy Father, Dracula is in a dark, cold, dirty cell, and given only bread and water. If we kill him, he will not pay us back for all the damage he caused. I assure you that, more than anything else, he wants to get out of that hole. If you want me to, I will bring him to you so you can see for yourself his condition."

The Holy Father shook his head. "I will ask a favor of you: as long as I live, please do not talk to me about that bloodthirsty man—do with him as you wish!"

Matthias left the Vatican frustrated. Dracula was still in jail, and this pope looked so healthy . . . there was nothing he could do but wait for time to offer a solution to his problem. Dracula would have to continue as his guest.

Erzsebet, Janos's widow, said to Matthias, "I would risk my life for Dracula, Son. He is a good man, and he has always been our most faithful ally. Remember when you were going to be decapitated? He always support you!"

Matthias sighed impatiently. "Mother, some letters were found . . . you read them yourself! I shouldn't have to explain what they said."

"That is a lie, Son!" Erzsebet said. "Do not believe your enemies. Some evil man wrote them to take way your strength—I assure you that Dracula would be a great asset to your army. He needs you, and you can help him. Free him!"

"You've read the book that Beheim was written about him—everyone has. If I free him, what are the people going to think of me?"

"You know better than anyone that Frederick hates Dracula; it is very likely that he is the one responsible for destroying his reputation by having his annoying court jester write that book."

"Mother, I am going to free him as soon as I finish investigating in depth the mystery of those letters."

"My lady," said Olagu, "I must remind you that you cannot talk about the book of Beheim, and you cannot mention the name of the pope during your visit to the guest."

Having received his instructions, Erzsebet went in to see the prisoner. "Son!" she said. "You do not know how happy I am to see you! How have you been?".

"Fine, Erzsebet," answered Dracula kindly. "How nice of you to visit me."

"When I am with you I remember my dear brother—he was so fond of you! He was always talking about you."

They talked and reminisced for hours, until Erzsebet finally rose. "I must leave, Son. Kneel down so that I may give you my blessing!" With that, she left.

One day Ilona said to her aunt Erzsebet, "I would really like to meet Dracula."

"He is a fascinating man!" Erzsebet replied.

"I don't know what it is it about him, but my father never stopped complimenting him," Ilona said. "I remember that at the end of his life he searched for him the way a thirsty man searches for water. I also admire him because he always was our ally. When are you going to take me to visit him, Aunt?"

"It will be sooner than you think," Erzsebet said.

One afternoon Dracula received an unexpected visit from Erzsebet and Ilona. When he saw the younger woman he was breathless; the world seemed to stop turning. He was struck speechless before such beauty.

"Son . . . Son?" He heard a voice, as if from a distance, and returned from his daydreaming. "This is Ilona, the daughter of my brother Mikhail," said Erzsebet.

Somehow Dracula could not make the connection with his brain. Without thinking he said aloud, "This woman is an angel!"

Ilona blushed. "Thank you," she said.

"Your father is and was one of the greatest Christian warriors I have ever met," he said. "I loved him like a brother."

"And he spoke a lot about you," she replied.

They dined and visited for hours. There was so much to talk about, so much to admire. By the end of the evening cupid's arrow had struck their hearts, and Dracula was a new man.

The women's visits became more frequent, and on one occasion Ilona said, "Tell me about your wife."

Dracula became thoughtful. His eyes filled with tears, and in a faltering voice he said, "She was the kindest, noblest woman who ever set foot on earth! Part of my heart died with her . . . I would gladly give my life for her to live!"

"To which noble family did she belong?" Ilona asked.

"Zalesha's nobility did not come from her lineage," he said. "It came from her heart. Her people were humble peasants, but with hearts as clean and pure as the most crystalline water." Then he added proudly, "I belong to that family, too!"

Ilona was amazed. Who was this extraordinary man? Where had he gotten his values? She wanted to hug him and tell him that she loved, admired, and respected him, and that she wanted to be part of his life, but her sense of virtue forced her to keep silent.

That visit lasted longer than usual. When they finally bid farewell and the women left, Ilona asked her aunt, "How many lovers did Dracula have?"

Erzsebet smiled. "Your father laughed at Dracula because he was faithful to his wife, and your cousin laughed, too, because Dracula did not want him to bring him the occasional feminine company. Even after she died, Dracula was faithful to the memory of his wife, and he said he would consummate a relationship only if he were married." The older woman looked at the younger one mischievously. "I think that you have a new boyfriend," she said playfully.

"Shush, Aunt!" Ilona laughed. "I would love for him just to notice me."

"Don't get your hopes up," Erzsebet said. "Dracula is an Orthodox and does not want to become a Catholic, so he won't ever be able to marry. Besides, why would you want a prisoner for a husband?"

The next day Ilona went to visit Matthias. "Cousin, when are you going to release Dracula?" she asked.

He answered her honestly: "I do not know!"

"What does his release depend on?"

Again, the emperor didn't know.

"Is he ever going to get out of prison?"

"Dracula is not a prisoner," Matthias said. "He is my guest of honor. He has servants, and everything he asks for we give him. It seems that you are interested in him. If you can convince him to convert to Catholicism, you can marry him and live in the town."

Dracula, meanwhile, was in his luxurious room, deep in thought. He did not have the least doubt that one day he would be reunited with Zalesha in heaven, and he had been faithful to his beloved wife even after death separated them. But now his body was reminding him that he was alive and needed a lover. He also wanted to have a family again. He considered himself a good candidate for a husband, as he was a widower and all alone, and he felt his heart beating only for Ilona. Now whenever he became quiet and thoughtful, his mind always returned to her: *Ilona, Ilona.*

Ilona, in turn, remembered the time when she was a child and saw Dracula—so strong, so brave, and so distant, as if he were an unreachable sun. She felt love in her heart, and her every thought was about Dracula.

That night after dinner, Dracula addressed Erzsebet in front of Ilona. "I would like your permission to get to know your niece," he said. "She is the most beautiful woman I know, and I know she is kind . . . I would like to marry her."

Erzsebet was impressed. "I am not the one who is going to marry you," she said. "It is Ilona who must decide if she wants to consider your proposal."

Ilona had been hoping for that offer and answered, "Aunt, if you allow me, I would like to spend more time with Dracula. You have always told me that he is a very good man."

And that way the engagement started, having as matchmaker the mother of the Roman emperor and the widow of one of Dracula's greatest friends and allies.

Matthias visited his guest and asked him, "How is your relationship with my cousin going?"

"I love her with all my heart," Dracula said. "I wish to marry her."

"Fine!" answered Matthias, "That news fills me with joy. I give my consent . . . are you going to become Catholic?"

"Over my dead body!" Dracula replied. "Bring the monk Barbat. He will marry us."

"And risk my position and create trouble with the Holy Father? Do not even think about that. Either you convert to Catholicism or you can continue hoping to get married!"

As time went on, what had been love at first sight became a torrid romance. Dracula and Ilona loved each other with all their hearts, and they wanted to consummate their love. "Please, my love!" Ilona begged. "Accept Catholicism and let us get married!"

Dracula's answer was always the same: "Over my dead body!" But now when she asked, he was silent. When Ilona saw this reaction, she kept insisting.

109

Things in Wallachia were reverting backwards, and the people's dreams of freedom from the Ottoman Turks had vanished. With Radu in power, they paid the sultan's tribute first and ate second. Every year, without excuse or pretext, Wallachia paid ten thousand gold coins and gave one thousand children of conscription to the Ottoman Empire. Only then were they assured of peace and freedom in Wallachia.

The peasants went right back to feeling oppressed and abused by the boyars and the Saxons. And now that the Ottomans were the ones giving the orders in Wallachia

The Saxons were at ease again, once again having a monopoly in the manufacture of many products and able to trade without paying taxes.

After greeting each other according to the stipulated protocol, Mehemed and Radu sought privacy, and when they were alone they kissed on the mouth, but their lips were cold. That old passion that once dragged them to the limits of sanity was no longer there; their minds were elsewhere now. Distance and time had done their usual work. The sexual relations that followed were almost automatic, and at the end the lovers lay next to each other.

Mehemed II spoke first. "Even though your brother is a prisoner of Matthias and there is no danger of any kind, I still dream every night that I am being impaled. It's horrible!"

Radu said, "Forget it—that's impossible," Radu said. "Wallachia is yours, and you can attack Rome whenever you want."

"It's not that easy," answered the sultan. "I assure you that as soon as we get organized, Matthias is going to release your damned brother. And who is going to stop him?"

"Our army," answered Radu.

"You don't understand! They don't want to fight against someone who is going to steal their soul. That demon exhumes the dead and impales them." Mehemed frowned. After a moment he said, "Because of your damned brother, people are saying that we are lovers. It is necessary for you to get married to shut them up and also to consolidate your power. We must look like men before our people! Look at me: I am married, I have children, and my harem has 650 women."

Radu knew Mehemed never would have made such a request if he loved Radu as before. He was overcome by sadness. "I assure you I am going to follow your advice," he said quietly.

When Radu arrived in Wallachia, he said to one of his boyars, "I am asking you the hand of Maria Despina in marriage."

"Gladly," the boyar answered, without consulting his daughter.

When the boyar arrived home, he said to his daughter, "You cannot imagine who asked for and received your hand in marriage!"

The daughter, alarmed, covered her face with both hands. "What have you done, Father? Your friends are really ugly!"

"If I tell you to who it is, you will not believe me!" he answered, heightening the suspense.

"Father, I have to do what you say," she said. "Even if you have given me away to the ugliest man you know, I will accept the engagement. But I swear I will never, ever forgive you!"

"I gave your hand to Radu!"

"Radu the Beautiful?" she asked, lowering her hands. Feeling faint, she murmured, "It is not possible." Then she shouted, "I am going to burst of happiness!"

And so the beautiful, powerful ruler of Wallachia was married in a solemn and elegant Ottoman ceremony. With Allah as the main witness, the union was made, and all Wallachia celebrated the important event.

The wedding night arrived, and Radu was nervous. He remembered that during his childhood he had had covert sexual relations with several women, but after that he had never voluntarily been with a person of the opposite sex, and he still was wondering how he had managed to end up where he was. When the wedding party was over and they got into the room, Maria Despina approached him with a warm smile, showing her desire for her husband. She put her arms around his neck and gave him a passionate kiss.

Radu felt so sick that he wanted to throw up, but he restrained himself. What would his wife say if he did? He closed his eyes and thought of Vajk, imagining his face, and everything started to change. He began to feel the fire that he felt every time he was with that vigorous man; his body consumed itself with pleasure. Everything was going fine until that silence was shared by the soft voice of his wife. "I love you," she whispered, and in a moment all the enchantment was gone. The night was a sexual disaster. Fortunately, there were no witnesses to his great failure.

Radu offered an excuse. "My love, you cannot imagine how much pressure I am under as a ruler . . . I hope you understand!"

"Don't you worry, my love. What matters is that I am your wife, and I already feel that I love you. I am proud of being the most envied woman in Wallachia!"

On one occasion when Radu was in the arms of Vajk, he asked, "Would you join me and my wife in the bedroom?"

Vajk, who was a fiery lover, answered happily, "You cannot imagine how much I would like that!"

So Radu built up his courage and approached his wife. "My love, I want to ask you a favor: would you mind if a friend were present while we got affectionate?"

"What are you proposing?" Maria Despina asked.

"That Vajk, you, and I enjoy each other in the bedroom."

Maria Despina knew of Vajk and thought he was very handsome. She smiled. "As you wish," she said."

That night the three entered the bedroom, and only they would know what happened there. Nine months later, a beautiful blond girl with blue eyes was born. The baby's resemblance to her beautiful mother was astonishing. She was baptized Maria Boichita.

Meanwhile, Radu's syphilis was latent but quietly getting stronger, waiting for the right moment to invade.

110

One night Ilona told Dracula, "I have orders not to talk to you, but you need to see this." And she gave him a copy of the book.

Dracula accepted it with curiosity and began to read it. "When this lie did come out?" he demanded. "Who wrote it?"

"It came out some years ago," she said. "A ridiculous man named Michael Beheim wrote it. He is a jester in the court of the emperor."

Dracula was silent for a moment. Then he said, "It had to be that damned Frederick! And why didn't anyone tell me?"

"My cousin forbade us to talk to you about this. He said he didn't want to disturb you. In fact, if he realizes that I gave this book to you, I will be in trouble and I might not be able to see you again."

Dracula remained quiet, keeping his thoughts to himself. He was no fool; he understood that something huge was behind this lie. But the more he thought about it, the more the mystery seemed to elude him, and he had more questions than answers. He never imagined that the reason for his disgrace was the one hundred thousand coins that Matthias had stolen.

"Then it is better to keep this secret," he finally said. "Because if the king forbade you from coming to see me . . . I would rather die!" And he hid the book so he could continue to enjoy the company of his beloved.

Ilona put her hands on his shoulders. "Convert to Catholicism," she said, "and let's get married! Look Vlad, if this were the other way around, if I were a prisoner in Wallachia and you visited me and we could only get married in the Orthodox Church, I would convert. My love for you is so big that I would go down to hell itself to be with you. I am not scared of becoming an Orthodox—I'm not scared of death, if it means I can be with you!"

Dracula felt the fire of his passion burning inside him. He had been abstinent for many years now, and only Christ gave him strength to keep his celibacy. *I am not going to convert to Catholicism!* He repeated that to himself time and again. But he also was made of the same material that all

411

men are made of, and his body, which had the strength of a bull, demanded a woman. Ilona was as beautiful and virtuous as his deceased Zalesha,—but she was Catholic! Still, her brave words struck a chord with him. She was daring to go to hell itself for him. Was he just as valiant? Would he go down to hell and fight against Satan and take Ilona from him if he had to? Of course! His love, his nature, and his conviction that his Christ, was also present in the Catholic Church inspired a big decision. Looking into her eyes, he said, "In order to prove to you how great my love is, I will convert to Catholicism. We will get married, and only death will tear us apart. But let me be very clear: the first chance we have, we are going to be married by the Orthodox Church."

Ilona burst into tears, and Dracula hugged her, saying, "Do not cry, my love."

"How can I help it? You agreed to become Catholic because of me!" She pulled away from her lover and walked to where a crucifix was hanging on the wall. Then she knelt down and said, "I knew you wouldn't fail me! Bless you, my God!"

In a private ceremony in which the main witness was Holy Roman Emperor Matthias Corvinus, Dracula and Ilona joined their lives. The bride and groom were happy: finally their hearts would beat together. The wedding night was unforgettable for both. The bride gave him her most valuable treasure, and the groom felt he was in paradise.

111

While Dracula was in prison, the book invented by his enemies had given him a terrible reputation. Nobody in Wallachia believed the lies, but everywhere else they were the favorite topic of conversation. From the humblest beggar to the most powerful king, people accepted the stories as truth, as sure as the sun rose every morning in the east. The jesters learned the stories by heart and told them in every European court. Soon Dracula was known as the evilest man in the world—the most savage and cruel man who had ever lived.

Emperor Matthias was happy. Now that Dracula had accepted the Catholic faith, he had the town as his prison, but Matthias already was preparing for the time when Dracula was completely free and could take command of the empire's armies against the Turks. The Holy Father was in poor health, and it was just a matter of waiting. One night the emperor came to visit Dracula for dinner. The hosts received him, and after they ate, Matthias asked Ilona to leave him and Dracula alone.

Ilona rose immediately. "I'll wait for you in bed, my love. See you, Cousin . . ." And with that she went to pray.

Matthias said, "It is time to prepare ourselves so that you can command a part of my army and put a stop to Mehemed's attacks."

Dracula nodded. "I can't get out of my head the idea that one day I will impale him. When that happens, I myself will introduce the stake through his body! His mouth has proffered so many heretical things against my Christ—I want to hear it crying from pain." Dracula's fury rose as he spoke. "I want to see him naked and ashamed, hanging from the tallest stake!"

Matthias was appalled by his vassal's words, but he also knew that it was Dracula's cruelty that the Ottomans feared so much and that kept them from fighting against him. After a brief silence he asked, "How are we going to face such a powerful enemy?"

Dracula answered, "With the faith that comes from Christ and the strength of good weapons."

"I have my army," Matthias said. "With it we can face him."

Dracula's reply had a certain tone of superiority. "Do you know the size of the sultan's army?"

"No," the monarch admitted. "I know it is very big, but I do not know the exact size."

"The day the sultan stops expanding its empire in other directions and concentrates on Europe is the day we are lost! Believe me, his is the biggest, best-equipped, best-organized, best-fed army in the world, and he constantly has new supplies of gold and children of conscription from the places he has subjected. If you want to defeat him, you must have a huge army, equip it with the most modern weapons and training, and then organize another army that can provide the necessary materials to the front lines, so you can fight nonstop, like the Ottomans. Only when you have done this should you face him."

Matthias heard the warrior talk, and his words sounded very convincing: make a huge army, buy the best weapons, and have another army to supply all the required materials. Without doubt it was an excellent plan. There was just one big problem: it would cost a fortune! So he asked, as if he were making a proposition, "And where would we get the money to do that?"

Dracula answered, "Whom are you going to defend? Your people! So who is going to pay? Your people! You have to establish a tax for them to pay. If they do not want to pay it, ask them, 'Would you prefer your sons to be Janissaries in the enemy army? Would you like your wives and daughters to end up in the harem or the prostitution houses of the sultan? Would you agree to being sold as slaves or suffering a dishonorable death at the hands of your enemies? Would you like to call Christ a prophet, not a God? If your answer is yes, then, do not pay the tax! If your answer is no, then you should work day and night, if necessary, to pay it. Fight for your freedom and your family. Fight for your religion. The defense of the faith in our God is worth a thousand times any sacrifice!'"

When he heard Dracula, Matthias was impressed: who was this vassal in front of him? "The next time I come for dinner, I promise you I will give you a project that you will like," he said. Then Matthias bid goodbye and left.

Dracula walked arm-in-arm with his wife through town. The ignorant people who saw him were scared; they made the sign of the cross and whispered, "That is Dracula—from Beheim's book!"

Dracula was amused by the treatment the town's inhabitants gave him, and he was pleased that they kept their distance. They were not his people anyway

After a few weeks, Emperor Matthias visited Dracula and told him about his plans. "I want to make a new army. It will be named the Black Army, and it will consist of twenty-thousand lightly armed cavalry, eight thousand infantry, nine thousand carts with horses, two hundred boats, and one hundred cannons. In order to sustain such an army we will eliminate the tax exemptions for the feudal lords and the clergy, and each family will give one gold coin. We will set up a tax collection system so that nobody will fail to give his contribution."

Dracula congratulated his monarch and said that such an army would be an excellent investment, because as they conquered new places they could force the inhabitants to pay taxes.

Matthias now had a clear objective and the plan to achieve it.

Dracula said, "There are people who spend all their lives making plans and never actually do anything. Those lame people have just one end: failure! Please, don't abandon this great project; it's the best one I've ever heard of! If you achieve this goal, you will gain my deepest respect and admiration. On the other hand, if you abandon this project, you will be the weakest emperor—with the most brilliant plan—ever."

Matthias new that Dracula was challenging him to show his abilities, as he was no longer a child and had matured. He looked Dracula in the eye and said, "Words are meaningless. You will see the facts!"

The monarch and the vassal took their leave, and from then on events would happen that would make Matthias a true monarch with a privileged and respected place in history, especially the history of Hungary. Thanks to his endeavors and actions, Hungary would become one of the most powerful and prosperous nations in Europe.

The years went by and the love between Ilona and Dracula bore fruit. "Look, honey!" Ilona said. "He looks just like you, and he has green eyes, too! This child can only be named Wladislaus, like his father."

Dracula held the little one in his arms, and the tears ran down his cheeks.

The next year God gave them another son, and when Dracula saw him he said, "This boy reminds me of my dear brother Mircea. What would you think if we named him after my brother?"

"As you wish," Ilona answered.

"Sons, you must make the sign of the cross with the thumb, index, and middle fingers together and the ring and pinky fingers folded. And the Holy Spirit comes from . . ."

Dracula instructed his children in the Orthodox faith, and he was always reminding them, "You must be the most ferocious defenders of the faith in our God."

112

On July 26, 1471, Pope Paul II died and the emperor of the Holy Roman Empire, Matthias Corvinus, went to offer his subordination to the new pope. "Holy Father," he said, "is there any pending issue about the one hundred thousand gold coins?"

The pope looked bewildered. "What are you talking about?" he asked.

Matthias threw up his hands apologetically. "Excuse me—I was confused, Holy Father!" He said nothing further, feeling relaxed. There was no longer a challenge to his crown and his reputation. Now he could set Dracula free.

When Dracula learned that Brother Jacob had helped the jester Beheim to write his infamous book, he remembered the day he went to a monastery to gather money for his crusade and was fooled by Brother Hans. That was a real chameleon! He could not stop thinking of Jacob, and he regretted not having had the monk impaled, as he was in part responsible for Dracula's bad reputation outside Wallachia. *One of these days I am going to find him and the jester and they are going to pay me back with their miserable lives for telling all those lies,* he said to himself. He began trying to think of a way to make impalement even worse so he could try it on the miserable liars who had done him so much harm.

In Wallachia the peasants had gone back to their former way of life. Radu continued to be a loyal ally of the Turks, and while it was true that they were no longer at war, they also saw a big difference from the way things were under Dracula's rule. In their hearts was still the fire of the

Christian faith, and neither the sultan nor anybody else could put it out. *Dracula, where are you?* they lamented. They knew he was a prisoner of the evil emperor, Matthias Corvinus; but there was nothing they could do against such a powerful man.

Between Radu and his dog, Corvinus, a solid relationship had formed. The dog followed his master everywhere he went, and Radu was happy because the dog reminded him of his beloved Vajk.

The Saxons were happy that everything has gone back to normal— that is, they had a governor who favored their interests, and in return they would support him to the end. They were also thankful to the good Emperor Matthias because he kept the demon in prison.

In 1473, Matthias was wishing he had his father to help lead the army, but Janos was at the right hand of his God. Who was even braver, shrewder, fiercer, and more intelligent than Janos? Without a doubt it was Dracula, so Matthias paid him a visit. "You will lead part of my army," Matthias said.

The soldiers who were under Dracula's command had read the sinister stories that Beheim wrote. As a result, they all thought of him as a monster, and they were scared of him. When Matthias presented Dracula to his army, the new commander introduced himself this way:

"I am Dracula! I will be your commander, and together we are going to fight the Ottoman infidels. We will fight for the glory, the honor, and the faith of God under the flag of our Christ and the Order of the Dragon. We should have as our maximum ambition to die on the field of battle with the name of our God on our lips. Our strength and our valor come from God; with him on our mind, defeat will turn into victory. From now on I want you to understand that before fighting for your emperor, you fight for our God. You will neither question nor argue against my orders; you will fulfill them even if you don't understand them. I will not accept any soldier of mine being wounded in the back in a battle. If that happens, it means that he ran, and nobody will run from the battle unless it is a strategy ordered by me. Those who do not obey will die as traitors—impaled—because it is not fair that as a result of their cowardice, a valiant soldier must stay and fight to the death.

"Death is the partner who will take us to the presence of our God. These wise words were spoken frequently by a sacred warrior who was braver and holier than anyone I've ever known: the great Janos Hunyadi, father of our Emperor Matthias, my master and best friend. He said that when we die valiantly in battle, we should not fear death. After all, we are fighting the enemies of the Cross, who want to destroy our faith—and are we going to allow that? We will offer our lives seeking the glory of our God, and if we are lucky enough we will die in the battle!"

When the soldiers heard him speak, they asked, "Who is this? Is he a saint or a demon?"

Matthias was astounded; the army had never heard any commander talk like that. Now he understood why Dracula was so often victorious.

"Today is a very special day for me," Dracula concluded. "I was born to defend the faith in Christ, and I have spent twelve years retired in prayer. Now I've come back to war, and you are my soldiers. Someday, in good time, you will become my friends, and as long as we continue in our victories, we will be brothers. To commemorate this special union, I invite you all to celebrate by going to holy Mass."

The soldiers could not believe it. What a pious commander! They asked themselves, *Is this really the monster that the mad jester referred to in his book? No! That had to be another man!* When he threatened to impale the cowards who ran from battle, the valiant soldiers considered the threat a fair and intelligent one: if nobody ran, the army had a better chance of victory.

At Mass, the soldiers watched their commander take communion with devotion, and when the final blessing was given they saw him cross himself the Orthodox way, with the last two fingers bent and the first three extended, representing God the Father, God the Son, and God the Holy Spirit. They were confused about his Orthodox ways, but of one thing they were sure: that man who spoke like a saint was going to defend with his life the very same God as theirs, Jesus Christ.

Dracula summoned the commander Litovoi and told him, "You served my brother Mihail, and now you will be my right-hand man. I appoint you general commander!" Litovoi was speechless from excitement; he could not even thank Dracula for the incredible promotion, he was so happy.

The soldier Jerzy said to his comrade Lactu, "We are ruined! Now we are not going to be able to stay in the rear and flee during combat."

"Of course we can!" Lactu said. "No one is going to notice us. You've seen how ugly the battle gets on the front lines. Dracula is crazy—I am not going to listen to him."

Jerzy shook his head. "The man's reputation for cruelty and shrewdness precedes him. We had better not run or we'll end up impaled—just imagine it!"

Lactu laughed. "*You* imagine it," he said. "Nothing is going to happen to me."

A few days later, King Matthias ordered Dracula's army to take some Ottoman squares.

Dracula asked several monks to join him in giving spiritual assistance to the soldiers: it was his habit that before every battle a solemn Mass would be celebrated.

When Mass was over, Dracula gave the battle cry: "For our God Jesus Christ!" And with that Dracula led his men into battle, with the bulk of the army behind him. At the end of the fight the Dragon banner fluttered from the highest place on the battlefield, and then came something new and horrible for Dracula's men: the impalements.

One of the soldiers from Matthias's Black Army pulled aside an experienced Wallachian soldier. "Why do we impale our enemy after we kill him? He is already dead—we're not causing further suffering."

"To send his soul to hell. This scares many of our enemies."

When the impalements were over, Dracula ordered his commanders to check their soldiers and identify any with wounds only on their backs. The order was carried out, and eight soldiers were identified, including Lactu. "You have dishonored our army!" Dracula said. "You abandoned the battle to spare your own miserable lives, risking the victory and betraying your God, your emperor, and your comrades! You knew the law, and now your actions are your executioners." He turned to his commander and said, "Impale them!"

"We are not going to flee again!" "Forgive us lord!" There were all kinds of pleas from men hoping to free themselves from their punishment, but Dracula did not seem to hear them. He just stared at the accused without speaking.

Soon Lactu was high up on a stake, his torment just starting. He looked down and saw that he had company: his faithful friend, Jerzy, with a bandage on his head, had knelt down in front of him, praying. He was so grateful for his friend's prayer. He wanted to complain of the pain but he could not. Now he regretted not having listened to his friend. If only he could go back in time . . . He felt the powerful claws of a vulture grab him by the skull, and then a beak ripped out his eye. He felt he was in hell and could not stand a moment of more pain. But the next four days proved him wrong.

Jerzy watched his friend and thought, *If only Lactu had listened to me, he wouldn't have ended up impaled.*

The witnesses watched the fate of the cowards and the lesson was clear: they had to fight the enemy with great ferocity and determination. They feared and respected Dracula in equal measures, and he was both obeyed and admired, especially by the brave ones who knew they could count on him.

113

Stephen from Moldavia was furious at his cousin for agreeing to command the powerful army of his hated enemy, Matthias. He knew that one day he would have to face that army, and he still didn't know what his reaction would be. He had made a pact with Dracula and twice violated it because of his cowardice. Now how could he attack Dracula? That was beyond his comprehension. Despite everything, he loved his cousin, who had always helped him. Now he should attack him? Never!

But Radu was his brother and now the declared enemy of Dracula. Stephen could attack him, and he did. In September 1473 in Tirgoviste, Stephen took hostage the wife and the daughter of the traitor Radu, who ran away. After Stephen took Bucharest, his military intelligence informed him that the sultan planned to attack Moldavia with his army, so he left immediately to defend it. He would worry about Radu later.

Radu was used to having everything; the only hard time in his life was when his brother attacked him when they were coming to Wallachia. He was used to a luxurious lifestyle, with good food and servants, and now suddenly he found himself alone: without friends, without a wife or daughter. His beloved Vajk had died of syphilis a year earlier, and that, for him, was the threshold of hell. His only support was his faithful dog, Corvinus, who followed him everywhere without protest, showing his value with his unconditional love.

Radu's depression lowered his body's defenses. That was the opportunity that his syphilis had been waiting for, and it started to manifest itself. The soles of his feet and palms of his hands became rough and spotted, and the disease preyed on his brain. He became delusional—he saw Vajk and Mehemed killing each other with huge swords—and then his hair fell out. He couldn't believe that the horrible monster in the mirror was him; he had always been the Beautiful! It was a nightmare, but the more he tried to wake himself up, the worse he got. The muscular pain and the fatigue were killing him; he had never been so thin. And that was logical, for syphilis was destroying his weak body.

He forgot about seeking refuge with Mehemed. How would he react, seeing Radu turned into this monster? Time went by, and looking like a beggar, Radu walked aimlessly without a home, praying all day and hoping to find refuge in Allah. He begged in the streets for his food. He was completely alone and missed Mehemed. If Mehemed had not left him in that place, he thought, they would still be lovers and he would have had a different fate. He turned around to see Corvinus, who meekly wagged his tail, acknowledging the attention.

Voica and Micul, two peasants, were coming home after an arduous day of work when they encountered Radu, who stretched out his hands and said, "Help me, for the love of Allah!"

The peasants looked at each other in amazement and Micul asked, 'How does this ragged beggar dare to ask us for help in the name of Allah?" But when they realized that the beggar was the once-powerful Radu—the Beautiful—they felt pity and disgust and gave him a coin. As they walked away, Voica said, "That man is an enemy of Christ, and I wanted to offend him, but I pitied him. He looks so helpless and sick—the poor thing."

Corvinus still had not left his master's side, and now Radu grabbed the dog by the head and said, "My faithful friend, what would I do without you? You are the only one who has not abandoned and rejected me."

The dog stood still, looking at him without blinking, and answered him in a demonic voice, "And do you think that you're going to get away? Dracula and Stephen will impale you!"

Radu went cold: that was impossible! Dogs never spoke, but this one not only spoke, but seemed to be the son of the devil. Shivering, Radu steeled his courage and asked in a trembling voice, "How do you know that?"

"I am a spy," the dog answered. "We are going to impale you—and then we are going to impale your boyfriend, the sultan!"

Radu then knew that his faithful friend was in reality his foe, and all it wanted was to betray him. He tried unsuccessfully to abandon the dog, finally beating it until he thought he had killed it, but the spy recovered from the savage aggression, found him again, and followed him everywhere. That started to get worrying, as a bitch was in heat and Corvinus was chasing after her, along with other aspirants for her company.

Radu could not believe it, but he was seeing it with his own eyes: the dogs were conspiring against him! He realized with horror that they were all accomplices of his enemies. Sure enough, among them were Dracula and Stephen, who turned to see him in a bad way and told him, "We are going to impale you!"

Fear started to dominate him. He looked up at the sky and saw in the clouds some black spiders the size of calves that were descending, also trying to kill him. He began running through the woods while Corvinus perfected the plot with his accomplices. He hid behind some trees until they came to life and told him, "You are a traitor of Dracula!" When the trees tried to stop him, Radu started to scream and run again, finally finding refuge in a cave. When he was inside he felt momentarily secure, but then he smelled the fetid odor of bad breath, and when he looked up and down he saw huge teeth . . . the cave was a big mouth that was going to eat him! He got out of there in a panic and fell down in the weeds, and then he realized that even the weeds were conspiring against him, encouraging the trees to catch him. There was nowhere safe to hide! He felt his eyes begin to fail him, and the last thing he saw was the traitor Corvinus coming to him and, with his presence, revealing him to his enemies. Finally he was caught by the trees, one of which entangled him in its limbs and stuck a branch into his anus. He could feel it working its way through his body . . . he was being impaled! Inside him, his brain was sending his nerves a series of confusing messages—paranoid, crazy messages leading to a sense of paralysis, which left him motionless. The dementia was complete. This was the third and final phase of his deadly syphilis, and he died in the throes of terrible nightmares—perhaps as he deserved, as he was a traitor to Christ.

114

The more Dracula's army fought, the better the results. Their victories came more easily, as did their opportunities to impale. On October 6, the army joined up with the army commanded by Matthias. The commanders of Dracula's army told the emperor about the victories they had achieved under the orders of the extraordinary crusader.

"I'm impressed!" Matthias told Dracula. "In just a short time my men have come to obey you, respect you, and love you. I am very satisfied with your performance. I want you to command the whole army, as I am going back to Hungary."

"Who is going to direct the taking of Srebrenica?" Dracula asked.

"You," answered the monarch. "I need to attend to some matters of state. I know I can trust you and your military strategy."

Matthias did not tell him the truth: that he feared attacking Srebrenica because it was protected by a huge wall—the army's failure there was almost guaranteed. He did not want people to say that Emperor Matthias had failed to take that important fortress.

Matthias does not seem like the son of Janos—he is too fearful of battle, Dracula thought. *But he is the emperor; he can do what he wants.* Later he evaluated the logistics of that difficult attack and sent some spies to develop a combat strategy. They decided that each boyar, dressed either as a Turk or a Janissary, would take a specific position. Some would enter the city with their weapons hidden from view, while others would arrive at the doors on horseback. Some riders would take position at the entry door to ensure that it would not be closed for any reason. Another group would surprise the guard, and when the bugler gave the signal, all the boyars inside the gates as well as the army that was outside would attack at the same time. But before any action, Dracula said, they would go to Mass, where everyone would receive Holy Communion.

The attack happened just as they had planned it, step by step, and it was a resounding victory. The soldiers were excited; they could feel the fervor, the valor, the bravery that can only come from God in battle, and they admired the intelligence, audacity, and wits of his commander. In the end they did what they always did, impaled the infidels, and there was the shame and the pain and, later, the birds feasting on eyes and other excruciating indignities. Afterwards Dracula asked his soldiers to bring him the bodies of the infidels. At Dracula's command they were torn into pieces and nailed to stakes in small stacks. The power of his army was too much to resist. Finally there were no enemy soldiers left to give their testimony of the battle, and at the highest part of the fortress a flag was raised representing the Order of the Dragon—a reminder that Dracula had returned.

In Wallachia, Basarab Laiota had taken power, helped by the Turks.

Meanwhile one of Mehemed's new spies rushed to deliver bad news to the powerful sultan. "The impaler demon has come back!" he said breathlessly.

"What are you saying?" the sultan asked skeptically.

"Dracula is leading Matthias's army!"

The Sultan put his hands on his head and remained silent, thinking, *If he does to me what he does to peasants and slaves, what is going to be my destiny?* In his subconscious, his fear of impalement was getting stronger and stronger.

Insomnia preyed on him. Amidst his men he frantically sought sleep, but it was useless. When he finally did sleep, his door banged open and there was Dracula with a huge stake in his hand, shouting, "Come here! I'm going to impale you!"

The sultan jumped out of bed, ran to the window, and shouted to his guards, but they did not appear. He ran desperately to a different window and jumped into the backyard, and when he landed he looked around and was horrified: he found himself amidst a forest of impalements. All the soldiers in his army were on a stake!

Dracula caught up with him and told him, "Come here, Mehemed. You wanted to destroy the Christian faith?" Turning around to see his boyars, he said, "Bring him to the main square!"

Then he was in front of all the people—defenseless, vulnerable, shaking with fear—and the demon's voice seemed to come straight from hell, giving the order Mehemed feared so much: "Impale him!"

They grabbed him roughly, and when he shouted for help, a hard blow with a huge stone knocked his teeth out. Then he was naked, and he felt the shame of being exposed in front of the people who had always seen him as the most powerful man in the world. The biggest stake was assigned to him, and Dracula began to stick it into his anus with his own hands. A shrill scream tore his throat.

"Wake up! Wake up!" He was violently shaken from that nightmare. Sweating and trembling, on the verge of tears, he grabbed the servant who had awakened him. "Please don't go!" Mehemed begged him. "I had a nightmare . . . Dracula was impaling me!" Night after night, the same scene repeated itself. There was no doubt that it was Mehemed's greatest fear.

"I am going to tell you about a dream the sultan has every night," the servant later whispered to his wife. "But please—don't tell anyone!"

Before long, everyone in the empire knew about the sultan's great fear of Dracula. When the people knew that their powerful sultan was afraid of the impaler, they concluded, as he had, that Dracula was an enemy they would never face, because after he killed them, he mercilessly threw their souls to hell.

The sultan summoned his chief falconers and announced "I will give a reward of fifty thousand gold coins to the one who brings me the impaler's head—I want it in my collection! I will also give him a city in my empire to rule."

The chief falconers were amazed by the offer—a reward that size would tempt a saint! Each man made his respective plans. Basarab Laiota, for one, wanted to get that juicy reward and please his master, as well. Soon afterwards, the sultan summoned Basarab. "I want you to destroy all of Stephan's army—and bring me his head!"

Basarab was confused. "Is not Stephan our ally?" he asked.

"He was until he attacked Radu!" Mehemed said. "Fulfill my command—but make a good plan. I don't want any little surprises!"

When Dracula led Matthias's Black Army, it was unstoppable: they had one victory after another. His infamy made Ottomans tremble just to hear his name, and his soldiers began to trust in him more and more. Now that he was commanding such a powerful army, he had no doubt that he would crush the infidels.

They approached Stephen's castle with Dracula at the vanguard, carrying a flag of the Order of the Dragon. There was not a white flag with them.

Stephen gave the order: "Open the doors! It is my cousin Dracula!"

Stephen and Dracula were once again face to face, and they hugged with affection. There was so much love in their past, so much happiness, so much reverence for the same God, that instead of being enemies, and despite the destiny that tried to pit them against one another, they couldn't help themselves.

"Let's forget ancient differences," Dracula said. "Let's face our enemy together."

"My enemy is Matthias—and you are his ally," responded stubborn Stephen.

"You are wrong," Dracula said. "Even if Matthias is Catholic, he believes in our same God. Our enemy is the Ottoman sultan! I will forget that you allowed passage of Mehemed's ships in the Danube when you controlled the Fort of Chilia, and forget your wound, cousin—and let's fight together."

"How can I forget my wound? I am lame! Besides, the defeat at Chilia is the only defeat in my military career. Is that a small thing to you? I hate Matthias!"

Dracula held out his hands. "Cousin, please think it over. We all have wounds—that is part of our job. We all have lost a battle. Don't think of yourself in terms of Matthias or me; think about the defense of the Christian faith! Have you thought what would happen if the Turks attacked you with the full strength of their army? You don't have the protection Constantinople had! They would destroy you—and they also would destroy Matthias and me. Remember, we are three, but together we are stronger than three. A well-braided rope is hard to break. That is written in the Holy Bible, and it is the word of God! Let's go talk to Matthias and fight together for the love of God!"

But Stephen was resentful. "No!" he said. "That is my last word. I will not make a pact with Matthias for any reason."

As a last resort, Dracula showed Stephen the palm of his right hand, reminding him, "We made an oath with Christ as our witness that we would always help each other and that there would never be a rivalry between us. I did my part when you needed me, and we recovered your throne—even though at that time I had more enemies than ever. However, I have asked for your help twice and haven't received it. Now this is the third time. Help me, Cousin!"

Still, Stephen answered categorically. "No, not with Matthias. And don't insist!"

The army led by Dracula would return to Hungary without an alliance. Dracula's deep sadness was reflected in his face. His heart was broken.

Meanwhile, Basarab Laiota waited like a vulture for Dracula to leave Stephen so he could destroy him. Basarab would fulfill the master's order.

The day after Dracula and his army left, Stephen's guards saw the enemy in the distance. They prepared for the fight, Basarab's army arrived, and the battle began. The numerical superiority of the Turkish army was evident immediately: soon Stephan's defeat was imminent.

Stephan understood that the fight was the last one of his life, and he was very sad. He had known defeat only at Chilia and against the hated army of Matthias. Now he was able to retreat, but where would he go from here? He was completely surrounded! It was time to accept defeat, and he began wondering about his destiny; he knew his head would enrich his enemy's collection. He was remembering the proposal Dracula had just made, and now he regretted not having listened to him. He knelt down to ask God for forgiveness for his cowardice.

Dracula was on his way to see Matthias, and since he was a good observer he noticed as he passed a hill that there were recent traces of a campsite behind it. He looked closer and knew by the tracks that they were Ottoman and very recent. His enemies had been there! "Alert for battle!" he told his bugler. "Attack!" The call went out, and everyone heard the strange order and prepared to face the enemy, although there was not a soul to be seen anywhere. Looking at each other, they wondered if Dracula had lost his mind. "What enemy?" they whispered to each other. "Where is he?" However, they knew better than to argue against his orders, and they obeyed blindly. They went at full gallop to Moldavia.

Stephan's dreams of greatness had come to an end. He knew he was going to die at the hands of his enemy; both his destiny and the destiny of his people were more certain now than ever. Suddenly, like an angel from heaven, and surely sent by his powerful God, Dracula arrived at full gallop. He had turned into a ferocious beast leading the Black Army of Matthias and carrying the banners of Jesus Christ of the Blessed Sacrament and of the Order of the Dragon. He threw himself fiercely at the enemy, with the braveness that was typical of him. The Turks were taken by surprise by the rear guard, and that changed the destiny of the battle. Once they realized that they were fighting Dracula, the Turks ran away, afraid for their souls. Basarab Laiota, who was known for his prudence and intelligence, wisely retreated, joined by his guard.

In the end there were new men impaled, but there was the same pain, the same humiliation, the same waiting vultures. As his soldiers were impaling the Turks, Dracula asked Stephen, "What do you think about Matthias's Black Army?"

"I have never seen braver or more determined men! "Said Stephan". Until that moment Stephan had never really understood his cousin. Now he apologized, saying, "I beg you to forgive me for being so stupid. I'm sorry for what had to happen for me to open my eyes! You helped me take Moldavia back and have already saved my life three times . . . I cannot believe my own ignorance."

Dracula hugged his cousin warmly. "Forget the past—it no longer exists! Let's go to Matthias. Together, the three of us will be invincible."

They got together with Matthias in Hungary, where they shook hands, asked for one another's forgiveness, exchanged gifts, and made a powerful alliance that only death and God's will could destroy.

115

Stephen went to Moldavia and Dracula to Tirgoviste, accompanied by Stephen Bathory and his army. When they got there they confronted the frightened hare, Basarab Laiota, who ran away—this time toward the Ottoman Empire. Once again he slipped through Dracula's fingers; there was no doubt that Basarab was the master of retreat. As a result, in November 1476, Dracula took power for the third time in Wallachia.

Dracula had turned into a legend among the Wallachian peasants, who were upset by the lies written by the jester Beheim and kept contradicting them with folk songs that stressed the courage, braveness, and godliness of their beloved Dracula. These songs would withstand the passage of the centuries, with some even lasting into the twenty-first century. Unfortunately they were sung only in Wallachia, and they never got out of that place. Suffice it to say that when Dracula returned to rule, the Wallachians welcomed their beloved and pious leader.

For the Saxons, however, their worst nightmare had come back from the grave. He had approached them with a compromise: he would tax their activities minimally on the condition that they not give refuge to Basarab Laiota. But if they did, the laws on the books would be applied. The sinister bullies trembled at the knowledge that they could not fool their ruler.

The Catholic Church in Wallachia, knowing that Dracula now professed the faith, hoped to be protected by him, but it also feared retaliation for the book written by Beheim and motivated by the lies of two Catholic monks.

116

A few days after having taken power for the third time two men and a woman—arrived at his quarters and asked to speak to their vovoid.

When the guard saw that they were humble people, he made them wait; the vovoid first had to attend to more important matters. However, Dracula also had instructed his guards that he would attend himself to all Wallachians, even the most humble. So the peasants waited until finally the guard said, "You can pass."

When they walked into the room and stood before them, Dracula was daunted. He felt like he was going to faint when he saw one of the visitors—it could not be! His legs were shaking and his heart was beating until it seemed his chest was going to explode. him. Setting aside any formalities or court customs, Dracula threw himself into the young man's arms and hugged him with such strength that it seemed he wanted to become one with him. Dracula thought his heart was going to explode from happiness, and he gave out a faltering cry, "Son of my heart!"

Minhea was crying, too, because of his father's emotional welcome. He had been remembering and missing his father for so long, and now he did not want to separate from him.

Finally Dracula held his son at arm's length, looking at him and trying to assimilate the news. Despite the high emotions, Dracula was still a keen observer, and he quickly scanned all three visitors, who were dressed humbly but cleanly. He wanted to know more from his son and his companions. Addressing the two strangers, he asked, "Who are you?"

The man answered, "Lord, we are Karijotas and Ruxandra. We work for your service in the fields."

Dracula then turned to Minhea. "Tell me son—what happened?"

"Father, the night that I got lost, I understood that if you left, it was only to protect me from the Ottomans—"

But Dracula interrupted him, anguished, "No, my son—I did not abandon you! I lost you! But I did not look for you because I wanted to protect you. I knew I was the one they were looking for, and so you had a better chance of survival on your own."

"I always trusted you!" Minhea said. "These good peasants found me and treated me like a son; in fact, I have come to love them like parents."

Dracula turned back to the peasants and asked Karijotas solemnly, "So you are the father of my son?"

The poor peasant looked ready to run away from fear. "Forgive me, lord," he answered timidly. "I only gave your child the love of my humble heart. I took care of him and loved him like a son. But now that you are here, I am not his father anymore. We are leaving—please forgive us!"

"Where you are going is to my table!" Dracula said to Karijotas. 'From now on you will be new members of my court. You will live in my palace and continue to be the parents of my son, and my son can keep calling you Father. I also had two." Then, turning to Ruxandra, he said, 'And he can keep calling you Mother, because my son's beloved mother died the day before I lost him."

Karijotas beamed with relief and gratitude. "God did not give us the joy of having children, and your son has filled our lives with light and happiness. Thank you, lord, for giving us the opportunity to keep seeing him—we love him very much. God bless you!"

Dracula silently thanked God for the unselfish love of those two peasants.

That day he suspended all his audiences, and he, Minhea, Karijotas, and Ruxandra went to the dining room and spent hours talking. "I am going to give you a reward for taking care of my son," Dracula said to the couple. "I am going to give you a great tract of land, and no one is going to take it from you: neither governors nor future ecclesiastical authorities." Soon Ilona and Minhea's half-brothers arrived; they were all delighted at the young man's return.

Members of Dracula's court helped the new nobles settle into the palace, where there was plenty room for the added family members.

Minhea told his father, "My adoptive parents instructed me in the Orthodox faith, and they also taught me how to sow and take care of animals. But I did not forget to practice my military skills!"

Dracula was pleased to hear that, as for years he had reminded his son, "Our main duty is to defend the faith of our God, remember our Orthodox tradition, and seek the freedom of Wallachia." Dracula had repeated to Minhea the same lessons his father, Dracul, had repeated to him again and again. Now Dracula was the parrot!

"Father, now that I am a man, I often think back on my favorite memory, and that is when you told me all those beautiful bedtime stories that made my childhood so happy. Now I am an adult and don't need bedtime stories, but the memories of them fill me with happiness." Then he said goodnight and made a respectful request: "Would you give me your blessing, Father?"

"First, let's pray together to our Christ to thank him for letting us find each other again," he said. They knelt down by Minhea's bed and before a crucifix said their prayers. Then the father gave his son his ceremonious blessing, and the two of them went to bed. It was the first day of their new life as father and son.

Dracula and Ilona set the date to celebrate their marriage in the Orthodox Church, agreeing that they would get married on February 18, and that their marriage would be a historic event.

Meanwhile, Bathory's army retreated to Moldavia.

117

The sultan's falconers devised a sinister plan. They had studied their shrewd enemy and analyzed various techniques to help them achieve their objective. Finally they decided to disguise some of their soldiers as Wallachian boyars, who would attack the demon when he was caught off-guard. They had to look for and seize some opportunity.

Soldiers in the Ottoman army got goose bumps just hearing the name Dracula; they refused to fight against the demon, as they didn't want to end up in hell. Wallachia was still filled with the impaled bodies of Turks. By order of Dracula, no one could take the impaled down, and the Ottomans did not dare do it because they were afraid to lose their souls.

On December 25, 1476, near Bucharest, Basarab Laiota and his great army went to fight the demon. They were not looking for a victory; they understood that they were again going to be sacrificed to Islam's Executioner, as he they had come to call him. Although they harbored the obscure hope of killing Dracula, this battle ended like all the others: the ferocity and bravery, the love of Christ, the impalements . . . and at the end, the victory of the monster's army, followed by the escape of Basarab Laiota and his personal guard.

Minhea is very happy, has tasted another victory in the name of his Christ, he goes to Dracula and said. "Father, I feel so proud to bring your blood in my veins. I will impale them!"

Dracula was just satisfied to have killed more foes in the name of his God. He left Minhea in charge of the impalements and went up a hill to watch the sweetest part of the battle, the desserts of his effort: the total destruction of the enemy! He listened happily to the cries of the infidels, who had once blasphemed against Christ. He was joined by his faithful van and seven boyars who served as his personal guards. He thought he did not need his other guards; the fight was over, and he had won. He noted with joy that Minhea was just like him: he was directing everything perfectly.

A group of enemies dressed as Wallachian boyars saw the perfect opportunity, and Dracula was caught completely by surprise. One of the boyars attacked him with his spear, managing to get just one blow through his back and right lung. The other soldiers saw what was happening and threw themselves into the battle against the small retinue.

Dracula drew his sword and, despite his mortal wound, began to fight. Ivan and the other boyars with him were also taken by surprise and ended up mortally wounded; however, they managed to kill numerous enemies.

The traitor Basarab Laiota waited for the moment of his victim's death like a vulture on the lookout, watching patiently from a distance, in the safety that his cowardice offered him. When he saw everybody on the ground, dead or dying, he decided to approach and capture the sultan's most prized trophy.

Dracula lay on the ground, feeling the excruciating wound in his back and chest. He realized his body was pierced—that was the objective of the infidels! He also understood that the moment had come for him to reunite with his creator, and he felt an indescribable joy. He could not believe he was so lucky: this was the reward that God had given him for having defended his faith with so much passion. He reminisced about his life, and a succession of scenes and people flashed through his mind: Mircea, his father, his mother, the traitor Radu, happy moments with his beloved Zalesha, his sons, his ordination, his brother Janos, his darling Ilona, and then his lifelong defense of his Christian faith. He was sure that as a result of his actions and his death on the battlefield defending the faith, the world would remember him for his true love of God and forget those ridiculous stories that portrayed him as a bloodthirsty maniac. He was sure that succeeding generations would remember him as Dracula, the most faithful and fierce defender of Jesus Christ.

One after another, the images kept flashing through his mind, and even as he gave up his soul, his mouth did not stop thanking God for everything he had given him. He was praying aloud, giving thanks for the opportunity to defend God's name, when suddenly he felt someone wrench his hair and saw the face of his foe, a traitor to Christ. "Let us see if your God saves you from this one!" With that, Basarab Laiota raised his sword.

Dracula was about to have the most important experience of his life: he was about to be in the presence of Jesus Christ of the Blessed Sacrament. He thanked his God again for having fulfilled his greatest dream, to die at the hands of his enemy, defending his faith. With eyes filled with tears because of the indescribable emotion, he said his last words: "Thank you very much, and blessed are you my Lord and God Jesus Chr—"

Basarab, roaring with laughter, beheaded him with a clean cut. His guards could not believe it: they now had the most valuable trophy in the world. They put it in a container filled with honey and headed to the Ottoman Empire.

The sultan received Basarab with great happiness. This was the day of his liberation, the day he stopped being afraid of dying impaled by Islam's Executioner. But his nightmares would not disappear for the rest of his life; only death freed him from that horror. For years afterward, Dracula continued to terrorize the Ottomans in their dreams.

From all over the Ottoman Empire, people traveled to Istanbul, formerly Constantinople, to see with their own eyes the most incredible sight in the world: driven onto a stake in front of the main palace was the head of the feared monster. People flocked there by the thousands.

Mehemed II now considered himself the holiest and most intelligent warrior in the world. To his pompous titles "Lord of Both Seas," "Conqueror of Constantinople," and "Master of the Horizons," he added yet another, which filled him with pride: "Killer of Islam's Executioner."

THE END?

Most biographical novels end with the death of the main character. However, in the case of Dracula, the real story seems to begin when he is murdered. His life and death are full of mysteries and legends that have continued to this day. In the centuries since Dracula's death, people have asked many questions about him:

1. Did Dracula exist in real life?
2. Was he a Christian?
3. Would Christianity have disappeared without his intervention?
4. Is Dracula's valuable contribution to Christianity recognized?
5. Where did his reputation for evil come from?
6. Did he drink the blood of the impaled?
7. Was he a vampire in Rumania (formerly Wallachia, Transylvania, and Moldavia)?
8. How did he become known as a vampire?
9. Where can I find more literature that tells the real story of Dracula?
10. Were there any other stories written about Dracula during his time besides the ones from the jester Beheim?

1. Did Dracula exist in real life?

Yes. Dracula was a man of flesh and blood who lived in Walachia, Transylvania, and Moldavia—an area known today as Rumania. He lived from approximately 1431 to 1476.

This is a biographical novel. and is based on the true story of Vladislaus III (Dracula), some names, events, and other details are different from the real story trying to make the novel amuse, but the main plot was respected; among many historic deeds we have to consider this real:

A. —The fall of Constantinople May 29, 1453; order from Mehemed II changing the name to Istanbul, and declaring Jesus Christ prophet as the same level of Mohammad.

B. —Mantua council in 1459 summoned by Pio II to conquer Constantinople, with the negative form all the envoys to face Ottomans.

C. —Proposal from Pio II to give one hundred thousand gold coins, in order to pay the expenses of the crusade against the Ottomans, to the one who has the courage to face them.

D. —Positive intervention of the Holy Inquisition to reunite this money with their brutal and savages methods.

E. —Mehemed's intention to conquer Rome, change its name and declare Jesus Christ prophet; same as he did in Constantinople.

F. —Dracula crusade in 1462; the impalement of thousands ottomans by 'the Impaler' and the great fear they have, it was so big. Than they fled in terror to the Ottoman empire, and they refuse to fight against him.

G. —At the end of his crusade Matthias put Dracula in prison 12 years. Beheim, a Jester from Frederick III, publish the book "History of a Bloodthirsty Madman Called Dracula from Wallachia"; destroying his crusade reputation and turn into a very evil man.

H. —Matthias Corvinus buy the saint Stephen crown in 80,000 gold coins, with this become in holy roman emperor.

I. —The violent dead of Dracula in 1476 by the hands of his enemies

And the historical fact that never happen: Mehemed never conquer Rome; never change its name and never declare Jesus Christ prophet at the same level than Mohamed in that place.

My personal conclusion through the analysis of this historical facts: Jesus Christ remain his divinity in West, thanks to Dracula.

2. Was he a Christian?

Yes. Orthodox, Catholic—however you want to categorize him—he was a devout and fervent worshiper of Jesus Christ, and therefore, he was a Christian. He also was the highest ecclesiastical Orthodox authority in Wallachia; during his second reign he named the metropolitan and bishops and founded five churches and eighteen monasteries. He also helped to pay a debt to the Turks in order to free Mount Athos, which was considered the Orthodox center of the ancient world after the conquer of Constantinople. He regularly made confession and received Holy Communion, and he always was accompanied by monks and bishops. He was a pious man who was well known for governing fairly.

3. Would Christianity have disappeared without his intervention?

It is difficult and risky to make an affirmation of that sort; we can only analyze the facts.

Mehemed II, commanding a powerful army and with new firearms technology, took Constantinople in May 1453. This event was so important that it is considered the end of the Middle Ages. From that moment on in that place, by the irrevocable order of the powerful sultan, Jesus Christ was no longer God but was, instead, an important and respected prophet, like Mohammad. The sultan also changed the name of the city from Constantinople to Istanbul.

Mehemed II had as his next military objective the conquest of Rome, in order to eradicate Catholicism there and establish Islam, as he had done in Constantinople. However, Dracula had one tool that horrified the Ottomans: he impaled, and by doing so he stole the souls of his victims. The Ottoman soldiers did not want to confront him because they knew that whoever died in battle against him would go straight to hell. To the people of that time, such matters were real-life concerns, and as a result, the Ottomans refused to fight against Dracula.

Maybe for his own convenience, Matthias did not kill Dracula but instead kept him captive, as having him there was a means of protection against Ottoman invasion. Matthias knew perfectly well the intentions of Mehemed.

The truth is that Dracula was an important factor in the Ottomans' failure to attack Europe. If it had not have been for him, certainly Rome would have fallen and probably the modern image of Jesus Christ would be something like our image of Zeus, who in his time was considered a real god by learned men like Pythagoras, Alexander the Great, Aristotle, Plato, and practically all the great thinkers of the ancient times. They questioned neither his existence nor his divinity, and they were sure of his power; certainly they would have given their lives to prove it, without thinking it twice. However, today Zeus is just another figure in Greek mythology—in other words, another lie from the greatest philosophers and thinkers in humanity, who were, of course, mistaken in their religious beliefs.

Perhaps it would not be too extreme to suggest that thanks to its fierce defense by Dracula, Christianity might not exist today. It is my opinion that the Catholic Church and all Christian churches owe their survival in great part to Dracula's military sacrifice of blood, sweat, and tears against the faith's powerful Ottoman enemies.

I also believe that no one deserves the title of saint more than Dracula, who should have been canonized long ago by the Catholic and Orthodox Churches. If nothing else, his name should be remembered with respect, since he dedicated his life to the defense of the Christian faith. Unfortunately, the personal interests of a single, more powerful man, combined with widespread publicity, turned Dracula into a "sanguinary and crazy man," and then into a bloodthirsty vampire.

It might be time for Christian churches to dedicate some time to analyzing the historical facts about this mysterious and largely unknown character. Maybe then they will restore his reputation and give him the justice he earned—and perhaps even the title of "saint."

One thing, at least, is clear: if the powerful sultan had taken Rome, by his order Jesus Christ would no longer have been God, and today Jesus would simply be a prophet, as happened in Constantinople, now known as Istanbul.

4. Was Dracula's valuable contribution to Christianity recognized?

Absolutely not. Stephen of Moldavia was canonized as a saint by the Orthodox Church in 1972, despite having made alliances with the Turks and paid them tribute with money and children of conscription (although this concession is justifiable in the face of aggression by more powerful enemies). Payment of the debt of Mount Athos, the Orthodox center that succeeded Constantinople, is attributed to Stephen, but few acknowledge that Dracula also contributed to that payment.

The history books prefer to conceal or omit the close relationship between Stephen and Dracula, probably so as not to stain the image of the saint.

It is said that history is written by the winners, and certainly Dracula died defending his faith while Stephen survived. As a result, Stephen became known as "Christ's athlete" while Dracula was known as a sanguinary crazy man and is now known as a bloodthirsty vampire.

5. Where did his reputation for evil come from?

Matthias Corvinus bought the crown of Saint Stephen, which gave him the title holy Roman emperor, for eighty thousand gold coins in order to validate his crown as king of Hungary. Where did he get the money to do that? Not just I, but also some perceptive historians, have carefully researched that subject and suspect that the money came from one hundred thousand gold coins Pope Pio II gave to Matthias to deliver to Dracula to help pay the cost of his 1462 crusade.

If Dracula had officially declared that he had never received the resources that Pope Pio II sent for the crusade against the Ottomans, he would have been excommunicated—and for that amount of money, possibly charged as a heretic before the court of the Holy Inquisition. In addition, Frederick III hated Dracula, whose brilliant and brave defense of Christianity made Frederick look like a mediocre and cowardly emperor. Besides, Dracula unwillingly supported Matthias as king of Hungary.

The book *History of a Bloodthirsty and Madman Called Dracula of Wallachia*, which made Dracula infamous as the cruelest, most wicked man of his time, was written by Michael Beheim, a court jester for Dracula's enemy, Emperor Frederick III. It would be a waste of time to go into the biography of this mediocre and shady character; suffice it to say that he was a failure who apparently wasn't even entertaining. But he did have the chance to become the voice of his master, Frederick III—surely with the help of Matthias Corvinus. This ignorant character never imagined that his defamatory work would become the first commercial best-seller in history and the inspiration for other authors to give voice to their fantasies. This poor imitation of a book was written when Dracula was in prison; otherwise, the vovoid certainly would have defended himself and explained away all those calumnies—and then we surely would have a different story.

This poorly written book enjoyed another natural advantage: it appeared at the advent of the printing press. The medieval people who saw the book printed so perfectly assumed that it was valid and authentic and that everything it said was true. And because the book was mass produced, Beheim's lies quickly spread throughout the known world. Nowadays people understand that any idiot can write all the lies he wants, and just because they are professionally printed and accompanied by graphic color illustrations doesn't mean we are going to believe them. But in the Middle Ages, people's way of thinking was different: a lie told a thousand times became truth. Dracula's bad reputation started as lies, and as they spread and were repeated, they consolidated into a portrait of a real monster! But even Dracula's ill-intentioned enemies never imagined him drinking blood; the wickedness of their brains was still evolving. The wild stories that would turn into the vampire legend were the product of later brains that were . . . more developed? You can make your own judgment about that.

Among the later stories were those by the Orthodox Russian monk Fedor Kuristisyn. He rehashed some of Beheim's stories and added some new ones, but in general they did not have as many lies and exaggerations. In the monk's stories, Dracula is occasionally praised for having fought against the Ottomans, but he still was vilified, too, and the stories affected his reputation. We should not forget that the Orthodox clergy were enraged by the fact that Dracula converted to Catholicism; if he hadn't, he would not have been able to marry Ilona. So let's put ourselves for a moment in the shoes of the prisoner: He was a widower and he was alone; he met a good woman; and in order to marry her he had to change his religion or stop seeing her and go back to his loneliness. He was in a golden cage that was still a prison. We also should not forget that the Catholic and Orthodox Churches worship the same God, Jesus Christ.

Later yet would come the Latin stories about Dracula, and those became the basis of many books, with every author writing what he wanted and changing the original interpretation to fit his own style.

6. Did he drink the blood of the impaled?

No. The ignorant jester, Beheim, and his angry teachers spread vicious rumors about Dracula in order to protect the interests of the most powerful men in that place and time (and, by doing so, protect themselves). These men were Dracula's bitter enemies, and they commissioned Beheim's book in order to defame his reputation with absurd and incredible rumors. For instance, they claimed that he impaled thousands and thousands of innocent people; impaled a donkey and a Franciscan monk on the same stake; and forced people to commit acts of cannibalism and other savage acts. Although his enemies were full of rage and jealousy toward Dracula, as well as frustration and a thirst for justice against him, they never imagined a scenario where Dracula drank blood. Some even crazier men who were only looking for fame and fortune wrote that.

7. Was Dracula a vampire in Rumania?

Dracula was forced to be the vassal of the king of Hungary, and as such he was obligated to pay tribute to the Ottoman sultan. He was a brave medieval prince who fought with all his resources to free his people from the oppression of these two powerful men who wanted to subdue him. In Rumania, therefore, he is known as a hero. But in the rest of the world, thanks to the jester Beheim and his book *History of a Bloodthirsty and Madman Called Dracula of Wallachia*, and to the disrespectful playwright Bram Stoker, his fantasy book of horror called *Dracula*, and the thousands of works based on these absurd and irresponsible "historical" sources, we now know Dracula as a bloodthirsty vampire.

I am Mexican, and the father of my native country is the priest Don Miguel Hidalgo y Costilla. He was considered a traitor by his enemies, the Spaniards from the Peninsula, who were upset by his fight to free Mexico from Spanish oppression; they disdainfully called him *cura* (priest), and it's safe to assume that they had a powerful interest in staining his reputation. What if they made up some absurd, sinister, mysterious, or even humorous violent stories about the priest, as Dracula's enemies did about him, and wrote a book that was published worldwide. By "telling" these stories thousands of times, they surely would have turned him into a monster— maybe even another sanguinary vampire!—in the eyes of the world. If a foreigner heard those stories, in which he was said to have done strange things like drinking human blood, he probably would believe that our most respected national hero, Father Don Miguel Hidalgo y Costilla, was a sinister, bloodthirsty vampire. He would probably be known as Mikey the Vampire, and any non-Mexican who heard people talk about Mikey would assume he was a vampire, while any Mexican would laugh at the person's ignorance and naïveté for believing such absurd lies.

If someone had written a book portraying George Washington as a diabolical and bloody man—say, a perverted serial killer who ate his victims raw and sucked their blood—surely any American would react as I would and either laugh or ignore it. Every American would have a different reaction, but no American would believe such stupid lies! (Chances are, we would also question the mental health of the writer.)

The same thing happened in Rumania. There Dracula is thought of as a medieval prince who acted in a heroic and just way; no one considers him a diabolical vampire. That characterization is an invention of minds that are perverted and perhaps even

8. How did he become known as a vampire?

The name Dracula became synonymous with *vampire* with the publication of the book *Dracula* by Braham Stoker in 1897.

It has always been the author's role to write about our dreams, our fears, and our frustrations in order to give some purpose to our existence. Authors also want fame and fortune. Therefore, in an attempt to give veracity to their fantastic novels, they have searched human history for characters whose actions might be classified as cruel and inhuman, and without analyzing the characters' motives or circumstances they distort them. The resulting works of terror have been incredible in the truest sense of the word.

At the end of the nineteenth century, Braham Stoker, a man dedicated to the theater and writing, spent eight years of his life writing a horror novel. He researched works such as *The Vampire of Polidori, The History of a Bloodthirsty Madman Called Dracula of Wallachia,* and some other books of the same style, and he wrote what many consider the most terrifying horror novel that has ever been written. He called this novel *Dracula,* and the main character is a sanguinary vampire that sucks the blood of beautiful women and steals their vitality. To represent this character, he chose a historical figure, the hero of Wallachia, Vlad III, without caring that he was staining the man's already stained memory. Stoker's book turned Dracula from a "sanguinary and crazy man" to a bloodthirsty vampire.

9. Where can I find more literature that tells the real story of Dracula?

In order to write this novel, it was necessary for me to consult the work of scholars who dedicated a large part of their lives to studying this controversial figure and as a result became true authorities on the subject. For anyone who would like to read more accurate and precise information about Dracula, I recommend the following works:

- *Vlad the Impaler: In Search of the Real Dracula* by M. J. Traw
- *Biography of Vlad the Impaler* by Radu R Florescu and Raymond T McNally (Hanthorn1973)
- *Dracula, Prince of Many Faces* (Little Brown 1989)
- *The Complete Dracula* (Copley 1992)
- "Dracula as a Hero" in *International Magazine* (August 1973)
- "The Manuscript of Kritiboulos of Imbros: From the 15 Century and the Historical Source of Dracula" in East European Quarterly (March 1987)
- *Dracula: Essays on the Life and Times of Vlad Tepes* by Kurt Treptow (Columbia University Press 1991)

- *The Real Dracula* by Stephen Czaba (1941)

If you want still more information, these books can provide an expansive bibliography.

10. Were there any other stories written about Dracula during his time besides the ones from the jester Beheim?

Yes. The Russian monk Fedor Kuristisyn, from the monastery of Belozersky, interviewed Dracula's widow, who told him in great detail all that her husband had told her. Working from this information and Beheim's fantastic stories, a monk named Efrosin published in 1490 nineteen stories that were indeed creepy but did not include the lies and exaggerations of the pasquinade (satire), *History of a Sanguinary and Crazy Man Called Dracula of Wallachia*. And that is logical, as neither Fedor nor Efrosin hated Dracula. They felt the way all the Orthodox monks did: hugely resentful because Dracula had married in the Catholic Church and never had an Orthodox wedding. (They never realized why their vovoid had to make that decision.) These stories also had a great impact; but since they were not bloody and exaggerated like Beheim's, they did not have the same success.

Let's look the first story, which goes something like this:

> Once upon a time in Wallachia there ruled a Christian prince called Dracula in the Wallachian language (or "demon" in our language). He was both cruel and smart. Some ambassadors from the land of the sultan paid him a visit, and when they entered the palace they bowed as was their custom. Dracula thought them disrespectful because they did not uncover their heads. "Why do you act like that?" he asked. "You ambassadors have come before a great sovereign, and it fills me with shame." The ambassadors answered with arrogance, "Because it is the custom in our land, which is dictated by the sultan." Dracula told them, "I want to reinforce your rude customs. Behave bravely." And he ordered their turbans to be nailed to their

heads with little nails. Then he said, "Go and tell this to your sultan, and tell him that he should get used to such shame from you. He should not impose his customs upon other sovereigns who do not want them, much less Wallachia's inhabitants."

Story number two goes like this:

The Turkish sultan was infuriated by this action and prepared his army against Dracula, invading Wallachia with overwhelming strength. But Dracula, with shrewdness and sagacity, took his few soldiers and attacked the Turks during the night and killed many of them, but with such mismatched strength, he could not conquer them. He examined his soldiers after they fought the Turks personally, and the ones who had wounds on their foreheads he honored as knights, but those with wounds on their backs he impaled, telling them, "You are not men—you are women." And when he fought against the Turks again, he told his army, "Anyone who even thinks of dying should not come with me but should remain there." The Turkish sultan withdrew in shame when he found out what Dracula had said. Besides having lost a great part of his powerful army, he also never dared fight against Dracula again.

In this story, the Russian monks praise Dracula for destroying a large part of the sultan's army and proving the sultan's fear of him. Of course, Beheim never would have included this story in his book of defamations.

Here's Russian story number three:

The sultan sent an ambassador to Wallachia to collect the annual tribute from Dracula. Dracula welcomed the ambassador with honor and showed good will to fulfill his commitment, saying, "I not only wish to pay the tribute to the sultan, but I also want my lord the sultan to have at his disposal myself, my army, and my treasure. We will gladly do what he orders, and you should let our sultan know that. When he comes I will put myself at his disposal, and when he gives us orders anywhere in his land neither I nor any of my men will disobey him." When the sultan heard from his ambassador that Dracula wanted to subject himself to the sultan's will—honoring him, giving him gifts, and smothering him with attention—he sighed in relief because at the time he was at war with powerful rulers from the East. The sultan sent a message immediately to all the fortified cities that when Dracula arrived, they should not harm him, but receive him as if he were their most valuable ally: they should honor him. Dracula traveled throughout the Turkish empire for about five days. Then he suddenly changed and started to rob and to attack the cities and towns. He captured many prisoners and cut them into pieces. He impaled a lot of Turks, cutting some in two and then burning them, and he also burned their crops. He did not allow any Turks to remain alive, not even the infants; but he displaced some others who were Christians. He returned home with great war booty, and before he honored the sultan's officers he said, "Go and tell the sultan that you came and I served him as best I could, and that if my service does not please him, I will serve him again with all my strength." And the sultan remained silent: he could not do anything against Dracula because he was defeated and ashamed.

Russian story number four:

Dracula was an enemy of wickedness. In his land if someone stole, raped, killed, or betrayed him, they did not have the chance to repeat their crime. Whether it was a rich nobleman or a pious priest, a devout and humble monk or a common man, the criminal could not escape death by impalement. Dracula was so feared and his law so respected that there were very few crimes. In a certain place there was a fountain visited by travelers and outsiders, and they drank the water from the fountain because it was cold and sweet. Dracula placed a gold cup next to this fountain, which was in a deserted place—anyone who wanted to drink took the cup and drank and replaced it again. While Dracula was governor, the cup was there all the time; no one dared to steal it.

This story describes a Wallachia where there is respect for the law and others. As the Russian monks told it, Dracula was a serious and respected ruler who inspired obedience to the law, as was to be expected. But Beheim's stories do not portray Dracula as a respected leader. Instead, the jester preferred to defame Dracula to serve others' interests, and also to fulfill his role as entertainer with his shocking stories.

Russian story number five:

> One time Dracula summoned all the old, sick, and poor in Wallachia to go to his palace, and so a great crowd of poor people, vagrants, and sick people arrived, expecting a great act of charity. Dracula ordered all his servants to gather those wretched people in a big wooden house that had been built especially to receive them, and he ordered his servants to feed them and give them drink according to their wishes. After they had eaten and drunk, they began to amuse themselves. Then Dracula appeared and asked, "What else do you need?" And they answered happily, "Lord, only God and your honor know what we need." Dracula asked them, "Would you like to live here until the day you die and never feel hunger or thirst?" They all answered, "Yes, my lord!" Then he promised, "You will never be hungry again!" And he ordered the house to be closed and set on fire. As everyone was screaming in agony, waiting for death in the middle of the flames, he told the nobles, "I did this first of all to avoid having these unfortunate people be a burden to others; there will be no more beggars or lazy people on my land, only rich people. Besides, I released those people from their poverty and suffering."

Russian story number six:

> Two Catholic monks from Hungary arrived in Wallachia, asking for alms. Dracula ordered them cloistered separately. He invited one of them to eat and then, showing him countless impaled people, asked, "Do you think I did a good thing? If you were judge, how would you judge these impaled?" And

451

the monk answered, "I would be merciful and would forgive them. You did wrong: you punished without mercy. It is better for a judge to be merciful, as certainly all the impaled are innocent martyrs." Dracula then called the second monk, invited him to eat, and asked him the same questions. The monk answered, "You are assigned by God as sovereign to do justice. You must punish the ones who do wrong and reward the ones who do well. Without a doubt these people behaved badly and so received their fair punishment." Dracula then called to the first monk and asked him, "Why did you leave your monastery and your cell to walk and travel to the courts of great sovereigns? You do not know anything about justice! You assured me that all these impaled were martyrs. I wish for you to be a martyr, too; you will be martyred along with these people." And with that he ordered his soldiers to impale the monk. Then he summoned the second monk and congratulated him, giving him fifty gold ducats. "You are a wise man," he said, and he ordered a carriage to be prepared to transport the monk with honor back to the Hungarian border.

Russian story number seven:

One day a Hungarian merchant arrived in the capital city of Wallachia. Following Dracula's orders, the merchant left his carriage on the street and slept inside a house. During the night someone came and stole 160 gold ducats from the carriage, and so the merchant went to see Dracula and told him about the theft. "You can leave without worries," Dracula said. "Your gold will appear before the end of tomorrow." Then he ordered his soldiers to look for the thief throughout the city, telling the townspeople, "If you do not turn the thief in, I will burn down the entire city." He then ordered his servants to put another bag of gold on the carriage during the night, but he added one more coin. The merchant got up in the morning, found the gold, and counted the pieces twice, both times counting one extra coin. He went to Dracula and said, confused, "Lord the gold has appeared, but I don't understand why there is an extra

452

coin." He then returned the coin to Dracula, saying, "Lord, this one does not belong to me." Right then the thief who had stolen the original gold was arrested and Dracula ordered him impaled. Then he said to the merchant, "Go in peace. If you had not returned to me the piece I placed there, I would have impaled you along with the thief."

This story from the Russian monks again shows us Dracula's sense of justice and the value that he placed on private property. While the thief died impaled, his punishment fit the law; he was his own executioner because of his action. It makes sense that this story was never told by Beheim, who wanted to discredit Dracula, not show him as a fair and honest man.

Russian story number eight:

If a married woman committed adultery, Dracula ordered her private parts and breasts to be shamefully cut, and then she was skinned alive and her skin was displayed outside, in the middle of the main square. The same destiny befell a woman who did not preserve her virginity, as well as any widow who fornicated: he ordered his soldiers to cut the nipples from her breasts and, in some cases, take the skin from the women's vagina and stick a hot-red poker in it. She would remain naked, tied to a pole, until her skin separated from her bones or she was eaten by the birds.

Russian story number nine:

When Dracula was riding through his land, he saw a poor man with a torn shirt and asked him, "Do you have a wife?" The man answered, "Yes, my lord!" "Take me to your house," Dracula said. At the man's house he saw a young and healthy woman, and so he asked the husband, "How is your sowing of grain?" And the husband answered, "Really well, my lord. I have a lot of grain," and he showed Dracula a cellar full of grain. Furiously, Dracula addressed the wife: "Why are you so lazy to your husband? It is his duty to grow grain and feed you, but it is your duty to fix your husband's clothes. You've resigned yourself to just washing his shirt, but you are not sick—you are lazy. The only one to blame for your husband's poor appearance is you. If your husband refused to sow grain, he would be considered guilty." With that Dracula ordered his soldiers to cut off her hands and impale her.

Russian story number ten:

It was typical for Dracula to eat with his table set among many men who had been impaled. One day he was bored and wanted to have fun. A servant arrived and stood in front of him, and when he could not stand the smell of the corpses any more, he covered his nose and bent his head. Dracula, enraged, asked him, "Why are you doing that?" The servant answered with disgust, "Lord, I cannot take this stench any longer." Dracula ordered his soldiers to impale him, saying, "Soon you are going to be really high where you cannot smell this horrible stench."

Russian story number eleven:

Dracula received a visit from an emissary of King Matthias Corvinus of Hungary. The ambassador was an intelligent nobleman from Poland. Dracula invited him to dine at his royal table set among the bodies of impaled people, and he placed in front of the king a long golden stake. Looking at him with malevolence, Dracula asked him in a somber voice, "Tell me—what do you think this special stake is for?" The ambassador was really scared and answered, "Lord, I believe that a nobleman has committed a crime against you, and you have reserved for him a more honorable death than these poor, unfortunate souls." And he pointed to the impaled. Dracula, still staring at him, said, "You speak with fairness. You are a great ambassador from a great sovereign, and this stake is destined for you." The ambassador, now terrified, said, "Lord, if I have committed a crime that deserves the death penalty, whatever law and punishment you've established will be fulfilled, because you are a fair ruler and you will not be guilty of my death—only I will be." Dracula laughed out loud and said, "If you had answered me differently, I would have really impaled you." Then he gave the ambassador gifts and allowed him to leave. As they said their farewells, Dracula said, "You are suited to be an envoy of great sovereigns, because you are smart and well-mannered and know how to speak to powerful men. But others should not dare to speak to me before they have learned to speak to great sovereigns, because their destiny will be the long golden stake."

Of course the jester Beheim never would have mentioned in his book a story like that one, in which Dracula is shown as a man who is cruel but also very intelligent.

Russian story number twelve:

Dracula did not like to talk with ignorant ambassadors. When he received one who dressed inappropriately or spoke nonsense, without knowing how to answer Dracula's difficult questions, he impaled him, saying, "I am not guilty of your death; the responsibility falls to your master. If I gave you information to take to your master, you would not have the chance to distort it with your stupid mind and you would not say anything bad about me. If your master knows that you are slow and not properly prepared to come to my court, then your own master killed you, and if someone dares to come here without being properly instructed, he is committing suicide. I will always have a long golden stake, and it will be used on the ambassador in front of everyone, and the following message will be written to the sovereign of that stupid ambassador: Do not be a murderer of fools, and do not send more ambassadors with ignorant minds to a wise sovereign."

Russian story number thirteen:

Once some virtuoso artisans made Dracula some steel barrels. He ordered the artisans to fill them with gold and place them in the bottom of the river. Then, to keep the secret, he had the artisans killed. That way no one knew about Dracula's crime except the demon who was directing him.

Russian story number fourteen:

On one occasion King Matthias Corvinus of Hungary shrewdly pitted his army against Dracula's. Dracula put up fierce resistance, but the intelligence of King Matthias Corvinus became evident when his army captured Dracula alive. Dracula was betrayed by his own man, who could not stand him anymore. Dracula was brought to the Hungarian king, who ordered him shackled and jailed. He remained locked up like an animal in Visegard on the Danube above Buda for twelve years. And the king of Hungary appointed another prince to Wallachia.

Russian story number fifteen:

After the death of that prince, King Matthias Corvinus of Hungary sent a messenger to Dracula, who was in jail. Putting aside their quarrels and without resentment in his heart, he offered to restore Dracula as prince of Wallachia on one condition: that he accept the heretical Latin faith. Dracula refused at the beginning, saying he preferred to die in prison, but he was more attached to the world than to eternity. That is why he abandoned the Orthodox faith, and the truth is, he abandoned the light and received the darkness to recover his power. He could not stand the temporary suffering of prison, and so he prepared for eternal suffering, abandoning the Orthodox Church and accepting the heretical Latin one. The king not only gave him Wallachia's principality, but also offered him his sister as a wife. Together they produced two children, and he lived ten more years and ended his life as a Catholic.

This story, told by the Orthodox monks, reflects their anger at Dracula for converting to Catholicism. It also says that he married the king's sister, but that is not true. His second wife was Ilona Szilagy, daughter of his brother Dragon Mihail Szilagy. But the point of this story is to show that Dracula is a monster for having committed the unforgivable heresy of converting to Catholicism—as if Catholics did not worship Jesus Christ, too. In Dracula's time, renouncing the Orthodox Church to embrace Catholicism was considered a heretical aberration, even though today it would seem an unimportant matter.

Russian story number sixteen:

> Dracula could not get rid of his bad habits when he was in prison. He spent the days chasing mice, and he asked his jailers to bring him birds from the market so he could torture them. He impaled some, cut the heads off others, and dropped them into the void.

Russian story number seventeen:

> When Dracula became Catholic, the king released him from jail and gave him a house located in Pest, past Buda. After a while, a criminal sought refuge at Dracula's house, and some guards entered Dracula's backyard to search for him. One of the guards found the criminal, but Dracula drew his sword and beheaded the guard with a single cut and then released the criminal without authorization. The other guards ran away terrified and went to the local judge. The judge, along with the guards, went to the king of Hungary to complain. So King Matthias Corvinus sent a messenger to Dracula to ask him why he killed a representative of the law. Dracula answered, "I did not commit any crime when I killed that intruder; he committed suicide. That is the destiny of anyone who invades the house of a great governor without permission. If you had come to me and explained the situation and I had found the criminal in my house, I myself would have decided the sentence and turned in the criminal or sentenced him to die." When the

king heard Dracula's answer he started to laugh, amazed by his courage and intelligence.

Russian story number eighteen:

Dracula died the following way: While he was a governor of Wallachia, the Turks invaded, wanting to conquer him. Dracula faced the Turks and began to fight, and his army killed many Turks without mercy, so Dracula went to the top of a hill to better see his men impaling Turks. When he separated from the army and his men, someone confused him with a Turk and hurt him with a spear, but Dracula saw he was being attacked by his own men and immediately he killed five of the murderers with his own sword. He received several wounds with a sword and several with a lancet, and that is how he died.

Russian story number nineteen:

King Matthias Corvinus took his sister and her two children from Dracula's home in Buda, Hungary. One of these children still lives as the king's son, while the other preferred to stay with Oradea's bishop to follow his religious calling. He died in our presence. I saw the third son, the firstborn called Mihail, in Buda; he ran away from the Turkish sultan and sought refuge with Hungary's king.

This was written first on February 13, 1486, and then on January 28, 1490, I transcribed the text, I Efrosin the sinner.

These are the stories of the monks Efrosin and Fedor Kuristisyn, who lived in the monastery Kirov-Belozersky in Russia. The stories seem very different from the ones written by the ignorant jester Beheim, although both sets of stories reflect the writers' serious issues against Dracula. Emperor Frederick III hated him and envied his courage, and the Russians hated him because the vovoid converted to the Orthodox faith. While today this may seem insignificant, at that time it was reason enough to die.

Brother Efrosin was seriously offended by the fact that Dracula had converted to the Catholic religion to marry Ilona. To the monks this was inconceivable, especially because Dracula was the highest representative of the Church in Wallachia. Nevertheless, the monks' stories are not as libelous as the lies written by Beheim.

The Russian monks never spoke of thousands and thousands of innocents impaled—not to mention children or donkeys. Stories like these were the product of one man's fertile imagination. The monks praised Dracula's successful military campaign in the Danube, and they wrote about the honesty and fairness with which he ruled his people. Still, Dracula's reputation was irreparably damaged by Beheim's book.

In 1477, Dracula was dead and his memory tarnished—in fact, nobody cared about his memory. The Orthodox were upset because of his conversion to Catholicism. For the Catholics, who took Beheim's book very seriously, Dracula went from being a saint to being Satan's favorite son. The Ottomans, of course, despised him for all the damage he had done to them; even when he was dead they feared his memory. The Saxons were happy to see him gone; now they managed everything as they had before. Dracula's memory and reputation were like a fallen tree: everyone makes firewood from a fallen tree.

History is written by the winners, and Dracula's history was written by the emperor of the Holy Roman Empire, Matthias Corvinus—variously described as wise, fair, intelligent, prudent, and a lover of books and fine arts, among other superlatives—who bought the crown of Saint Steffen with money of uncertain origin. We will never know the truth.

So let us continue to discuss the man. Let us canonize him, demonize him, or do whatever seems appropriate in relation to his memory. From my point of view, the energy of Vladislaus III—or Vlad III, or Dracula—followed its due course, the course that cosmic energy had assigned to him. And our efforts to modify that divine will have been, in my opinion, completely in vain.

End